QUEEN OF THE WITS

Queen of the Wits

A Life of Laetitia Pilkington

∞

NORMA CLARKE

faber and faber

First published in 2008
by Faber and Faber Limited
3 Queen Square London WC1N 3AU

Typeset in Minion by Palindrome
Printed in England by Mackays of Chatham, plc

The right of Norma Clarke to be identified as author
of this work has been asserted in accordance with Section 77 of the
Copyright, Designs and Patents Act 1988

A CIP record for this book
is available from the British Library

ISBN 978–0–571–22428–9

2 4 6 8 10 9 7 5 3 1

In memory of my father, William Clarke
1918–2006

Contents

CONTENTS

Plates

Acknowledgements

My first debt is to the Swift scholar, A. C. Elias Jr, whose densely annotated edition of Mrs Pilkington's *Memoirs* made this biography possible. I am grateful to friends, family and colleagues who read all or part of the manuscript and responded enthusiastically: Tracy Bohan, Kathryn King, Julian Loose, Adam Phillips, Michal Shavit, Barbara Taylor, Nick Tosh, William Tosh and Henry Volans. Also to Toby Barnard, Clare Connolly, Cora Kaplan, Alison Light, Jack Lynch, Bob Mahony, Anthony Malcomson, Ian McBride, Natasha McEnroe, Hallie Rubenhold, Jenny Uglow, Carolyn D. Williams, Clair Wills, Frances Wilson and others upon whose expertise I have drawn. Mrs Pilkington travels well and I have enjoyed speaking about her to many and varied groups including: Chawton House 'Wild Irish Girls' conference; Johnson Society, Lichfield; Institute of Advanced Study in the Humanities, Edinburgh; Irish Studies Group, London University; Queen Mary Graduate seminar; Kingston Readers' Festival; London University Extra-Mural Literature Group; Riverside Book Circle, Sunbury; Swift Symposium, Dublin; University College, Dublin; University College, Cork; University of British Columbia, Vancouver; Keogh Institute, Notre Dame, Indiana.

Kingston University English department continues to be able to fund a rotating leave scheme for which I am profoundly grateful; my turn came round twice in the course of writing this book. I have depended on the British Library and the London Library, making forays to the Dublin City Archive and the National Library of Ireland. In all these institutions the courtesy and helpfulness of

ACKNOWLEDGEMENTS

librarians has smoothed the way. I specially want to thank Adrian Le Harivel, Curator of British Painting at the National Gallery of Ireland, for taking me into the vaults where we viewed James Worsdale's painting of the Dublin Hell-Fire Club, and to the temporary exhibition where the Limerick Hell-Fire Club portrait was on display. Alec Cobbe, direct descendant of Matthew Pilkington's patron, Archbishop Charles Cobbe, welcomed me to Newbridge House and showed me round Donabate church. He also gave me the relevant chapter of Mark Broch's thesis, translated into English. Brian Lynch and Mary Shine Thompson were great company and generous hosts in Dublin. Derek O'Shaughnessy, verger of St Ann's church, entertained and helped me.

Working with Faber has been a special pleasure. Julian Loose understood at once that Mrs Pilkington's life would be a literary biography not a scandalous romp and supported that vision throughout. Kate Murray Browne assembled the plates. Paula Turner was a superb copy-editor and designer. The brilliant cover was drawn by Neil Fox and designed by Gavin Morris; it has gone on making me laugh ever since I saw the first draft.

NOTE ON SPELLINGS

In quoted matter the sometimes idiosyncratic usage of the eighteenth century in spelling, use of capitals and punctuation has been retained.

But I have been a Lady of Adventure, and almost every
Day of my Life produces some new one . . .
Memoirs of Laetitia Pilkington, vol. 1, p. 213

the life of a Wit is a warfare upon earth
Alexander Pope, *Works*, 1717, Preface

A *saucy, proud, impertinent person*

On a bitter winter day in 1744, a tiny Irish woman trudged through snow to deliver a petition to the Lord High Almoner, Bishop Sherlock, at his house in the Temple, off Fleet Street. She was hoping he would add her name to the list of candidates for the Royal Bounty. The pleasant Bishop of York had recommended her, so she expected a successful outcome. She had to knock several times before anybody came and when an old porter opened up it required half a crown to get him to take the letter. Eventually Bishop Sherlock, fat and carbuncled, his face all 'Knobs and Flames of Fire', appeared, and in a vile temper demanded to know why she, a 'foreigner', felt herself entitled to royal charity when there were beggars enough in England. She answered with spirit that she was indeed Irish, but that Ireland was 'not a foreign Country' it was 'equally a Part of his Majesty's Dominions with Great-Britain'. This the bishop denied; he called her a liar and sent her packing. She was 'a saucy, proud, impertinent Person'.

Laetitia Pilkington got her revenge a few years later when she wrote about the imperious bishop in her *Memoirs*. English disregard of Irish interests and the corruption of the clergy were among her darker themes. There was a story behind the encounter: she had written a political pamphlet that was rude about Tory bishops like Sherlock. But Sherlock's adjectives were apt, as she herself observed, and they can be reclaimed. Mrs Pilkington was proud and impertinent and exceptionally gifted. In her three volumes of *Memoirs* she left an unprecedented record of her life and times. This biography is based on those memoirs and it tells a remarkable tale.

When she went to call on the bishop, Laetitia Pilkington had been a struggling writer in London for four or five years. To the everyday problems all writers faced – hard work, poor rewards – she added several more. She was a woman, Irish, without family protection or funds, and of infamous reputation. She was 'the famous Mrs Pilkington' who had been caught in flagrante by her husband, Matthew, a Dublin curate, in their bedroom late at night with a young surgeon, Robert Adair. She couldn't deny it – twelve nightwatchmen were the witnesses – but she said her husband had been scheming to be rid of her, and that he had a 'buxom' lover of his own. Formally separated by order of the Dublin Consistory Court, she was not allowed to re-marry; and though she was supposed to receive a token maintenance from Matthew, that never materialised. Keeping herself alive was no small challenge, especially as a lone woman in London. Mrs Pilkington had a further agenda. She was determined to expose the hypocrisy and venality of a society that condemned her for faults which men got away with; worse, for sins which women were required to commit to meet men's desires. She had learnt by harsh experience how men's use and abuse of women was enshrined in law: or, as she put it, how men 'our seducers' were also 'our accusers'.

The Royal Bounty, though only a modest sum of money, would have been significant as a mark of official favour and it was not unrealistic to hope for it. (Needless to say, she didn't get it.) Mrs Pilkington had respectable supporters, some of them highly placed in church and state, who viewed her as a woman of merit ruined by a bad marriage. They too thought society was in need of reform and that men were to blame. They sympathised with her sorrows and were amused by her anecdotes. The 'little Irish muse' made it her business to be entertaining; in some company she even joked about the night she was discovered and thrown out of her home – she confessed to indiscretion, but 'solemnly declared' she was just trying to finish a book the young man was reluctant to let her borrow.

In a culture that valued wit as highly as England did when Pope and Swift were its most admired writers, sauciness could be an asset. Mrs Pilkington, a poet, had been a protégée of Jonathan

Swift in Dublin and she had stories about him too. The elderly dean of St Patrick's had taken an interest in the curate and his wife because they impressed him with their talent and ambition; and they, as a young couple keen to get on, understood perfectly the value of intimate friendship with the author of *Gulliver's Travels*. The scandal of divorce in 1738 put an end to the friendship. Swift repudiated them, calling Matthew a 'rogue' and Laetitia (more damagingly) 'the most profligate whore in either kingdom'. He tried to erase their names from his correspondence and remove all trace of the connection. But Mrs Pilkington had stored her memory. She was able to create an unrivalled portrait of a most peculiar genius. As Swift's first biographer, her name will always be linked with his.

For eighteenth-century readers, Mrs Pilkington's brilliant evocation of Swift's oddities was compulsive reading. The vicissitudes of her life, too, astonished and enthralled them. From curate's wife to 'a Lady of Adventure' nothing was quite as expected. The sense of being slightly off-balance is one that readers today may share, for Mrs Pilkington doesn't fit neatly into familiar categories. She was disgraced but not ashamed, an outcast but well connected, a rejected wife and mother who would not go quietly. Her *Memoirs* testify to unshaken self-belief; her story displayed how badly people could behave towards one another but also how the bonds of community stretched across the Irish Sea. She blamed her husband for exposing her to the world, sardonically thanking him for enlarging her horizons (she had seen life 'from the palace to the prison'), but she relished her independence. Few women had the freedoms she had. If she was a bit like her fictional semblance, Moll Flanders, she was even more like Moll's creator, Daniel Defoe, and other male writers of the period. The fallen daughter of Irish Protestant gentry – an awkwardly situated class at the best of times, as Swift, who felt himself an exile in Dublin, often had cause to complain – her wit was her weapon. The pen was very much in her hand.

I first came across Laetitia Pilkington as one of the so-called 'scandalous memoirists' and assumed, wrongly, that she wrote as a courtesan and offered titillating fare. She did not. She wrote of her 'follies' and 'faults' as her friend Colley Cibber did in his auto-biography, *An Apology for the Life of Colley Cibber, Actor*, and she did not claim 'immaculate chastity' any more than he did, but the real scandal in her view was the sexual double standard and English treatment of Ireland, not any sexual behaviour of her own. From childhood she had dreamed of literary fame. Reading Dryden and Pope – that other early starter – at the age of five set her on the path to poetry and she became an admired (still admired) poet. In Dublin she gained a reputation for quick-fire wit and clever impromptu rhyme. Some said she was better than her husband, which did not improve relations between them. She was able to support herself in London by raising subscriptions towards the cost of printing a volume of her poems. Though the volume never appeared, people's willingness to give is an important sign of how they viewed her. Mrs Pilkington's originality, polished simplicity and precision continue to be praised by critics today.

But it is the *Memoirs*, a 'minor classic of the eighteenth century', that makes it possible to write a biography – and it is surprising that nobody has done so yet. Of course, it is a problematic source: Laetitia Pilkington wrote to vindicate herself and blame others. Nor did she pretend otherwise, wanting to give both pleasure and offence – in her own words, 'lemon and sugar is very pretty'. But she also wanted to leave a record and claim a place in literary history. The *Memoirs* mix fact with fiction, prose with poetry (almost all her own poems are skilfully incorporated), sincerity with artifice and satire with panegyric. Working the mock-heroic vein of Gay's *Beggar's Opera*, Pope's *Dunciad*, and Hogarth's *The Harlot's Progress*, she created a glorious and exciting new form, full of vivid characterisation and worldly shrewdness. There are no longueurs, although for the uninitiated it can be difficult to follow at times: figures who loomed large in the 1730s are barely remembered today; and a number of Mrs Pilkington's targets were obscure even then. More importantly perhaps, we have nothing in our literature that is remotely like it. Respectable Dublin and rakish London, seen from the perspective of the fallen woman, appear fascinatingly askew. 'Good' men, like the famous philanthropist Dr

Richard Mead, prove villains; priestly robes are no guide to sanctity; the debauched behave with respect. In the Marshalsea prison, she listens to interesting sermons. In lodging houses she is robbed; on the streets she is protected. Gradually Mrs Pilkington makes us realise that the society she describes is full of fallen women like herself, struggling with limited options and shamed into silence. Hers is a rare voice, a distinctive voice, and one that refused to be shamed.

If she was 'poor Laetitia . . . the Foot-ball of Fortune', she was also fortunate in being born in a time and place which rewarded wit in women. She cultivated story-telling gifts that provided a rattling good read for her contemporaries. I have tried to emulate her (truly it would be an achievement to make her life story dull) while at the same time bearing in mind that the early eighteenth century, and especially Ireland in that period, is much less well known than later eras. I have depended on the magnificent modern edition of the *Memoirs* edited by A. C. Elias Jr. Elias explained that when he began his work he expected to keep the explanatory notes short and refer to established scholarship, but he discovered there was little such scholarship available. His notes are extensive. Without Elias's groundbreaking efforts, Mrs Pilkington might have stayed buried in the 'deepest obscurity' Virginia Woolf lamented in her 'Lives of the Obscure', when she ringingly pronounced, 'If ever a woman wanted a champion, it is obviously Laetitia Pilkington'.

There is an irony here that Mrs Pilkington would have been the first to appreciate. She had never needed bolder souls to speak for her. As the heroine of her own romance she occupied centre-stage. She told the male writers of her day – the 'bastard Sons of Wit' – to stand aside and take their 'false Heroes' with them. She was the self-appointed 'genuine Successor of . . . immortal Swift'. And just as *Gulliver's Travels* was 'a faithful history' and 'absolutely true', so too was the story of the Irish curate's wife who dreamed of beating the men on the battleground of literature.

PART ONE

Ireland

CHAPTER ONE

Doctor's Daughter

Laetitia Pilkington claimed to have been born in 1712 but it was probably 1708 or 1709 in Co. Cork where both her parents had family connections. Her father, Dr John Van Lewen, was the son of a Dutch physician, Guisebert Van Lewen, who had settled in Co. Cork and established a successful practice there. Guisebert did well enough to send John, the elder of his two sons, to Trinity College, Dublin, in 1701 and afterwards to the famous medical schools at Leiden and Utrecht. On 17 August 1705, at the age of twenty-one, John Van Lewen received his MD after satisfying the examiners at Utrecht with his defence of an eleven-page thesis on the un-romantic subject of purges and emetics, *De Emeticis seu Remediis Vomitoriis*. A few months later he married Elizabeth Corry, 'his faithful Mistress', who had been waiting for him.

Her family were not pleased. On her mother's side, Elizabeth could trace her ancestry back several generations, laying claim to an earl – the Earl of Killmallock – as her great-great-grandfather. In fact he held the lower rank of viscount, but he had been the first baronet created in Ireland, in 1619, and when he was made a peer, in 1625, he took the title Viscount Sarsfield of Killmallock. Being 'descended of an antient, and honorable Family, who were frequently inter-married with the Nobility' was important to Elizabeth Corry, perhaps not least because so little seems to have been known about her actual parents. Her mother died giving birth to a second child and her father, a Catholic soldier who had come over to Ireland with the deposed Stuart king, James, abandoned her. In 1690, the Protestant William III's victory at the

Battle of the Boyne put an end to James's hopes of recovering the throne. Like other Jacobites, Elizabeth Corry's father fled, first to France and then into England where later he married a Catholic heiress. Little Elizabeth was taken in by her maternal grandmother Meade, a colonel's widow, who brought her up as a Protestant, thus entitling her to claim the money settled on her by her mother at her death.

Though effectively an orphan, Elizabeth was embedded in an extensive network of relations and connections, those 'Friends' who were displeased at her choice of a husband. One of her uncles, Sir John Meade, first baronet and progenitor of the Meade earls of Clanwilliam, was an eminent lawyer; he was reputed to be one of the finest orators at the Bar. Wealthy, successful, a classical scholar and patron of the arts, he had a high sense of personal and family pride not a little tinged with Irish nationalist feeling. The contempt with which the English regarded the Irish – 'that natural Contempt for the whole Country, which those of the English, who have not been resident amongst them, are but too apt to express, on every Occasion' as his great-niece later put it in her *Memoirs* – enraged him. The Meades were cultivated, polite gentry. They lived in comfortable houses, visited a great deal, held musical evenings, discussed books and current affairs, were interested in science and politics, and probably expected Elizabeth to marry into an ancient Irish family like their own or even into the nobility. She was well educated, well bred, graceful, witty and intelligent. She also happened to have 'a handsome Fortune'.

Elizabeth, however, fell in love with a Trinity College student of Dutch lineage, 'accidentally' Irish, who could boast neither family nor fortune. She had plenty of other admirers; but, free to make her own choice, since by then her grandmother had died, she chose the eighteen-year-old John Van Lewen and she waited three years for him to complete his studies. We can be sure that during that time she had opportunities to change her mind, and that there were those in the family who muttered that she was throwing herself away. A story about Guisebert, the immigrant 'old doctor' as he was known, suggests something of what the Meades objected to regarding the marriage: when neighbours complained that his younger son, George, was sexually rampant and a menace to their daughters, Guisebert responded unsympathetically. He was a proud father of sons. He advised his neighbours: 'Coop up your hens, I let my game cocks loose.'

If the Van Lewen boys had a mother alive at the time, no mention is made of her. From this febrile masculine household emerged an energetic, ambitious and sensitive young man who, with the example of his father before him, set about building a successful medical practice. For John Van Lewen, it made sense to begin in Co. Cork where he was already known and he stayed there for five or six years; but his sights were on Dublin. Sir John Meade, who died in 1707, had left a young widow, Lady Meade, who lived in William Street; and in about 1711 it was to William Street, a few doors down from Lady Meade, that John Van Lewen brought his wife and child, a move which suggests that if Elizabeth's family were annoyed with her they had got over it and were prepared to use their society contacts to help her husband on in his profession.

From purges and emetics, Dr Van Lewen had turned his attention to a new field. In a radical departure from customary practice, he began to specialise in obstetrics. At the time, childbirth was in the hands of midwives and surgeons (it required no formal training to be a surgeon or a midwife). A trained doctor would only be called in if there were complications. Evidently there were mixed feelings about medical men taking over these practices: while Van Lewen was himself to become well respected within the profession, as witnessed by his election to the College of Physicians on 3 November 1729 and subsequent service as Vice President and President, the College was uncomfortable about its members doing the work of midwives, perhaps because they feared a loss of status. (It is unlikely that they were concerned to protect the livelihoods of the women who would be squeezed out.) The College passed a resolution within a few weeks of Van Lewen's death in 1737 that 'no man for the future shall have a License to practise Midwifery and Physick [medicine] together'.

However ambivalent the College of Physicians might be, fashionable Dublin welcomed Dr Van Lewen as its first male midwife. He quickly acquired a reputation for gentleness and skill. His success can be measured by his progress up the property ladder: from the modest but respectable house in William Street (substantially smaller than Lady Meade's – her house was assessed at ten shillings on the local cess list, while the Van Lewens had to pay only three shillings and sixpence) he moved to a larger house in Church Street and later, as Dublin grew eastward, to Molesworth Street. These moves reflected social as well as financial success: the doctor, moving with his well-heeled clients, was welcomed in the drawing room no less than at the bedside. As early as March 1714, he had been elected a churchwarden of St Bride's, a sure sign of his standing in the community.

Laetitia was the second child but her older brother died in his infancy and until she was six or seven she was the only one. She was tiny, pretty and precocious. Often poorly in her early years, she nevertheless survived a bout of smallpox which left her with weakened eyesight but none of the usual scarring. When she wrote about her childhood in her *Memoirs* she recalled her father in tender, loving terms as an indulgent parent, ready to listen and observe, quick to kiss and comfort. Of her mother, by contrast, she remembered only cruelty and violence. Elizabeth Van Lewen, according to her daughter, 'strictly followed Solomon's Advice, in never sparing the Rod, insomuch that I have frequently been whipt for looking blue of a frosty Morning; and, whether I deserv'd it or not, I was sure of Correction every Day of my Life'. It was not unusual for children to be beaten in this way and few people made any connection between physical chastisement and emotional damage, but looking back as a parent herself Laetitia condemned her mother's brutality towards a vulnerable child. She was grateful for her father's gentle treatment, not only because he saved her from whipping but because his kindness kept her soul alive: 'I was by my Father greatly indulg'd; indeed I cannot say, but it was in some Measure necessary, he should, by his Gentleness qualify my Mother's Severity to me; otherwise it must have broke my Heart.'

Her earliest memories were of desire and restraint. Having 'a strong Disposition to Letters', she longed to be able to read, but her mother refused to teach her on the grounds that reading would weaken her eyes still further and mar her beauty (no doubt convinced that her daughter would go cross-eyed and get frown lines on her forehead). Determined to learn, Laetitia pored over printed materials and pestered her mother for help: 'my Mother us'd to tell me the Word, accompanying it with a good Box on the ear', a response that made the child all the more insistent, so that by asking and being corrected 'Twenty times a day' she taught herself to read before her mother realised she even knew all her letters. And then, one memorable day, there came a change:

I was at this Time about five Years of Age, and my Mother being one Day abroad, I had happily laid hold on *Alexander's Feast*, and found something in it so charming, that I read it aloud; – but how like a condemn'd Criminal did I look, when my Father, softly opening his Study-door, took me in the very Fact; I dropt my Book, and burst into Tears, begging Pardon, and promising never to do so again: But my Sorrow was soon dispell'd, when he bade me not be frighten'd, but read to him, which to his great Surprize, I did very distinctly, and without hurting the Beauty of the Numbers. Instead of the whipping, of which I stood in Dread, he took me up in his Arms, and kiss'd me, giving me a whole Shilling, as a Reward, and told me, He would give me another, as soon as I got a Poem by Heart.

With her mother safely out of the house, the little girl had crept into her father's study and helped herself to a volume of Dryden. 'Alexander's Feast, or The Power of Music: an Ode in honour of St Cecilia's Day', with its repetitions and chorus, demands to be read aloud:

> Happy, happy, happy pair!
> None but the brave,
> None but the brave,
> None but the brave deserves the fair.

Not all of the language is as simple as this chorus, however, and if at five she was able to read Dryden's entire ode clearly and with a feel for the rhythm of the lines then it is not surprising that her father was impressed. The poem he then handed her to learn by heart was

Pope's 'Messiah', 108 lines in imitation of Virgil's 'Pollio'. Nothing daunted, she memorised the whole thing before her mother returned, recited it to both parents, and rendered them speechless with astonishment: 'from that Day forward, I was permitted to read as much as I pleas'd'. She was the genius in the family.

As well as giving her free access to his own library, Dr Van Lewen made sure his clever daughter had a plentiful supply of new books – 'the best, and politest Authors' – and took pleasure in explaining whatever she could not understand. It appears that this was the extent of her education. No mention is made of schooling, or masters or mistresses. Laetitia already knew what she liked best: 'chiefly was I charmed and ravish'd with the Sweets of Poetry; all my Hours were dedicated to the Muses; and from a Reader, I quickly became a Writer.' Like that other early starter, Alexander Pope, she 'lisp'd in Numbers, for the Numbers came' and like Pope she was admired and encouraged: 'My Performances had the good Fortune to be look'd on, as extraordinary for my Years, and the greatest and wisest Men in the Kingdom did not disdain to hear the Prattle of the little Muse, as they call'd me, even in my childish Days.'

Perhaps it didn't happen quite like that, but we can probably trust the essential elements of the story: an avid, intelligent child with a remarkable memory who loved poetry and was loved for the entertaining manner in which she expressed it; a born performer, showing off; a father captivated, a mother wary and perhaps rivalrous. The story displays how much Laetitia adored her father and feared and resented her mother.

In her daughter's account, Elizabeth Van Lewen comes down to us as capricious, bad-tempered, capable of ill judgement, intrusive and – above all – the person to be blamed for the disastrous marriage to Matthew Pilkington. Home life during Laetitia's adolescence was probably stormy, but other sources suggest that adults considered Elizabeth a reasonable person. Mary Pendarves, the future wife of Patrick Delany, Dean Swift's close friend, enjoyed an evening with the Van Lewens in 1731, finding them a 'sensible and cheerful' family. She described how Mrs Van Lewen encouraged the company to play a sophisticated party game inspired by Mme de Scudery's popular romance, *Clelie*: one by one they each owned up to what they most liked and disliked about themselves. This made everybody 'very merry'.

Laetitia's favourite author was Shakespeare. She read him voraciously. Years later, having claimed to know all of Shakespeare by heart, she invited Jonathan Swift to read out any line from any Shakespeare play, confident that she would be able to identify and continue the speech. Apparently she carried her point, not once but several times. Swift, in return, handed her Samuel Butler's *Hudibras,* and she made the same experiment on him. People habitually memorised verse in the eighteenth century; they read it aloud in company, quoted constantly from the most popular authors and, to some extent, thought their own thoughts through the poetic expressions that encapsulated them in Thomson or Pope, Young, Swift or Gay. But Laetitia's memory seems to have been exceptional. Though she had no formal schooling, she laid in a stock of learning ('I never forgot what was once told me') as well as a habit of reading that stayed with her all her life.

When she was about six or seven, Laetitia acquired a brother, Meade, who was baptised at St Bride's on 2 May 1715, and the following year a sister, named Elizabeth after her mother. She was wildly jealous of them both and seems to have disregarded them as much as possible. She was not short of companions. The widowed Lady Meade was bringing up a large family a few doors away; as a child Laetitia probably spent time with them, though they were older than her. She also had friends of her own age, 'two young Ladies, in particular, for whom, from my Childhood, I had a very tender Affection, and whom, as often as I could, I visited'. These young ladies were to be instrumental in bringing about the 'Misfortune' of her marriage, for it was at their house that Laetitia Van Lewen first met Matthew Pilkington. Even so, there were to be no harsh words for the friends of her youth, in striking contrast to the bitterness of the references to her mother, brother and sister.

It was a short childhood. Though she was 'unaffectedly innocent' and 'much more pleased with my Female Friends, than with the Company of Men', she soon had admirers and offers of marriage:

By the Time I had look'd on thirteen Years, I had almost as many Lovers; not that I ever was handsome, farther than being very fair. But I was well-drest, sprightly, and remarkably well-temper'd, unapt to give or take Offence; insomuch that my Company was generally coveted; and no Doubt, but I should have been happily disposed of in Marriage, but that my Mother's capricious Temper made her reject every advantageous Proposal offered . . .

None of these 'lovers' who coveted her company made any impression on her heart, though they fed her self-esteem. Intellectually precocious, leading a busy social life, she was also sexually confident. If she was not handsome, she was certainly pretty and vivacious. While, by her own account, 'entirely sub-missive' to her parents, she seems to have had considerable freedom to come and go, even if she often had to take her younger brother with her since otherwise he would cry and make a fuss. Meade, as the only boy, was the focus of the family's future hopes. Both parents idolised him: they were 'fond even to Extravagance' and whatever he wanted he was 'constantly indulg'd in'.

One of the friends Laetitia was allowed to visit was a remarkable young woman a few years older than herself who lived in lodgings nearby. Constantia Crawley, the daughter of 'poor illiterate country people', had somehow scrambled herself into an education. Her knowledge of ancient and modern languages, history, philosophy, mathematics and divinity impressed all who met her. In her teens she left Co. Kilkenny where she grew up and made her way to Dublin, probably after initiating a correspondence with the printer, George Grierson. In Co. Kilkenny Constantia was a celebrated prodigy, and it may be that local worthies recommended her and gave her the money to travel; in any case, Grierson had not been slow to appreciate her value to him. Not only did Constantia have a huge appetite for the contents of books, and a quickness of understanding beyond her years, but her imagination was also caught by everything to do with the production of books. She was to become an adept at selecting, arranging, editing, introducing, proofreading and seeing volumes through the press.

In 1721 when Constantia came into Laetitia's life she was about eighteen and working for Grierson in some capacity. Grierson was married and Constantia was not his mistress, but she was obviously in love with the print (one of her poems was a celebration entitled 'A Poem on the Art of Printing') and possibly with the printer. Meanwhile, for reasons that remain obscure, she wanted to study midwifery. Grierson had taken her to call on Dr Van Lewen.

Constantia's command of Latin and Greek meant that she would be able to read medical textbooks, which may have been what prompted her to seek out a qualified doctor for her lessons in midwifery rather than one of the many women practising at the time. Dr Van Lewen had no hesitation in accepting her as a pupil. He went further still, extending an open invitation to his dinner table. Perhaps he saw at once that Constantia's intellectual serious-ness, her drive, and her passion for learning would appeal to Laetitia and that they would become friends in spite of the difference in age. If so, he must have been pleased for soon they had become so intimate that they were 'seldom asunder', studying hard, talking, going to church, writing, visiting, and testing their wits on the Dublin 'beaux'.

Though constantly in her company, Laetitia never satisfactorily resolved the mystery of Constantia's unusual acquirements. She was told that Constantia's father had encouraged her reading, and that the minister of the parish had taught her now and then, when Constantia could escape the drudgery of needlework 'to which she was closely kept by her mother'; no other explanation was forthcoming. What was puzzling to the doctor's daughter living in the kingdom's second-largest city, in a house full of books, with educated parents and cultivated friends, is even more puzzling at this distance in time. One thing we can deduce, however, is that Constantia herself had little interest in dwelling on the details of her past. Her energies were directed outward and into the future. Nor was she willing to be confined by conventional notions of appropriate feminine behaviour. She had left home, taken herself and her dreams to Dublin, formed a working relationship with one of its leading printers, and decided to study midwifery by apprenticing herself to Dublin's most fashionable male midwife.

At every stage of her progress she found decent men who welcomed and encouraged her, believing – as she did – that God had given her unusual abilities which it would be a sin to waste. Deeply religious, living a life of 'continual Application' as the poet Mary Barber later wrote, she was not solitary, for, as Laetitia put it, 'Curiosity engaged every Person to see' her. She had a reputation as a natural genius.

Nobody doubted Constantia's propriety. Her aim was to be constantly working and always improving. She immersed herself in the classics: her editions of Terence and Tacitus printed by Grierson were to be favoured by scholars for many generations. She kept up with the latest ideas in philosophy and religion: in 1726 she provided an admiring foreword to a new edition of William Wollaston's *The Religion of Nature Delineated* which first appeared in 1722. For light relief, she read and re-read Addison and Steele's essays in *The Spectator* and in 1728 composed a long critical essay introducing an eight-volume reprint. By that time she had married Grierson, whose first wife died in 1726. The two worked closely together. By 1729, when Grierson applied for the patent to be the king's printer in Dublin, the wording of the patent recognised her share in their achievement: 'Mr George Grierson of the city of Dublin, printer, and Constantia, his wife, have brought the art of printing to a greater perfection than was ever heretofore done in this kingdom.'

Not averse to lecturing other young women on their trivial pursuits, it was probably Constantia who characterised Laetitia as the 'gay' and flirtatious one in their friendship. Or perhaps the younger Laetitia, awed by Constantia's achievements while fiercely ambitious on her own behalf, found it more comfortable to play light to Constantia's heavy. Both enjoyed the attentions of the many men 'of the Gown' who were regular visitors at the house of Laetitia's two special friends whose elder brother was a clergyman. It was through this connection (the name of the family has not come down to us) that they met Matthew Pilkington, who took his BA from Trinity in 1722, and was ordained as a deacon a year later. Matthew held a position as a reader in the local parish church of St Andrew's while he studied to become eligible for a full curacy. He was good-looking, clever, musical – he composed, played harpsichord and organ, and sang – and, most compelling of all, he was a poet. To these agreeable accomplishments he added a quick wit, ready humour, and a directness of address and sense of his own worth that made people notice him even though he was very short. Laetitia viewed him as one of the crowd. He was someone she liked without counting him among her 'lovers' for he was 'of obscure Birth, and low Fortune' and she was a girl with at least a dash of slightly noble blood in her veins. Perhaps for this reason, Matthew saw in her a potential wife. He was ready to marry. He probably calculated on a decent dowry and, because she was young and little, assumed she would be malleable.

She was fourteen or fifteen and he was twenty-two or -three when he singled her out. One day Matthew invited all the girls to come to the evening service at church and to stay behind afterwards for a musical entertainment. He sang and played on the organ and then took them into the vestry where he had arranged 'a little Collation' of fruit and wine. Laetitia, who loved to hear music in church and had begged her mother to let her go to the impromptu concert, was no doubt on especially charming form, her complexion heightened by pleasure ('all the Beauty I ever had consisted in Complexion') and her strawberry blonde hair flashing gold by candlelight. Matthew, she recalled, 'began to address me in a very passionate Stile'. He asked permission to visit her. She explained that she was leaving the next day to spend the summer in the country and in any case did not receive male visitors except those her parents had approved.

Throughout that summer of 1723 while she was away in Co. Cork, Matthew sent her letters and poems signed only by the pastoral pseudonym 'Amintas'. Her mother, who kept a close eye on her correspondence, was impressed by the standard of compliment – 'they were really very elegant' – and suggested she should reply if only to thank the poet. Laetitia preferred not to, and pretended she didn't know who her admirer was, in case her mother should find out where she had met him and bar her from the house of her favourite friends.

Returning to Dublin she went as usual to these friends. As often happened, she was forced to take nine-year-old Meade with her. Hardly seated before Matthew arrived, she found herself being upbraided for failing to answer any of his letters. A duel of coquetry followed. She thanked him for the entertainment provided but excused herself: other than her father, she had never written to any man; and besides, she could hardly be considered 'Mistress of Wit enough' to begin a correspondence. These exchanges pleased her – she was flattered and excited – but what followed revealed Matthew's ability to exploit an opportunity and manipulate a situation in pursuit of his own ends:

A good many civil Things were said on either Hand, during Tea time; after which my Brother growing urgent with me to return Home, I happened to say he was so great a Favourite, I durst not contradict him; upon which, Mr Pilkington made his Application to him, and gave him an Invitation to his Lodgings; where he entertain'd him so kindly, that the Child return'd in Raptures with him; and loaden with Toys and Sweet-meats. Upon this Civility to my Brother, my Father sent and Invited Mr Pilkington to Dinner (and you may be sure, he did not refuse him); but quickly found the Art of making himself so agreeable to my Parents, that they were even uneasy whenever he was absent; which seldom happen'd, except when his Duty required his Attendance. He now began openly to court me; and, to my great Surprize, neither of them seemed averse to it; but allow'd him as much Liberty of conversing with me, as a reasonable Man could desire; and for my own Part, he gained so large a Share in my Esteem; that as they seemed to approve of him, I was very well satisfied.

And thus the courtship began. She was surprised at how easily he insinuated himself into her parents' affections and not less so at their willingness to countenance as a suitor a man who brought little beyond his personal qualities. Matthew's father, William Pilkington, was a watchmaker who had come to Dublin when Matthew, the only child, was a boy and put him through school and university. Of Matthew's mother we know almost nothing except that as an old woman she was frightened of her son. A career in the church was costly (one estimate from the 1730s reckoned it cost £400 to educate a boy to become a cleric) but it was cheaper than a training in law or medicine since it could all be done at Ireland's sole university, Trinity College; and all clergymen, by virtue of their office, were accounted gentlemen.

There had been enough money to support Matthew through Trinity as a pensioner, that is, a paying student, not a sizar, a charity case. (Oliver Goldsmith, by contrast, was a sizar when he was at Trinity in the 1740s.) William also owned three plots of land on Lazer's Hill (now Townsend Street) although unlike fashionable Church Street, where by this time the Van Lewens were living, Lazer's Hill was barely genteel.

In the year that followed his strategic wooing of the family through Meade, Matthew came daily, a young man in love. He wrote poems to Laetitia and she to him. They played music and sang together, read and discussed books. She listened to him in church. He mourned with her when her pet canary died. When Mrs Van Lewen took summer lodgings for the bathing a mile away at Blackrock, settling there with children and servants, Matthew rode out every afternoon with Dr Van Lewen to visit. Friends and family questioned the doctor's willingness to indulge the relationship, especially when more promising suitors were turned away. The public nature of the courtship led to talk: from Van Lewen's professional eminence and standard of living, it was assumed he could bestow a fortune on his daughter, so why did he countenance the watchmaker's son? True, Matthew was a respectable and promising clergyman. But he was Irish. And, as everybody knew, in colonial Ireland, the plum jobs always went to the English; it did not matter how much merit an Irish clergyman had, advancement depended on interest. Every English functionary who came over, from the viceroy down through the judges, bishops, clerics and assistants brought their own long trail of dependants. Who was going to help Matthew advance? What kind of future did Dr Van Lewen suppose this Irish curate without means or connections could offer his daughter?

Matthew's circumstances probably aroused sympathetic memories in John Van Lewen, who had also married above himself and made a successful career by combining talent and drive with some well-placed in-laws. But more importantly, there seems to have been a question mark over how much ready money Dr Van Lewen had and what he could bestow on his daughter as a marriage portion. Matthew's poverty may have recommended him; a wealthier suitor could command a higher price. Most of Dr Van Lewen's income went to maintain the necessary appearance of success: house, coach, servants, fine clothing. Anything that could be set aside was reserved for Meade's future expenses. If it came to drawing up a marriage settlement the true nature of his finances would be revealed.

Dr Van Lewen may have wilfully deceived Matthew. Matthew may have deceived himself, choosing to believe that Laetitia would have some sort of fortune; or it might be that her family's social cachet was as significant to him as immediate cash. Matters came to a head when Dr Van Lewen, pressed yet again on the subject by his wife's relations, panicked and tried to pull back. He denied that he understood Matthew Pilkington to be coming to the house as Laetitia's avowed lover; the young man came as a clergyman visiting the family, his parishioners. And then, in a subtle twist, the doctor announced that since people *were* saying there was an 'amorous Correspondence' between the two young people, he would henceforth forbid the man his house, or at least tell his wife not to let him in. Mrs Van Lewen was instructed accordingly. Matthew, arriving as usual to find himself refused entry by an implacable Mrs Van Lewen, fainted clean away. Laetitia's state was not much better. Too scared of her mother to protest, she stood sorrowfully by as Matthew picked himself up and departed, declaring that he had nothing now to live for.

More histrionics followed. Matthew appealed to Constantia to help them meet secretly at her lodgings and with Laetitia's collusion this was arranged. Amid sighs and tears and much tender talk and violent outbursts, Laetitia consented to marry Matthew. It seemed the only solution, but she was in no hurry; snatched meetings and clandestine letters were thrilling enough. Dr Van Lewen, however, had come to a decision. He would send his daughter out of town and out of reach. He announced that she was to go at once and stay for a year with her grandfather Van Lewen in Co. Cork. The moment Laetitia heard this she quickly wrote a letter telling Matthew of her father's plans and gave it to Meade to deliver. Meade came back with the alarming news that Matthew had stabbed himself with a penknife. This turned out to be more theatre than self-harm ('a Scratch, on purpose to terrify us') but it was enough to earn him re-entry into the house and into Elizabeth Van Lewen's good favour, especially as Matthew managed to suggest that he had, after all, some prospects of his own. He was, he announced vaguely but impressively, 'next Heir to a good Estate'. This, according to Laetitia, was 'the most prevailing Argument he could make use of' to her mother.

Convinced that Matthew was sincerely in love, fond of him yet conscious that he was socially beneath them, Elizabeth Van Lewen came up with a proposal that disconcerted and offended her daughter. The young couple should marry at once, and the parents would pretend to the world that they disapproved. The parents would then display forgiveness and help them as much as they could. Laetitia, happy to deceive her mother when it suited her, was shocked at being expected not to mind being publicly regarded as a disobedient daughter. True, she had decided she would marry Matthew, but she did not want to do so immediately, and definitely not at her parents' insistence. Her objections, when she explained them, were dismissed as trifling.

There were other reasons why by this time the Van Lewens might have been happy to accept Matthew as a son-in-law. He was on the verge of qualifying for a full curacy, meaning that with luck and sufficient interest he might obtain a comfortable post; and a poem of his had been published, 'A Pastoral Elegy on the Death of a Lady's Canary-Bird: Inscrib'd to the Fair Mourner', which named his beloved, 'Laetitia'. Protestant Dublin – the Dublin that mattered – was small; it fed on gossip and scandal. It may have been this poem that troubled the relations, for it had made the romance public no matter how much Dr Van Lewen might try to deny it. Laetitia's prospects had been compromised.

Early next morning, called down to breakfast, Laetitia was surprised to find Matthew in the hall with her father. In a state of great excitement Matthew announced that he was off to buy a ring and get a licence and they were to be privately married that evening. She thought he was joking until she noticed that his harpsichord was standing in the parlour 'which, with a Cat and an Owl, were all his worldly Goods'; he had already moved in. Her father gave her the choice: marry immediately by special licence at home or give Matthew up entirely. 'I was too much confounded to make any other Return than to give my Hand to Mr. Pilkington, who kiss'd it with great Extasy; and my unfortunate Nuptials being thus concluded on, we were married privately in the Evening.' Apart from the vicar, there were no witnesses besides her parents and Matthew's father. The date was Monday, 31 May 1725, and she was probably still only sixteen.

CHAPTER TWO

Curate's Wife

The family arranged a honeymoon in Co. Meath, some twelve miles north of Dublin. The newly-weds were packed off to stay with a relation of Lady Meade, Brigadier Patrick Meade, and his wife, Charlotte, who had recently bought themselves a substantial country estate at Curraghstown near Ashbourne. The house, which stood in 177 acres, was described when it was sold on the brigadier's death in 1732, as 'a good wainscoted Dwelling-House, Coach-Houses, Stables, Cow-Houses, Brew House and Dairy, all slated and in good Repair, with Gardens, Fish-Ponds, Dove House and Warren, and all other Conveniences fit for a Nobleman, or Gentleman'.

In these pleasant surroundings, warmly welcomed by the brigadier and his wife who had no children of their own and were affectionate and generous, Mr and Mrs Pilkington stayed till about the middle of June. Matthew, arriving as a published poet as well as a husband, surely carried some copies of his 'The Progress of Music in Ireland', an ambitious poem over 200 lines long, which had recently gone on sale, along with the 'Pastoral Elegy on the Death of a Lady's Canary-Bird', which had named Laetitia.

The young couple came prepared to oblige the company with musical entertainment. Matthew played and Laetitia was an accomplished singer – good enough to please a lover whose musicianship was of professional standard. The 'Pastoral Elegy on the Death of a Lady's Canary-Bird' opens with praise of her voice:

> One Ev'ning mild as fair Laetitia sung,
> And pour'd melodious Sweetness from her Tongue . . .

Less happily, the poem goes on to make use of a telling conceit: the pet bird's death is attributed to a fit of envy at hearing how well his mistress could sing:

> His Heart with Envy burn'd,
> With jealous Rage his tender bosom swell'd,
> To hear his Song surpass'd, his Voice excelled . . .

The lines flattered 'fair' Laetitia's singing while at the same time hinting at Matthew's ambivalence about her wit and poetic ambition. Their two-year courtship had offered opportunity enough for him to discover how badly she wanted to excel and surpass all competition – including him. She meanwhile had learned something about his capacity for envy.

If the evening was for music, the days were spent rambling about in the gardens and fields, loitering by the brook, admiring the prospects:

> Groves, Rivers, Hills with Verdure crown'd,
> And Nature smiling all around

and, for Matthew, wandering further afield, gun in hand. Once when he was gone the whole day, Laetitia composed a poem, 'The Petition of the Birds', in which the 'plum'd Inhabitants of Air' begged him to stop shooting them:

> What Phrenzy has possest your Mind,
> To be destructive of your Kind?

In its application to herself and her children, this was a question that was to beat through later years. For now, though, Matthew was delighted when his wife presented the poem to him, and 'with the raptures of an enamour'd Bridegroom', read it aloud to every acquaintance or visitor who showed the slightest interest.

Back in Dublin, they settled into the Van Lewen family house in Church Street. Returning as a married woman to live with her parents alongside her ten-year-old brother and nine-year-old sister cannot have been easy, but Laetitia claimed that her mother made things worse by deliberately humiliating her. Elizabeth Van Lewen had done what she said she would do, letting it be known that her daughter had married without consent; indeed, she 'said it so often, that at length she persuaded herself it was so; and made it a Pretence for giving me all imaginable ill Treatment, both in public and private'. Feeling ill-used 'both in public and private' because of stories people believed about her was to be a recurring motif in Laetitia's life, and perhaps in these undescribed episodes, when she felt her own powerlessness and her mother's willingness to exploit it, we can discern some of its early formation.

How long the couple continued to live with the Van Lewens is not known but it might have been two or three years. Restive and resentful, having nowhere else to go and insufficient income to rent anywhere decent, Laetitia consoled herself with Matthew's caresses and by spending as much time as possible with her friends. Constantia, friend to them both, heard many complaints about Mrs Van Lewen, and when Constantia visited the house in Church Street Laetitia was glad that she could see for herself, 'how severely both Mr Pilkington and I were us'd, or rather abus'd by my Mother'.

Among other households which offered relief from these 'Vexations' was that of the Percival family who had lived on William Street during Laetitia's childhood. By 1725 they had moved to St Stephen's Green – Dublin's best address. Literary and musical and very sociable, they made their house a centre for talented people, and both Laetitia and Matthew were welcomed there for their own abilities, but also because Dr Van Lewen was Mrs Percival's physician. The connection between the families, if not deep, was a long-standing one: Mrs Percival's brother-in-law, Sir John Percival, later Earl of Egmont, was the dedicatee of Dr John Van Lewen's doctoral thesis. One of Mrs Percival's daughters, Ann Donellan, was the special friend and correspondent of Mary Pendarves, the future Mrs Delany, whose letters provide much information about Dublin at this time. The Percivals were well placed to help Matthew in his poetical and musical ambitions. Since 1716 Philip Percival had been in charge of supervising the king's music in Ireland. It couldn't be said that he always enjoyed this role: in 1723 he grumbled that 'there is not in the King's Dominions a more vexatious Employment, having to do with such a pack of sorry Wretches as fiddlers & Trumpeters'. Of those fiddlers, Matthew's friend Matthew Dubourg was acknowledged as one of the finest violinists in the kingdom. (He was to take over from Percival as master of state music in Dublin in 1728.) Dubourg composed as well as played. He was frequently to be found at the Percivals' house and among his compositions were settings of Matthew's poems.

Like Dubourg, Matthew understood how to distinguish himself from the 'pack of sorry Wretches'. He could combine the obsequiousness, charm and talent required of an Irishman in those unpropitious times with a capacity for hard work that was vital if he wanted to make his way up. Matthew's interests were wide-ranging: in later life he became a noted authority on the lives and works of European artists, producing an important book, *The Gentleman's and Connoisseur's Dictionary of Painters* (1770) that held its own as the standard reference work for almost a century. From his poems it is clear that he was studious: in 'The Candle' he depicted himself 'by Thirst of Wisdom led' poring over Homer, and Flaccus (Virgil) and Anacreon far into the night, enjoying 'Sapho's Soul-subduing Tongue', and improving himself as a man of the 1720s by reading the leading writers of the day. His father's investment in his education, which may have demanded some sacrifice, was not wasted. Egotistical but humorous, convinced of his own importance, Matthew was always busy, always keeping one eye on the main chance. He used his child-like appearance to good effect; when he was a young man most people responded well to him. Perhaps he was also child-like in his cruelty. He cared neither to seem honourable nor courageous. He was breathtakingly indifferent to the feelings of those closest to him; and it was not only his wife who had cause to note that his morals left something to be desired.

Matthew began as an appreciative husband, proud of his wife and pleased with himself. Soon after the honeymoon, in June 1725, a reprint of 'The Progress of Music in Ireland' had been announced, prompted, apparently, by the existence of a pirated 'incorrect' version. Building on this sign of popular appeal, the publishers took the opportunity to put out with it a revised version of the poem on the death of the pet canary and another poem 'written to the same Lady' which depicted Matthew giving his loved one a volume of Pope as a present: 'To Mira, with the Miscellaneous Works of Mr Pope'. Matthew's name was not on the title page but his authorship was known. On 28 August a poem appeared in the *Dublin Weekly Journal* 'Humbly dedicated to the Revd. Mr Ma—ew Pi—k—g—ton, Author of a Poem call'd the Canary Bird'.

In the autumn, a curacy fell vacant at St Andrew's church, where Matthew was already serving as reader and occasional preacher. It is possible that the vicar, John Travers, who was also Chancellor of Christ Church Cathedral and a prebendary of St Patrick's, and who died in 1727, was already ailing and therefore decided he needed a full curate at St Andrew's. John Van Lewen may have put in a word. Matthew was appointed, taking up his post on 17 November 1725 (he was to keep it until 1741 when he became vicar at Donabate). Matthew's signature in the St Andrew's parish registers between March 1726 and March 1728 suggests that he, not the vicar, was managing parish affairs. One of his poems, 'To Lycidas in the Country', bemoans the lack of that 'Ease and Solitude' necessary to pursue his writing. In place of 'calm Delights' were 'harras'd Thoughts', and what with weddings and funerals and the sick beds of the poor, his was a life of 'never-ending Labours'.

He was also at war with his mother-in-law and had become a father. The evidence suggests that fatherhood was not a role which brought Matthew any pleasure. Laetitia meanwhile, pregnant for the first time by mid-November when Matthew took up his curacy, tells us nothing of what it was like to become a mother, nor whether she and Matthew were still living with her parents, nor what arrangements were made for the birth (did her father deliver the baby?). In the *Memoirs* she occasionally observes in passing that she was pregnant, and says once that she was 'always a-breeding'; but mostly we have to remind ourselves that the witty young woman portrayed there gave birth to six children altogether, three of whom died in infancy. There may also have been pregnancies that did not go to full term, especially in the first few years of the marriage.

How did marriage and motherhood suit her? If we judge by a poem Constantia sent when Laetitia was away in Co. Cork in the summer before she married Matthew, the domestic arts of household management were not likely to be her *forte*. In this verse epistle, 'To Miss Laetitia Van Lewen', Constantia poured scorn on the idea that her sophisticated, Dublin friend could find any entertainment in the country, and especially not in grave conversation 'with some serious Matron' about

> Possets, Poultices, and Waters still'd,
> And monstrous Casks with Mead and Cider fill'd

let alone that she would pretend to care

> How many Hives of Bees she has in Store
> And how much Fruit her Trees this Summer bore.

Not the stillroom nor the pantry but amid

> the Grandeur of a Town,
> Where Beauty triumphs, and where Pleasure reigns

was where Constantia felt her friend belonged. (Perhaps we can read into this how much Constantia herself preferred the printshop to the kitchen or garden.)

Laetitia's youngest son Jack, however, who was to be the closest to her of her three surviving children, lauded his mother's maternal qualities. Traumatised by his parents' break-up and divorce when he was seven, Jack looked back on his early years as a haven of peace with an affectionate, attentive mother who liked nothing better than to teach her children their letters. On the other hand, he claims that when he was about three his godfather, Dr Clayton, the bishop of Clogher, offered to take him off his parents' hands and raise him, promising to give him a good education and place him in the world. Reflecting on this, Jack regretted that his parents refused. By then he was able to compare his own rootless life and patchy education with that of his elder brother William. William, the firstborn, baptised on 9 June 1726, had been given to his Pilkington grandparents to bring up. It was not uncommon at the time for children to be passed around family members in this way. The decision may have been taken when Matthew's father gave the couple a home of their own on Lazer's Hill. Of the three properties William Pilkington senior owned there, he lived on one plot himself, rented out a second, and the third he made available to them, rent-free, sometime before 1729. Living just two doors away, this did not mean that William junior was entirely removed from his parents but the arrangement had significant consequences. It provided him with a measure of stability and some detachment. William grew up more rough and less polished than if he had been kept with his parents or handed over to his Meade relations (or so Jack, who shared his mother's pride in her maternal connections, implied). The cost of his education was borne by his grandfather, who could probably only just afford it. Just as old William Pilkington had ensured that Matthew was well educated, so too he gave his eldest grandson and namesake 'the best tuition money could procure' while Jack got nothing.

∞

Ireland after 1690 was a colony governed from England and in the Protestant interest. There was an Irish parliament, presided over by successive lords lieutenant, which sat every other year in Dublin Castle; and in the Irish House of Lords the bishops of the Church of Ireland had some influence, but never enough to counter a government policy expressly designed to keep Ireland weak. In his great biography of Jonathan Swift, Irvin Ehrenpreis explained it thus:

The Irish represented most of all a threat, and less often a resource, but never a nation to be sympathized with. In times of war or unrest, invaders and trouble-makers might come from Ireland; so the country had to be kept under strict military surveillance. If Ireland grew prosperous, she might provide enough royal revenue for the King to make himself independent of Parliament; so she must be kept poor. If the Irish made a success of any industry that was already established in England, their lower wages and costs might give their products a competitive edge; so manufacturing had to be discouraged unless it was in some sense non-competitive.

Prevented from developing its rich natural resources, its trade ruthlessly controlled, land shockingly mismanaged, and economy burdened by carpetbaggers of every description, Ireland in the early eighteenth century existed to be plundered. In 1717, the Primate of Ireland, Archbishop King, observed that the kingdom was 'more miserable' than ever, 'the poor squeezed to death by excessive rents to maintain the luxury of a few'. Within a few years, matters had become even worse. The 1720s was a decade of economic crisis. There was a financial crash, a shortage of silver coin because it suited the merchants and bankers to ship it out, failed harvests, famine and fever. Archbishop King blamed 'the griping landlords who grind the faces of the poor', by which he meant English landowners who lived for the most part on the English side of the Irish Sea, and who 'drained us of our money and contribute nothing to the burthens of the kingdom or the employment of the poor or their relief, so that we that live here are forced to maintain the beggars they make, or let them starve'.

If they were not a nation to be sympathised with, nor were the wretched Irish to be accorded respect. The paradox was that English-born Protestant Irish suffered along with the native Roman Catholics over whom they ruled and whose land they had appropriated, for, with six or seven Catholics to every Protestant, their only security was felt to lie in English military might and deference to English policy. But English policy was avowedly antagonistic to Irish interest, and that included the interests of English-born families who had settled in Ireland, had children, and looked to place younger sons in the church, government, law, farming or business. The Anglo-Irish gentry were a ruling minority denied any real power of self-government. Jonathan Swift, who had been dean of St Patrick's Cathedral in Dublin since 1714, had many friends in this class and understood the frustrations of their ambiguous position. Time and again when a place became vacant, he lobbied on behalf of promising home-grown candidates only to find that an Englishman – and not necessarily a talented one – would be given it.

Swift himself had once hoped to be granted an English bishopric and play a direct part in government by sitting in the English House of Lords. But by the mid-1720s he had reconciled himself to the fact that neither the Crown – the House of Hanover – nor the government – a Whig hegemony under Robert Walpole – was ever going to look favourably on him. Even before the huge fame of *Gulliver's Travels* in 1726, Swift was a well-known high-Tory pamphleteer. Through the force of his pen he had risen to be one of the most influential figures in the 1710–14 Tory government of Queen Anne. He had been a close associate of Robert Harley, Earl of Oxford, Anne's chief minister, and Viscount Bolingbroke, both of whom were in disgrace in the years following Anne's death in 1714.

It may have been true that Swift considered Ireland 'a scene too little for his genius', as Patrick Delany put it, but in some ways it suited him well. Identifying with a community of people ill-treated by the English ruling class and taking up its cause was a convenient way of revenging himself on that ruling class for treating him badly. In 1724 Swift became a popular hero in Ireland, and especially in Dublin, when a series of his pamphlet letters addressed to the Irish people and signed 'M. B. Drapier' prevented the introduction of cheap currency. Swift intervened in an affair that was typical of the times, involving bribery and corruption at the highest levels and the prospect of huge private gain from robbing the public purse. A hefty bribe to one of the king's mistresses had bagged for a speculative ironmaster, one William Wood, the patent to manufacture copper coins for Ireland. Ireland needed coins (though it needed silver more than copper) but this monopoly would have been a licence to debase the currency. Swift appealed to shopkeepers, farmers, 'common-people', warning them to refuse to handle the 'filthy trash' and assuring them that resistance was not treason. His cleverly calibrated words produced what government observers and church leaders called an 'epidemical frenzy', a 'general con-flagration': mobs on the streets, public declarations, pamphlets, broadsides, poems and petitions, arrests of printers (including Swift's printer) and rioting in Cork where a ship was waiting to unload the coins. Everybody knew that Swift was 'the Drapier', but the government was reluctant to finger him. The fourth Drapier letter, *A Letter to the Whole People*, was timed to be hawked and cried about in the very precincts of Dublin Castle when the new viceroy, Lord Carteret, arrived to take up his post in the autumn of 1724, and its contents were blatantly seditious. After that, the government announced a reward of £300 for anyone who would reveal the author's identity, but this was no more than a face-saving gesture. In response, all over Dublin pieces of paper were fixed up in public places bearing a verse from the Bible: 1 Samuel 14, verse 45: 'the people rescued Jonathan'.

In the years that followed, bonfires were lit and church bells rung on Swift's birthday. His minor ailments and indispositions, his comings and goings, were reported in the press. Ostentatious celebration of Swift as the people's hero was, among other things, a way of expressing protest against English rule.

For a poetical young curate like Matthew Pilkington, Swift's eminence was an obvious draw. They may have encountered each other through the church: St Andrew's and St Patrick's were neighbouring parishes. They would certainly have been at some of the same cultural events. There were potential family and friendship overlaps: Meade was a pupil at the school in Capel Street run by Swift's closest friend, Dr Thomas Sheridan, and a contemporary of Swift's godson, Thomas Sheridan junior. But Matthew no doubt recognised that he had taken his best step towards the dean when Patrick Delany, Dublin's most popular preacher and a long-time fellow of Trinity College, began to take an interest in him. Delany, a close friend of Swift, had been told about the Pilkingtons by Constantia Grierson, who took copies of their poems for him to read, and reported on the difficulties 'the poor young Couple' had been having with Mrs Van Lewen. As a Trinity classmate of John Van Lewen, Delany was not unacquainted with the family. Now his notice extended to all of them and was regarded as a mark of status. It was 'a Favour we were all extremely proud of' when, one Sunday after preaching at St Andrew's, Delany walked home with them. Better still, he issued an invitation to dinner at his country villa, Delville, just on the edge of Dublin.

At Delville Patrick Delany self-consciously lived the life of a cultivated, polite gentleman of letters, raising the tone of society by promoting literature and patronising writers and doing everything he could to advance himself. Music and art were important to such a life, as were landscape gardening and home improvement – on which Delany spent well beyond his means. Those means were ample enough to irritate the archbishop, Hugh Boulter, who objected to Delany's insistence on keeping a church incumbency at St John's along with his college fellowship that Boulter calculated paid no less than £700 per annum. There were other sources of income, all needed to feed a habit of high-minded high living: along with his country estate, Delany maintained elegant rooms in Stafford Street where the virtues of moderation were extolled at regular Thursday evening gatherings.

Delany's known friendship with Swift gave a special éclat to his literary coterie. Indeed, he had already interested Swift in some of his protégées. Mary Barber, a wool-draper's wife with four children, who had published poems in 1725 and 1728, and who was a neighbour of Delany's at Delville, as well as being a close friend of Constantia Grierson, had been introduced to Swift by 1728. Swift thought highly of her writings and promoted the subscription volume of her poems that was eventually printed by Samuel Richardson in London in 1734.

A generation older than the Pilkingtons, Mary Barber was 'Saphira', the senior poet of the circle. The newcomers treated her with deference, seeing her as more of a patron than a peer. Delany's literary circle was unusual in being so friendly to female aspiration and in numbering among its members many gifted women. Others we know of include Frances-Arabella Kelly, Martha Donellan Percival and Mrs Sican, a grocer's wife; also, Dr Van Lewen's wife, Elizabeth, who on at least one occasion argued with Delany about whether Christians should follow the practice of Jews and abstain from eating blood or things strangled. (Delany, who thought they should, published his views in *Revelation Examined with Candour*, 1732.) All took a lively and intelligent interest in books, poetry, music, art and ideas, discussing them with the clergymen and scholars – the 'Men of Genius' – who gathered around Delany. For the poets there was in addition what Delany liked to call his 'Senatus Consultum', an inner circle who read and advised on each other's writings.

Having edged their way in, both Matthew and Laetitia at once wrote and circulated poems to charm and flatter the coterie and reinforce the sense of their own worth. Matthew's 'The Lost Muse' eulogised Delville as a place 'where all the Wise resort, / Where oft the Muses keep their Court', and praised Delany's 'Learning,

Elegance and Ease'. It was the job of the poet invited to the patron's country retreat to sing the praises of place and person (the beauties of the place serving as an emblem of the virtuous owner). Laetitia's poem, 'Delville the Seat of the Rev. Dr. Delany', composed, she claimed, 'in one of his lovely Arbours', hailed Delville as an earthly Paradise of Christian inspiration. Delany, attuned to Nature's beauties, finding God's image 'in each Insect, Plant and Flow'r', and creatively developing his open prospects and winding walks, flowers and meadows, was like God himself, seeking to 'bless and beautify the earth'. To be at Delville was to be elated by 'Nature improv'd and rais'd by Art'. She tells us that this early poem was well received: 'from the Candour of the Company [it] met with great Applause'. She had made her mark. She became one of the 'Senatus Consultum', along with Matthew who was dubbed Thomas Thumb, or Mighty Thomas, she meanwhile being 'his Lady fair'.

If Mary Barber was the senior poet, Constantia Grierson was the intellectual. Intense and driven, pale and perhaps already sickly, Constantia published her edition of Terence in 1727, the same year she gave birth to her first child, a son baptised George Primrose Grierson. A few months later, the little boy died, accidentally smothered by the nurse. Both parents were heart-broken. Constantia memorialised this 'Unhappy Child to early Sorrows born' in a touching poem which was circulated:

> Ah Lovly harmless shade Couldst thou but see
> How much thy wretched mother mourns for thee.

The whole group mourned the baby's death. Mary Barber commemorated the tragedy in lines 'Occasion'd by seeing some Verses written by Mrs Constantia Grierson, upon the Death of her Son', which registered Constantia's learning while calling on Heaven to soften the bereaved mother's woes:

> This Mourning Mother can with ease explore
> The Arts of Latium, and the Grecian store:
> Was early learn'd, nay more, was early wise . . .

Mary Barber herself made no claims to being learned. Her skill lay in colloquial light verse and her poetic persona drew on her daily life as the mother of school-age children. Like Swift she enjoyed speaking through the voices of others. A number of her poems, among them one of her most anthologised, adopted the voice of her elder son, Constantine, who was to grow up to be a doctor and president of the Irish College of Physicians. The lively and informal 'Written for My Son, and Spoken by Him at His First Putting on Breeches' begins,

> What is it our mammas bewitches
> To plague us little boys with breeches?

and goes on to argue for rational dress: no tight trousers to impede the circulation, no narrow shoes with peg-like heels, no hat-bands cramping the brain, no close-bound wrists, no cravats. In other poems she displayed characteristic feminist views, as when advising her son on the qualities he should look for in a wife – 'let her principal care be her mind' – and good humour when ventriloquising an unnamed reverend gentleman whom she imagined disapproving of her writing:

> I pity poor Barber, his wife's so romantic:
> A letter in rhyme! – Why the woman is frantic!
> This reading the poets has quite turned her head;
> On my life, she should have a dark room and straw bed.

Progressive and enlightened, self-consciously superior, the group made fun of old-fashioned attitudes and promoted each other's work. In 'The Lost Muse', Matthew depicted 'Saphira' as the embodiment of the goddess Clio, full of goodness and gaiety, excellence and wit, charm and delight. Mary Barber's poems do indeed reveal her as witty, charming and original, but she was tough and worldly too. A businesswoman working in what seems to have been a failing enterprise in the cloth trades, she was determined that her children would not spend their lives behind a counter. (Her husband, Rupert, seems not to have been much help.) With the encouragement of Swift and Delany, she was putting together a volume of her poems in the hope of publishing it by subscription. To this end, many gatherings at Delville, and at Delany's regular Thursday evenings at Stafford Street, were devoted to correcting Mary Barber's verses.

Matthew, who was also working on his first collection of poems, circulated his writings and vied for attention. By the autumn of

1728 he had been introduced to Swift, probably about the time he composed an ode for the king's birthday celebrations that was set to music by Matthew Dubourg. This 'Ode on his Majesty's Birthday' was accepted and performed in pomp and state at Dublin Castle in October. Like most official verse it is undistinguished poetry, but it was a great mark of the parson's progress. There would have been festivity in the Pilkington households on Lazer's Hill. Dubourg's musicianship and connections were crucial to this success. Swift, meanwhile, took note of the ode in two ways, both of them gratifying: he made fun of it in his own 'Directions for a Birth-day Song', and he helped Matthew revise the ode when it was chosen again for performance the following year.

Official recognition of this sort paid well. On its second time around, in 1729, Matthew received £50 from the viceroy, Lord Carteret, as a 'premium' for the ode, a sum of money that threw him and Laetitia into a fever of anxiety and excitement. Matthew wrote about the experience in a self-mocking letter-diary addressed to Dr Delany. His narrative about how awful it was to be given £50, *The Plague of Wealth, or the Poet's Diary: occasion'd by the Author's receiving £50 from His Excellency the Lord Carteret, as a Premium for the foregoing Ode on His Majesty's Birth-Day. In a Letter to Dr Delany*, is a far more interesting piece of writing than the ode. *The Plague of Wealth* purports to teach that wealth is more troublesome than poverty and it does so by using some of the techniques of the sermon: the Biblical moral that money is the root of all evil being expressed through personal anecdote. In the exchanges with the poet's wife we glimpse his abjection and fear of her tongue which, though formulaic, tell us something about the relationship as Matthew experienced it. Matthew describes how he had to keep calling at the viceroy's secretary's office for a week before he actually got the promised bill, and then in his excitement managed to tear it before he got home:

Dismally frightened – I came home – shew'd it to my Wife – was more terrify'd at hearing that it would now be of no Value – receiv'd several compliments from her for my Care of it – and, *that I was likely to be rich, since I took such Pains to preserve what I got* – and the like – went directly in a Fit of Anger and Vexation to Henry's Bank – smil'd a little and spoke submissively to the Clerk – obtain'd a new Bill – return'd again in great Joy – all Things settled amicably between us.

Sleepless nights follow. His wife nags and berates the hapless poet, waking him three times in one night convinced that burglars are in the bedroom. The pleasure of spreading the money out on a table and gloating over it is easily overwhelmed by unease. 'Went round my House to inspect the Doors whether they were all safe – perceiv'd a great deficiency of Bars, Bolts, Locks, Latches, Door-Chains, Window-Shuts, Fire-Arms, &c which I never had taken the least Notice of before.' Finally, after eleven days of this, the 'dreadful Narration' closes with an arithmetical calculation of the exact amount of pleasure and pain that the £50 had brought him. There was the hour spent with Lord Carteret, the three hours and one minute telling his friends about it, the three minutes of actually receiving the bill and three hours of peace with his wife after obtaining the new bill in place of the torn one. A total of seven hours and four minutes of happiness. On the debit side, 'All the Remainder': ten days, sixteen hours and fifty-six minutes of misery.

The Plague of Wealth makes good comedy out of what was already a stock theme: the inability of the poor to handle wealth, especially if they were poets and even more so if they were Irish. It may have been written with his wife's help. As a married couple Matthew and Laetitia projected stylised versions of themselves that drew on Irish stereotypes – foolish, useless man, scathing woman. They developed a double-act that was to provide material for the entertainment of others for years to come, working as a pair and using the visual gag of their diminutive size for comic effect. Whether this would have been so much of a temptation had it not been for Swift's *Gulliver's Travels* with its Lilliputians as a ready reference point is debatable; but the fame of Swift's book must have made it irresistible. Beyond the coterie, harping on their smallness was a convenient way of reminding readers that they were part of a circle that included one of the most famous writers in the kingdom. Matthew's verse epistle, 'The Invitation. To Dr Delany at Delville', written in 1729, which invites Delany to dinner at their house at Lazer's Hill – the 'humble Cell' where 'Mirth,

Innocence, and Peace can dwell' – compares himself and Laetitia
to toys in a toyshop:

> Oft in a Toyshop have you seen
> A gawdy-painted, small Machine
> Where Man and Wife are plac'd together,
> To tell by turns the Change of Weather;
> No Simile could half so well
> Describe the House in which I dwell.
>
> O! wou'd some Zephyr waft, with Care,
> My House and Garden thro' the Air,
> To Lands encircled by the Main,
> Where Lilliputian Monarchs reign,
> How wou'd it glad my Heart to see
> Whole Nations – somewhat less than me?
> My House wou'd then a Palace rise,
> And Kings with Envy view my Size.

Could zephyrs have wafted the house to another part of the city
it would probably have pleased them both. For the girl who had
grown up in William Street and Church Street, and whose father
was planning to move to a new house on fashionable Molesworth
Street, Lazer's Hill was a comedown. Neighbouring properties
included a chandler's shop and a whisky distillery; and William
Pilkington himself seems to have augmented his watchmaking
business by keeping an ale-house. (Perhaps this was a fund-raiser
for William's future college bills.) Close to the south quays of the
river Liffey, the area was full of boatmen and fishermen. In term-
time, it must also have been full of students, since it bordered
Trinity College on its eastern side. Still, it was a convenient
location for Matthew's duties at St Andrew's church and near
enough to George Grierson's printshop in Essex Street for Laetitia
to visit Constantia, while Delany and other Trinity men had to do
no more than walk across a field to pay a visit.

The toy-sized couple delighted in their toy-sized house with its
long, narrow garden. They took a pride in making a genteel home.
They had books, prints and musical instruments. Following the
example set by Delany and Swift, both of whom were keen
gardeners, Matthew saw to it that the garden was beautifully laid
out and maintained. He supervised the building of a summerhouse that doubled as a reception area and shared study, giving

them extra space. The summerhouse was where they entertained their friends and where they retreated to write – or, in Laetitia's words, where 'we both invoked the Muse'. As a curate, Matthew's secure income would have been perhaps £50 per annum. Dr Van Lewen had agreed to make a contribution to the couple's finances, though that may not always have been paid. Swift estimated in 1732 that Matthew was getting about £100 from different sources. It was enough to keep a maid and a footman, though not enough to maintain a carriage; the ready availability of her father's carriage was one of the luxuries Laetitia feared she would miss after leaving home.

There was certainly mirth in their married life together at this time, and perhaps even innocence and peace along with the turbulent energies of competing ambitions. But in the *Memoirs* Laetitia observed that when Matthew published his poems in her praise he was privately saying 'every thing disagreeable' to her, which suggests that the marriage turned sour early. Her pregnancies put a strain on the relationship; they took off her bloom and led Matthew to look elsewhere for female company.

In the winter of 1729, Mrs Sican travelled to England. She carried with her a letter from Swift to Alexander Pope in which Swift bragged about Dublin's literary women. 'Can you boast such a Triumfeminate in London,' Swift challenged Pope, as Mrs Sican, a grocer's wife, Constantia Grierson, a printer's wife, and Mary Barber, a wool-draper's wife? Laetitia Pilkington was not included in the list, probably because Swift had only very recently made her acquaintance.

Through Delany, Swift had begun to interest himself in Matthew's prospects. Of all the young clergy Swift met in his capacity as dean of St Patrick's at that time, Matthew seemed to him the most promising. He found him intelligent, well-read, a good preacher, and 'of so hopefull a genius' that he was worth nurturing. Swift's support was invaluable: Matthew was preparing his poems and building up a list of subscribers for a first volume. Constantia, too, was making headway in her writing career. We know that Laetitia was writing hard, and that visitors might expect to hear her recite her own verses when they came to Lazer's Hill to be entertained in the summerhouse. But she had given birth to a second baby, Elizabeth (Betty), baptised on 28 January 1729, whom she was caring for, and by the autumn of that year she was pregnant again. Mrs Pilkington was jealous of the others and made no secret of it. She complained that she was being excluded, especially when Matthew and Constantia were invited to go with Delany to St Patrick's deanery to celebrate Swift's birthday that November. Exasperated, she accused them of deliberately keeping her away from the dean because they knew she would monopolise his attention: her wit would outshine theirs. 'As I spoke this but half serious, I set them all a laughing,' she commented, but it was clearly no laughing matter. With so many examples before her – not only Matthew, but also Mary Barber whose achievement in bending so many men of genius to her cause was truly remarkable – it was frustrating to be left out. She knew the benefits that would accrue from having Swift as a patron. Characteristically, Laetitia's complaint was made after she had devised a retaliatory action. She was not just a wife left to mope at home but a poet, and birthdays were occasions that a poet could always mark with celebratory verses. She had composed twenty elegant lines praising Swift. These she gave to Delany to present. Delany played his part well, telling Swift the story of her 'saucy' speech. ('Give me my Due,' she wrote smugly later, 'I was pretty pert.') Swift sent back a message that he would see her whenever she chose to visit him.

Thus began a relationship which, on her side, was indeed to prove profitable. Swift at this time was in his sixties. He had never married, and the evidence suggests that he feared and was disgusted by adult sexual relations. Women were important to him, however, especially young women, and he valued female company; he had maintained the companionship of Esther Johnson (the 'Stella' of his poems and letters, whom he had first met when she was a child) throughout her life. Esther had left England and settled in Dublin to be near him. Some scholars claim they married secretly, but there is no evidence to prove this and the leading Swiftians dismiss it. Perhaps, like Esther

Vanhomrigh, the 'Vanessa' of Swift's poems and another young woman whose relationship with Swift had been important and is hard to fathom, 'Stella' pined and longed for marriage; or perhaps she was content living with her older companion, Rebecca Dingley, seeing plenty of company, enjoying books and conversation and having, through her well-known connection with the dean, a public identity which was more like being his ward than his lover.

Stella's death in January 1728 had devastated Swift. There was a space in his life for a bright young woman whom he could tease and play with in his own peculiar way; and it is to Laetitia Pilkington that we owe much of our knowledge of just how peculiar Swift's ways could be.

CHAPTER THREE

Dr Delany's Set

Laetitia's first meeting with Swift took place at Delville. The dean invited himself to dine at Delany's and requested that Delany also invite the Pilkingtons. Matthew made his own way there while Mary Barber called for Laetitia and accompanied her, possibly in Dr Van Lewen's coach.

On arrival, Delany's servant directed the women out to the garden where they found Matthew, Delany and Swift walking on the terrace. Below the terrace, a lawn sloped down to a little brook; beyond was a high bank with a hanging wood of evergreens, and beyond that a glorious view of hills and sea. The terrace wound its way round the garden; there were fruit trees trained along the wall, and what Mary Delany later described as 'several prettinesses': 'wild walks, private seats, and lovely prospects'. Much levelling and raising had produced a 'natural' aesthetic modelled after Pope's garden at Twickenham. Later there was to be a grotto and a folly built as a miniature temple of Apollo; already the terrace was carefully designed to lead the eye of the visitor to 'a magnificent Portico, where Painting and Sculpture display'd their utmost Charms'. Dr Sheridan, who was probably envious (his home life was squally and he was always short of funds), and Swift, who was not, both made fun of what they deemed grandiosity: Delville was an eleven-acre suburban plot, not a handsome landed estate. The nakedness of Delany's ambition made them uncomfortable.

Portico, paintings and sculptures testified to Delany's appreciation of the arts while at the same time sending a message about status: one sure sign of a gentleman was the building up of a private collection of art. Delany's was the first collection that Matthew was able to study and learn from; we can imagine him developing his connoisseurship by examining the works, and picking up from Delany some knowledge of the business of acquisition. The group boasted that the viceroy, Lord Carteret, would occasionally drop in for convivial chat. They exaggerated the informality of this, but there was something for Carteret – a serious scholar and even more serious wine lover – in the company at Delville; and no doubt the presence of paintings and sculpture helped smooth what might otherwise have seemed a dangerous abandonment of pomp and circumstance.

Corpulent and cheerful, Patrick Delany brought the art of being comfortable to a high pitch. Of a modest background – he was a farmer's son and had been a sizar at Trinity, which meant that unlike Matthew, whose father had paid his fees, he had been required to be a servant to the other students – he had by this time added the Chancellorship of Christ Church Cathedral to his list of preferments and was soon to gain St Patrick's. Swift described him to Pope as 'a man of the easiest and best conversation I ever met with in this Island, a very good list'ner, a right reasoner, neither too silent, nor talkative, and never positive'. These qualities served Delany well: the combined support of Dean Swift and Lord Carteret was crucial to his rise, although in 1743, when he wanted to marry Mary Pendarves, a cousin of the viceroy, he discovered the limits of easy conversation and elegant hospitality. Lord Carteret was among those of the family who vehemently objected on the grounds that no matter how learned he was, how good his conversation, how elegant his hospitality, Delany was not a gentleman. He was low-born and Irish. The marriage went ahead and proved to be a happy one. (Mary Pendarves was a widow of forty-three at the time, and Delany a widower of fifty-eight.)

Presented to Swift by the matronly Mary Barber, Laetitia, aged about twenty, found herself facing a well-built, tallish man of sixty dressed in clerical black, with piercing blue eyes under shaggy brows. His demeanour was grave. It was a point of principle with Swift that he rarely laughed, even when – or especially when – cracking a joke. He, meanwhile, looked down and apparently saw someone he mistook for Mrs Barber's daughter. Mary Barber, knowing Swift's ways, smiled and explained that the very small person beside her was Mrs Pilkington. Swift expressed his astonishment. In her *Memoirs*, Mrs Pilkington rendered the scene in dialogue, so that the first words she claimed Swift spoke to her were full of wise portent: 'What,' says he, 'this poor little Child married! God help her, she is early engag'd in Trouble.'

The day passed in 'a most elegant and delightful Manner'. This is all we know about it except that Matthew was asked to preach at St Patrick's the following Sunday morning and all the company were invited to the deanery for dinner afterwards.

Of that Sunday visit to St Patrick's, which was Mrs Pilkington's first full-length exposure to Swift on his own ground and which included three hours alone with him, we know a great deal. She remembered it in vivid detail. The day began with morning service at the cathedral where Matthew preached and Swift administered communion. After the service, they met the dean at the church door and saw how he gave money to beggars. There was a coin for every outstretched hand except one, an old woman whose hand was dirty. Swift reproved her: water was not so scarce that she couldn't have washed. They then processed behind the silver verge from the cathedral to the deanery, a commodious mansion that still stands in Lower Kevin Street. Once inside, Swift immediately separated Mrs Pilkington from the rest of the company and took her off to his study. Matthew, who tried to come too, was 'merrily' repulsed. Swift was excited. He had something to show the awe-struck little person by his side. Like an adult with a special toy he knew would please a child, he guided her into the library promising to produce trinkets and medals, souvenirs of his glory days when he was advisor to the most powerful men in the land. He opened the drawers of a bureau filled with presents he had been given by his famous friends: the Earl and Countess of Oxford, Lady Masham, Lady Betty Germain. He let Laetitia hold some medals and invited her to choose two for herself (instinctively she weighed them to see which was heaviest and therefore, as she thought, most valuable). Then he directed her towards a cabinet, explaining that he wanted to show her all the money he had got when he was 'in the Ministry', but she had to promise she wouldn't steal it. She promised. He opened the cabinet and then, one by one inside it, she was shown 'a whole Parcel of empty Drawers'. Swift had got nothing from his time 'in the Ministry' except an Irish deanery – a cabinet of empty drawers. 'Bless me,' he said, pretending to be surprised, 'the Money is flown'.

Swift loved wordplay and practical jokes of all kinds. He 'amused' Laetitia in this way until they were called for dinner. During dinner, she observed him watching his servants through a mirror above the sideboard. Just as he knew very well that the cabinet in his library was empty of money, so he knew that the butler would help himself to a glass of ale, and there was a routine theatricality about catching the man in the act; as there was when the cook, who had over-roasted the meat, was hauled up to the dining-room to be told to take it back and cook it less. These squabbles with the servants were a regular part of the entertainment. She found them a trial.

Nor was Swift's conversational style a restful one. After thanking Matthew for his sermon and observing that neither of the Pilkingtons smoked – a sign 'you were neither of you bred in the University of Oxford; for drinking and smoking are the first Rudiments of Learning taught there' – he turned to Mrs Pilkington and demanded she tell him her faults. When she begged to be excused he asked her husband to reveal them. Matthew politely claimed he had yet to find any faults in his wife. Dr Delany protested that the dean was being 'unpolite' in supposing Mrs Pilkington had any faults, upon which Swift explained his logic. Whenever he saw agreeable qualities in any person he was always sure they had an equal number of disagreeable ones and in her case he wished to know at once what they were. She took his words as a compliment. Trying to compliment him back or know how to behave when in the grip of his attention was more complicated. Her account of what happened next became one of the most celebrated passages in the *Memoirs*:

The Dean then asked me, 'If I was a Queen, what I should chuse to have after Dinner?' I answered, 'His Conversation'; 'Phooh!' says he, 'I mean

41

what Regale?' 'A Dish of Coffee, Sir'; 'Why then I will so far make you as happy as a Queen, you shall have some in Perfection; for when I was Chaplain to the Earl of Berkley, who was in the Government here, I was so poor, I was obliged to keep a Coffee-house, and all the Nobility resorted to it to talk Treason'; I could not help smiling at this Oddity, but I really had such an Awe on me, that I could not venture to ask him, as I long'd to do, what it meant? The Bottle and Glasses being taken away; the Dean set about making the Coffee, but the Fire scorching his Hand, he called to me to reach him his Glove, and changing the Coffee-pot to his Left-hand, held out his Right one, ordered me to put the Glove on it, which accordingly I did, when taking up Part of his Gown to fan himself with, and acting in Character of a prudish Lady, he said, 'Well, I don't know what to think; Women may be honest that do such things, but, for my Part, I never could bear to touch any Man's Flesh – except my Husband's, whom perhaps,' says he, 'she wish'd at the Devil.'

'Mr Pilkington,' says he, 'you would not tell me your Wife's Faults; but I have found her out to be a damn'd insolent proud, unmannerly Slut': I looked confounded, not knowing what Offence I had committed. – Says Mr Pilkington, 'Ay Sir, I must confess she is a little saucy to me some-times, but – what has she done now?' 'Done! Why nothing, but sat there quietly, and never once offered to interrupt me in making the Coffee, whereas had I had a Lady of modern good Breeding here, she would have struggled with me for the Coffee-pot till she had made me scald myself and her, and made me throw the Coffee in the Fire; or perhaps at her Head, rather than permit me to take so much Trouble for her.'

This raised my Spirits, and as I found the Dean always prefac'd a Compliment with an Affront, I never afterwards was startled at the latter (as too many have been, not entering into his peculiarly ironical Strain).

Both the Pilkingtons had the knack of entering into Swift's play-acting and 'peculiarly ironical strain' but it required a nimble wit. She was glad when dinner was over.

Most of the company left after the meal. Then shortly before 3 p.m., when the bells rang for church, Matthew and Dr Delany, who had preaching engagements elsewhere, also left. Laetitia was able to avoid going with them and sitting through another sermon. There was no service at the cathedral till six, so she stayed alone with Swift the rest of the afternoon. He brought out the manuscript of his *History of the Four Last Years of the Queen* and asked her to read it aloud to him. This history of 1710 to 1714 was one of a number of accounts Swift wrote about his own 'four last years' of intense and high-powered political involvement which had ended with the death of Queen Anne, the collapse of the Tory ministry and his exile in Ireland. Wanting to publish it, he had taken it with him to London in the summer of 1727 and given it to Pope and Bolingbroke to read, both of whom told him to put it away and forget about it. It was not only the money from those days that had 'flown'.

Bright-eyed and receptive, Mrs Pilkington was a more obliging reader than either Pope or Bolingbroke. Some of the wounds her presence salved may be heard in Swift's rudeness to her: as she read, he stopped her periodically to ask if she understood what she was reading, explaining that he wanted the account to be intelligible to 'the meanest Capacity', and adding, 'if you comprehend it, 'tis possible every Body may'. She noted the insult with a smile, recognising the honour he paid her and making sure she showed, by the aptness of her comments, that she was well versed in history and the rudeness of men.

When the bells rang for evening prayer they went together to the cathedral, where the music from choir and organ put her in mind of Milton, whose lines she had by heart, and then they returned to the deanery to find the usual Sunday evening company gathering. Dr Delany and Matthew had returned, Dr Sheridan and several clergymen had arrived, along with Swift's close friends John Rochfort and Charles Ford. At this point, the Pilkingtons began to say their goodbyes, but were told they could stay for supper. Swift took out a corkscrew from a golden case he kept in his pocket and decanted a bottle of wine. He handed Matthew the lees in a glass to drink, 'For,' says he, 'I always keep some poor Parson to drink the foul Wine for me.' Matthew gamely declared he was grateful to get any wine at all, and couldn't tell the difference anyway, at which point Swift removed the glass from his hand and congratulated him on being wiser than some other 'paultry Curate' who, dining with him a few days earlier, had been offended at such treatment 'and so walk'd off without his Dinner'.

Charles Ford dominated the conversation at supper, contradicting everybody in a manner Mrs Pilkington found deeply annoying. She was no longer the centre of attention although

Swift singled her out when, wanting to open another bottle, he couldn't at first find the golden corkscrew. He accused her of stealing it on the grounds that she was the poorest person in the company. When at last she and Matthew left, Swift pressed into her hand enough money to cover the hire of the coach and make up what she had given in the offering at church. She was puzzled but dared not refuse. Perhaps it was charity; perhaps it was a payment for services rendered; or perhaps it was a reward for passing an unspoken test.

There was a further test to be passed when the couple returned the invitation and the dean came to them at Lazer's Hill – to their 'Lilliputian Palace' as he called it. Dressed as always in his black gown with the pudding sleeves, periwigged and plump-jowled, unsmiling, he was ready to find fault. Instead of sitting politely in the parlour he rapidly inspected the entire house: garret, bedroom, study and basement kitchen. He complimented his hostess, explaining that it was from the cleanliness of the garret and kitchens that he judged a woman's standards since even 'a Slut' would make sure to clean rooms where guests were to be entertained.

Mary Delany said that time went pleasantly in Swift's company though he was 'a very odd companion'. He talked all the time, she noted, 'and does not require many answers; he has infinite good spirits, and says abundance of good things in his common way of discourse'. The Swift that Mrs Pilkington recalled was a less bland construct: his volubility, his need to give offence and desire not to have offence taken, the restless unease – all had a manic quality. Unlike Mrs Delany, who was neither young nor child-like in appearance, Mrs Pilkington found herself at the sharp end of Swift's attentions.

That Sunday at the deanery was the first of what were to be many dinners and suppers in Swift's company, sometimes with Matthew, at other times alone. Swift also drew the couple into his wider circle. On one occasion, the play-acting took place at the home of Swift's friends the Grattans. The Grattans were a clan of

talented brothers, mostly clergy, of whom the bachelors Robin and
John were closest to Swift. At the family home at Belcamp, some
five miles north of Dublin, their cellars were extensive and well-
stocked; John knew best about beer and Robin about wine. Staying
there for Christmas in 1729 or 1730, Swift invited Delany and the
Pilkingtons – 'mighty Thomas Thumb' and 'her serene Highness
of Lillyput' – to drive out to Belcamp for a tipsy dinner. On arrival,
'by Agreement', Laetitia hid her face behind a fan and the
newcomers pretended she was a girl they had picked up on the
road. (Whose idea was this, one wonders?) Swift knew it was her;
the pleasure was in the pretence, and in introducing a 'wench' or
prostitute into a parlour full of black-gowned clergymen. 'We were
very merry on this odd Introduction', Laetitia wrote, and Swift was
in 'infinite humour', addressing her in his vigorous reversed way
with compliments that sounded like insults, to which she
retaliated with her famed 'Sauciness'. 'Pox on you, you Slut,' said
the dean, and the parlour rang with laughter.

Happy to pretend that the curate's wife was a prostitute
charitably being given a dinner, the company do not seem to have
been surprised when Swift, 'meditating revenge' on her for her
witty answers, progressed from words to actions. He had set some
bottles of wine by the fire, and their corks, sealed with resin and
pitch, had begun to melt. Swift 'slyly rubbed his Fingers' on the
black stuff and 'daubed' her face 'all over'. His intention, as she
understood it, was to provoke her from wit to anger. She, however,
produced a quick pun: she pretended to be happy that he had
'sealed' her for his own. 'Plague on her, said he, I can't put her out
of Temper,' she remembered him saying, but he appeared
determined to do so if possible. His next gambit was to ask everybody if they had ever seen such a dwarf. He made her take off her
shoes so that he could measure her. When she asked him why he
wanted her to take off her shoes he said he anticipated she might
have holes in her stockings or smelly feet and he would be able to
mock her in front of everybody. He made her stand against the
wall and put his hand heavily on her head, crushing her down to
mark her height on the wall. Already, in her own words, 'one of the
most diminutive Mortals you ever saw, who was not a Dwarf, or

disproportion'd', she shrank under the weight of his hand 'to almost half my Proportion' so that Swift, making a mark on the wall with his pencil, announced that she was only three feet two inches high. Lilliputian, indeed. The sadistic, uncontrolled aspects of Swift's behaviour, the compulsive elements – he was seemingly unable to leave her alone, wanting to pummel her, shout at her, insult her, tease and squeeze her – suggest he really did experience her as a creature of his own imagination, a plaything sprung to life.

At Belcamp, amid clergy, Laetitia was the only woman present, pregnant (again) and unable to eat. Asked by the other guests ('the gentlemen guessing at my Circumstances, by my decreasing Face, and increasing Waist') what she would like, she replied that she wished she could be a man so as to get less of their ceremonious attention. The idea appealed to Swift. Perhaps she *was* a man. Quickly falling in with Swift's line of thinking, she asked him to put it to the company and let the men take a vote to determine her sex:

I will, said he; Pilkington, what say you? A Man, Sir: they all took his Word; and, in Spite of Petticoats, I was made a Man of after Dinner: I was obliged to put a Tobacco-pipe in my Mouth; but they so far indulged me, as to let it be an empty one, as were the Dean's, Doctor Delany's, and my Husband's.

In Swift's company, the foolery was invariably acted out in some way. The dean's 'agreeable whims' included giving his friends and servants titles like 'sock washer to the blackguard Boy who waited on the under Butler's under Butler', or 'Inspectress-general of all the drinking Vessels'. The latter was a position conferred on Laetitia one Sunday evening at the deanery when the usual set of intimate friends were gathered and Swift, in high good humour, deciding he would treat them all, sent her to the cellar to bring up some special ale, a present from John Grattan. Entrusting her with the key, he gave precise instructions about how exactly to draw the beer off from the cask:

After receiving his Commands, which I promised punctually to obey, I went down, but had scarce open'd the Door, when Doctor Delany and Doctor Sheridan were with me. O Breach of Trust, unpardonable! We sat down on a Bench, and each of us drank; but we laughed so heartily at cheating the Dean, that he stole down, having some Suspicion, that where there was a Woman, and two Clergymen, there might be a Plot, and surprised us; I, in Imitation of his Servant, told him, the Parsons seduced me, and I did drink: Pox choke you all, said he.

That was the last time she was trusted with the key to the cellar.

∞

Swift was a feminist after the fashion of his time: he believed passionately in the power of education to improve women. In his *Letter to a Young Lady on her Marriage*, which had been addressed to Deborah Staunton on her marriage to John Rochford in 1723, Swift blamed the young lady's parents for 'too much neglecting to cultivate your Mind; without which it is impossible to acquire or preserve the Friendship and Esteem of a wise Man'. (The mature Mrs Pilkington commented drily, 'which by the bye, the Lady did not take as a Compliment, either to her or the Sex'.) An eager reader and quick learner, Laetitia easily acquired Swift's friendship and esteem, though she was under no illusion about her status. She knew that as people 'sans consequence', she and Matthew were but a cut above the servants: they were to come when called, listen when Swift wanted to talk, be impressed when he wanted to boast, and be grateful when he condescended to advise on their reading or correct their verse. Swift suffered from Ménière's syndrome which caused periodic fits of deafness and giddiness, symptoms he hated to display and which were worsening as he aged. Often morose, in company he needed to feel free to ask people to speak up, repeat what they had said and generally submit to his bad temper. 'It was owing to this', Mrs Pilkington candidly explained, 'that Mr Pilkington and I frequently pass'd whole Days with him, while Numbers of our betters were excluded'. They were among the people 'of middle understanding, middle rank, very complying, and consequently such as I can govern' that Swift told Pope he liked to have around him.

Towards Laetitia, Swift took on the role of tutor. She attributed her skills as a writer to 'the Pains he took to teach me to think and speak with propriety'. She recognised that his attentions were a compliment – 'had he thought me incorrigibly dull, I should have escap'd without Correction' – but he was 'a very rough sort of a

Tutor'. Swift cared passionately about language and had no patience with woolly thinking. He also enjoyed hurting her. When she used an inelegant phrase he pinched her so hard she ended up 'black and blue', often without knowing what she had said or done wrong. This was Swift's custom: Stella and Vanessa had been treated the same way. Even Mary Pendarves, thanking Swift for the honour of allowing her to correspond with him, wrote to say she would 'submit to any punishment' he wanted to convey through English friends, now that she was too far away to receive his usual 'favours' of 'pinching and beating'. (Swift's answer to this was among a number of letters that were destroyed by Fanny Burney when she helped the elderly Mrs Delany sort out her correspondence and, with Mrs Delany's agreement, eliminated 'all that could not be saved every way to Swift's honour'.)

Under Swift's tutelage, Laetitia read and discussed a number of recently published books, including contemporary philosophers like the Dublin-based Francis Hutcheson whose *Inquiry* of 1725 had been widely praised but whose later *Essay on the Nature and Conduct of the Passions and Affections* some judged incomprehensible. They read the classics in translation – Xenophon and Plato in particular, Swift pointing out how much Lord Shaftesbury in his *Characteristics* and Pope in his *Ethic Epistles* had borrowed from Socrates. Most exciting, however, was to be privy to Swift's recollections of his years in England, when among his companions were Pope and Gay and Bolingbroke. From these days he had material remains of real value, not medals and 'trinkets' or non-existent money, but a treasure trove of unpublished letters from his famous friends. One morning he sent for her to come to him very early and explained that he had a job for her to do. He brought from his study a large, beautifully bound book. It was a new translation of Horace which had been sent to him by the author as a present. He invited her to admire its 'special good Cover' of Turkey leather and fine gilt. Then, explaining that he had decided it needed something more valuable inside it, Swift took out a penknife and cut all the pages close to the margin. Horace was thrown on the fire. He then brought out two drawers filled with old correspondence and gave her instructions:

Your Task, Madam, is to paste in these Letters, in this Cover, in the Order I shall give them to you; I intended to do it myself, but that I thought it might be a pretty Amusement for a Child, so I sent for you.

He knew what sort of 'amusement' it would be for a woman of her interests to be handling manuscript letters from Pope and others. It was a mark of honour and an opportunity. Laetitia displayed appropriate reverence, gratifying Swift with some exaggeratedly child-like deference, but at once asked if she could read the letters as they went. After some banter – 'Are you sure you can read?' – Swift agreed that she should do what had clearly been his intention all along and handed her a letter recently received from Lord Bolingbroke. She read it with 'unspeakable Delight'. And then there was a feast: letters from Pope, Gay, Addison, Congreve, Bishop Burnet, Dr Arbuthnot, Lady Masham, the Earl of Oxford were passed to her – 'a Noble and a Learned Set! So my Readers may judge what a Banquet I had'. Intoxicating exchanges and some careful flatteries on her part followed:

I cou'd not avoid remarking to the Dean, that notwithstanding the Friend-ship Mr Pope profess'd for Mr Gay, he cou'd not forbear a great many Satyrical, or if I may be allowed to say so, envious Remarks on the Success of the *Beggar's Opera*. The Dean very frankly own'd, he did not think Mr Pope was so candid to the Merits of other Writers as he ought to be.

She then broached the subject of Pope's dedication of *The Dunciad* to Swift. It had been widely remarked that Pope's lines were cold and even dismissive, especially when compared with Swift's effusive praise of Pope. This was what Swift thought too. He, Laetitia assured him, revealed himself a warm, sincere and generous friend, whereas Pope, 'according to the Character he gives of Mr Addison, damns with faint Praise'. This pleasing exchange prompted Swift to bring out a recent letter he had received from Pope. She read it and gave the desired response:

I own, I was surprised to find it fill'd with low and un-Gentleman-like Reflections both on Mr Gay and two noble Persons who honoured him with their Patronage after his Disappointment at Court. 'Well, Madam,' said the Dean, 'what do you think of that Letter?' (seeing I had quite gone thro' it): – 'Indeed Sir,' returned I, 'I am sorry I have read it; for it gives me Reason to think there is no such Thing as a sincere Friend to be met with in the World.' 'Why,' reply'd he, 'Authors are as jealous of their Prerogative as Kings, and can no more bear a Rival in the Empire of Wit, than a Monarch could in his Dominions'.

From the time of the Scriblerus Club in 1713, Pope and Swift had maintained the fiction that as satirists they were engaged in a shared endeavour to reform the world. Their letters were full of protestations of affection, each urging the other to cross the Irish Sea and visit – Delany was ready to host Pope at Delville, Pope and Bolingbroke came up with a decent clergy living for Swift in the Buckinghamshire countryside (Swift preferred to stay in Ireland, 'a freeman among slaves'). The friendship was deep-rooted but it had been put under pressure by the publication of the joint *Miscellanies*, an edition of miscellaneous writings in several volumes which Pope put together between 1727 and 1732. Swift had given Pope carte blanche – 'despotic' power, in his own words – to edit and organise these materials as he chose, but he was not satisfied with the result. Pope claimed the *Miscellanies* showed them as equals, peers, 'friends, side by side, serious and merry by turns, conversing interchangeably, and walking down hand in hand to posterity'. Swift felt that Pope was upstaging him.

Swift had plans to bring out his own selection of his writings. He saw in Mrs Pilkington an intelligent, biddable assistant, an amanuensis who could help him sort and think about his manuscripts; and in Matthew Pilkington an envoy who might usefully serve his purposes in London. Some serious scheming was going on behind what appeared to be an old man's foolery with an amusing young couple. Meanwhile, their excitement at being found worthy of whatever use Swift might have of them is well conveyed in Mrs Pilkington's description of the rest of that visit:

The Dean running into the Parlour, threw a whole Packet of manuscript Poems into my Lap, and so he did for five or six Times successively, till I had an Apron full of Wit and Novelty, for they were all of his own Writing, and such as had not then been made publick, and many of them, I believe, never will. Mr. Pilkington coming, according to the Dean's Desire, to Dinner, found me deeply engaged, and sat down to partake of my Entertainment, till we were summoned to Table, to a less noble Part. 'Well, Mr Pilkington,' said the Dean, 'I hope you are jealous; I have had your Wife a good many Hours, and as she is a likely Girl, and I a very young Man' (*Note*, he was upwards of Three-score), 'you don't know what may have happen'd: Tho I must tell you, you are very partial to her; for here I have not been acquainted with her above six months, and I have already discovered two intolerable Faults in her; 'tis true, I look'd sharp, or perhaps they might have escaped my Notice: Nay, Madam, don't look surpriz'd, I am resolved to tell your Husband, that he may break you of them.' 'Indeed, Sir,' returned I, 'my Surprize is, that you have not found out Two and Fifty in Half that Time; but let me know them, and I will mend of them, if I can.' 'Well put in,' says he, 'for I believe you can't; but eat your Dinner, however, for they are not capital.' I obeyed, yet was very impatient to know my particular Errors; he told me, 'I should hear of them Time enough.'

The Things being taken away; 'Now good Sir,' said I, 'tell me what I do amiss? That I may reform'; 'No,' returned he, - 'but I'll tell your Husband before your Face to shame you the more: – In the first Place, Mr Pilkington, she had the Insolence this Morning, not only to desire to read the Writings of the most celebrated Genius's of the Age, in which I indulged her; but she must also, forsooth, pretend to praise or censure them as if she knew something of the Matter; indeed her Remarks were not much amiss, considering they were guess Work; but this Letter here of Mr Pope's she has absolutely condemn'd . . . If you don't take down her Pride, there will be no bearing her.'

'Indeed, Sir,' said Mr Pilkington, ' 'tis your Fault that she is so conceited; she was always dispos'd to be saucy, but since you have done her the Honour to take Notice of her, and made her your Companion, there is no such Thing as mortifying her.' 'Very fine,' said the Dean, 'I have got much by complaining to you, to have all your Wife's Faults laid at my door.' 'Well, Sir,' said I, 'all these Misdemeanours may be included under the article of pride: Now let me know my other Crime': 'Why,' said he, 'you can't walk fast; but at present I excuse you.' [She was pregnant.] 'Well, Sir, if I can't mend my Pride, I'll try to mend my Pace.' 'Mr Pilkington,' said he, 'I have a Mind to clip your Wife's Wit.' 'Indeed, Sir,' said I, 'that's Death by Law, for 'tis Sterling.' 'Shut up your Mouth, for all Day, Letty,' said Mr Pilkington, 'for that Answer is real Wit.' 'Nay,' said the Dean, 'I believe we had better shut up our own, for at this Rate she'll be too many for us.' I am sure, if I was not proud before, this was enough to make me so.

It was heady stuff. Swift was the most famous writer in the kingdom, and he teased her, allowed her to browse his unpublished manuscripts, invited her comments, and praised her wit.

The little curate's wife understood well the combination of reverence, intelligence and docility required to keep the door of the deanery open to her. Through it she tripped for five or six years, playing the prattling child within and boasting about it elsewhere. Sexually experienced, she had her own views about the dean, which were those of a grown woman not a child. Remarking that there was no risk to her reputation in spending hours closeted with Swift because of his advanced years she added a word about what she called 'love' but by which she clearly meant lust: 'to speak my Sentiments, I really believe it was a Passion he was wholly unacquainted with, and which he would have thought it beneath the Dignity of his Wisdom to entertain'. Swift's companion was a woman shrewdly observing the world of men, making comparisons and drawing conclusions. Serving as a Stella-substitute in the deanery, she was no more an actual child than Esther Johnson had been, though, as with Stella, Swift took pleasure in treating her like a child.

When Swift took Laetitia to 'Naboth's vineyard', a field south of the deanery that he had walled and planted up with fruit trees, she found it hard to keep up with his pace. She was heavily pregnant. It was spring and the trees were in blossom. She sat and rested while Swift, a compulsive exerciser, walked 'or rather trolled, as hard as ever he could drive', around the field, his movements reminding her of the horses he had written about in *Gulliver's Travels*. Her condition provoked more than usual levels of verbal aggression from him, and she recalled an exchange driven by repressed sexual energy. Swift declared 'what a fool Mr Pilkington was' to marry her, since he could afford to keep a horse for less money than she cost him; and a horse, he invited her to agree, 'would have given him better Exercise and more Pleasure than a Wife'. The big-bellied wife, self-evidently more knowledgeable about such things than the clergyman who had never married and might never have had sex, replied, 'Pray how can a Batchelor judge of this matter?' It began to rain and the exchange about whether men got more pleasure from riding horses or having sex ended. Telling the story later, and writing it up for a public familiar with the joke that Swift preferred horses to humans, Mrs Pilkington used imagery suggesting his arousal, anxiety, and relief. The rain had made him agitated. Keen to avoid spending on a coach, he hurried her back (although any money unexpectedly saved he would then give to a beggar). He urged her on with the words, 'Come, haste, O how the Tester trembles in my Pocket!' A tester was a coin, and 'spending' means ejaculation among other things. 'I obeyed', she recalled, 'and we got in a Doors just Time enough to escape a heavy Shower.' Swift immediately started running up and down the front and back stairs in the deanery. He ran so frenziedly she was afraid he would fall and hurt himself.

The baby she was carrying was Jack, and he was born some time in mid- or late April, 1730. He was baptised on 1 May and his parents gave him the middle name Carteret, in homage to the Lord Lieutenant. Whatever hopes prompted this naming were not fulfilled and Jack later lamented that Lord Carteret had never taken any notice of him. There was some suggestion that Swift would stand godfather to the child, but in the event he did not. Jack's sponsors were Dr Clayton, Dr Delany, Mrs Barber and Mrs Grierson, wishing him respectively fortune, power and eloquence, poetry and learning. They were 'poetical people' Jack wrote; it was 'a fairy christening'.

With Swift as their patron, Dr Delany's poetical people were planning an onslaught on London. Mary Barber was fed up with the hard work and confinement of the woollen drapery, especially when compared to the leisured existence of those who had begun to take an interest in her because of her poetry. In several poems written to 'a Lady in the Country', Mary Barber depicted herself as

> A Wretch, in smoaky Dublin pent,
> Who rarely sees the Firmament.

She was 'Doom'd by inexorable Fate' to the weary, dreary world of trade,

> Sick of Smells, and dirty Streets,
> Stifl'd with Smoke, and stunn'd with Noise

and would love to 'quit a life I hate':

> How gladly, Madam, would I go,

> To see your Gardens, and Chateau;
> From thence the fine Improvements view,
> Or walk your verdant Avenue;
> Delighted, hear the Thrushes sing,
> Or listen to some bubbling Spring;
> If Fate had given me Leave to roam!
> But Citizens must stay at home.

No doubt she did dream of babbling brooks and birdsong, but Mary Barber's urge to roam was driven by stern economic and social considerations. She had four children living (another five had died in infancy). Her eldest, Constantine, early showed his academic aptitude. Con's future prospects could not be secured in a land where, no matter how well qualified its 'sons', the best positions were always filled by English placemen. Poetry by itself was hardly a way forward, and she took care to dissuade Con from ever thinking it might be, no matter how impressed he was by his mother's extraordinary success. In a poem of 1727, written in the voice of a school friend of Con's, she told him not to waste his time on such activities: 'Fly the fair, delusive Nine' (the nine Muses) she urged him,

> They talk of an immortal Name,
> And promise you the Realms of Fame:
> A mighty Empire, Con, 'tis true
> But wondrous small the Revenue!

Compared with the wool trade, poetry did offer Mary Barber revenue of potential value, measured in the connections it enabled her to make as well as in immediate monetary gain. She had brought her business experience to the task of building a support-base among the leading families in Dublin. London, however, was the centre of literary life; and in England there were many more, and grander, country houses where the powerful gathered and where a charming Irish poet might be welcomed, especially so unusual a one as the draper's wife. Swift encouraged Mrs Barber in these hopes. Her light verse – unpretentious, domestic, amusing – had some of the qualities of his own. No less important, a shrewd and reliable woman might, like Matthew, be useful to him in his own affairs.

In July 1730 Mary Barber took a tearful leave of her friends and sailed with her younger children to England. Lucius was ten; Rupert, already showing his talent as a painter, eleven; and Mira, 'a melancholy, drooping young woman' according to Mary Pendarves, thirteen. Con, at sixteen, was enrolled at Trinity where he was soon to begin winning prizes that his mother was able to boast about in her poems. Suffering from what was variously described as 'arthritis' and 'gout', Mary Barber's health was not good and she was planning to spend the summer taking the waters at Tunbridge Wells, continuing, meanwhile, to solicit subscriptions for her volume of poems from the 'Persons of Quality and Distinction' to be found there. Rupert delivered at least one petition to Swift's friend Lady Betty Germaine. 'I was Gaming,' Lady Betty explained to Swift, apologising for having done nothing. Glancing at the paper and noticing verses, she simply 'slunk' them into her pocket and forgot about them. Perhaps these were the flattering lines later printed in Mrs Barber's *Poems*, 'To the Right Honorable the Lady Elizabeth Germain, upon seeing her do a generous Action. Written as from the Person reliev'd'.

From the perspective of elegant Tunbridge Wells, where Mrs Barber mixed with holidaying 'Britons void of care, / A happy, free born Race', Ireland and the Irish seemed ever more wretched. Poverty was 'relentless' in Ireland for reasons that were not at all mysterious; those who tried to advance themselves were blocked and those who did not were despised; all participated in their country's 'cruel Fate', all were defined in racist terms as 'abject, grovelling'. She knew whereof she spoke when she warned Con to beware the siren call of the Muses:

> They'll tell you too, to gain their Ends,
> That Verse will raise you pow'rful Friends.
> Believe me, Youth, this is not true:
> The *Great* think ev'rything their Due.

The general truth had a local application when the 'Great' were English and the supplicant Irish.

Dancing attendance, waiting for favours, hoping for relief: this was not what Mrs Barber wanted for Con. Poetry provided her with a life outside the confines of the drapery and enabled her to imagine and put in place a better life for her children. She was remarkably successful in her subscription – especially if we bear in mind the words of her contemporary Mary Davys, 'To Tell the Reader I was born in Ireland, is to bespeak a general Dislike to all I write' – but she was lonely and in England she felt alienated. In a short poem, 'Written on the Rocks at Tunbridge Wells', Mrs Barber articulated a poet's despair for the mother-country. She wrote about being homesick and the fact that politically and socially Ireland provided no real home to go to. Like any other tourist she scratched her name in the rock, a symbol of endurance. Printed in the volume she eventually produced with the aid of over 900 subscribers, 'Written on the Rocks' suggests not so much enduring fame as the stony road she trod.

At Tunbridge, canvassing the same exclusive, moneyed circles, was an amusing painter named James Worsdale. A few years later, Worsdale was to play a significant part in Mrs Pilkington's life. Mary Barber may already have come across him in Dublin. He seems to have been known to John Van Lewen and the family. He may be the painter addressed in Matthew's poem, 'To Mr — on seeing a Friend's Picture of his Painting', in which there is a standard compliment echoed later by Mrs Barber: both poets praised Worsdale's ability to convey character through portraiture, 'At once to paint the *Face* and *Mind*'.

The facetious Mr Worsdale could sing and act, and was a brilliant mimic and all-round entertainer. He had been apprenticed to the court portraitist Godfrey Kneller. He some-times claimed to be Kneller's illegitimate son; most authorities agree he was the son of a colour-grinder in the studio. Apparently, he secretly married Kneller's wife's niece in a Fleet wedding in 1722, upon which Kneller sacked him. It is impossible to be sure of anything about Worsdale, whose life was devoted to what Samuel Johnson later (disapprovingly) described as the 'perpetual masquerade' of the times. Artifice and travesty were his element. He loved dressing up and acting out parts – sometimes for days at a time; symbolically, he camouflaged himself so effectively that he can barely be found outside Mrs Pilkington's *Memoirs*, and yet he was actively involved in many aspects of eighteenth-century cultural life. A libertine who fathered at least four illegitimate children by various women, a would-be playwright and poet, an artist building himself a reputation (at Tunbridge he was painting the Duchess of Newcastle) and a showman of immense charm, Worsdale was well established in London's theatrical and musical circles. He had taken lessons in singing from Henry Carey, the most prolific English song writer of the period, who in 1727 had dedicated his *Six Ballads on the Humours of the Town* to his 'Dear Friend and Scholar Mr James Worsdale' whose 'agreeable Performances' had enhanced the songs. Worsdale's detractors, of whom he had a number including another follower of Kneller, George Vertue, said he was better at acting than painting, a judgement reflecting the relative status of the activities. A small man – 'a little cringing creature' according to Vertue who noted that the successful painters of the day were all under five feet tall – Worsdale was full of energy and industry. He devised an original method for collecting payment on his portraits. Like a writer gathering subscriptions, he asked for half the agreed sum at the first sitting and then, when the painting was completed (and dry) he chalked white prison bars on it until the sitter came to collect and pay up. Perhaps he didn't do that to his portrait of the Duchess of Newcastle, which Mary Barber praised in a poem full of the virtues of the duchess:

> Say, Worsdale, where you learn'd the Art
> To paint the Goodness of the Heart . . .

The duchess later put her name down for seven copies of Mrs Barber's *Poems*. This is how it was done.

The gentry amused themselves with amateur theatricals at Tunbridge and Worsdale was the sort of man they needed. Vertue sourly observed how with 'his many artful wayes' Worsdale pushed himself 'into a numerous acquaintance'. How much acquaintance the Pilkingtons had with him at this stage is unknown, but Laetitia was soon to meet him.

∞

All summer, while Laetitia cared for the baby, Matthew busied himself with the final stages of preparing his manuscript for the press. Where Mary Barber went, he had every intention of following; indeed, as far as publication was concerned he was determined to get there first. He had enough poems for a volume. Swift read them over and gave advice which Matthew heeded, keen to impress as a young man willing to listen and learn. Swift's patronage was a valuable commodity that could be exploited in a number of ways. Hearing the old man's stories, reading his writings, catching his idiom, Matthew began to take a pride in being able to imitate the dean's style.

By August, 247 subscribers had been signed up, paying for a total of 288 books. Mary Barber had put herself down for four copies before leaving, Constantia Grierson and Elizabeth Sican each subscribed for one; John Van Lewen and at least one of the Meade relations subscribed, along with Delany and his future second wife, then still Mary Pendarves.

On 25 August, Matthew sat down and wrote a short preface. 'I am now committing my self to the judgement of the public, un-certain what the fate of these trifles will be,' he wrote, and thanked his 'generous encouragers' for their support. He assured them his work had already profited from the comments of his 'judicious acquaintance', at the head of whom stood 'the admired Doctor Swift'. Matthew devoted a quarter of the preface to this theme:

Inexpressible are the Obligations (and unpardonable were the Folly and Humility of concealing them) which I have to the admired Doctor Swift, who condescended to peruse the following Poems with the greatest Kind-ness and Care, and honour'd them with his Corrections and Remarks; and I hope he will forgive me the Vanity of telling the world how much Candour, Humanity, and Accuracy of Judgement he testified on that Occasion.

Truly, it would have been 'unpardonable' folly to conceal his obligations to Swift, a mistake that was never likely to happen. Swift's publisher, George Faulkner, printed the volume in a modest octavo edition, embellishing the title page with tags from Horace and Anacreon. There were eight pages of subscriber's names headed by Lord Carteret. The collection was dedicated to Robert Fitzgerald, 19th Earl of Kildare, holder of one of the oldest titles in the Irish peerage. Kildare, a wealthy man of formal manners and pious tendency, had probably not been asked; nothing in the wording of the dedication suggests that Matthew had any acquaintance with him. However, as the head of Ireland's 'first' family, Kildare was something of a figurehead for Protestants especially because, unlike many others, the Kildares had long resided in Ireland and considered themselves Irish. In his fulsome dedication, Matthew played the nationalist card in the hope that it might win him Kildare's patronage. He wrote:

Your sincere Love to your Country has been sufficiently shown in your constant Residence among us, when the greatest Part of our Men of Titles were deluded into different Kingdoms, to purchase Vanity at the Expense of their own Interest and the Happiness of their Country.

In that note of aggression towards the 'Men of Titles' blissfully deluded by English comforts we might hear Swift's voice. He too, perforce, was in 'constant residence'. A 76-line poem by William Dunkin hailing Matthew as the chosen poet in a revived Irish tradition, come to 'tune Ierne's ancient Harp', completed the preliminaries.

Matthew Pilkington's volume, *Poems on Several Occasions,* was a considerable achievement. To some extent it was a group endeavour. As such, it is noticeable that though Mary Barber was the better poet and had Swift's support, it was to be another four years before she saw her volume into the world. Similarly, while Laetitia's wit was acknowledged, there seemed not to be much talk at this stage of publishing her work though she was becoming ever closer to Swift. Swift's first mention of the couple in his letters to England occurred in October 1730 and there he gave equal weight to their ambitions, describing Matthew to Lord Bathurst as 'a little young poetical parson' who had a 'littler, young poetical wife'. But it was Matthew whose poetical career was to be promoted. Swift's letter to Bathurst continued:

The young parson aforesaid hath very lately printed his own works, all in verse, and some not unpleasant, in one or two of which I have the honour to be celebrated, which cost me a guinea and two bottles of wine. Thus we strive to keep up our spirits in the most miserable country upon earth . . . if any kingdom was ever in a right situation for breeding Poets, it is this, wither you and your crew unpardonably sent me 16 years ago, and where I have been ever since studying as well as practicing Revenge, malice, envy and hatred, and all uncharitableness.

Bathurst was meant to laugh at Swift's self-description, and see the truth in it.

In England, Mary Barber made sure that the new Lord Lieutenant, the Earl of Dorset, who was due to take over from Lord Carteret, was presented with a copy of Matthew's *Poems*. Serving Matthew in this way was also, of course, an opportunity to promote her own cause. Swift's letter to Lord Bathurst mentioned Mrs Barber: 'there is an Irish Poetess now in London, soliciting the Duke of Dorset for an Employment, though she be but a woollen-draper's wife'; and, for good measure, Swift also told Bathhurst about Constantia Grierson, 'who hath lately published a fine Edition of Tacitus with a Latin Dedication to Lord Carteret'. Swift intended that both women should be included in a volume of the Pope–Swift *Miscellanies.*

What he might have been hoping for with regard to Matthew is perhaps suggested by the success of Stephen Duck who in 1727 was an unknown thresher in Wiltshire, using a dictionary to enable himself to get through *Paradise Lost* and writing poems about the lives of agricultural labourers. By 1730 Duck was a favourite at court. On 11 September that year, he presented a poem to the Queen at Windsor and stood by while the Earl of Macclesfield read it aloud. The Queen showed her appreciation by awarding Duck a pension of £30 per year and a small house in Richmond Park. There was intense public interest in the Thresher Poet. When Laurence Eusden, who had been poet laureate since 1718, died that autumn, all the newspapers predicted that Stephen Duck would be appointed to the post. Swift thought so too. Over in Dublin they followed events closely. In November 1730 the choice fell not on Duck but on the well-known actor-manager and long-standing butt of Pope's satire, Colley Cibber. The *Grub-Street Journal* first denied it and then expressed bewilderment:

> But guessing who would have the luck
> To be the b[irth]day fibber,
> I thought of Dennis, Theobald, Duck,
> But never dreamt of Cibber.

On 3 December, Colley Cibber was officially notified and presented at St James's Palace where, exquisitely turned out in satin and frills, he knelt and kissed the royal hand. The post, which gave Cibber the social standing he desired, was the formal, institutional version of what Matthew had been doing at Dublin Castle: the holder's main task was to compose odes for the royal birthday or New Year celebrations. Cibber's first official composition, the new year ode, set to music and sung by the choristers of the Chapel Royal on New Year's Day, was mocked by the *Grub-Street Journal* and other newspapers for weeks afterwards, but the new laureate, mingling with the distinguished throng at court, was untroubled. He could console himself at another exclusive venue which his elevation made available: the doors of White's Club in St James's were now opened to him. This haunt of dukes and peers was notorious for its faro tables where high spending gamblers passed the time in between appearances at the king's levee or attending on the queen in her apartment. Ten years later, Cibber's contacts with the fine gentlemen of White's were to be crucial to Mrs Pilkington's survival in London.

CHAPTER FOUR

Dean Swift's Little Helpers

In March 1731 the respected London printer William Bowyer brought out an expanded edition of *Poems on Several Occasions* by Matthew Pilkington, MA. A few extra pieces had been added, most notably the self-mocking *The Plague of Wealth* which was announced on the title page, along with the information that it had been written after Matthew was awarded £50 by 'his Excellency the Lord Carteret' for the birthday ode. As a further selling point, readers were informed that the volume had been 'Revised by the Reverend Dr Swift'. The London edition also boasted a frontispiece, an engraving commissioned from the most sought-after engraver of the day, George Vertue. Vertue made a speciality of portraits of poets. His series of prints, 'The Effigies of Twelve of the Most celebrated English Poets', had been published by subscription between 1726 and 1729. As a newcomer Matthew did not qualify for a portrait. Instead, Vertue composed a flattering allegory which emphasised his association with Swift and suggested (though there is a certain ambivalence) that Pilkington, too, might one day reach the heights. Vertue showed the Muses picking out volumes of poetry from a heap on the ground and handing the selected few to the winged messenger to carry to the Temple of Fame behind him. Thomson, the poet of the moment whose 'Autumn', fourth and final book of *The Seasons*, had appeared the previous year, is still lying on the ground waiting his turn; Dorset is being handed over (a compliment to the new Lord Lieutenant, descendant of the witty Restoration poet, Charles Sackville, sixth Earl of Dorset); the messenger holds Pope and

Gay; and Swift has already been installed. The volume of Swift – larger than the volumes of Pope, Gay and Dorset – rests on a podium in the centre of the temple and centred in the picture. It is ringed by the company ranged on the shelf: Homer, Virgil, Horace, Chaucer, Milton, Dryden, Addison.

Everything about the presentation of the book signalled a high-end production. There was trouble, however, over *The Plague of Wealth,* which had almost certainly been sent to Bowyer by Matthew for inclusion in the London edition. The two had corresponded about the volume. The advantage the narrative offered of being able to use Lord Carteret's name on the title page would not have been lost on either of them. Swift had probably been consulted. The letter-diary had circulated in manuscript in Dublin and London; it had provided amusement in Lord Carteret's circles. Delany puffed it and Matthew was proud of it. But one person who was not amused was Thomas Tickell, Carteret's secretary, the official blamed in the piece for making Matthew wait a week for his payment.

Tickell, once the protégé, now literary executor, of Addison, and himself a poet whom Swift had known for many years, was in general well disposed. He had early made himself useful by speaking well of Mary Barber and bringing her into viceregal favour. Swift understood his value. Hence, when Tickell went to him and complained about the 'foolish Scribble printed in Mr Pilkington's Poems', Swift went to some trouble to smooth matters out. He wrote a long, emollient letter to Tickell in which he portrayed himself as properly investigating a matter of which he had had no prior knowledge. Swift told Tickell he had summoned the curate to the deanery to explain himself. The explanation had satisfied him: the piece had been included without Matthew's knowledge 'and much to his Vexation'. Lord Carteret had shown the letter-diary about in London, someone had copied it and 'by the impertinence of the Bookseller' it had been printed. Swift offered a plausible reason why Matthew would not have wanted *The Plague of Wealth* to be printed – that its self-revelations were not calculated to improve his prospects in his chosen career: 'the character he gives himself in it is a very mean one, and must be remembered, much to his disadvantage if ever he rises in the world'. Tickell, Swift implied, was making a fuss about nothing. Matthew was the main one hurt:

The young man was sorry, as he had reason, to see it in print, lest it might possibly offend a Person of your reputation and consequence. He appears to me to be a modest good natured Man; I know but little of him: Dr Delany brought him to me first, and recommended him as one whom I might safely countenance. He is in the utmost pain at hearing that you imagine that there was the least design to affront you. Since, as it would be the basest thing in itself, so such treatment would be the surest method to ruin his interests. I could not forbear telling you this out of perfect pity to the young Man.

There was a postscript to say that he was sending Mrs Tickell peaches and nectarines from his orchard.

Swift's 'perfect pity' for Matthew was genuine up to a point, though with his own name on the title page of Matthew's London edition it was important to satisfy Tickell, and beyond him Lord Carteret, that he himself had done nothing to cause offence. Distancing himself from Matthew ('I know but little of him') made sense strategically: via Delany there was a straight line to Lord Carteret, whose £50 gift and circulation of the letter-diary was a form of endorsement or patronage in itself. In his capacity as dean of St Patrick's taking a kindly interest in a modest, sober young parson who happened to have poetical talent, whose private communication, a low joke at his own expense, had become public property of a sort that might hinder his career, Swift could imply that lordly people had behaved carelessly and, whether true or not, he brought all his weight to bear in persuading Tickell to this view.

A letter of this sort was a literary exercise to Swift. The challenge was to catch the tone, play the part. He had spent a lifetime honing just such skills. His commitment to a policy of support for Irish writers, combined with his penchant for literary trickery, ensured that they were well employed. In the spring and summer of 1731, he apologised twice to Pope on Mary Barber's account. Working Swift's contacts in London, Mrs Barber had approached Pope. Pope and his mother each dutifully added their names to her subscription list. But Pope was not Swift and had no desire to take up the Irish woman's cause. When Mrs Barber went a stage further and tried to leave her manuscripts with him for his comments she clearly became, in his eyes, one of the poetry-writing pests besieging him at Twickenham whom he lambasted in 'Epistle to Dr Arbuthnot'. Swift wrote : 'Mrs Barber acted weakly in desiring you to correct her verses, I desired her friends here to warn her against everything of that kind. I do believe there was a great Combat between her modesty and her Ambition'. Perhaps there was. Swift claimed she had 'only one defect, which is too much bashfullness', but anyone who reflects on what Mary Barber achieved is likely to conclude that he was joking.

Impatient at the slow progress being made by her sponsors, Mrs Barber decided to forge Swift's signature and write her own testimonial to the queen as if it were a letter from Swift, adding, for good measure, another letter abusing one of the queen's favourites for blocking her access. (This courtier's verdict on the poet? 'A strange, bold, disagreeable woman.') 'Swift' told the queen there was a genius of Irish birth at large in London, one who was every bit the equal by merit in her sphere as the queen was by birth in hers. Mysteriously, this genius had yet to be brought to the attention of royalty. Her name was Mrs Barber and she was 'the best female poet of this or perhaps any age'. The queen, who disliked Swift, passed the letter to the Countess of Suffolk, who sent it to Pope, who sent it to Swift, who at once disclaimed all knowledge of it in a carefully worded letter. He assured Pope that to imagine he could have done something so grotesque would be to think him 'fit for Bedlam'. But he did not renounce Mary Barber.

All sorts of forgeries and anonymous writings were fathered on Swift, a compliment to his celebrity which kept up his spirits in 'the most miserable country on earth', and a practice he could exploit. *An Infallible Scheme To pay the Publick Debt Of This Nation in Six Months*, a sixteen-page pamphlet that appeared in Dublin and afterwards in London, suggesting that vice should be taxed, was widely assumed to be by Swift. In fact it was Matthew's, an imitation calculated to please the dean and draw on his fame. The proud author confessed to his London publisher: 'I have the honour to see it mistaken for the Dean's, both in Dublin and in your part of the world'. We can disregard Matthew's dismissive, 'It was a sudden whim', but take seriously the statement that Swift had read the pamphlet before it went out: Matthew had known he could depend on 'the approbation which the Dean, my wisest and best friend, expressed when he read it.'

We have no record of what his wife thought when she read it, as she undoubtedly did. *An Infallible Scheme* proposed that if a tax were levied on swearing, drunkenness and fornication – 'now made an essential part of the polite gentleman's character' – the public debt could be wiped out in 182 days. (As in *The Plague of Wealth*, Matthew used precise calculations for comic effect.) There were concessions: soldiers and sailors were to be allowed a tax-free forty or fifty oaths per day and women taxed half as much as men, while bachelors were to be regarded as public benefactors since they, unlike married men, did not 'furnish the land with beggars'. Indeed, a law that forbade marriage until the age of forty offered a double benefit: people would transgress and could be fined; and a lower birth-rate would eventually wipe out the Irish requiring the land to be 'new peopled from England', a consequence that might 'cure that Nation of its inveterate antipathy to the inhabitants of this'. The anti-English satire, so much in the spirit of Swift's *A Modest Proposal*, has bite; the adoption of a Swiftian voice ensured there was nothing 'mean' about the character Matthew gave of himself. But his wife might have read something personal in a sentence towards the end of the pamphlet:

I would also earnestly request, that all young clergymen, who, with more passion than prudence, shall dare to marry before they are beneficed, may be liable to a most severe tax, equal to a prohibition; because such offenders must inevitably multiply beggars, live in contempt, and die in poverty.

Matthew was resolved that the fate of the average Irish clergyman would not be his, even though (as he now thought) he had married too soon. In favour at Dublin Castle, in demand as the coming poet of the day, in cahoots with Swift, writing, pamphleteering, keeping abreast of literary and political affairs at coffee-houses and taverns, he was busy and it is unlikely that he was much at home. When a consignment of books arrived from London – ninety-four copies of *Poems on Several Occasions*, and some other publications Matthew had asked the bookseller to supply him with – it took him six weeks to write in thanks because he had 'the misfortune to live in a scene of great hurry, and between attending those who live in high stations who honour me with their friendship, and discharging the duties of my profession, I have scarce a moment disengaged'.

There was also the delicate matter of payment. Assuring Bowyer that he 'would not for any consideration seem to forget my creditors', Matthew directed him to Delany for the miscellaneous publications; and, for his own books, told him he was to charge Faulkner. The proud author explained that he couldn't sell the volumes, he could only give them away: 'for when any of my friends are desirous to have one, and ask me where they are to be had, I am always too generous or too bashful (which is a great rarity among us Irish) to accept of payment for them'. And in any case he had only asked Bowyer for thirty, the number he had calculated he needed to give away as presentation copies and gifts. Promising to send what he owed for thirty copies and suggesting that Faulkner should advertise the rest in *The Dublin Journal* as recently imported by him, Matthew signed off with some more requests. Bowyer was to send him, care of Robert Clayton, the lord bishop of Killala, 'any catalogues that are now selling in London . . . any other little pamphlets', and, for 'another gentleman in town' the *Monthly Chronicle* for March, and the *Historia Literaria*, both of which had been asked for, neither of which had arrived. A postscript provided some trade gossip that was likely to interest Bowyer: a new bookseller had come from London, one Green, with an interesting collection of books. Matthew had taken Swift to Green's shop the first morning he opened ('I made the Dean of St Patrick's go with me there') but the bookseller had priced everything too high and also had a haughty manner so Matthew did not think he would last long in Dublin.

During the spring and summer of 1731, Laetitia was pregnant

again. In August she gave birth to a son. Swift, who had agreed to be godfather to the child if it was a boy, was holidaying in Co. Wicklow. He had taken with him two manuscripts begun several decades earlier and which he was trying to put into a satisfactory form, one of which, a satire on conversational commonplaces and clichés later published as *Polite Conversation*, he had read aloud at Belcamp over Christmas. Laetitia, listening intently and building up her own abilities as a satirist in the Swiftian mode, had offered a 'hint' that Swift pursued: she had suggested that it would work well as a dialogue in an aristocratic household. Swift re-fashioned the piece, inventing characters such as Lord Sparkish, Lady Smart, and Lady Answerall who might have wandered in from a play by Congreve, and depicting exchanges which for a modern reader evoke *Alice in Wonderland*.

As soon as the baby was born Laetitia wrote with the news, telling Swift that he was to be named Jonathan after him. Alas, the child died within a few days. Swift returned to Dublin two weeks later and came at once to visit her. He was, she thought, relieved: Irish babies were potential beggars and wretches. They sat and 'drank a little caudle' together. An hour after he left, Swift's servant brought a letter and a package, 'a great bundle of brown paper, sealed with the utmost care, and twisted round with I know not how many yards of packthread'. The letter explained that he was sending her a piece of plum cake for the dead child's christening. Stranger still, inside the package was a piece of gingerbread with four guineas, wrapped in white paper, stuck into it. On each of the guineas Swift had written the word, 'Plumb'. It is hard to know what he meant, but the money, the clumsy, excessive packaging, the pun (a 'plum' or 'plumb' was slang for £100,000) suggest his desire to comfort and be helpful, all the while striving to govern unmanageable feelings of his own.

Irvin Ehrenpreis refers to Swift's 'infatuation' with the Pilkingtons. 'How thoroughly the childlike couple mastered him', Swift's biographer observes, 'one may reckon from his exertions on behalf of the little husband'. We will come to those 'exertions' in a moment; because of his involvement with Swift, Matthew's life is relatively well documented at this period. The same cannot be said for Laetitia. Her *Memoirs* give us little help in trying to picture her connection with the dean in the context of her daily round as a young mother and curate's wife; but we can read some things between the lines. Being known as a friend of Swift – a 'much envied Honour' – raised her stock. When Mary Pendarves arrived in Dublin in the autumn of 1731, staying with the Claytons in their 'magnifique' house on St Stephen's Green and paying court to her viceregal cousin the Lord Lieutenant up at the castle, she was proud to have 'begun an acquaintance among the wits'. The 'wits' were Mrs Grierson, Mrs Sican and Mrs Pilkington. She singled out Mrs Pilkington as 'a bosom friend of Dean Swift's'. Meeting Dr Delany's set was, the future Mrs Delany felt, to be admitted to a company that included 'those of the best learning and genius in the kingdom' and she was honoured. She sent her sister Ann Granville a sheaf of Matthew's poems and promised to send more. With Mrs Clayton and others she was entertained by the Pilkingtons at Lazer's Hill. Oysters were served. It was a rather stiff affair at first but things improved when the music began. 'We were not very merry at Mr Pilkington's till after supper,' she told her sister, 'when our spirits danced, and *we sung* most harmoniously.'

There was scope for Laetitia to imagine a future in which she and Matthew progressed in parallel as Swift's favourites. Connections like the Claytons and Percivals seemed full of promise. Like Constantia Grierson, she might produce books as well as babies. Constantia had given birth to a second son and in 1730 she brought out her major work, the three-volume edition of Tacitus. In addition she not only worked in the print as the partner to her husband but wrote poems, broadsides and tracts of various kinds. Or there was the example of Mrs Sican and Mary Barber, mothers of families, whose exceptional abilities had enabled them to forge social lives as 'wits' independent of their duller husbands. Whatever complaints Laetitia later made about Matthew – 'self-willed', 'plagu'd with envy' – she never accused him of being dull; and at that stage, though he was progressing faster than she, she could still hold to a vision of themselves as a golden pair, being geniuses together.

That Swift was charmed by her and considered her worth

nurturing, and that she could handle his odd ways was a source of pride, but it is misleading to say that the 'little', 'childlike' Pilkingtons 'mastered' Swift. The phrasing suggests that they exerted an improper power over him. The power, of course, ran in the other direction. For a number of years they were his favourites, woven into his thoughts and figuring in his schemes much as earlier protégés had done. To the usual range of responses an older man might feel for a young couple was added the special entertainment the Pilkingtons offered in seeming to have sprung from the pages of *Gulliver*. Swift liked to set them in motion. He recognised the potency of their ambitions and the underlying rivalry: Laetitia's quickness, the sharpness of her wit, gave opportunities for humbling the cocksure husband which Swift did not resist. She, meanwhile, made as much as she could of the relationship. What she brought to it was a hunger for a life that might fulfil her imaginative and creative needs, her sense that she had singular poetic gifts. When she looked back nostalgically many years later, across the chasm of a catastrophic divorce, everybody else had fallen away. She and Matthew were the only ones, together on equal terms in the innermost circle: 'I believe there never was any Set of People so happy in sincere and uninterrupted friendship,' she wrote, 'as the Dean, Doctor Delany, Mr Pilkington, and myself; nor can I reflect, at this Hour, on anything with more Pleasure, than those happy Moments we have enjoyed!'

Swift was searching for a way to get Matthew to London. In June 1732, having to explain to Pope that the pamphlet, *An Infallible Scheme*, was not his but by 'a young gentleman whom I countenance', Swift implied that Pope might countenance him too: 'The utmost stretch of his ambition is, to gather up as much superfluous money as will give him a sight of you, and half an hour in your presence; after which he will return home in full satisfaction, and in proper time die in peace.'

Within a month, something concrete presented itself. Swift's old friend, the ex-printer and now wealthy City alderman John

Barber, had been elected mayor of London. It was a one-year position, due to begin at the end of October, and the mayor was entitled to select a chaplain of his choice. In Swift's opinion, it was an ideal opportunity for Matthew. Others did not agree. The archbishop of Dublin, for example, had grave doubts: John Barber was a Tory, a suspected Jacobite, fully identified with the opposition to Walpole's government. Serving him would not improve Matthew's career prospects in the church. But for Matthew, as for Swift, the chaplaincy was no more than an instrument to get him to the heart of literary London and fulfil his 'great longing to see England, and appear in the presence of Mr Pope, Mr Gay, Dr Arbuthnot'.

In July Swift wrote to John Barber care of Mary Barber (no relation) and Delany, both of whom were in England, asking them to present his letter. This they failed to do. Delany had an excuse: he was preoccupied with courting a rich widow, Mrs Tenison, whom he married that month. Swift had to write a second letter. By then it was almost too late. There were other candidates who had been promised things, and numerous 'little difficulties' John Barber had to sort out; Barber warned that there was not much money in the position and he could not provide accommodation. But for Swift's sake, and because his obligations to his old friend were considerable, he would take Matthew on and 'show him all the civilities I can'. A jubilant Matthew rushed home to tell his wife the news.

The London chaplaincy represented the first major gain of the Pilkingtons' friendship with Swift, except that Laetitia saw it as no gain at all. She was 'sunk in Sorrow' at the prospect of such a long separation. She felt betrayed and abandoned. On a proper wifely level, she took seriously the general view that it was a poor career move, 'contrary to everybody's Advice who had any Regard for him'. (Her parents probably disliked a scheme that removed the protection of a husband from their daughter.) Less properly, she was furious that Matthew had an exciting opportunity and she did not.

Anxious to see him in post, Swift urged Matthew to sort out his affairs and go, telling Barber that the young man was ready to attend the mayor's commands and that for his part he wanted him to go 'as soon as possible, that he may have a few weeks to prepare him for his business, by seeing the Tower the Monument and Westminster Abbey, and have done staring in the Streets'. What he didn't say was that he wanted to be sure that Matthew had time to attend to his, Swift's, business.

Serving as Swift's amanuensis and agent, Matthew was to carry over to Bowyer a collection of Swift's writings to be published in London. Matthew would see them through the press and take the profit. This simple-sounding scheme had one drawback: Swift had already agreed with Pope that most of the pieces assigned to Pilkington were to be included in a fourth volume of the Pope–Swift *Miscellanies* which Pope was editing. Swift had become increasingly unhappy about this arrangement and had been stalling all year, assuring Pope he would send him materials and not doing so. But he did not want to oppose Pope openly. His hope seems to have been that if Matthew moved quickly he could get his own edition out first and pretend he knew nothing about it. Everything could be blamed on 'the impertinence of the printers', or on someone like Matthew who, it would readily be believed, had used his intimacy with the dean to take advantage of him.

Throughout August, Matthew and Swift were busy preparing the manuscripts for publication. A large parcel was sent to Bowyer. Meanwhile, Pope had become discontented with his publisher Benjamin Motte and was dealing with Lawton Gilliver. Motte wrote complaining to Swift. Saying nothing to Pope, Swift assured Motte that his firm would have the *Miscellanies*. Pope and Swift were playing a delicate game with and against each other. Matthew wrote with assurance to Bowyer, promising him the copyright of Swift's *Modest Proposal* among other things already listed for Pope's *Miscellanies*. As Bowyer's friend Clarke was to observe sardonically, the 'great affairs about property in Irish Wit' were a 'dangerous controversy' when men like Pope and Swift were involved. 'Have you come off safe?' Clarke asked Bowyer. Bowyer was fine, but Matthew, and in consequence Laetitia, were to be badly damaged by Swift's use of them in his publishing schemes.

Laetitia, watching Matthew hurrying about puffed up with his own importance, noticed that the more Swift ordered him around the more servilely complaisant Matthew was to him while treating everybody else, including herself, with 'Contempt'. Relations became increasingly strained between them. Matthew did little to soften his departure for his wife, though he agreed to take some of her poems with him and promised to show them to Pope. Repeatedly, she tried to argue him out of going, accusing him of being reckless, obstinate, selfish, rash. He was not to be persuaded, especially not by a wife who, he knew perfectly well, would have done exactly as he was doing had their positions been reversed and who alternated her insistence that he should not go with a plea to take her with him.

By mid-September Matthew was ready. The government yacht sailed on the 23rd. Among the passengers due to travel then was the Prime Minister's second son, Edward Walpole, MP, returning on his father's orders to take up a vacant parliamentary seat at Great Yarmouth. An artistic, insecure young man with little interest in public life (though his father had also appointed him a joint secretary of the treasury) his potential as a patron seemed beyond compare. Matthew had probably met him through Mrs Percival at one of her entertainments, or at the Claytons' house. Edward Walpole's musical knowledge would have impressed him – Walpole later went on to invent a bass viol called a pentachord. Music was his first love. Walpole composed and played, but he also sketched, painted and wrote. It was easy for two such men to strike up a friendship; and it was characteristic that Matthew who, encouraged by Swift, was writing anti-government satires and was on his way to be chaplain to an anti-Walpole lord mayor of London, should begin by trying his luck with someone belonging so emphatically to the other side.

The day before his departure was a wretched one in the little house at Lazer's Hill. The misery and quarrels of the preceding months came to a head and the couple had a fierce row. Laetitia again proposed that Matthew should take her with him. Excited at the prospect of escape and adventure, he delivered a cruel blow:

he told me plainly he did not want such an Incumbrance as a Wife, that he did not intend to pass there for a married Man, and that in short he could not taste any Pleasure where I was. As this was a Secret I did not know before, I receiv'd it with Astonishment; for amidst all his wayward

Moods, I ever imagin'd till then that he lov'd me, and that the many ill-natur'd Speeches he made me were rather the Effect of a bad Temper, than any settled Aversion he had taken against me.

It was an acrimonious parting. Matthew could not wait to be off and Laetitia could not bear being left behind. By the end they were hardly speaking. He 'left me and my three Children almost without an Adieu'.

∞

She mourned him, she missed him, and she resented the fact that he could so easily leave her. She called him cold, proud, neglectful. She wept bitter tears. Then a kind letter from him posted from Chester on his arrival, combined with the attentions of her friends who made sure she was seldom left alone, dispersed some of the rage and melancholy. An even kinder letter from London, 'passionately tender' this time, inspired her to write him a poem:

> These Lines, dear Partner of my Life,
> Come from a tender faithful Wife . . .

in which she expressed the hope that their love would endure for ever, and told him that in the meantime,

> To soothe my Woe and banish Care
> I to the Theatre repair.

She had seen some Shakespeare, possibly *Macbeth*, *Hamlet* or *Othello*, all of which played at Smock Alley in the 1732–3 season.

Matthew, meanwhile, had also been amusing himself at the theatre, being less interested in Westminster Abbey and the Monument than in Drury Lane, Covent Garden, taverns like *The Shakespear's Head*, where actors and playwrights gathered, and the Bedford coffee-house. His letter contained a portrait sketch of himself drawn by his 'ingenious Friend', James Worsdale. The sketch was a good likeness, or so Laetitia thought, asking her husband to convey her praises and thanks.

Worsdale mixed with a hard-drinking, heavy-gambling set that included Edward Walpole. Henry Carey was another. Like many English musicians, Carey resented the craze for Italian opera, which he had satirised in his *Faustina* (1726), several years before Gay's *Beggar's Opera*. Together with the composer Thomas Arne and Frederick Lampe, Carey formed the English Opera Company which took the Haymarket in 1732 to stage their own productions, including the successful *Amelia* with Susannah Arne in the title role. Iconoclastic, facetious, aggrieved (his biographer suggests he suffered from a persecution complex), Carey welcomed the new arrival and very soon all three were planning collaborative writing and acting schemes.

Earlier in the summer, Worsdale's studio in Marylebone Street had been one of the places where tickets could be bought for the grand opening of Vauxhall Gardens, the *ridotto al fresco* concocted by the Bermondsey entrepreneur, Jonathan Tyers. Worsdale may have been one of the 'several painters' employed to finish the temples, obelisks, triumphal arches and grotto rooms by 7 June when the Prince of Wales and 400 of the finest families graced the official opening with their presence. These newly opened Gardens would have been high on Matthew's list of sights to see, and if he was taken there by Worsdale and Carey they are unlikely to have been without female company. The 'passionately tender' letter from London probably owed as much to the soft light and sweet airs of Vauxhall, or the excitements of Drury Lane, where the leading actress, Mary Heron, soon caught Matthew's eye, as to any conjugal longings.

Most urgent for Matthew was to present himself at Twickenham, but unfortunately he went without sending Pope warning and the poet was not at home. Next day, 17 October, Pope, all hospitality, wrote inviting him to pass the fortnight before he was due to take up his chaplaincy as his guest. Given that Pope distrusted Matthew and was prepared to dislike him, the invitation seems extraordinary; and can only be understood as a gambit in the ongoing manoeuvres about the *Miscellanies*. Pope was feeling triumphant. He had moved fast and foiled Swift: Lawton Gilliver had brought out the *Miscellanies* on 4 October thus rendering Matthew's project with Bowyer valueless.

Pope's invitation dazzled Matthew. He was thrilled by it and accepted at once. Lodged at Twickenham as Swift's protégé and Barber's chaplain, the ambitious Irish curate was introduced into the highest circles. Perhaps he was not altogether sorry that the

Miscellanies volume had appeared, for it included his own *An Infallible Scheme*, positioned just before Swift's *A Modest Proposal*, and though his name was not given, since none of the pieces were signed, Pope and others knew that he had written it. Matthew's Swiftian pamphlet had been lodged for posterity alongside those of the two most famous writers of the age. Pope showed him 'extraordinary regard', seemed indeed to be 'even oppressing him with civilities'. Attributing this welcome to 'Mr Pope's Respect for the Dean', Matthew wrote to Laetitia, regaling her with his success, praising Pope and acknowledging his obligations to Swift. His wife thought this a letter 'very proper' to take to the deanery. Swift's reaction was not what she expected:

> The Dean read it over with a fix'd Attention, and returning it to me, he told me, he had, by the same Pacquet, receiv'd a Letter from Mr Pope, which, with somewhat of a stern Brow, he put into my Hand, and walk'd out into the Garden. I was so startled at his Austerity, that I was for some Minutes unable to open it, and when I did, the Contents greatly astonish'd me.

In the letter, which does not survive, Pope apparently expressed surprise that Swift had recommended as a modest ingenious man who might be an agreeable companion, 'a most forward, shallow, conceited Fellow' whose impertinence had sickened Pope before three days were out. There was more in the same vein. Pope 'heartily repented' having invited him.

Laetitia, reading the letter, stunned, would have recognised the portrait of her husband, and could well imagine him in Pope's drawing room, talking too much by English standards, being too pleased with himself, overplaying his hand. But she also knew that Swift had been making use of Matthew to deceive Pope. And Pope, in return, was making use of him to vent his anger at Swift. These perceptions were explosive and she did not utter them. Even to hint a criticism of Pope's deplorable treatment of Matthew was too much:

> the Dean return'd, and ask'd me what I thought of it? I told him, I was sure Mr Pilkington did not deserve the Character Mr Pope had given of him; and that he was highly ungenerous to caress and abuse him at the same Time. Upon this the Dean lost all Patience, and flew into such a

Rage, that he quite terrify'd me; he ask'd me, Why did I not swear that my Husband was six Foot high? and, Did I think myself a better Judge than Mr Pope? or, Did I presume to give him the Lie? and a thousand other Extravagancies. As I durst not venture to speak a Word more, my Heart swell'd so that I burst into Tears, which, he attributing to Pride and Resentment, made him, if possible, ten Times more angry, and I am not sure he would not have beat me; but that, fortunately for me, a Gentleman came to visit him.

In 'a violent Passion of Tears' she made her escape.

If Swift's rage, which had little to do with Matthew and everything to do with his own relations with Pope, included some guilt it would not have been inappropriate, for he knew very well he had set Matthew up. Laetitia, meanwhile, spent an anxious night fearing that Pope's bile would lose them Swift's good will. The dean's 'favour' was crucial to them. Next morning she wrote an apology and begged Swift to reassure her of his continuing regard. Having by this time recovered his composure, Swift was able to reply graciously that she had been the one at fault:

Madam
You must shake off the Leavings of your Sex. If you cannot keep a Secret and take a Chiding, you will quickly be out of my Sphere. Corrigible People are to be chid, those who are otherwise, may be very safe from any Lectures of mine . . . I desire you may not inform your Husband of what has past, for a Reason I shall give you when I see you, which may be this Evening, if you will.

She went to him at 5 p.m. when she knew he was likely to be alone. He received her in avuncular fashion, said he would write 'a Letter of Advice' to Matthew, and urged her to keep the matter secret for Matthew's sake: so long as Matthew thought Pope was his friend he might still get some advantage from him, whereas to reveal that he knew what Pope had said behind his back would be to make of him an enemy. Pope did indeed continue to pretend friendship for Matthew and Swift continued being able to use him. Pope and Swift continued to assure each other of their mutual affection, though Pope's disdain for Swift's apparent liking for 'low' company broke out on a number of occasions in subsequent letters.

Matthew's charms worked better on Dr Arbuthnot, who

specially appreciated him for his music and reported him 'a very agreeable ingenious man'. As for John Barber, it was never likely that they would get on but to begin with at least Matthew's reports to Swift were upbeat: the modest demeanour Swift had instructed him to adopt was effective and the mayor was proving all helpfulness.

∞

For Laetitia there were advantages in being an abandoned wife. Matthew's absence removed some of the pressures of rivalry. She no longer had to fear his jibes when others compared their productions and rated hers superior to his, as their friend the lawyer John Smith had done, tactlessly complimenting Mr Pilkington 'on having a Wife who could write better than himself'. Matthew was easily riled by such remarks. Pride in his wife's unusual abilities shrank when it seemed to take away credit from his own. Stung, he would say that her head had been turned by the dean's attentions; and even, stooping to the hoariest cliché, inform her – as she witheringly recalled – that 'a Needle became a Woman's Hand better than a Pen and Ink'. Laetitia had Swift's authority for retorting that all poets notoriously envied one another:

What Poet wou'd not grieve to see
His Friend cou'd write as well as he,

wrote Swift, and we can hear his caustic common-sense views in her reflection in her *Memoirs* that a 'poetically turn'd' woman was best advised not to marry a poet, for:

If a Man cannot bear his Friend should write, much less can he endure it in his Wife; it seems to set them too much upon a Level with their Lords and Masters; and this I take to be the true Reason why even Men of Sense discountenance Learning in Women, and commonly chuse for Mates the most illiterate and stupid of the Sex, and then bless their Stars their Wife is not a Wit.

Progressive thinkers keen to raise the general tone of society by improving women's educational standards would have nodded in agreement. There was support for such views; attacking men on these grounds was becoming standard practice in advanced circles.

What it obscured, of course, was the no less powerful envy of the 'poetically turn'd' wife and the real difficulties of managing two straining talents within the framework of marriage.

She had the 'scribbling Itch'. She was 'most incorrigibly devoted to Versifying' and she used the time that Matthew was away to write, read and think. She wrote poems about sitting in a library ('Vain, deceitful World, adieu') and on 'sacred Solitude', but she was not naturally drawn to solitude nor introspection; her own feelings, envious and otherwise, were not her subject matter. She was an observer, an extrovert, a talker, an entertaining performer 'fond of Admiration to a Fault', and even if she had tried to be alone company would have sought her out for she had always been in demand. Men who blessed their stars their wives were not wits did not necessarily dislike wit in other men's wives. As a self-proclaimed 'coquette', Laetitia had a reputation to keep up. In the early eighteenth century, the word 'coquette' was used to describe women who met men on equal terms as raconteurs and wits. It did not necessarily convey a strong sexual meaning, though inevitably it inclined in that direction. Embracing the term as she pursued her literary ambitions in a city notorious for its love of backbiting and scandal, engaging in witty contests with attractive, clever young men, she began to be subject to as much criticism as praise. The gossip was under way well before Matthew left, but her sociability during his absence intensified it.

It was not only literary satisfactions she sought. Matthew's 'ill-natured speeches' in recent years had included expressions of physical distaste for her body. Perhaps he was one of those men who find it hard to adjust when their sexual partner bears children and becomes a mother. It would not be surprising if the admiration Laetitia enjoyed for her rattling wit included solace from the company of men who told her she was still attractive, a detail which, in Matthew's absence, would be all the more remarked. She was, she admitted, 'a little too much upon the Coquette, for a married Woman'.

∞

Mary Barber returned to Dublin on 21 October 1732, travelling with Dr Delany and his new wife, wealthy Margaret Tenison, the first Mrs Delany. Mrs Barber, troubled by her gout and asthma, did not intend to stay: her plan was to go back to England and settle in Bath and if necessary let lodgings. Her husband had sold what was left of their business and intended to go too. Inspired by Swift's success in getting Matthew the chaplaincy, Mrs Barber urged him to write to John Barber in hopes there might be some sinecure in the mayor's gift that would suit her husband. Meanwhile, she also seems to have suggested the mayor might take on Rupert and teach him how to become a successful City businessman. A coolly pragmatic poem tells what she wanted for the boy: he should have a 'heart set on gain', be 'industrious and orderly, prudent, and smart', not too 'scrup'lous', and not have 'too much conscience'.

As usual, Swift's birthday at the end of November was celebrated across Ireland with bells, bonfires and illuminations. Many healths were drunk, many poems written. A new young friend, Lord Orrery, presented him with verses and an expensively bound manuscript book. Delany gave him verses and a silver inkwell. Mary Barber mentioned these gifts to Laetitia and prompted her into action. Remembering 'a fine Eagle Quill' she happened to have, Laetitia wrote some verses on the 'matchless' pen it would make, and sent the quill wrapped in the verses, along with a cutting from a London newspaper that had recently arrived in the post from Matthew. The cutting contained a poem of her own, wrongly attributed to Catherine Talbot. (Matthew had evidently taken the poem with him and seen it into print.) Swift dutifully passed all these specimens around among his 'Friends of Genius and Taste'; by January Laetitia's poem had been printed in the *Dublin Evening Post*; and very shortly afterwards, Faulkner put out a four-page pamphlet where Mrs Pilkington's, 'Sent with a Quill to Doctor Swift, upon hearing he had receiv'd a BOOK and a STANDISH', appeared alongside the birthday tributes from Orrery and Delany.

Delany gave a party to mark his return and to introduce his wife to the 'easy, gay, polite' society of Dublin, about which he had no doubt been boasting. It was then, or on another occasion in the early summer of 1733, that the elderly Irish dramatist Thomas Southerne, famous author of *Oroonoko*, was there and Laetitia enjoyed his company, staying the whole day 'in Delville's sweet inspiring Shade'. (The following year Southerne sat to James Worsdale for his portrait.) Constantia Grierson put in an appearance to meet the first Mrs Delany: wraith-thin, always coughing, sleepless, increasingly dependent on laudanum, her health had never been good and it had worsened during 1732. She had given birth to two daughters, one of whom died in 1731 and the other not long after. The strain was too much, especially as she seems to have maintained a punishing regime of study, writing and translation throughout. Like Mary Barber, she had become more outspokenly political. In a poem dated 5 January 1732 which Mary Barber preserved and published in the introductory pages of her own *Poems on Several Occasions*, Constantia Grierson attacked those who:

> Squander vast Estates at Balls and Play,
> While public Debts increase, and Funds decay;
> While the starv'd Hind with Want distracted lives,
> Nor tastes that Plenty, which his Labour gives.

She added that the people of Ireland were quite used to seeing their wealth drain away, their gold flowing 'to Albion with each Tide'.

Delany's party was probably Constantia Grierson's last social outing and perhaps her friends could see death in her features. Still only twenty-seven, her edition of Sallust unfinished, she died shortly afterwards and was buried in St John's church on 4 December 'in a very handsome manner'. George Grierson was devastated. Mary Barber and Laetitia Pilkington felt her loss deeply, not just as a friend but as a key figure in the set. Constantia had helped them all. She had enjoyed acting as an agent for literature in every respect. Mary Barber memorialised her by including six of Constantia's poems in her *Poems on Several Occasions* and, in the preface, providing some biographical details. It was appropriate that Constantia should figure largely in the volume; along with others in the group she had worked hard to improve many of Mrs Barber's poems. Laetitia, similarly, was to pay homage to her exceptionally gifted friend in her *Memoirs*, taking the opportunity for a swipe at Mrs Barber, whose poems, she observed, were 'dull' but would have been much worse without the help she received.

Coincidentally, in England on the day of Constantia Grierson's funeral, John Gay died. Pope and Dr Arbuthnot wrote to tell Swift but he, guessing the contents of the letter, couldn't bring himself to open it for five days. Gay's funeral, conducted at night as funerals often were, was a grand affair, his coffin having been carried from the Strand to Westminster Abbey in a magnificent hearse 'trimmed with plumes of black and white feathers', with three mourning coaches in attendance, and peers of the realm serving as pall-bearers. Among those who attended to show their respect for the celebrated author of *The Beggar's Opera*, perhaps we can imagine the lord mayor's chaplain, staring about him and taking it all in. For Matthew, Gay's career carried the special message that persistence and patience in the hunt after aristocratic patronage, along with a willingness to seize whatever opportunities presented themselves even if it meant switching political allegiance, really did pay off. Gay's beginnings were no more propitious than Matthew's own: he was a draper's apprentice. He died worth more than £6,000, a huge sum, especially for a man who never ceased to lament the insincerity of his court connections and the false promises of his wealthy friends.

If Matthew wrote his wife or Swift an account of the poet's grand funeral the letter has not survived. Swift complained he barely heard from his protégé, but the mayor seemed pleased enough, judging by his reports back to Swift. 'Mr Pilkington gains daily upon us,' John Barber wrote in February, suggesting that his first impressions had not been altogether positive, 'and comes out a facetious agreeable fellow'. In March, Lord Carteret saw him at a 'great entertainment' given by the mayor in Goldsmith's Hall where Swift was the first toast. 'I like the Young man very well,' he told Swift, 'and he has great obligations to You, of which he seems sensible'.

There was a reason why Swift was being toasted. The mayor was leading the City aldermen in a major campaign opposing Walpole's Excise Act, mainly a tax on tobacco. John Barber was 'the darling of the people'. On 11 April feeling ran so high in London that there was a night of rioting in the streets. Swift's famous anti-government interventions in Ireland in the 1720s made him a symbolic figure, and there was a buzz of expectation in the spring of 1733 that he would suddenly appear in London. Matthew was Swift's representative and when he was among the 'patriots' – that is, the opponents of Walpole – Swift's name was ever in his mouth. Presumably, when he was with Edward Walpole and his cronies he was more circumspect.

Meanwhile, Matthew was busy planting Swift's verses, as requested, in the press. At the height of the Excise crisis, he arranged publication of 'The Life and Genuine Character of Dr Swift', a poem supposedly acquired by an unnamed lawyer of the Inner Temple from a copy transcribed by a disloyal servant, sent from Dublin, and printed without the dean's permission. The date was April Fool's Day. As Swift told Carteret: 'I will not deny that I take a malicious pleasure in being anyway Instrumental in making some thousands of fools at least for a season.' 'The Life and Genuine Character of Dr Swift' was a spoof version of one of Swift's major poems, 'Verses on the Death of Dr Swift', completed the previous year, trailed in the press, frequently shown about, much talked of but not yet printed. Having sent Matthew the spoof, Swift brought Laetitia into his scheme of making fools of thousands. It had become customary at the deanery for her to read his works aloud. On this occasion, he produced the manuscript of his 'Verses on the Death of Dr Swift', which she duly read, and afterwards she asked, or Swift hinted that she might like, to take it home with her. They went through a little pantomime of promises and demands: she had to promise not to copy it out, and to bring it back first thing next morning. Swift knew very well the social value of what he was lending and the purpose to which she would put it. Laetitia kept her word and did not copy the poem out: she sat up most of the night memorising it. In no time at all she was out reciting it in company; others memorised it in turn from her and very quickly it spread round town. Swift, of course, summoned her to explain herself, pretended to be angry, accused her of breaking her promise for she must have copied his poem, and then, with a flourish, produced the printed 'Life and Genuine Character' which had been sent to him from London. The London printers, he fumed, could only have got this inferior version to print by garbling the original which she had put into circulation.

This was a classic Swift hoax and Laetitia, knowing him well by now, saw through it at once. He made her read the 'Life and Genuine Character' out loud to him:

I did so, and could not forbear laughing, as I plainly perceiv'd, tho' he had endeavour'd to disguise his Stile, that the Dean had burlesq'd himself; and made no manner of Scruple to tell him so. He pretended to be very angry, ask'd me, did I ever know him write Triplets? And told me, I had neither Taste nor Judgment, and knew no more of Poetry than a Horse. I told him I would confess it, provided he would seriously give me his Word, he did not write that Poem. He said, Pox take me for a Dunce. I then assur'd him, I did not copy his Poem; but added, when I read anything peculiarly charming, I never forgot it, and that I could repeat not only all his Works, but all Shakespear's.

The interview concluded happily with the two of them testing each other on their recall of lines from Shakespeare. When she got home there was a letter from Matthew confirming what she had 'plainly perceiv'd': Swift had sent the 'Life and Genuine Character' to Matthew and told him to place it in the press.

As well as giving printers writings by Swift which Swift denied having written, Matthew gave them pieces of his own which he claimed were by Swift. Matthew was a good mimic of Swift's style: the pamphlet, *A Serious and Useful Scheme to Make an Hospitable for Incurables of Universal Benefit* by 'A Celebrated Author in Ireland' was assumed to be by Swift. It promulgated Swift's ideas, drawing on Matthew's intimate acquaintance with him and their many hours of talk. It is quite likely Swift knew what Matthew was doing and unlikely that he minded; these were the services he had sent him to perform and for which he paid: Matthew was given leave to draw £20 from Benjamin Motte on Swift's name.

The money was soon used up. With James Worsdale, Matthew was out and about at clubs and theatres; and in pursuit of Edward Walpole he was undoubtedly living too high for his means. Now and then at Drury Lane or Covent Garden he might have caught sight of a familiar face, a small boy dressed in the long double-breasted jacket and breeches of Westminster School, who was also spending beyond his allowance. Fourteen-year-old Thomas Sheridan, Swift's godson, had been sent over early in 1733 and left pretty much to his own devices. Young Sheridan made no apology for wanting to see all the shows, no matter how much it cost nor how little time was left over for his studies. He was to grow up to be a controversial manager of Dublin's theatre royal, Smock Alley, his arrogance remarked by many and his determination to raise the tone of the stage bringing him into conflict with Mrs Pilkington in her last years.

Instead of lodging in the City close by Goldsmith's Hall, where his expenses would have been less, Matthew lodged in the West End near Worsdale, paying an extravagant £30 a year, keeping a servant, and maintaining a distance between himself and the mayor. Barber told Swift, 'had he lived in the city, I should now and then have had the favour of his company in an evening'. The mayor was not short of company at this time: the great political leaders of the opposition saw his importance and were taking care to flatter him – he was 'caressed by great courtiers', his name ever in the newspapers. What he would have liked from Matthew and was surprised not to get was active political support. He offered to pay him to write against the government during the Excise crisis, an offer Matthew flatly refused. Worsdale, however, had begun painting the mayor's portrait which he seems to have hoped Vertue would engrave. (Vertue declined.)

John Barber reported punctiliously to Swift on his own proper behaviour towards his chaplain, sending Swift a full account of Matthew's earnings for reading prayers and preaching sermons (£130 for the year, more than any other chaplain before him) and taking care not to mention politics or hint at a criticism. Matthew was not so restrained. Of Barber he declared he abhorred his principles, and 'despised him for his follies and vices'. Swift, whose behaviour seems to have been driven by casual malice, urged Matthew to send him an 'impartial' description of the mayor's character, a strange request considering that Swift knew Barber very well. Matthew duly wrote a savage satirical portrait, stressing Barber's vanity, love of publicity, avarice, greed, lust and unscrupulousness. Far from being 'impartial' it was a character assassination, a politically motivated hatchet-job: John Barber as the Walpolians saw him. Matthew told Swift that Barber had spoken 'disrespectfully of the Irish', and for good measure told Barber he had told Swift this, and that Swift considered Barber one of his 'ungrateful' friends.

In Dublin, Matthew's 'true' account of John Barber, shared with the set, gave a great deal of pleasure. Dr Delany and Mary Barber were 'transported with the justness of the character', and Mrs Barber read it over to herself several times. She then reproduced as much of it as she could remember in a letter to a friend in London, Mrs Drelincourt, telling her to take it to the mayor and read it to him, making sure he knew that the original had been written by his own chaplain. According to Matthew, and later Edmund Curll who published Matthew's abusive portrait of John Barber after Barber's death in 1741, this revelation produced an 'uneasiness' between the two men.

John Barber was a shrewd operator, a sophisticated political animal. He had no intention of openly quarrelling with the man Swift had sent him, no matter what the provocation. In Matthew's not very believable account, their 'uneasiness' was amicably resolved. Barber, we are told, admitted the truth of the portrait and his chaplain asked pardon for any offence he might have caused. The person at fault was 'that female Judas', the treacherous Mary Barber.

∞

In betraying Matthew, Mary Barber was probably hoping to prod the mayor to reward her. She had taken to claiming cousinship with John Barber, on the strength of their name, a piece of information that filled him with horror. He already had a list of pensioners, a 'set of ungrateful monsters called Cousins'. When Swift put in a request on her behalf early in 1733, indicating that the Barbers intended to settle in England, it provoked an unusually forceful refusal from John Barber.

Mrs Barber turned her attentions to Robert Boyle, fifth Earl of Orrery, the dim and disappointing scion of a lineage of high achievers in the arts and sciences, who, upon the recent death of his father, had come into title and wealth. Orrery had a hunger for literary immortality by association which made him amenable to those who had wit. He was putty in Swift's hands. Swift flattered him, and Orrery gave Mrs Barber large sums of money as well as the use of his name. John Barber was no doubt pleased to hear about it when Swift told him.

Swift was tireless in his support for Mary Barber. By the summer she was well enough to travel again and was getting ready to take her final leave. Swift wrote letters of introduction for her to all his friends, soliciting money from some, such as Sir Andrew Fountaine, a well-placed courtier, whom he had not seen for decades. Embarrassingly, the subscription had remained open for over three years and there was no sign of a book. Swift laid the blame on illness, telling Mrs Caesar how their friend had had 'so many repetitions of the gout, that her limbs are much weakned, and Spirits sunk'. Oxford, who had already subscribed, was similarly informed that the gout had delayed everything, and reminded that Mrs Barber remained 'by far the best Poet of her Sex in England, and is a virtuous modest Gentlewoman, with a great deal of sense, and a true poetical Genius', so Oxford was to ensure that all his family, friends and relations subscribed. The Duchess of Queensbury, browbeaten by Swift, agreed to believe what he said about his protégée, though it went against all her instincts: she had 'hitherto ever had a naturall aversion to a Poetess'.

As usual, Swift had his own agenda and Mrs Barber did not get this help for nothing. Swift put together a parcel of new poems for her to carry over and give to Matthew to see into print. The poems Mrs Barber packed in her bags were among the most inflammatory works Swift wrote: 'On Poetry: A Rapsody', 'An Epistle to a Lady' and 'On Reading Dr Young's Satires'. He knew what the consequences might be: carriers, printers, booksellers and writers all ran risks. As it happened, everybody involved in handling those manuscripts, with the exception of Swift, ended up in jail.

Unaware of her friend's base treatment of Matthew, Laetitia continued to see a good deal of Mrs Barber. They met at the deanery, at Delville, at their own homes. There was constant talk about Tunbridge, London, Bath. The more Laetitia heard, the more she shared in the preparations for departure, the more restless she became. Life without Matthew was boring. Constantia was dead, Mrs Barber was leaving to begin a new life.

'London,' Mrs Pilkington wrote in her *Memoirs*, 'has very attractive Charms for most People'; and she was 'a young lively Woman' whose mind had been turned towards London for almost a year. Matthew had written with the compelling news that he had shown her verses to Pope. Pope had said he 'long'd to see the writer'. True or not, it was wonderful to imagine herself among the company. Matthew went so far as to say he missed her and wished she could be in London. She was conscious that the year of his chaplaincy was coming to an end. There was another, less appetising, reason for wishing she could be there: rumours had reached her of Matthew's infatuation with the actress Mrs Heron.

Mary Barber's return to England began to seem like an opportunity not to be missed. Mrs Barber's new and generous patron, the Earl of Orrery, was also travelling back to England. Going with them, Laetitia could travel as the companion of a respectable older woman and a peer of the realm; and as for coming back, she would return with Matthew. There was the question of her three little children, of course. William was already being cared for by Mr and Mrs Pilkington senior; the Van Lewens would look after the younger two once the servants told them she had gone. She persuaded herself that it was reasonable for a young wife to miss her husband so much that she had to be with him, but she recognised that others could not be trusted to view the matter in the same light, especially not her parents who, if they knew what she planned, would forbid it. She told no one.

On 7 August, the government yacht was at anchor off the coast hoping for a fair wind to set sail next morning. Laetitia packed her portmanteau. That evening, she confided in one servant whom she directed to take the bag and see that it was loaded on board along with the luggage of the other passengers. Next day, on the pretext that she wanted to wave them all off, she travelled down river to Ringsend with the Barbers, their children and Lord Orrery and his retinue. When they reached the yacht and went aboard, she went too, explaining that she was curious to see what it was like. Once on board and no longer in danger of being pursued and stopped, she told her friends that she planned to go all the way to London with them. It was a 'frolic'. She was excited and pleased with herself. Some of the company cheered her on, some disapproved. But she didn't care. 'I was very chearful and easy, and little regarded what was thought of my Frolick'. Like Matthew a year earlier, she also left her family 'without an Adieu'.

CHAPTER FIVE

London Frolic

The crossing was pleasant and easy. Once landed at Parkgate, then a port outside Chester, Laetitia wrote to Matthew telling him what she had done, confident that he would be pleased. A few days later, as the travellers approached London, Matthew and James Worsdale drove out to meet them. Matthew, all smiles, received her 'very obligingly'. Teasingly, he called her his 'little Fugitive and Run-away', perhaps a reference to Mary Davys's book, *The Fugitive*, which related an Irish woman's adventures travelling alone in England. Matthew's endearments, however, and his pleasure in seeing his wife after so many months apart were as nothing compared to Worsdale's: 'A Stranger would have thought Mr Worsdale was my Husband,' she wrote, recalling that first summer evening with the man who was to figure largely in her future life, 'he welcom'd me so kindly, and paid me so many Compliments.'

Paying compliments was Worsdale's *forte* and he kept them up as her belongings were transferred into his coach and all three drove not to Matthew's lodgings but to Worsdale's studio. She had been up and travelling since 3 a.m. and was tired, but the men were in party mood. She had to be shown Worsdale's paintings which were stacked about and to hear about his commissions. If she expressed admiration for anything she saw, he immediately urged her to take it, keep it, have it as a present. High-spirited, successful, funny, the painter was currently in funds so he could afford to be generous. Worsdale loved the idea of himself as a benefactor, showering gifts and promises on those less blessed than he was, though he was already depending on Matthew for verses and songs which he passed off as his own. Matthew hoped for great things from him. He whispered to Laetitia to invite Worsdale to go back with them for supper, an invitation which threw Worsdale into transports of joy. Laetitia watched as he loaded the coach-box with 'as many Bottles of Wine . . . as it could conveniently hold', and then all three drove off to Matthew's 'very handsome and convenient' lodgings in St James's where they drank, talked and laughed till midnight.

It was an appropriate beginning. London had become Matthew's playground. His term as chaplain was coming to an end: his final duty was to preach a sermon on 29 September, the day the new mayor was elected. His interest in returning to Dublin, family responsibility and the chores of a curate's life was nil. He spent all his spare time at the theatre. Matthew, Carey and Worsdale were co-writing a ballad opera, *A Cure for a Scold*, inspired by Shakespeare's *Taming of the Shrew* – a choice which might have sounded a warning note. The world Matthew moved in was aggressively antagonistic to respectable married life: the wife who was a wit, like Kate in the *Shrew*, had to be tamed; better still was no wife at all, as in Farquhar's version of the popular ballad 'O'er the hills and far away' in *The Recruiting Officer*, where Kite leads his men in the song:

> We all shall lead more happy lives,
> By getting rid of brats and wives,
> That scold and brawl both night and day,
> O'er the hills and far away.

Matthew had happily got rid of his brats and wife for a year, and, though Laetitia had pursued him 'o'er the hills and far away', he had no intention of changing his habits. That first night, the moment Worsdale took his leave, she learned that her husband would not be spending much time with her. He explained that his duties as chaplain required him to attend on the lord mayor from nine in the morning until six in the evening, after which he always went to the play at Drury Lane and after that to supper with Mrs Heron. 'Though I thought this but an odd manner of Life for a Clergyman,' she commented drily in the *Memoirs*, 'I did not say so, being unwilling to offend him.'

The understatement conveys a great deal. His indifference to her feelings was stunning, but it was necessary not to offend him since she required his protection. By joining him in London, she had made herself vulnerable; he could easily have received her other than 'obligingly'. The law gave husbands more or less complete control over wives. As the historian Lawrence Stone put it, in English law 'until the nineteenth century, a married woman was the nearest approximation in a free society to a slave'. No matter how badly a husband behaved, a wife's duty began and ended with submission to him. Furthermore, as she had no legal existence apart from him, there was nowhere to go to complain, no rights to lean on. If Matthew chose the company of an actress 'of no very good fame' over his wife, there was absolutely nothing to be done about it. And if he sent a friend to entertain his wife while he amused himself elsewhere, and the gentleman proved charming and the wife succumbed, then the fault was entirely hers. Marriage was ostensibly sacrosanct; but male adultery was condoned, while female adultery was severely punished – if proven, it gave grounds for divorce and made a social outcast of the woman.

Early next morning, before Matthew left for the City, Mary Barber called and had a private conversation with him. She delivered the poems Swift had entrusted to her along with a letter of instructions: Matthew was to 'dispose of' the poems and take the profits. It was a hurried meeting. Matthew was late. As he rushed out, stuffing the poems into his pocket to read later, his wife reminded him that Worsdale had said he would spend the evening with them: 'He laugh'd at my believing it, and said he was a Man so uncertain in his Temper, that perhaps I might never see him again while I liv'd.' See him she did, however. Worsdale arrived, as arranged, while Matthew was at the play, bringing the news that Matthew, forgoing the pleasures of Mrs Heron's company, would return for supper, and in the meantime they were to entertain themselves. Worsdale exerted all his charms, complimenting her 'at an unmerciful rate', singing 'the tenderest Love Songs he could think of, in the most pathetic manner' and generally behaving like the gallant that he was, addressing a vivacious, excitable and pretty young woman whom he hoped to seduce. She did not dislike it, but it made her uneasy. The extravagant flattery, 'so much in the Stile of a Lover', and then, upon Matthew's return, Worsdale's pointed astonishment that Matthew could bear to be a moment away from such a paragon, verged on contempt: it made too clear her position as a snubbed wife, especially when Matthew showed no displeasure. That was humiliating enough, but Matthew had further plans:

When we were alone, he told me, he believ'd his Friend was in Love with me. I answer'd, if he thought so, I wonder'd he gave him so warm an Invitation. He said, he was a very generous Man, and that his liking to me, if well manag'd, might prove very profitable; for he valued no Expence where a Lady was in the Case.

Matthew's willingness to pimp her ('So, it seems, I was to be the Bait wherewith he was to Angle for Gold out of a Rival's Pocket') came as a shock, though only perhaps because she was the bait; she was as keen on angling for gold as he was. Over the next few weeks, while Matthew spent his evenings with Mrs Heron, James Worsdale made it his business to entertain Mrs Pilkington. She swore, 'as I shall answer it to Heaven', that Matthew 'did every thing in his Power to forward and encourage an Amour between his Friend and me' and implied that she resisted. Whether an 'amour' took place at this time cannot be known, but Worsdale's attentions, the full force of his charm, the exciting range of his connections, his usefulness in squiring her around town and the guineas that spilled from his pockets, laid the basis of an intimacy that was to be as intense as any marriage.

The mayor invited his chaplain's wife to dinner at his house in Queen Square, where his long-time lover, Sarah Duffkin, did the honours of the table. Whatever John Barber privately thought about Matthew he kept to himself, and as a man of the world who enjoyed the company of witty, strong-minded women – the writer Delarivier Manley had been his mistress and lived in an apartment above his print-shop in Ludgate Hill until her death in 1724 – he was delighted by Laetitia. He invited her to dine at Queen Square whenever she wished. Sarah Duffkin, meanwhile, took the opportunity to tell her everything she knew or had heard about Matthew's infatuation with his actress. Perhaps Matthew had anticipated some such exchange: he boasted that Sarah Duffkin was madly in love with *him* and was furious that Laetitia had turned up. Or perhaps that was a fantasy Matthew nursed having daily had to witness the good fortune of the former servant and her unprepossessing old printer, now wealthy and powerful as lord mayor of London. A wife in all but name, Sarah Duffkin was appropriately rewarded when Barber died in 1741: she was left £20,000 and the house in Queen Square, along with Barber's country property at East Sheen. (She married an actor and lived happily ever after.) Matthew may well have tried to foment trouble between the couple. The 'uneasiness' Laetitia felt as she listened to story after story about 'my Husband's extraordinary Regard for the Player' suggests some score-settling, and was probably exactly what Sarah Duffkin intended.

Still, the two women became friends. Together, they went to the theatre to see Mrs Heron in action. Matthew and Worsdale were also at the play, but seated elsewhere. Aaron Hill judged Mrs Heron a self-conscious actress whose natural charms were spoiled by affectation and whose voice, with its 'swallow-like risings and windings', was horribly squeaky. She was the leading lady of the day, however, having inherited Anne Oldfield's parts. The season of 1733–4 was a strenuous one for Mrs Heron: she was among the players who, led by Theophilus Cibber, Colley's rambunctious son, had staged a revolt and been locked out of Drury Lane. They had formed themselves into a new company – the Company of Comedians of His Majesties Revels – at the unlicensed Haymarket. There she played Lady Brute in Vanbrugh's *The Provok'd Wife*, Mrs Fainall in Congreve's *The Way of the World* and Lady Townly in *The Provok'd Husband*. It might have been on 6 October that the mayor's lover and his curate's wife went to scrutinise the rival (whom Sarah Duffkin, a keen theatre-goer, had seen many times before) and if so they would have been watching her play Berinthia to Colley Cibber's Lord Foppington in Vanbrugh's *The Relapse: or, Virtue in Danger*, an appropriate play in a number of ways, featuring a reformed libertine who lapses, an unscrupulous mistress, a virtuous wife, a pressing lover and a crooked parson. It was a gala night, that 6 October: Corelli's first concerto followed the play and there was a new trumpet overture with Susannah Arne singing and Miss Robinson dancing. They might have seen Mrs Heron in any number of parts through October and November, some of them comically apt: Lady Lurewell in *The Constant Couple*, Lady Betty in *The Careless Husband*, even Laetitia in *The Old Batchelor*, and, perhaps most gratifying of all, as Lady Sadlife in *The Double Gallant*. Whatever Laetitia thought on seeing her, and whatever she said then, her comment on Mrs Heron in the *Memoirs* was restrained: 'To do her Justice,' she wrote, 'she was a graceful, fine Woman, at least she appear'd such on the Stage, and had a peculiar Skill in dressing to Advantage.' The restraint probably had more to do with the fact that Mrs Heron, by then long dead, had been trained by Colley Cibber, whom Mrs Pilkington did not wish to offend.

The trip to London was a sobering one. If being well known in a small and gossipy community like Dublin – 'a Place of the least sin, and the most Scandal, of any City in the World' – was constraining, it did at least provide support: family and friends who, watching her own and Matthew's behaviour, exerted the pressures of familiarity. In Dublin, the clever Mrs Pilkington had a defined place as her father's daughter and the witty favourite of Dean Swift. She was the protégée of Dr Delany, admired by Lord Carteret and kept company with aristocrats like the Earl of Orrery. In London Mayor Barber and Sarah Duffkin took an interest in her, and as an older couple gave her some protection, but Matthew's hostility to Barber, his decision to lodge in St James's rather than in the City, his identification with Walpole and hopes of preferment from Edward Walpole, all had the effect of isolating her. She was a dependent wife, subject to her husband's wishes. Her husband wished her to keep company with a notorious libertine, a man for whom sexual conquest was integral to his sense of identity. When Matthew 'obliged' her to go with Worsdale to see the sights at Windsor, a trip of twenty miles, which in winter necessitated an overnight stop, Laetitia claimed she could not refuse.

What happened at Windsor? As she told the story in her *Memoirs*, this was the moment when the scales fell from her eyes. Travelling to Windsor, alone in a coach with an attractive, 'importunate' man whose 'tenderness and passion' were those of an avowed lover, who pressed her to respond in kind and enjoy a holiday weekend of sexual pleasure, she was tempted. But she managed to resist. Over dinner she realised, with horror, that the expedition could be a trap. Matthew, like a number of husbands at the time, might have planned to catch his wife in a lover's arms. Or perhaps Worsdale was in a conspiracy with him. She became suspicious, angry and fearful; every sound of horsemen pulling up at the inn made her start with terror. In this mood, all Worsdale's 'soft endearments' were wasted; she was 'obstinately sullen'. Pretending to be tired, she asked to be shown to her room and there discovered that Worsdale had booked only one room with a double bed for them both:

I was now in a manner convinc'd there was Treachery intended against me, and reproach'd my desiring Swain in such bitter Terms, that he had no way to prove his Innocence, but by retiring, tho very reluctantly, to another Apartment, and I took special Care to barricade my own, not only double locking it, but also placing all the Chairs and Tables against the Door to prevent a Possibility of being surpriz'd.

The etiquette among gallants did not absolutely forbid rape, but under the circumstances, rape was not in Worsdale's interest. Nor was it necessarily sexual assault that she feared – she admitted that in the coach there had been dalliance of some sort. If Worsdale was in collusion with Matthew to prove his wife an adulteress, then all it needed was for them to be discovered in compromising circumstances. Equally, if the Windsor trip was, as she claimed, the first of Matthew's artful 'schemes' against her which were to culminate four years later in the discovery of Robert Adair in her bedroom, their lodging in a room with but one bed would be enough. Matthew would be able to press for damages against his friend on the grounds of criminal conversation. 'Crim. con.' was a method of 'angling for gold out of a rival's pocket' that could net a husband dazzling rewards. In a famous case of 1730, brought by Lord Abergavenny against Mr Lyddell for sleeping with

Lady Abergavenny, the fact that the two men had been friends made the wrong unpardonable and the price immense. Lord Abergavenny was awarded damages of £10,000. As a later judge put it, 'the breach of friendship enhances the guilt'.

Henry Fielding's triumphant 1732 comedy, *The Modern Husband*, put a cynical spin on the matter and may provide a surer guide to Matthew's fantasies. In that play a willing cuckold, Mr Modern, sells his willing wife.

It was a jaundiced pair of tourists who went out early next morning to see what Windsor had to offer (nothing much in her opinion). Worsdale, still playing the gallant, reproached her for her 'cruelty' the night before, but was otherwise well behaved. The episode had the unexpected effect of uniting them against Matthew. Worsdale became something of a protector whom Laetitia could lean on, and with her stronger personality she could, to some extent, control the relationship. Unlike her husband, Worsdale had no legal power over her; she did not have to obey him. One of the lessons she had learned was that Matthew was prepared to treat her as property; he would 'gladly dispose of me to the best Bidder'. This was a 'Shocking Thought!' not least because the law countenanced it. She was better protected by a libertine painter who hoped to seduce her than by her clergyman husband.

The law favoured husbands. Worsdale, a man of 'an avowedly dissolute character' with regard to women, was reckless, pleasure-loving and opportunistic. He was a prankster and a schemer, and later events confirm his relish for the dramatic, but he did not want to play Lyddell to Matthew's Abergavenny. If they had become more intimate than was safe by the time of the Windsor trip, and she had the sense (or greater knowledge of Matthew) to put the brakes on, he would have seen the point. Matthew could spin a convincing tale of dutiful care: he, the hard-working curate; she, the volatile wife whom he had sent on a 'Party of Pleasure' for her health; Worsdale, the trusted dear friend who betrayed him. No tale she told would carry any credit, for she was the woman in a story about sex, and neither law nor language allowed her to be on the winning side.

There might or might not have been 'a Failure in Point of

Chastity' during the little fugitive's frolic in London; there was certainly a hardening of her understanding of her position as a woman in a man's world. Men blamed women – they were 'severe in their Censures on our Sex' – for giving them what they wanted. Men used deception and force, arts and wiles, to get their way and then loaded women with 'every opprobrious Term with which our Language so plentifully abounds'. All men were a threat; dependency, a trap.

In two linked poems written at this time, Mrs Pilkington expressed the feminist anger Matthew's behaviour aroused in her. Both poems are about sexual rejection but in neither does the woman beg or plead. In 'To Strephon' it is spring and the lady feels desire, but Strephon, busy pursuing 'Some senseless, tasteless, Girl', is cold towards her. He prefers to 'rove' and buy his sexual pleasures. The speaker first berates him for his betrayal and then thanks him for setting her free. 'A Song' offers a plausible picture of Laetitia's mood by the end of her London stay. Indignant, cool and defiant, she recognised that her marriage was over and, at some level, was determined to embrace her freedom:

> Strephon, your Breach of Faith and Trust
> Affords me no Surprize;
> A Man who grateful was, or just,
> Might make my Wonder rise.
>
> That Heart to you so fondly ty'd,
> With Pleasure wore its Chain,
> But from your cold neglectful Pride,
> Found Liberty again.
>
> For this no Wrath inflames my Mind,
> My Thanks are due to thee,
> Such Thanks as gen'rous Victors find
> Who set their Captives free.

She had been a captive, freely wearing the chains of matrimony, but through her husband's betrayal she regained liberty. Strephon's failure epitomised the failings of all men, and from her vantage point she viewed their antics with some disdain. She claimed to feel no 'wrath' but 'To Strephon' ended with the word 'Revenge':

Go then, Inconstant, go, and rove,
Forget thy Vows, neglect thy Love;
Some senseless, tasteless, Girl pursue,
Bought Smiles befit such Swains as you;
While for the worst I see you change,
You give me a compleat Revenge.

∽

On 29 September 1733 Matthew delivered his departing sermon at the new lord mayor's election, and on 30 October his term as chaplain expired. Without position or income, but still hoping for some benefit from Edward Walpole, he resolved to stay on in London. There was also the matter of Swift's poems to see through the press.

It was too expensive to keep up rooms in St James's. Worsdale offered the couple a share of his studio, and Matthew accepted, an arrangement which more or less forced Laetitia to go home. Pregnant once more, it was some time in late November or early December that she began the long trek back alone, via Chester and Parkgate, to Dublin. John Barber, who told Swift that he had been trying to get Matthew a living in Coleraine, gave vent to some indignation about this in a postscript: 'Why Mr Pilkington should send his wife home in the midst of winter', he grumbled, 'or why he should stay here an hour after her, are questions not easily answered. I am not of his council.'

Going home was not a frolic. Laetitia had to face the disapproval of friends and family, some of whom had heard rumours, all of whom had complaints to make, so that she was 'both traduced for going to London, and for returning from it'. Wealthy Mrs Clayton, wife of the bishop who was Jack's godfather, invited her to dine at her opulent house on St Stephen's Green where, amid the marble and gilt, carved oak and Genoa damask, pictures, busts, and fine Persian carpets, she launched into a tirade of abuse. Shocked and upset – Mrs Clayton used language 'I should have scorned, in respect to my own Gentility, to have given to the meanest Servant I was ever Mistress of' – Laetitia ordered a chair to be called, burst into tears and ran out of the room. Gossip between London and Dublin being what it was, Mrs Clayton knew about James Worsdale; Matthew was making no secret of his affair with Mrs Heron. Gentility was precisely what was in the balance. Laetitia's prudent decision to leave London when Matthew gave up his own lodgings counted for very little. The damage had already been done.

The explosive encounter between the women, Laetitia's exit in tears, the bishop's discovery of her in the hall in her 'disordered' state, was quickly spread about town. In Laetitia's version, it was not her behaviour in London that provoked the quarrel but her big belly: the childless Mrs Clayton was 'barren' and cruelly envious. Meanwhile, Bishop Clayton, as Laetitia knew from her own experience, was one of those jovial prelates a visitor to Ireland described as being in thrall to both 'Venus and Bacchus'. Seymour Conway, cousin of Horace Walpole, complained about how much hospitable eating and drinking went on in Dublin, especially among the senior clergy: 'A primate will toast his nymph with all the gaiety of one and twenty.' No blame attached to such men; only the nymphs stood to lose. In the *Memoirs*, Laetitia got her revenge on the Claytons by identifying Mrs Clayton (though not actually naming her) as 'the first to attack my Character', and accusing the bishop of having ravished her maid on the carpet.

Back in London, Matthew sold Swift's poems as a job lot to Benjamin Motte who published them through the *Grub-Street Journal* in November and December. By January, they had come to the notice of the government. Not pleased by the anti-Walpole mockery in 'On Poetry: A Rapsody' and 'An Epistle to a Lady', they arrested Benjamin Motte, Lawton Gilliver of the *Grub-Street Journal*, the printer, the trade publisher and Matthew. Once in custody, Matthew wasted no time in informing on the carrier, Mary Barber. Perhaps he would have done so anyway, but he had become convinced that she and Patrick Delany had deliberately tried to sabotage his chances for the chaplaincy by not delivering Swift's letter to John Barber in the summer of 1732. Mary Barber was arrested on 30 January.

Swift's name stayed out of all legal proceedings, although most people guessed that he had written 'Epistle to a Lady'. Matthew, however, became what a recent scholar calls 'the Government's star blabber', and his name was on everybody's lips. It was taken for granted that he had betrayed the dean. To understand what this meant for Matthew's reputation, we need only consider the story that went around and which was recorded in Thomas Sheridan's much later *Life of Swift*. Sheridan claimed that Walpole had been determined to apprehend Swift, but a friend 'better acquainted with the state of Ireland' told him he would need 10,000 men to do it, for 'no less a number would be able to bring the Drapier out of the kingdom by force'. In fact, the government was never going to arrest Swift, even if they did think his poems were 'scurrilous and scandalous Libel', and probably were not all that interested in him. They were far more interested in Matthew's former employer, John Barber, because of his opposition to the Excise scheme and because he continued to be a focus for anti-government feeling.

The first Laetitia heard of these developments was at St Ann's church on the Sunday following. She was happily talking to friends after the service when Sir Daniel Molyneux whispered to her brother, Meade, in French, that he was surprised to see her so cheerful considering that her husband was in the Bastille. Meade reported the incomprehensible aside to her, but it wasn't until she saw a newspaper report that she knew what had happened. And very quickly she understood that they were ruined. Nobody had a good word to say for Matthew. 'The Notion of his having betray'd Doctor Swift incens'd the whole Kingdom of Ireland against him.' There was no proof he had been an informer, nor indeed that he had anything to tell the government that it did not already know from its own network of spies. 'But certain it is, his Character suffered so much that it almost broke my Heart, as it depriv'd me of any Hopes even of his having Bread for his Family.' No letter came from Matthew to help her explain events and justify him. She had to cope with rumour, some unpalatable facts and much fantasy. She had to deal with other people's rage and malice, anxiety and curiosity. Dr Hoadly, the archbishop of Dublin, sent for her and demanded an explanation; all she could do was cry. Swift did nothing. Dr Hoadly and his wife, loyal supporters of Walpole, were kind. They told her to feel free to dine with them as often as she liked: it would be a sign to those who – ominously – were coming to the archbishop and blackening Matthew's name.

Hoadly, speaking with the official voice of the well-placed government stooge, promised that if and when Matthew returned to Dublin he would do all he could to help.

At last a letter came. It was sent under cover to someone else to avoid it being intercepted by officials and taken to be examined at the castle. Matthew had been held for about two weeks and released on recognisance on 7 February. (Mary Barber and the others had all been released earlier, pending formal charges against them.) Frightened and broken in spirit, Matthew was suffering from rheumatism, had no money and wanted only to get away from London where prison loomed. He needed the fare to get home. Laetitia appealed to her father whose first reaction was to wish Matthew a long way away; he 'bade me let the Fellow go to the West Indies, and he would take care of me and the Children'. Crying, desperate, she pestered her father, following him about till he gave her £20 to send over. With this, Matthew was able to come back. He arrived on or about 1 April 1734, 'so pale and dejected, that he look'd like the Ghost of his former self; and the Disregard he met with from every body went very near his Heart. Every Day there was a new Abuse publish'd on him.' All Matthew's hopes of a bright future as the protégé of Swift were blasted; his dream of a new life – a comfortable Suffolk rectory, perhaps, in the gift of Edward Walpole – in tatters. Unwelcome notoriety intensified his gloom. Dr Van Lewen defended his son-in-law (possibly through gritted teeth) at the bedsides and in the drawing rooms of his influential clients – he 'battled' for him, Laetitia wrote, adding that she herself did all she could 'to chear and comfort his Spirits'.

The future looked bleak. Heavily pregnant, she was about to give birth to their fourth child and there was a chance Matthew would lose all his sources of income. One curacy he held, which paid £20 per annum (about a fifth of their income) was withdrawn, and she feared he would be deprived of the curacy at St Andrew's also. Hanging over them was the immediate anxiety about whether charges would be pressed. Matthew was supposed to go back to England for a court appearance. On 20 April 1734, Laetitia wrote to Worsdale (a letter addressed to 'Dear Worry' and complaining that an earlier one of his to her had been 'a very formal odd sort of a letter') telling him about Matthew's plight. There was a postscript from her father. John Van Lewen asked Worsdale to use his influence with Edward Walpole and to hire a lawyer – Van Lewen would pay – in order to get Matthew excused from returning to face charges. 'Matt' was ill: his rheumatism was bad, and besides, the winds were contrary and he would surely not be able to return in time. The excuses were feeble, but as Matthew did not go back to England and was not prosecuted, presumably they sufficed. Between them, his wife, friends and father-in-law got Matthew off.

As for Swift, we have no record of his behaviour towards the Pilkingtons during this time. He was receiving letters from England that bluntly told him he had been foolish. Bolingbroke wrote to him on 12 April, carefully not mentioning any names:

Pray Mr Dean be a little more cautious in your Recommendations. I took care a year ago to remove some obstacles that might have hindered the success of one of your recommendations and I have heartily repented of it since. The fellow wants morals & as I hear Decency sometimes.

A little later, Pope complained to him about the 'hurt' done to their friendship by what he described as the 'intervening, officious, impertinence of those goers-between us, who in England pretend to intimacies with you, and in Ireland to intimacies with me'. Pope went on:

I cannot but receive any that call upon your name, and in truth they take it in vain too often. I take all opportunities of justifying you against these friends, especially those who know all you think and write, and repeat your slighter verses. It is generally on such little scraps that Witlings feed; and 'tis hard the world should judge of our housekeeping from what we fling to our dogs, yet this is often the consequence. But they treat you still worse, mix their own with yours, and print them to get money, and lay them at your door. This I am satisfied was the case in the Epistle to a Lady; it was just the same hand (if I have any judgement in style) which printed your Life and Character before, which you so strongly dis-avow'd in your letters to Lord Carteret, myself and others.

Pope was clearly referring to Matthew Pilkington and perhaps also to Mrs Barber.

Mary Barber, stuck in London waiting to be charged, blamed

her plight not on Swift, who had given her the poems to carry over, but on the absent Matthew and his wife. On 28 May 1734, Mary Pendarves reported that 'poor' Mrs Barber 'has not yet finished the troublesome affair that the Pilkingtons' ingratitude has involved her in'. Ill and anxious, Mrs Barber was completing her subscription list and making final preparations for printing the handsome volume of poems that bore testimony, among other things, to her own vast talents in obsequious gratitude. As Swift put it, getting on in life was 'a very dirty road'. Too much mud was being spattered in the Pilkingtons' wake, and Mary Barber washed her hands of them. Editing the manuscript, which incorporated poems by Constantia Grierson and other testimonies to the group, she seems to have excised references to the Pilkingtons. This task may have delayed the volume's appearance, for though Samuel Richardson began printing it later that year and the title page bore the imprint 1734, copies were not available for distribution until the following summer. Meanwhile the Duchess of Queensberry who was on her way to Edinburgh, knowing something of the 'good deal of trouble' Mrs Barber was in and presuming that was why she hadn't seen her in company, left some gowns for her with Pope, so that when the poetess was ready to appear again she would at least be able to do so in aristocratic style.

Matthew had tried to play both sides and he failed catastrophically. His opportunism rebounded on him. Perhaps if he had been more prudent there might have been more sympathy for him, but he was a bumptious character. Dublin was unforgiving, and few bothered to make any distinction between the presumptive sins of the curate and those of his wife. Ostracised, enduring 'Misfortune's rude, impetuous Shock' on a daily basis as friends turned away and doors were closed to them, they both suffered. Matthew plunged more deeply into depression. His despair frightened and moved Laetitia. He wept, and she wept with him. The compassion she felt drew her closer to him, as love had once done, and it inspired a poem written to him 'by way of Consolation', in which she combined a reminder that he should trust in God and put his faith in the afterlife with a tough pragmatism and willingness to look adversity in the eye. Urging

Matthew to learn from experience and make the most of what life threw at them, the poem drew on conventional morals while revealing the emotional strength that was to carry her through even wilder storms. Their situation made available to her the role of loyal wife, a persona she was to employ for a range of responses to the vicissitudes of her life:

> No more, lov'd Partner of my Soul,
> At Disappointments grieve,
> Can flowing Tears our Fate controul,
> Or Sighs our Woes relieve?
>
> Adversity is Virtue's School
> To those who right discern;
> Let us observe each painful Rule,
> And each hard Lesson learn . . .
>
> Ill Fortune cannot always last,
> Or tho' it should remain,
> Yet we each painful Moment haste
> A better World to gain.
>
> Where Calumny no more shall wound,
> Nor faithless Friends destroy,
> Where Innocence and Truth are crown'd
> With never-fading Joy.

They told themselves they were innocent and unlucky, destroyed by 'faithless friends' ('friends' used here in the eighteenth-century sense of those with power to help lesser mortals on in the world). Both had been true disciples of Swift, creatures whose fortunes it seemed he could make or mar, and it may be that his indifference to the 'calumny' unleashed upon them was felt as the unkindest cut of all. Relations with Swift could never be the same for either of the Pilkingtons, for they knew more than anybody how he had used Matthew. Although the connection was not yet broken, it had been irretrievably damaged. Swift found other favourites. His last recorded communication with the Pilkingtons is a pleasant one. A letter survives from October 1736 which accompanied a gift of fruit and which promised a visit when his health was better. The letter ended 'my humble Service to the little woman's little Man', suggesting that though Swift felt under pressure to repudiate them ('my fault is, what my Enemy's give out, that I use you too well') it was not something that came easily. Matthew, meanwhile, with the support of Archbishop Hoadly (that 'eager Government understrapper') retained his curacy at St Andrew's and did not lose court favour: by autumn he was again writing the birthday ode for the king. The following spring, he wrote the official ode sung at Dublin Castle to celebrate Queen Caroline's birthday, and in October 1736 his was the ode sung for the king's birthday. These can probably be viewed as rewards for his co-operation with the authorities.

The baby, a girl, was born in the spring of 1734 and named Charlotte. She was to live for three years, arriving at a time of trouble and dying at a time of worse trouble. We know little about this period in the Pilkingtons' lives, but it is clear that any healing effect of misfortune on their relationship was short-lived. As Matthew's confidence returned, so he began to plot alternative possibilities for his future. Laetitia's health, meanwhile, gave way under the strain. She failed to recover her strength after the birth – the fifth baby she had carried to term. Poorly, and in low spirits, she seemed 'very much inclined to a Decay'. Her father, wisely judging she would be better away from Dublin and from Matthew, prescribed a trip to stay with his brother George in Cork. It is possible that Meade, who had graduated from Trinity College the previous spring, went with her, but there is no mention of the children, five-year-old Betty and four-year-old Jack, nor do we know if she took little Charlotte. Most likely the baby was put out to a wet nurse under the supervision of Dr Van Lewen, and the children were cared for by servants and grandparents as they had been during her trip to London.

George Van Lewen was, like his older brother, a successful doctor and midwife, although probably untrained and with no prospect of being elected a Fellow of the College of Physicians as John had been in 1729. He lived in Hanover Street, Cork, with his wife, Catherine, and her two sisters, Betty Donevan and Peggy Crofts, who between them ruled his household. He also seems to have supported their brother, Barry McGomery, whom he trained in midwifery, and a nephew. George Van Lewen was a kindly, hard-working, hard-drinking, eccentric character, peculiar-looking and full of 'whims', as Jack Pilkington later wrote. Jack ran away to his Cork relations when he was about eleven and was taken in by them. He left a vivid account of 'the doctor' coming home drunk – he was 'a bon companion wherever he went, and never started from his bottle till pretty late at night' – and singing very loudly till he fell asleep. 'It generally happened,' Jack recalled,

that at his return he found the ladies at cards, perhaps, with some of the neighbours who were to sup: he used, at his entrance, to salute them in a friendly manner, and then, taking me on his knee, by the fireside, behind them, every now and then he loll'd out his tongue at the company, and whisper'd softly to me – Bitches! Bitches! As I had no conception of this being the effect of drink, I was quite at a loss what to think of it; nor could I get from him, for he held me fast, saying, now nephew, you are undoubtedly my flesh and blood, and I am determined to tell you the whole affair: – then he'd look at the company and put his tongue again out, in an ironical and contemptuous manner, which the homeliness of his face, and the gravity of his wig, rendered so whimsically absurd, that I could not forbear laughing at: this pleased the old gentleman infinitely, as he imagined I laughed at the company . . . the same scene was acted almost every night.

It had also been acted pretty frequently when Jack's mother stayed at Hanover Street in the mid-1730s. Jack's great-aunt told him how he 'used to teize my mother in the same manner, when she was there; and my uncle, Capt Vanlewen, used to steal off to bed the moment the doctor came in'. Dublin-bred Meade had no patience with the country doctor and his gross behaviour. Laetitia, child-like in appearance and ailing, pinned on her uncle's knee, was probably subjected to more of his 'vagaries' than was comfortable, especially given the nature of domestic politics suggested by George Van Lewen's behaviour. Mostly, Uncle George was content to be governed by his three women who took the line that he 'meant no harm' (Jack implied that they controlled him and that the doctor was easily manipulated). But they in turn were wary when the Van Lewen relations came looking for support; it was their own nephew who was in line to inherit.

Laetitia stayed in Co. Cork for several months and while there went with the family to Mallow for the season. Mallow was becoming popular as a spa town, its mineral waters attracting visitors in the summer months in much the same way as Tunbridge Wells and Bath in England. It was John Van Lewen's birthplace, so there were family associations, and George Van Lewen was a well-known figure. Plenty of 'good company' gathered in what was 'once reckoned to be the best village in Ireland'. They filled the hours between drinking the waters with pleasant walks, card-playing, dances, assemblies and the usual intrigues and gossip. At spas like this, poems written by, about and to named individuals of the company were a recent trend, giving rise to published collections – the 'spa miscellany' – which listed the leading belles of the season, and printed ballads and songs and riddles. It was a sure route to local celebrity, which might spread further as groups dispersed at the end of the season and re-formed the following year. Mary Barber had contributed at least six poems to *Tunbrigiala; Or, Tunbridge Miscellanies for the Year 1730*, later included in her *Poems on Several Occasions*.

Mallow received Laetitia Pilkington as a known wit. Evidently she had recovered enough by then to make her mark – or the waters had been effective. There were some tensions: Jack was told that his mother had cost them 'fifty pounds at Mallow', a sum of money which, if true, suggests some extravagant re-stocking of her wardrobe and her library. Well-dressed and with restored health, Laetitia shone at all the best gatherings and was a target for witty combat and poetic exchanges. One young man, Freeman Murray, became obsessed with her, constantly making her the butt of a new game, 'selling bargains', in which people were tricked into asking innocent questions which drew indecent replies, usually involving posteriors. Swift said it was fashionable among the maids of honour at court. For example, someone would absently remark, 'It is white, and it follows me,' and when asked, 'What?' would triumphantly reply, 'My arse!' When young Murray wouldn't stop pestering her, Laetitia asked him why and he explained that he had heard she was a wit and he wanted her to write a satire on him. She obliged with 'The Mirror', in which barren-minded, empty-headed 'Strephon' is shown his resemblance in 'Truth's polish'd Mirror', advised to leave off the 'Rude and Rash', and told to employ his talents to better purpose:

> Bounteous Nature fram'd your Mind
> Fit for Sense and Taste refin'd.

Echoing Shakespeare's *A Midsummer Night's Dream*, ('If we shadows have offended . . .') she displayed her own ability to be scatological while lecturing him against it:

> How can you to Fame ascend,
> If your Course you downward bend;
> You, indeed, may hope, in Time,
> To achieve the low Sublime:
> And suppose the Bottom gain'd,
> What but Filth could be obtain'd?
>
> If my Freedom here offend you,
> Think it kindly meant to mend you.
> In your Mind are Seeds of Worth,
> Call their latent Virtues forth:
> Nor need you far from Wisdom roam,
> Your best Examples are at home.

For Mrs Pilkington herself, there was a plentiful supply of books to aid the improvement of her mind. We do not know how she imagined her future at this time but it clearly included literary success of some kind and to this end she set herself to read systematically and write. She may have spent successive summers between 1734 and 1736 in Co. Cork as a way of living apart from Matthew. It does not seem that the children ever went with her; Jack makes no mention of it. Her reading included Shakespeare, Milton and Dryden, Swift and Pope and Thomson; but she also had some knowledge of women writers like Katherine Philips, Delarivier Manley and Aphra Behn who were coming into focus for her as important forebears.

The poem 'Verses Wrote in a Library', a self-conscious attempt to situate herself in a tradition of learning that reached back to classical times, registers this reading. The library was the 'Sacred Nursery of Wit' and books were faithful friends:

> Friends who ne'er were known to shun
> Those by adverse Fate undone.

Meanwhile, 'Calm philosophy and Truth' wooed like lovers:

Let me here enwrap'd in Pleasure,
Taste the Sweets of learned Leisure . . .

Here immortal Bards dispense
Polish'd Numbers, nervous Sense;
While the just Historian's Page
Back recals the distant Age . . .

Come then, all ye sacred Dead,
Who for Virtue wrote or bled,
On my Mind intensely beam,
Touch it with your hallow'd Flame.
And thou chaste and lovely Muse,
Who didst once thy Dwelling chuse
In Orinda's spotless Breast,
Condescend to be my Guest . . .

'Orinda' was Katherine Philips, whose translation of Corneille's
Pompey had been successfully staged in Dublin in 1663. She was
the most famous female poet of the day. Elsewhere the poem
praised Swift and Stannard to say that Ireland could produce great
poets and patriots to vie with those of Greece and Rome. Mrs
Pilkington wanted to include herself in that company and may
have begun to think it a not wholly fantastical dream. By 1735, her
reputation had spread beyond Ireland. 'Verses Wrote in a Library',
appeared under the title, 'To My Study', in the *London Magazine* in
February 1735, and in the *London and Dublin Magazine* the same
month, and it was reprinted in London in *The Bee* in March. One
person at least thought enough of it to copy it out, for there is a
handwritten version in the Bodleian library, Oxford, with the
superscription, 'A Poem in Pambaic Verse written by Mrs
Pilkington, a very ingenious Lady in Dublin'.

During one of Laetitia's absences from Dublin, Matthew began
an affair with a wealthy widow. Officially, he became Mrs Warren's
private chaplain, spending much time with her at her town house
on St Stephen's Green, travelling in her private carriage, and
visiting at her country house. To Matthew, marrying money
probably seemed his only way forward at this point, barring the
awkward fact that he was already married. No longer charmed by
Letty's 'real wit', he could hope that she would die and leave him
free, or – what Laetitia believed – continue to devise schemes for

her destruction. Frustrated and angry, he was not inclined to be sweet-tempered in his dealings with her family; and they, in turn, probably knew more than they liked about his relations with the widow Warren. For example, it was Matthew's habit to send his lover a new-laid egg from one of the thirteen hens he kept proud watch over in the garden at Lazer's Hill. One evening after Laetitia had returned to Dublin he came home late to discover that she had eaten two of his eggs. He created a scene, abusing her in front of her brother and sister who were visiting. Worse still was the time she provided a custard for her father and Matthew ate it before it could be served, 'telling us to our Faces, we should not liquor our Chops at his Expence'.

Like many unhappily married women whose husbands enjoy the exercise of prerogative and who desperately try to maintain a decorous surface, Laetitia was generally in a state of 'Fear and Terror' if she invited family or friends to her home, 'being well assured, they would never depart without receiving some gross Affront'. The memorable affair of the custard occurred on All Hallows' Eve, probably in 1734, before the advent of the widow Warren (whose husband died in February 1735) but at the same time that another sexual drama was unsettling the Van Lewen household in Molesworth Street. That evening Laetitia had invited her parents, and Dr Delany who was dining with them, to Lazer's Hill for dessert so that her younger siblings could entertain their own guests without the inhibiting presence of 'old folks'. Among those guests was a Trinity College undergraduate, George Frend, a contemporary of Meade's, whom the youngest Van Lewen daughter, Elizabeth, had secretly married some time in 1734.

When Mary Pendarves had come to Dublin for the first time (in 1731) she had commented on the 'great sociableness' that she found among the Irish there, and guessed that from it would arise 'a good deal of tittle-tattle'. It is all the more surprising, then, that George Frend's family do not seem to have found out about his marriage. As an undergraduate, he was not allowed to marry, yet the service was performed (though not recorded) by the vicar of St Ann's, John Madden, who lived next door to the Van Lewens in Molesworth Street where the married Elizabeth continued to live

– just as her sister had done almost ten years earlier. It seems likely that the Van Lewens knew about the marriage, and might have been party to it all along (especially given their behaviour over Laetitia's wedding), keeping it secret but allowing Frend to come and go as an acknowledged husband. Their obliging behaviour on All Hallows' Eve might reflect a willingness to take themselves out of the house sometimes; and if they didn't know about the marriage at the time, they were surely told when Elizabeth became pregnant.

The baby, a boy, was born in the middle of December 1735. The following spring, George Frend graduated; and a few months later he enlisted in the army and was posted abroad. He was not to return for thirteen years. Effectively, Elizabeth was abandoned.

We learn almost nothing of Elizabeth from Laetitia's *Memoirs*, and the glimpses of the sisters' relationship suggest awesome levels of sibling rivalry. Laetitia continued to resent her younger sister's arrival in her life. Elizabeth, as she grew up, might have been jealous of her older sister's reputation; perhaps she tried to emulate her. Certainly, by the time Laetitia wrote her *Memoirs* she had reasons for wishing to keep Elizabeth out of the picture, for in the years of George Frend's absence Elizabeth gave birth to a number of babies which were obviously not his, thus providing him with grounds for divorce. Frend's return and litigation against Elizabeth followed shortly after Laetitia's return to Dublin in 1747 and the publication of her story in which she represented herself as an erring but meritorious and wronged woman, who had endured 'all imaginable ill Treatment, both in public and private'. Elizabeth's life uncomfortably mimicked her own. One fallen Van Lewen daughter could claim misfortune; two looked careless. Some such explanation would account for her impulse to downplay Elizabeth, though not for the extreme hostility of the characterisation.

In practice, at this time Laetitia seems to have remained closely involved with all members of her family, often having her meals with them and accompanying her mother and sister on visits. Matthew, too, going about his duties as local curate, was a regular visitor. Quarrels and harsh invective were a part of daily interaction. The social circles of the two households overlapped; they went to the same church, attended musical evenings together, met at the theatre. John Van Lewen's professional progress, as reflected in his house moves, from William Street, to Church Street, to the newly built Molesworth Street, was steadily upward. He could afford to send Meade off to Leiden to study medicine, which he did in July 1735, and as well as keeping his carriage, wearing fine clothes, buying books and claret, and entertaining company, he could afford to invest in property: in 1734, just a few years after moving into Molesworth Street, a house that was expensive to keep up, he spent £700 on a little housing development called Temple Court, just off Church Street.

Outwardly, all looked prosperous and thriving. And if we find ourselves asking how a family which seemed to be doing so well could manage to fail its daughters so abysmally, we should perhaps turn the question around and recognise how fragile the achievement of gentility could be, how much it required to sustain it and how easily the props could be kicked away. In the case of the Van Lewens, things went catastrophically wrong for all of them after Dr Van Lewen had a fatal accident at home on the morning of Sunday, 17 October 1736.

CHAPTER SIX

Death, Adultery, Divorce

Laetitia had been spending the summer with the relations in Co. Cork. In the week before her father's accident she travelled back as planned, reaching the outskirts of Dublin on Thursday, 14 October. Her aunt's sister, Peggy Croft, came with her. Matthew met the stagecoach a mile outside town, and all three transferred into a hackney to drive to Lazer's Hill.

For the husband and wife, it was not a happy reunion. Matthew was in a towering rage, and she soon knew why. There had been an exceptionally violent quarrel with the Van Lewens, and he now came to issue instructions: in obedience to him, she was to break off all connection with her family. Matthew commanded her, if she had any regard for him, never to set foot inside Molesworth Street again.

We do not know what the quarrel was about, nor if Matthew had deliberately fomented it to alienate his in-laws and provoke his wife, but he had profoundly offended John Van Lewen. Probably the doctor had thrown his son-in-law out and told him he wanted nothing more to do with him. Matthew's behaviour had long since ceased to be moderated by any concern for what his in-laws might think, although it seems that by this time they blamed Laetitia as much as him. When 'at all Hazards' she went next morning to call on her parents – informing Matthew that a daughter's duty came before that of a wife – she discovered that she was fully included in her father's fury. The doctor, the 'best natured Gentleman in the World', received her with a coldness that struck her to the heart:

He said, Mr Pilkington had used him so ill, he did not desire to see his Wife. 'Dear Sir,' said I, 'am I not your Daughter?' 'Yes,' said he, 'and had you taken my Advice in letting the Villain go to the West-Indies, I should have regarded you as such; but, make much of him; and remember, the Hour will come, when you will wish you had follow'd your Father's Counsel.'

He 'walked to and fro in a sort of distracted Manner, and looked so ill' that she thought it best to leave; and departed 'in such inconceivable Sorrow, as I never in my Life experienced before, because I really loved him more than any thing in the World'.

All that day, Matthew was out and she spent it 'in Tears'. Matthew did not return until midnight. The following day, and the next, she sent notes to her parents, asking after their health, conveying her desire to see them and her misery at the situation. They politely acknowledged her notes but did not invite her to go to them nor did they visit her.

By Sunday morning the strain of this had made her so ill she could not go to church. Matthew, due to preach in the afternoon at St Peter's, left early to dine with the widow Warren. She herself had an invitation to dinner with the Dubourgs whom she counted as among her closest friends. Arriving at their house at about 2 p.m., she noticed that her friends greeted her 'with as much Surprize as if they had seen an Apparition'. They sat her down then both left the room; she could hear them talking urgently behind the door, but could not fathom what was going on. John Smith arrived and there was more mysterious whispering. 'In short', she recalled, 'everybody behaved themselves so oddly to me, that I knew not what to make of it.'

Nobody explained anything because nobody had the courage to tell her what she ought already to have known. A servant was sent to fetch Matthew, presumably on the assumption that he would break the news kindly. The company had seated themselves for dinner when Matthew turned up. His wife was the only one who was surprised to see him:

'My Dear,' said I, 'you are better than Promise.' 'Why,' says he, 'I am not come to dine; but to tell you, your Father is stabbed.' Had he plunged a

Dagger in my Heart, it could not have given me a deeper Wound.

The Dubourgs had already heard the terrible news; by two in the afternoon, 'all Dublin' knew that Dr Van Lewen was lying close to death, his life 'despaired of'. Neither her mother nor her sister had sent to tell Laetitia. What Matthew callously called a stabbing was apparently an accident that had happened at home at about nine o'clock that morning. John Van Lewen was handling his surgical instruments, perhaps checking them, preparing them, when he slipped and fell while holding a very sharp surgical knife in one hand. The knife entered his body – either in his side or his belly, newspaper accounts differ on this detail. Whether he was in the parlour or the dining room, if it was a caseknife or a penknife, nobody seems to have been sure, and Laetitia, as she tells graphically in her *Memoirs*, was unable to find out the simplest details of what happened:

I rose from the Table, had a Chair called, and went to my Father's: Three of the Servants sat in the Hall, and my Sister, excessively dirty, walked to and fro in it. She would willingly have kept me out; but, however, the Servant knowing me, opened the Door. The first Noise which struck my Ear, upon my Entrance, was the deep and piercing Groans of my dear Father. When I attempted to go up Stairs to offer my Duty to him, my Sister by Violence pulled me down; but the Agony I was in for my Father, and the Resentment I conceived at her gross Usage of me, supplied me with Strength to get up in despight of her. When I opened the Dining-room Door, the Floor was all besmeared with Blood; my Mother, in an arbitrary Voice, asked me, what Business I had there? I told her, I had a Child's Right to pay my Duty to my Father. She said, if I spoke to him, it would kill him. Upon which, for the first, and indeed the only time that ever I gave her an impertinent Answer: I said, that if every Person about my Father had loved him with half my Tenderness, he would not have been reduced to the Condition I was then too sure he was in. Upon this, I offered to go into the Bed-chamber, but was not only forcibly withstood, but even beaten by my Mother, and again asked, if I intended to kill my Father? I made her no Reply, but sat down, and assured her, that the first Person who opened that Door, I would go in. In about three Minutes time Dr Cope, Dr Helsham, Mr Nicholls, and in all seven Physicians and three Surgeons (as my Father was universally esteemed) came of their own Accord to visit him; when I heard them on the Stairs, I took that Opportunity to open the Bed-chamber Door, in which neither my

Mother nor my Sister could well oppose me, as the Gentlemen were come into the Dining-room, before they were appriz'd of my Intention; but, Heavens! how shall I describe the Agony that seiz'd me, when I beheld my dear Father pale as Death, and unable to utter any thing but Groans? those only who have lov'd a Father as well as I did mine, can judge of my Condition: I kneel'd down by the Bedside: Weak as he was he kindly reach'd out his hand to me: he ask'd me if this was not an unhappy Accident. I begg'd he would not speak, because Mr Nicholls had told me, his Lungs were wounded, and that every Word was detrimental to him.

She asked him to lay his hand on her head and give her his blessing. He asked her not to leave him. That, however, was impossible because Mrs Van Lewen – in a frenzy of anxiety which her subsequent fate fully justified – had decided that her elder daughter must be kept from the bedside at all costs. Frantically she pulled her away, dragging her out of the room and out of sight. Determined not to let her near her father, she insisted that Laetitia go to bed with her, leaving Elizabeth, younger and stronger, to wait up and fetch whatever was needed. In the days that followed, Laetitia was kept a virtual prisoner. Though the women of the house would expect to take turns in nursing, her mother never once let her leave her side, and if she tried to she 'tore her hair, and scream'd like a Lunatick'.

Mrs Van Lewen was perhaps hysterical from grief alone. Perhaps she was keeping an errant daughter from her father for what seemed to her good reasons. Blame and guilt may account for Laetitia's lack of sympathy even ten years later when she coldly observed that she didn't know if her mother 'was really mad, or counterfeited to be so'. Then again, if the accident were a bungled suicide attempt that would account for some deranged responses, though there is no reason at all – other than the peculiarity of the incident – to suppose that it was.

These were desperate days at the house in Molesworth Street. There was much coming and going as Dublin's top physicians took turns to view the patient and gathered in the dining room to consult. When the news reached Cork George Van Lewen mounted his horse and rode night and day to Dublin. He arrived in the early morning, took a large glass of Madeira to fortify him, then went in to see his brother. He judged at once that there was no hope of saving him. Shocked, still carrying his whip and wearing his hunting cap, he appeared in the dining room where the Dublin medical fraternity stared at him. In that company he felt his inferiority. He was afraid to suggest remedies and in any case he was convinced that nothing could be done. Helping himself to some cold rice pudding from a dish on the sideboard, George Van Lewen turned to 'the grave eminent gentlemen of the faculty', rice pudding in one hand, knife in the other, and with his mouth full congratulated them on killing his brother. He 'put out his tongue, took a pinch of snuff' and turned to Laetitia – who was ready to sink with shame – and scornfully dismissed the physicians, saying 'are not these a parcel of pretty little gentlemen? It's apparent to me they know nothing of the affair'. Then he left. Jack was told the story by his aunt, as a sample of George's 'whims'. Laetitia did not mention it, perhaps because she found the whole episode so excruciating. Jack asked his Uncle George why he had behaved in such a self-demeaning way, and his uncle explained, with tears in his eyes, that he had been overwhelmed with misery and trying to hide it. He thought the Dublin faculty would have 'a contemptible opinion' of him, an untrained doctor from the south. In fact, they seem to have responded with sensitivity and gentleness.

Laetitia gave herself the credit for her father's first apparent turn towards recovery. She said that on the fourth night she heard her father's bell and was able to creep down to him without waking her mother. He was surprised to see her, having been told she had gone back to her own house. Finding him in a cold sweat, and having overheard the doctors say they did not think he would last the night, she decided to 'turn Physician' herself. She told him the doctors ordered him to drink 'some Hock and Sack made warm'. She plied him with the mixture all night, and it put him into a deep sleep. Next morning the fever was gone and her father's eyes were 'quite lively'. The physicians were amazed.

It appeared he was on the mend. Soon he could sit up all day and receive visitors. 'The whole Town seem'd to participate in our Joy'. On 22 October he was strong enough to draw up his will. On the 23rd *Pue's Occurrences* reported hearing 'that Dr Vanluen, is in a fair way of Recovery'. The *Dublin Daily Advertiser*, carrying the good news that he was out of danger, described him as 'the most Understanding Man of his Profession in this Kingdom', one who used his skills 'as well for the Poor as Rich, and as willingly dedicates his time to Charity as to his Interest'.

But by 29 October, the *Dublin Daily Advertiser* had to report that he still continued 'dangerously ill'. The *Dublin Gazette* feared he would not recover, and the *Dublin Evening Post* for 9–16 November declared him 'past hopes of Recovery, he being in a deep Decay'. But he rallied, and throughout the rest of November seemed to be gaining strength. There was talk of him being allowed to get up and about and even that he would begin to practise medicine again. The changing reports and attendant conversations wearied Lord Orrery, who told Bishop Clayton, then in Cork, that Dublin was now 'quite tir'd of curing and killing, and killing and curing Doctor Vanleuen'.

The end came in late December. Laetitia had ceased keeping watch at Molesworth Street. She was at Lazer's Hill when a message came from Matthew that her father was very bad. She hurried over to find 'all things in Confusion, and he so ill, that there was now not the least Hope of his Recovery'. He was coughing the whole time, 'seiz'd with what they call a galloping Consumption'. He died a few days later, leaving her, as she put it, 'in inconceivable Sorrow.' It was 3 a.m. on New Year's Day, 1737. About an hour before he died she left the room, unable to witness his last agonies, and went upstairs to her mother whom she found fast asleep.

Like George Van Lewen, they were all inept at grief. In a clumsy attempt to protect her mother, Laetitia pretended that her father was still alive. It was six in the morning and she had been busy locking up all the valuables and sending the chest of plate next door into Dean Madden's house for safe keeping – a wise precaution as it transpired. Her mother, waking, asked how her father was:

I told her, he had been very ill, in the Beginning of the Night, but was now very quiet. She said, she hop'd Sleep would do him good. I answer'd,

I trusted in God it had. So she arose, and would not put on her Shoes, lest she should disturb him: Nay, so strong was the Force of her Imagination, that she even said, she heard him cough as we pass'd by his Chamber Door.

But it was not possible to hide the truth from her mother for long:

when we came into his Dressing-Room, which opened to the Garden, as it was now Day-light, my Mother easily perceiv'd the Concern in my Countenance; she shriek'd when she look'd at me, and with great Impatience, ask'd me, what ailed me: 'O Lord!' cry'd she, 'can't you give me one Word of Comfort?' I answered very faintly, I wish'd it was in my Power: But, alas! her worst Fears were but too true; all was over. I really thought she would now have run quite mad.

As the eldest daughter, and with Meade away in Paris (her father had insisted he was not to be told or called home), Laetitia took command. Unable to express her sorrow – 'my Tongue refus'd its Office' – tense and overwrought, it was a relief to be active. She sent for Dean Madden whose prayers and spiritual advice helped calm her hysterical mother. She instructed the nurse to wash the body and lay it out. Laetitia could not bear to look at 'the Clay-cold Figure of him who, under God, was the Author of my being' but Elizabeth, to her sister's disgust, not only helped the nurse but laughed and made jokes as she boiled the kettle for tea. No doubt that was Elizabeth's way of dealing with things.

It had been a harrowing night, and New Year's Day brought fresh horror. Laetitia was upstairs with her mother, having just persuaded her to drink some tea, when a servant beckoned her to follow him downstairs. She found the ground floor of the house filled with bailiffs, one of whom, named Williams, behaved in an exceptionally offensive way. She again sent for Dean Madden, who was also abused, and then for Counsellor Smith, who was not at home. Meanwhile 'those licens'd Robbers' were taking an inventory of the furniture. Counsellor Smith arrived at about 7 p.m. and the 'Wretches' abused him too.

The bailiffs had been sent in by a litigious neighbour, widow Ford, to secure a bond of £200 Dr Van Lewen had either borrowed from her or stood surety for. The matter was settled relatively quickly, though not before the bailiffs had created a great deal of anxiety and the bailiffs' fees had mounted to £20.

The funeral took place at midnight on 2 January, in St Ann's church, privately, as her father had requested. Counsellor Smith and his wife came to look after Mrs Van Lewen who, having been weeping non-stop for two days, was half-asleep in a chair. The noise of the men carrying the coffin downstairs alerted her to what was happening: 'She started up, crying out, they were carrying her dear Husband to the Grave, and that she would go and be buried with him. We were obliged by Violence to restrain her.' They pretended the internment had already taken place and that the noises she heard were the servants tidying up. The visitors did all they could to help alleviate her anguish, including persuading her to drink some wine which, as Laetitia hoped, would make her sleep. Meanwhile, Matthew also put in an appearance. He attended the funeral, paying his respects in proper fashion. It was a gesture his wife appreciated.

Elizabeth judged it was time to make herself known to her husband's family. Dean Madden was again called on, this time to confirm that the marriage had taken place and that Elizabeth's little boy, now a year old, was the legitimate offspring of George Frend. Once satisfied on that point, Mrs Frend welcomed her daughter-in-law and Elizabeth did not return to Molesworth Street, nor, according to her disapproving elder sister, did she even send a message to her mother, for three weeks. She probably returned for a family conference when Meade at last arrived from Paris. By then, the 'melancholy' fact that there would be no money had become clear to all of them. Judging by an entry in the minutes of the College of Physicians for 31 January 1737, Mrs Van Lewen was already feeling the pinch: the treasurer was instructed to give £10 to Mrs Van Lewen 'in charity'.

In his will, John Van Lewen made no special provision for his wife or daughters, leaving everything to Meade with a recommendation that he maintain and support his mother. Meade seems to have done what he could ; what is surprising is how little cash there was in reserve. His hopes of following the family tradition and becoming a qualified doctor were over. By the end of May 1738, he had auctioned their goods, dismissed the servants, sold off Temple Court for the price his father paid for it, rented the Molesworth Street house at £50 per annum to the Rev. Dr Arthur St George, and settled his mother as a boarder in a clergyman's house 'in the Country' with an annual maintenance of £30; 'after which,' Laetitia recorded tersely in her *Memoirs*, 'I never saw her more'.

There was another death to endure before the miseries of the grim winter and spring of 1736–7 were over. In March, three-year-old Charlotte sickened and died. Still grieving for her father and oppressed by the impending break-up of the Molesworth Street house, uncertain what was to happen to her mother, afraid for her own future in the light of Matthew's continuing affair with Mrs Warren, Laetitia succumbed to stress – or, in eighteenth-century terms, 'the vapours'. She could neither eat nor sleep. The conviction that Matthew sought to destroy her became an obsession. Just as in London she believed he had hoped to catch her in incriminating circumstances with James Worsdale, so now she saw his scheming everywhere. Her father's death led him to throw off 'all Disguise'; he showed himself 'in his proper Colours'. He wanted money, 'and as nothing but my Death, or a Divorce, could accomplish his Desires, the latter seem'd the safer Method. To this End, he set all his Engines to work'.

Although the Matthew of the *Memoirs* is something of a stage villain – appropriately enough perhaps given that both Pilkingtons were intoxicated by theatre in all its forms – it is not far-fetched to believe he had determined to be rid of his wife by tormenting her at home and blackening her name out of it. Dumped by Swift, he needed a new patron if he was to have any chance of rising in the church; and if a wife whom he no longer loved or even liked *was* 'too much upon the coquette for a married woman' he might reasonably have viewed her as an obstacle. In a later age such a couple would have been able to separate and make new lives for themselves. In 1737 divorce and re-marriage required an Act of Parliament and was so expensive that only the very wealthy or well-connected even contemplated it. A private deed of separation could be granted, however, through the ecclesiastical courts. Quite properly, the courts required husbands who wished to live separately from their wives to go on supporting them: an innocent wife might be awarded up to a fourth of a husband's income in maintenance. This arrangement did not appeal to Matthew. A wife proved guilty of adultery would be entitled to nothing at all; furthermore, if doubt was cast on the legitimacy of the children of the marriage he could wash his hands of them too.

Gone were the days when Matthew composed pastoral verses – 'Love-excited Lays' – figuring himself as a shepherd, Colin, and Laetitia as Mira, his 'matchless' nymph. Disillusioned with poetry and poets, he had gravitated towards a new group of friends which included at its extremes the most hardened libertines of a libertine culture. These men, connections of James Worsdale and Edward Walpole, were founders of the Dublin Hell-Fire Club. Sir Richard Parsons, first Earl of Rosse, who had been a neighbour of the Van Lewens on Molesworth Street, a man 'fond of all the vices', was a central figure, along with Henry Barry, fourth Lord Santry, who later murdered a porter in a drunken brawl. Vicious, arrogant, blasphemous and violent, the 'Blasters' took as their motto 'do as you will'. Mostly what they wanted to do was drink, whore, fight and gamble. They performed rituals that demonstrated their contempt for religion and life – proceedings at the Eagle Tavern on Cork Hill might begin by pouring hot scaltheen (a mixture of whisky and butter laced with brimstone) over a captured cat and setting it alight – and they commemorated themselves through objects such as medals and jugs and group portraits. Worsdale painted the portrait now in the National Gallery of Ireland which shows some of the club members gathered round a drinking bowl. He also painted the portrait of the Limerick Hell-Fire Club.

Worsdale, who arrived in Ireland sometime later in 1737, was 'Master of the Revels' according to an inscription on a surviving glass drinking bowl belonging to the Club. We can be sure he participated in the 'rackets, brawls and midnight confusion' that were brought to the streets of Dublin by these wealthy thugs. Matthew presumably had to be more careful, but he was friendly with the painter Peter Lens of whose 'vile, atheistical conversations and behaviour' George Vertue complained, and whom Swift knew as one of the founders of the Club. Matthew was re-inventing himself, developing a new specialism designed to carry him upward. This was the cultivation of 'taste' or connoisseurship and it drew him into circles that overlapped with the Hell-Fire Clubs. In London the Society of Dilettanti, formed in 1732 by men who had met while on the Grand Tour in Italy, was to become an important force for disseminating the values of 'high' art as well as patronising artists. In its early years Horace Walpole described it as 'a club, for which the nominal qualification is having been in Italy, and the real one being drunk; the two chiefs are Lord Middlesex and Sir Francis Dashwood, who were seldom sober the whole time they were in Italy'. Sir Francis Dashwood was one of the London Hell-Fire Club enthusiasts. He later became notorious for the large-scale orgies he hosted at Medmenham Abbey.

In this company, decency was a joke. Laetitia knew rakish *mores* well enough (and she was to come to know Lord Middlesex, eldest son of the Duke of Dorset, very well later in London) to know that a husband scheming to free himself from the bonds of holy wedlock would have plenty of support. He would hardly worry about the scandal of divorce. And if, like Mr Modern in Fielding's play *The Modern Husband*, his pride could bear being branded a cuckold, cuckoldry was the most convenient route. She claimed that Matthew schemed her ruin. He encouraged a young poet, one William Hammond – 'a very troublesome coxcomb' – to make advances in the belief that she would be willing. Once she had managed to disabuse Hammond, this is what she claimed he told her:

Mr Pilkington describ'd you to me, as a Lady very liberal of your Favours, and begg'd I would be so kind as to make him a Cuckold, so that he might be able to prove it, in order to [get] a Separation from you; promising to give me Time and Opportunity for it: he assur'd me, it would be no difficult Task; that I need but throw myself at your Feet, whine out some Tragedy, and you would quickly yield.

Hammond later denied all knowledge of this in a pamphlet of 1748. He said he visited and sat quietly while she recited her verses to him. Hammond had some connection with the Duke of Dorset, then the outgoing Lord Lieutenant, and Matthew might well have hoped for advantage through him. When Laetitia wrote about Hammond's alleged seduction attempts, she set the main scene on the day of little Charlotte's funeral. She pictured herself, the mourning mother, sitting weeping in the summerhouse so as not to witness the removal of the baby's coffin, only to have her grief intruded upon by the 'popinjay' Hammond into whose mouth she put the message she wanted conveyed, that Matthew was 'a very great Villain', and 'very unworthy' of her. The scene effectively dramatised her circumstances at that time. Similarly, it is easy to imagine Matthew having 'drank a glass too freely' speaking contemptuously of her and raising the hopes of a poetical young spark whom he despised for being young and still loving poetry. But Hammond's version is interesting too in the way it reminds us that Mrs Pilkington was a poet of renown in these same circles and that she might be visited by men who expected to sit and hear her recite her verses to them.

Whether Matthew was laying 'snares' as she believed, he had clearly given up pretending to show any consideration for her or for his employers and parishioners. Shortly after Charlotte's funeral on 27 March he left Dublin, accompanying Mrs Warren on a two-month country holiday, without leaving word where he could be contacted or when he would be back, and without providing for his wife, children, maid or footman, and without telling the vicar of St Andrew's, the Rev. Dr Bradford, that he was going. The parish was 'quite in an Uproar'. Laetitia stepped in and with her brother's help found a young man who had recently been ordained to read six o'clock prayers and visit the sick. Her own situation was dire. Matthew had spitefully locked up his study into which he had moved all the books, including those which were legally hers (which she had brought into the marriage). The tea chest was locked and so was the garden, he 'rather chusing it should be overgrown with Weeds, and the Plants and Flowers die for Want of Water, than that either I or the Children should have the Pleasure of amusing ourselves in it'. She was left 'like a tame Cat, with the Liberty of walking about through two or three empty Rooms'.

Matthew's father, who was now keeping an ale-house next door, paid for the children's schooling and fed them, but there was no money to pay and feed the servants and they soon ran into debt. For her own meals Laetitia depended on her neighbours on the other side, Mr and Mrs Lindsay. We can be sure she had other resources too; and, with Matthew gone, though she had no money and no idea if or when he would return, she did not have to answer to him for her whereabouts.

Needy, lacking in judgement and even a little unhinged, Laetitia was furious at being abandoned for a 'buxom old Widow', old enough to be her mother 'and big enough to make four of me'. Rage fed recklessness. Her father's authority in Dublin had been important to her reputation; with his death she had only Matthew to stand between her and a scandalmongering world, and Matthew, far from protecting her, was doing all he could to besmirch her name. That she was not sitting quietly at home like a tame cat we know; where she spent her time and with whom we do not know, but it was public enough for there to be disapproving talk. Some of this would have been a mere by-product of the talk about Matthew, although Mrs Warren for one made a distinction when she informed Matthew that his wife was 'a Woman of so bad a Reputation, that she would not for all the World countenance' her.

∞

After Matthew's return in the early summer, by which time Laetitia may have decided to pay him back in kind, there was open hostility between them. He continued his attentions to Mrs Warren. Laetitia came under the spell of a charming young surgeon, Robert Adair.

It is possible that she knew or had known of Adair for some years. As a medical man beginning to make his way, in 1735 he advertised a series of public lectures on surgery, to be held at the main Dublin hospital, Dr Steevens's hospital. The Barber-Surgeons Company were at this time trying to establish a legal monopoly of the profession and they took out a lawsuit against him which on 18 July 1737 they voted to continue financing. Dr John Van Lewen was one physician who would have had views on this long-running issue.

Adair was ardent and eager, and though not especially good-looking he was an attractive and dedicated philanderer. His biographer was sure he had 'no enemies but his passions' and a 'constitutional penchant for female society'; or, in more ribald terms, he 'played the devil with the women'. He would have been hard to resist; added to which, if Laetitia did find herself melting under his seductive gaze, there was the extra pleasure of feeling she had done better than Matthew in *his* choice of lover. Some evidence for Adair's high-voltage sex appeal has come down to us from later in his life when an earl's daughter, Lady Caroline Keppel, fell in love with him at first sight: her emotions were 'singular, sudden and violent'. Her father, the Earl of Albemarle, tried to shake Adair off but to no avail and the two were married. Adair rapidly acquired the position of Inspector General of all Military Hospitals. His fortunes contrast dramatically with those of the curate's unhappy wife who in the autumn of 1737 may have allowed herself to be seduced – and 'in a moment of giddy rapture was undone', as the romantic and unreliable *Life of Robert Adair* put it; may have fallen in love; may have deliberately embarked on an affair; may have hoped for a happier life with a man who liked her, was sexually appreciative of her and gave her pleasure; or may have been, as she said, just reading with him in her bedroom. It would be nice to think that she had a bit of rapture before it all went so horribly wrong. She was pregnant again that autumn and the baby might have been Robert Adair's.

This is what she said happened. They were in her bedroom at Lazer's Hill, well after midnight. She was reading a book that belonged to Adair. He was waiting for her to finish it. Suddenly, the door was broken down and a crowd of armed men burst in. She thought they were burglars. Adair leapt up, drew his sword; there was a scuffle in which she was hit on the head and two of her fingers were pulled out of joint. Then Matthew appeared. Adair recognised him. He threw down his sword. Matthew hit him – first making sure that two of the night watchmen were holding Adair's arms.

Matthew, in jubilant mood, told his wife she had to go, but first he sent for a bottle of wine and drank their healths. He said he was making a present of her to Adair, and added that once he had obtained his divorce he would, in his capacity as a clergyman, gladly marry them. He tried to kiss her as they left.

It was 2 a.m. She was evicted from her home without being allowed to take any of her possessions since they did not belong to her but to her husband, without a change of clothing, with no money and no means of acquiring money, and without being able to say goodbye to her children. She was forced into entire dependence on Adair. Unsure what to do, in shock, the two of them went to Adair's lodgings where his servant had been waiting up to let him in. Once there, they 'sat like Statues till Day-break'.

In the morning she wrote to Matthew asking him to send on her clothes, or at the very least some clean linen. Meanwhile, to avoid being accused of co-habiting with Adair, she wasted no time in finding herself a cheap lodging 'up two pair of Stairs' across the river in Abbey Street. The clothes arrived, along with a letter in which Matthew explained that he intended to sue for a legal divorce and did not expect her to contest it. He sent her no money, nor her jewels, watch or books.

Word quickly spread and the wits had a field day. Peter Lens soon had a good story: he claimed that he went looking for Matthew a few nights later and not getting any answer when he called, went up to the bedroom at Lazer's Hill where he found Matthew and Mrs Warren 'administering Christian Consolation to each other' in bed. He said they offered him some punch, which he refused. He quipped that his action in bursting into the bedroom was a case of following the parson's example.

Everybody knew that the Rev. Pilkington had caught his wife in compromising circumstances and was pressing for a divorce. Dr Edward Barry wrote to Lord Orrery, in London, that she 'was found by her husband and brother in the close embraces of a young surgeon' who loved her – evidently the version of the story that reached Cork, from where Dr Barry wrote on 28 October.

If Adair loved her, or had some feeling for her, we can presume he continued to protect her in the weeks that followed, while friends like the Dubourgs fell away, and family, notably Meade, who may have been with Matthew that night, turned against her. However, we cannot be certain. All we know is that once ejected from her home and cast off by her husband, she became prey.

It is shocking to read about what happened next. Laetitia was shocked herself. She wrote, 'it was quite the mode to attack me', and by 'attack' she meant physical as well as verbal, attacks on her person as well as her reputation. She detailed a number of terrifying episodes which took place in the winter and spring of 1737–8. With her name 'publickly known through all the Coffee Houses in Dublin', there were many who wanted the honour of ravishing her or the chance to boast they had done so. Her attackers were not coxcombs or popinjays like Hammond but violent sexual predators. Pregnant, in real fear for herself and her unborn child, she was pursued by well-born louts who answered to no restraint. One wealthy MP burst into her lodging-house bedroom early one morning, ugly and six feet tall. She was terrified: 'I started up and threw my Gown about me, but I was not quite so quick in putting on my Cloaths as the Gentleman was, in taking his off'. Drunken young aristocrats including the Earl of Rosse 'and several other Persons of Distinction' rampaged through her lodgings bent on raping her: 'When those worthy Peers could not find me, they threatened to kick the Landlady'.

Part of the shock was in discovering what a commodity she became when no husband owned her. As a writer she liked to think she could meet and beat men on their own ground, but she had always had the protection of Matthew's name, and before that her father's. The violence to which she was subjected taught her the limits of wit as weaponry. She had to learn quickly when to hide, push a heavy trunk against the door as a barricade, ask another woman to share her bed, or simply move lodgings, which she did frequently. Once when she took rooms in the house of a sheriff's officer in Michael's Lane, the local minister and curate blackmailed the landlord so that he had to expel her. She was the subject of lewd verses, repeatedly circulated, and lies, to some of which she responded; well-turned answers had a strategic function even if they couldn't ward off actual blows. A prosperous lawyer who pestered her with his attentions, one Callaghan, was informed that he could keep his gold and his 'Wine three Doz'n' for she was a star beyond his sphere. This poem, 'To Counsellor Callaghan', was followed by a scatological ballad directed at Callaghan which she arranged to have delivered to the Rose tavern at a time when she knew that many lawyer friends of Callaghan would be there. It came with instructions to one Taaffe that he should read it aloud 'for the amusement of the company' and to humiliate Callaghan. If Taaffe failed, he would be her 'next subject for satire'. This 'Taaffe' might have been the gambler and card shark Theobald Taafe, a rake whose sexual prowess was celebrated in a well-known story. Taafe was said to have bet the actress Peg Woffington five guineas that he could perform five times in a single night. Having done so, he claimed his winnings upon which she challenged him: double or quits.

By entering into combat, making men laugh at other men, Laetitia kept alive a version of Mrs Pilkington, poet and wit, which was in danger of being submerged under the category of fallen woman. Such tactics would not protect her, however, from becoming a target for the procuresses and bawds who, often in league with landladies, ran the all-pervasive prostitution trade. As a repudiated wife without income, her obvious resource was to sell her body; as a 'name' she could command a high price. The landladies with whom she lodged probably expected this; the bawds who ran whorehouses and the procuresses who dealt at the luxury end of the market, seeking out high-quality goods for wealthy men – fourteen-year-old virgins, singers, dancers, wits – knew her circumstances. They soon had her in their sights. Perhaps she was prepared to contemplate going into keeping if a rich-enough offer was made. She was visited by a very well-dressed 'matron-like' female of about fifty who claimed to be housekeeper to the young Earl of Antrim. The earl apparently wanted to apologise for being among the worthy peers who had terrorised Mrs Pilkington, and said he wished to meet her so that he could compensate for his behaviour with a generous gift of money ('a prevailing Argument to one not worth a Shilling'). Laetitia believed the story and agreed to a meeting. No earl appeared, only a hopeful client. The woman was a celebrated procuress. Many other such callers tried their luck.

At the mercy of wild importuning men on the one hand and

calculating women on the other, the horror of her situation was brought fully home. She had 'no Protector, no Friend, no Guardian' and no money. For all her bravado, she was afraid. She told the MP who burst into her bedroom that far from being willing to entertain strangers, she 'never wished to see any Human Creature, and should be glad I could hide myself even from myself', adding that if he was a gentleman 'he would not insult Misery'. He left.

In a poem written at this time, titled simply 'Sorrow', she starkly catalogued absolute loss. Her father was dead, her mother had been packed off to the country, her children had been taken from her, and her husband was in the process of severing a supposedly indissoluble tie. Her reputation was in shreds. Stripped of her social identity, she stared ruin in the face. She did not claim to be an innocent victim: she acknowledged 'Frailties' and 'Faults'. A casualty of the 'tumultuous War of Passion' she had been 'undone' and in the language and cadence of eighteenth-century senti-mental poetry, she appealed for sympathy for a suffering woman:

> While sunk in deepest Solitude and Woe,
> My streaming Eyes with ceaseless Sorrow flow,
> While Anguish wears the sleepless Night away,
> And fresher Grief awaits returning Day;
> Encompass'd round with Ruin, Want and Shame,
> Undone in Fortune, blasted in my Fame,
> Lost to the soft endearing Ties of Life,
> And tender Names of Daughter, Mother, Wife;
> Can no Recess from Calumny be found?

'Sorrow' mixed bitterness at the hypocrisy of 'cruel Human-kind' with acquiescence in God's will. It depicted a fallen woman appealing to God for forgiveness and mercy – God would 'Regard the lifted Hand and streaming Eye', God would keep her 'from the Horrors of Despair' now that her husband had villainously resolved to 'loose that Knot which God has join'd'. The poem implied that it had been left to her, a weak woman, to remind others that there was a higher authority. Those who attacked or slandered her were themselves guilty of the same errors or had condoned similar behaviour in others. Whatever her faults she was not alone, yet she had been made an outcast. And not only was there no recess from calumny, but 'Fate' had a yet deeper wound to inflict: her friends had deserted her.

Among those friends was Jonathan Swift. The Pilkingtons had come into Swift's life as a pair through Patrick Delany who, it now suited Swift to think, had been a 'very unlucky recommender'. Writing to John Barber, Swift rejected his former protégés in words that showed no pity and took no responsibility. It was Delany, he wrote, who

forced me to countenance Pilkington; introduced him to me, and praised the Witt, Virtue and humour of him and his Wife. Whereas he proved the falsest Rogue, and she the most profligate whore in either Kingdom. She was taken in the fact by her own Husband. He is now suing for a Divorce.

Barber must have smiled to himself as he read this, since it was Swift who had forced *him* to 'countenance Pilkington' in exactly those terms. Ex-mayor Barber's reflections on Laetitia's fate are likely to have been more sympathetic, given his experience of Matthew, than those of the dean of St Patrick's. Later, going through his papers, Swift scratched out the name 'Pilkington' wherever he found it.

Laetitia's misfortunes as a wife were public knowledge, but it may be possible to read in this poem an additional reason for despair. A closer friend than Swift had abandoned her. Whatever degree of intimacy she had enjoyed with Robert Adair ended abruptly in mid-January 1738 when he fled Dublin giving no warning that he was going, leaving a letter and five guineas with a local Dissenting Minister.

We do not know if she missed him, or if she was angry at him; nor if the baby she was carrying was his. The hurt she acknowledged was that of friends and family who, wanting nothing more to do with her, knowing she had lost everything, were prepared to watch her descend into absolute want and starvation or prostitution.

Adair's passage from Dublin to Holyhead was a gloomy one. He too had, after all, received a shock 'from striking on the shoals of unlawful passion'. But he cheered up when he reached England, reasoning that though bruised he was not wrecked. Indeed. The man who was to be nicknamed 'the fortunate Irishman' had a fairy-tale encounter on the road to London with a courtesan whose carriage had overturned: she gave him £100 for his tender attentions, invited him to her house in London, and – among other favours – was to introduce him to Lady Caroline Keppel, facilitating his rise into the nobility.

Meanwhile, in another twist that may throw light on Adair's departure and which reveals that God was not Mrs Pilkington's only provider, James Worsdale was still in town. As a friend of the Earl of Rosse – Jack later said that he pimped for him – and a leading light in the Hell-Fire Club, his antics came to Swift's attention that winter. Swift complained to John Barber about the 'Brace of Monsters called Blasters, or Blasphemers, or Bachanalians (as they are here called in Print) whereof Worsdail the Painter and one Lints (a Painter too, as I hear) are the Leaders'. Worsdale took it upon himself to give Laetitia some sort of protection, though it might also have been through Worsdale that the Earl of Rosse knew where she was lodging. Still nursing his 'strange ambition to be thought a poet' and knowing well her skill in light verse, Worsdale paid her to write for him. Compared to her other options, it was 'an easy and honorable method of getting a subsistence'.

It was rather an odd one, however, since Matthew was also ghost-writing for Worsdale who passed everything off as his own. Being a 'Blaster' seems not to have affected Worsdale's ability to charm the quality. Cutting a dash and busying himself with theatrical schemes as well as successfully angling for painting commissions – among them a portrait of the Duke of Devonshire, new Lord Lieutenant (whose official secretary was Edward Walpole) – he was able to keep his minions busy, a state of affairs that suited Laetitia well enough: she enjoyed being 'full of poetical business'. Given Worsdale's conviviality, and the character of his friends, it is unlikely that she was as solitary as 'Sorrow' suggests. Vengefully, Matthew spread the word that she and Worsdale 'conversed unlawfully together'. Whether they did so or not, Worsdale's presence reinstated the entanglements of 1733, the husband and wife competing for his bounty while their divorce proceedings were scheduled in the Consistory Court. Matthew priced himself out of business by demanding £50 for expenses in London four years earlier that Worsdale supposedly owed him.

Perhaps he also felt entitled to a cut of the profits from *A Cure for a Scold*, the adaptation of Shakespeare's *Taming of the Shrew* which, according to Laetitia, Matthew had mostly written and which Worsdale had succeeded in getting staged in London in 1735, with himself in the cast along with Colley Cibber's daughter, Charlotte Charke. Having carefully preserved the script and brought it with him, Worsdale now mounted it in Dublin.

On 16 January, the very day Adair left Dublin, the 'new operatical farce' *A Cure for a Scold*, 'written by Mr Worsdale', opened at the Smock Alley theatre. It was played at least fourteen times over the next four months, making it a considerable success. For Dublin audiences, some of the play's appeal lay precisely in its connection with the Pilkington scandal. Keen to exploit the promotional value of Mrs Pilkington, Worsdale encouraged her to write a prologue for his benefit (traditionally, the third-night performance) and 'insisted' that she appear in person, in a box he would keep entirely for her and her guests – the two daughters of her landlady.

She did so. She wrote what she described as 'a flaming prologue . . . in honour of my fair country-women'. We can assume that it contained her rage at the sexual double standard by which she, an erring wife, had been condemned while Matthew, a no less erring husband, continued to benefit from his curacies and his mistress. The prologue was never printed and does not survive, but we know from its impact that, combined with her appearance – seven months pregnant and three weeks short of being divorced – it was dramatically effective, serving as a counterpoint to songs in the opera that warned men against taking wives, celebrating the 'lick it, or leave it' pleasures of bachelor dogs. Worsdale failed in his promise to keep her box empty: her former friends the Dubourgs were there in the crowded theatre, along with Rev. Hugh Graffan and others. They were as shocked to see her as she them. Words were exchanged. Mrs Dubourg, the former singer, called her an 'odious creature'; they fled, she stayed. After the play, Worsdale accompanied her from the theatre, saw her into a chair and promised to come and have supper with her, a promise which, she notes, he kept.

∞

The *Dublin Newsletter* of 7–11 February 1738 and the *Dublin Evening Post* carried exactly the same information: 'Last Tuesday [7 February] came on in the Spiritual Court the trial of Mrs Letitia Pilkington, alias Vanlewin, for adultery with Mr Adair, which being fully proved, sentence of divorce was pronounced against her by Dr Trotter, vicar-general of the diocese, and judge of the Consistory Court.'

The trial records were among the archives burned in 1922 in a huge fire at the Four Courts so we cannot reconstruct that day's proceedings – a sad loss to the biographer. Laetitia made no effort to contest Matthew's 'vigorous prosecution' (and would not have been present in any case) but the specificity of trial records are often a wonderful resource and these might have told us much about her movements, friends, family – did Meade testify against her? Was anything said about the children? – as well as providing another sample of Matthew's rhetorical skills. Before winning the case, Matthew had 'solemnly declared' that he would provide some sort of maintenance. Afterwards, puffed up with triumph, delighted at having beaten her, he felt free to be as obnoxious as usual and retracted his promise. She lodged an appeal. The church courts had the power to impose maintenance orders; and they could revoke a divorce if it could be shown that the husband had connived or if the wronged party had also been adulterous. Mrs Pilkington's appeal was for maintenance (since she did not want to return to the marriage) probably on the grounds of Matthew's adultery. Swift, in his last surviving utterance about the Pilkingtons, told John Barber, 'she is suing for a maintenance', adding that Matthew 'hath none to give her', which was not true.

In March, before the appeal came on, Worsdale acted as a go-between and brought her the information that Matthew would settle privately, having agreed to pay her a small annuity and a lump sum of £30. Desperate for immediate cash she withdrew the appeal. The baby was due and she had to pay the expenses of her lying in which were more than expected because the landlady had doubled the rent upon discovering that her tenant was about to go into labour. Finding another lodging to give birth in was no easy matter; she stayed where she was at the higher rate. Worsdale advanced half of the £30 Matthew had agreed to pay. The rest was not forthcoming, nor was there ever any annuity, and nor did Worsdale get his £15 back. Matthew made a contribution which felt like mockery and no doubt was intended as such: he sent eleven-year-old William round with sixpence and a letter piously reminding her of 'the Temptations to which Want exposes our helpless Sex'. This occasion is one of the rare glimpses we get of the Pilkingtons' eldest son and it is hard to imagine what he made of it all.

Having paid the 'exorbitant' price demanded by the landlady, Laetitia gave birth to a daughter at her lodgings. She was attended by a doctor, James Arbuckle, an independent-minded, humane Dissenter, well known for serving the poor and those 'in concealed distress of circumstances'. There was nothing concealed about her distress but she was grateful for his kindness. Matthew refused to recognise the child as his. He advised her to abandon it.

Late in the theatrical season that year, on 3 May 1738, a new afterpiece was put on at Smock Alley. It was a farce entitled *No Death but Marriage*, described as 'an entire new comic opera', and 'written by a Lady'. Advertising it, one newspaper predicted that there would be 'the greatest appearance of nobility and gentry' that had been seen all season. Why would such a play attract such an audience? And who was the lady author? No other known lady playwrights were in Dublin at the time. The title seems designed to capitalise on public interest in the Pilkington case, and the genre, comic opera, was that of the popular *A Cure for a Scold*. The play was not printed and we know nothing more about it, but it seems plausible that in the months after giving birth to her sixth child, while *A Cure for a Scold* was pulling in good houses, Laetitia developed her 'flaming prologue' into a full-scale farce based on recent events in her life. Worsdale might have suggested it and they might have worked it up together, for he would be in a position to present it to the company. There is no record of the performance, however, and no indication of how the 'nobility and gentry', if indeed they flocked to see it, received the piece.

That summer, Worsdale went to Mallow and promptly got

himself chosen poet laureate for the season. Since in Laetitia's words, 'Mr Worsdale never wrote a poetical Line in his Life', his 'Subalterns, or under Strappers in Poetical Stock-jobbing' were kept busy. It took little skill to mimic the language of the languishing beau. From Mallow Worsdale sent Laetitia the names of the reigning 'charmers' and relevant details about them, and she wrote them into poems like 'Mallow Waters':

> In Dunscomb's faultless Form and Mind,
> A thousand winning Charms we find;
> And graceful Bond, whose easy Air
> Bespeaks the unaffected Fair.
> O Lysaught! Such a Form as thine
> In Homer's deathless Lays should shine
> [*etc.*]

Under normal circumstances, a man like Worsdale needed a constant supply of light verse for social occasions: sometimes merely to help him on, other times to get him out of social embarrassments. But when he decided that it was time to publish a book, and began collecting subscriptions for it, his demands became impossible. Laetitia failed to send him enough ballads (her version: he wanted a hundred by return of post, and proposed to pay two guineas for them). He wrote her a letter which she quoted in full in her *Memoirs*. Perhaps she made it up. It could have come straight out of Henry Fielding's *The Author's Farce*, or Matthew and Worsdale's *A Cure for a Scold*, or her own *No Death but Marriage*; and if Worsdale wrote it he was probably drunk, but then he was drunk quite a lot of the time:

Damn you! sink you! God fire you! I have beggar'd myself between your scoundrel Husband and you, all to support a little dirty Vanity. When I want any thing from him, his damn'd Spirits are sunk: Nor has he given me any thing worth a Farthing, for the monstrous Sums he has drawn out of me. I could write before I ever saw either of your ugly Faces; tho' not quite so well – and damn me, if I ever write another Line of Verse – You understand me – I shall be in Town so as to meet the Parliament. The Eyes of all Europe are on me, and damn me, if you don't send me the Ballads, but I'll despise, and defy you for ever.

There was a postscript:

By God, I can't stir out, for my Landlady has beat me through the Town with a hot Shoulder of Mutton, which she snatched from the Fire, Spit and all, only for catching me a little familiar with her Daughter.

Laetitia commented that she feared Worsdale had lost his sanity. In fact, the bombast reflects their shared farcical vision and gives a good idea of how she and 'Worry' got on. As comic writers they were well suited. Scabrous and enterprising, her spirit reached for the freedom he had: a licence to speak and be whatever he desired at a particular moment. It was the libertine philosophy parodied by Swift and his friends at Belcamp when they stuck a pipe in her mouth and pronounced the pregnant young woman 'a man' for the occasion.

Not being a man, she struggled to make up a new life in Dublin. She claimed that she lived quietly – 'I lived the Life of a Recluse' – but this was certainly not true of spring and early summer 1738 and if it was so later that was only by default. It was not how she wanted to spend the rest of her life. In any case, it did not stop the talk: 'I had every Day some new Story invented of me. If I went out to take a little Air, they said I had great Impudence to shew my Face; and if I stay'd at Home, I was then in Keeping with some Man who confin'd me.'

The 'some man' was probably Worsdale, though judging by his letter he was not sending money. Matthew spread gossip, continuing to attack her character in the hope of driving her away. Censured by those whose fine Georgian drawing rooms were off limits – families like the Claytons, her Meade relations, Dr Delany and Dean Swift – Laetitia tried to put a brave face on an impossible situation. She repented having dropped the appeal, 'like an easy Fool as I was', as it became clear that Matthew's persecutions would not cease.

There is no record of Worsdale being in Dublin in the autumn of 1738. He may have gone on to Limerick from Mallow. She was left to find what money she could by writing. Her speciality was the complimentary poem to a named individual, a form to which she covertly brought the satirical talent nurtured under Swift. Poems like 'Sorrow' which presented her in repentant mode were for the quality; and they drew some support as the poem 'To a Lady, who defended the Author's Character' attests. But even if she managed to raise enough to pay for lodgings and food, any hopes of real success as a writer in Dublin or of regaining any sort of status must soon have faded. London increasingly came to seem the only option. She had thought about going as soon as the baby was born but the widow Warren's eagerness to get rid of her ('This Lady sent a Captain of a Ship to me, when she heard I was going for England, to hurry me out of the Kingdom') made her stay longer. It was probably Mrs Warren who persuaded Matthew to agree to give his irritating ex-wife funds to cover the journey. Matthew sent £9, making a point of telling her he had raised the money by selling her possessions: her diamond ring to Mrs Dubourg, her watch chain to Mrs Warren. She asked about her father's snuff-box. Matthew pretended it was lost, but she knew he had given it to Mrs Warren. Legally he was within his rights although morally most people would have found such behaviour repugnant. Mrs Pilkington affected a philosophic disdain: he was not the first man to have 'plunder'd his Wife' to oblige his whore.

Removing herself from the Dublin scene was in some ways an admission of defeat. It hurt to know that Matthew's life would be easier once she was gone. There was anguish for the children she could do nothing to protect. But by the autumn of 1738 she seems to have been ready to strike out alone. Loss, grief, fear and rage had taken their toll, but at barely thirty her appetite for life was undiminished and she felt some excitement in planning for a future. Like others before her, she would go to seek her fortune in a place that promised excitement and potential recognition. And if London received her as a writer, which she had every intention of ensuring that it did, it would not only provide a chance to deliver herself 'out of calamity', but also to do better than Matthew whose metropolitan ambitions had ended so disastrously.

There were some advantages in not being a man, and these could be worked up. Her story was good material for an unprotected woman so long as it was presented in the right way: not through rage and attack but through submissive suffering, using the confessional tone she had adopted in 'Sorrow' to engage the reader's sympathy. Late that autumn as she prepared to go she wrote a companion piece to 'Sorrow' – 'the last strains I sung in

Ireland' – giving it the title 'Expostulation'. In 'Expostulation' Laetitia pictured herself as a female Job submissively protesting to God about her hard fate:

> O God! since all thy Ways are just,
> Why does thy heavy Hand
> So sore afflict the wretched Dust,
> Thou didst to Life command?

God made her and God, for whom past, present and future are one, must have known what her fate was to be. It seemed that He had singled her out for woe at every stage of her progress:

> Thro' ev'ry Scene of Life distress'd,
> As Daughter, Mother, Wife . . .

As in 'Sorrow', she accepted culpability for some of that distress: she had allowed her passion to govern her reason. But God might have ordered things differently. 'Expostulation' remonstrates with God, finding fault with the Almighty much as its author found fault with mortal men:

> 'Twas thou gav'st Passion to my Soul,
> And Reason also gave,
> Why dids't thou not make Reason rule,
> And Passion be its Slave?

But the Bible taught that it was a sin to repine at God's will. The poem asked pardon for her presumption in complaining about the fate, or 'doom', that had been ordained for her; it accepted the painful experiences of the previous year as God's 'correction' for her 'errors'; and in a restrained final quatrain of humble heroism asked to be made worthy through penitence:

> Lord, give me Penitence sincere
> For ev'ry Error past,
> And tho' my Trials are severe,
> O give me Peace at last.

By expressing the hope that reason would henceforth rule passion, Mrs Pilkington, fallen woman and serious poet, made a bid for redemption and even – though it might seem rather unlikely – moral leadership. 'Expostulation' announced that not the body of the woman but the mind of the poet would now rule. In eighteenth-century thinking it was a commonplace that passion should be the slave of reason; applied to women, strong mental capacity was identified as the source of moral virtue. Female sentimental verse that displayed a controlled expression of private feeling – anger governed, aggression subdued – and a dutiful response to God could reach beyond the personal. It could command respect and carry authority.

Reading 'Sorrow' and 'Expostulation' one feels intense sympathy for a woman whose trials were, as everybody knew, severe. This was the effect intended. But peace was never Mrs Pilkington's natural element. The reflective, prayerful persona of these poems was as much a weapon in the blame wars as the lost feminist voice of her 'flaming' prologue to *A Cure for a Scold* and the afterpiece, *No Death but Marriage*. Poetry of every kind conferred status. It enabled her to go on holding her head up high, providing an alternative and more dignified version of the Mrs Pilkington whose name had been dragged in the mud through Dublin streets.

Matthew's £9 was not in fact enough to clear her debts and pay travel costs. She wrote more letters. Charles Stanhope, fifty-five-year-old cousin of the Earl of Chesterfield, 'the first, and best of Men' as Mrs Pilkington's complimentary verses 'To the Honourable Mr ****' hailed him, stepped forward. Stanhope had been secretary at the Treasury until 1721 when his government career ended after he was tried for taking bribes in the South Sea Bubble scandal. He was acquitted, but only just, and he was rumoured to have made a quarter of a million pounds during his four years in office. (Since bribery and corruption were more or less structured into the system, the real surprise is that he was prosecuted at all.) He could afford to be generous. Her self-description – 'Forsaken, comfortless, distrest' – framed with the usual flatteries touched his sympathetic nerve. From the apex of the Protestant Ascendancy, Stanhope put some money in a bag and sent it to her. It was a lavish gift. She made arrangements to go.

PART TWO

England

CHAPTER SEVEN

Lady of Adventure

Jack, the youngest son, remembered vividly his mother leaving Ireland. He had not seen her since her eviction from Lazer's Hill when his life as the favourite child, who loved to sit and read with his mother, was turned upside down. Through all the months before and after the court case, Matthew refused to allow access to the children; and it was only when Laetitia resolved to go to London that he relented and allowed them to spend a day with her at her lodgings in order to say goodbye. 'The sense I felt of our separation,' Jack wrote later, 'even at that age, is scarcely imaginable'. He remembered being held: how his heartbroken mother would frequently 'gather us in her arms, and folding us in the most passionate grief, invoke the Almighty to be a father and mother to us . . .' His last view as he and Betty were bundled off home was of his mother 'in a flood of tears'. She told him later that she had tried to keep him so as to take him with her to London but that her attempt was foiled by the servant.

There were more tears on the day of departure some time in November or December. The coach taking Laetitia to the yacht went along Lazer's Hill and passed the door of the old house. It was painful to know that inside was 'all the Treasure of my Soul enclos'd; namely, my dear little ones', and that she could not protect them and might never see them again. She had no rights, the children belonged to Matthew.

The last of the little ones, the daughter born in the spring of 1738 and by then eight or nine months old, had also to be left behind, though not with Matthew who refused to acknowledge her. Whatever arrangements Laetitia made for this baby went unrecorded.

Stanhope's money had enabled her to equip herself for the journey. Her trunk was packed with clothes. Fair copies of her most important writings, including a long poem entitled 'The Statues', went with her. Perhaps she took some books, not only because she was a voracious reader but because books, like expensive clothing, were marks of gentility. She boarded the yacht with just five guineas in her purse.

It was a rough crossing. As she stood on deck watching the shores of her homeland disappear from view, she hid her face and cried. Seasick as well as homesick and heartsick, weeping – 'I thought my very Heart would split with Sorrow' – she asked the steward for a cabin. The cabins were all taken. An elderly gentleman offered his and she was relieved to be able to lie down but alas, recognising her, he resolved to share the bed. She escaped back on deck. The gentleman – 'handsome, well-bred' – followed. They talked; indeed, he kept her company throughout the journey and provided pleasant distraction. When they landed at Parkgate they dined together. She described how he propositioned her, offering not just £50 if she would spend the night with him but 'a Settlement for Life'. She said she had 'Chastity enough' to refuse him. Whatever actually took place between them, the detail owed as much to artistry as memory, for the encounter provides a bleakly satirical comment on her circumstances. Stripped of family, no longer daughter, mother or wife, unprotected and unprovided for, Laetitia Pilkington, the notorious Mrs Pilkington, had decided to leave Dublin and venture into the unknown. What awaited her? That her options were limited to the time-honoured female career of prostitution, whether 'high' as in agreeing to be kept by a handsome well-bred man, or 'low' as in street walking, was a view she could be sure her readers shared. 'Who this same Gentleman was, may, in due Season, be revealed,' she wrote slyly. (It never was.) 'I can only assure my Readers, that I believe, had I accepted of the Offers he made me, poverty would never have approached me.'

Romantically, heroically, she chose to refuse the gentleman and brave poverty, and armed with 'Chastity enough' trust in her merits. It was the stuff of cliché and she treated it as burlesque – could a woman be an adventurer? Could she be heroic? What form would her heroism take? She pointed the moral in a dialogue which parodied popular stage plays and fictions about innocent country girls going to be debauched in the city, and familiar enough from Hogarth's 1730 series of prints, *A Harlot's Progress*. It was given to the gentleman to speak 'prophetic' words:

'Well, Madam,' (said he) 'you don't know London; you'll be undone there.' 'Why, Sir,' (said I) 'I hope you don't imagine I'll go into any bad Course of life?' 'No, Madam,' (said he) 'but I think you will sit in your Chamber, and starve'; which, upon my Word, I have been pretty near doing.

∞

She reached Chester on a Tuesday only to discover that the weekly stagecoach to London departed on Mondays. With the dismaying prospect of using up her guineas before even reaching London, she took a room at an inn and prepared to while away six days. It was winter; she hung over the kitchen fire with the landlady and felt like a prisoner until 'Providence' came to her rescue in the shape of another traveller, a gentleman on his way back to Ireland, forced to wait until the winds changed direction. He was someone who knew her family and her story and was prepared to sympathise. Along with the landlady, 'who was really a Gentlewoman', they diverted themselves with card games, books and conversation, and what had been tedious became an agreeable and even welcome interlude, especially because the gentleman made it clear that he would pay for everything. When they parted he gave her three guineas.

In a society that made women dependent on men, it was not unusual for men to assume financial responsibility in social situations, even for complete strangers. According to these conventions, no gentleman could feel comfortable watching a lady pay for herself. On stagecoach journeys, a lady travelling alone might expect the men to sort out between themselves her part in the reckoning for meals and drinks. Hence it was disappointing to board the coach the following Monday and discover that her fellow passengers, an MP and two lawyers, were 'Brutes' who sneered at her for being Irish, assumed she was a fool, talked pro-Walpole politics among themselves, drank heavily, farted freely and, to cap it all, made her pay equal shares in wine she hardly saw. Things improved when they picked up a Welsh parson who responded to her charms, and paid for her, although he became over-amorous. At Barnet where they stopped for dinner a rich relation of the 'Brutes' met the coach and seemed resolved to treat them all, especially 'that little Hibernian Nymph', but his charms diminished when she discovered that though he wanted to flirt and enjoy her company, he didn't want to pay.

All in all, the journey was more expensive than she had bargained for. She arrived in London with three guineas. Since she went straight to fashionable St James's, the part of London she knew, and took lodgings in Berry Street, those guineas were unlikely to last her long.

She had decided for general purposes not to go by the name of Mrs Pilkington. It was doubly associated with scandal: her own, and Matthew's in 1732–3, which many in London were likely to remember. Instead, she made use of the 'ancient and honorable' family name on her mother's side and called herself 'Mrs Meade'. This was a precaution inspired by her experiences in Dublin, a defence against hot-blooded rakes and opportunistic procuresses; she was not hiding her identity nor did she hesitate to tell her story. She had every intention of becoming well known.

We know little about these first few months in London except that, predictably, they were very difficult. She was reduced to writing begging letters back to Ireland, to no avail. Soon she was desperate. She needed a wealthy patron and perhaps that was why she tried her luck with Edward Walpole, from whom Matthew had hoped so much, and to whom Worsdale later dedicated the printed version of *A Cure for a Scold*, praising him as 'an excellent judge of books and men' and thanking him for 'favours'. As Secretary to the Duke of Devonshire when he was Lord Lieutenant, Walpole had been back and forth to Dublin, annoying people along the way. Personally unambitious, he was an MP whose vote could be depended on and in return the Duke of

Newcastle tried to meet his many requests for places or commissions for protégés. These included his alcoholic ex-tutor, a local carpenter, a master sweep, and various poor clerics and struggling artists. Conveniently, he lived nearby: he had recently moved into a new house at 71 Pall Mall built by his father for the express purpose of spiting his old enemy the Duchess of Marlborough by cutting off direct access to Pall Mall from her palace, Marlborough House, behind. Edward shared the house with his four illegitimate children by the beautiful milliner's apprentice, Dorothy Clement, with whom he had fallen in love, much to his family's chagrin. Dorothy died in 1738. Edward had withdrawn into a semi-retirement cushioned by the gift through his father's interest of a rich sinecure in the Treasury as clerk of the pells. He responded to the note from his friend Pilkington's ex-wife by visiting her and staying for several hours, but when she came to the main point he affected a vagueness that seems to have covered sadism: asked to promote her planned volume of poems and gather subscriptions he replied that he was not very good at that sort of thing and was bound to forget, so would she mind taking money instead? He pulled five guineas out of his purse, looked at them, then put them away again saying he couldn't spare them after all.

She fared better with a less likely candidate. Further east on Pall Mall one of the large houses backing on to St James's Square had recently been turned into a linen warehouse and tea emporium. A sign in golden capital letters announced Benjamin Victor as an importer and proprietor of Irish linens. No ordinary merchant, Victor was a busy writer and unsuccessful dramatist who had for many years rubbed along on the edges of literary society. Friendly with poets Aaron Hill, Richard Savage and Edward Young, he had been taken up by Richard Steele and claimed some acquaintance with Pope. His tragedy *Altamira* was never staged, to his great distress, but he drew on his friendship with the actor Barton Booth to write *Memoirs of the Life of Barton Booth* (1733) and he was later to write an important book on theatre history. More than anything Victor loved to be backstage, mingling with actors, collecting anecdotes, circulating gossip and generally being important. It had been Victor's idea to bring Joseph Highmore, a gentleman-amateur, to Drury Lane in 1733, when Barton Booth was dying and wanted to sell his shares. Highmore became a manager and Drury Lane, which had for several decades balanced its books and even been profitable under the managership of Colley Cibber, Robert Wilks and Booth, went into rapid decline, leading to the walkout led by Theophilus Cibber.

Hoping for a position in the Prince of Wales's household, Victor wrote birthday odes and congratulatory verses and attended the Prince's levees with 'unremitting assiduity'. Frustrated, unrewarded, he had turned his experiences into a satire, *The Levee Haunter*, and sent it to Sir Robert Walpole as something likely to please (the Prince was the centre of the Opposition). The poem was passed around and for a while Victor was 'the favourite of the town', but it didn't lead to a post in the Excise, which is what he had then been hoping for. City friends urged him into the linen trade and helped him start up. Between 1734 and 1736 Victor had twice gone over to Dublin where Dr Van Lewen was among those who showed him hospitality, possibly because he had helped Matthew during his London troubles. Laetitia had met him then, when he was in 'low' circumstances and she was still comfortably situated. This, Victor later wrote in a carefully self-serving account of their relationship, gave her 'a sort of right to assistance from me' in her distress.

In the winter of 1738–9, Victor's business acumen in relation to linen was proving better than his instincts about running a theatre, and when Mrs Pilkington came to call he was in a position to help. They fell out later when she returned to Dublin, by which time he had become treasurer and joint manager with Thomas Sheridan of the Smock Alley theatre. She was rude about him in her *Memoirs*, but it seems likely she depended on him during these early months. He was well connected. According to Victor, she sent for him the moment she arrived in London. He was not sorry to see her: still hoping to get something from the court, he was quick to exploit her facility in writing panegyrical verse. (In *her* version, he was another Worsdale: sadly untalented but desperate for the reputation of a writer.) It was an ideal friendship for both of them and soon Victor was giving her money to write poems he passed off as his own. With his customers Victor liked to play the lettered gentleman, while with literary friends he did the sober businessman; and with an un-protected Irish woman he would have played the beau. She was given lots of warnings about the streets of London being full of knaves and sharpers, and heard often of his important friends: Sir William Wolseley, who sent venison to Mrs Victor from Stafford-shire; the famous Admiral Vernon, with whom Victor claimed 'the honour of an intimate acquaintance'; not to mention all those associated with the theatre, as well as out-of-town poets with whom he kept up correspondence such as Aaron Hill and John Dyer. The Prince of Wales was his neighbour at Norfolk House; from his counter, Victor could see the prince driving out in a one-horse chair or setting off on his morning ride. He dole-fully kept an eye on him. William Pitt was his tenant in the part of the house that fronted St James's Square.

The linen warehouse was an emporium of political and literary gossip where Victor was constantly busy wrapping parcels and keeping up with current affairs. It was a social as well as a business sphere and one that was easier, perhaps, for a woman to be part of than coffee-house or tavern sociability. Writing for Victor would have been done on site, especially when they began to collaborate. Together they started a comedy adapted from Marivaux's, *Le Paysan Parvenu,* which Victor eventually published under his own name, and two satires. Victor's advice, as he recalled it, was that she should concentrate on two kinds of writing if she wanted to make money: a successful play, preferably comic; or 'dangerous satire', by which he meant political pamphleteering. It was with the second of these suggestions that Victor was most able to help her and for which her access to the linen warehouse, with all its comings and goings, was critical. Mrs Pilkington had arrived in London at an exciting time.

In February 1739, the word went quickly round: Robert Dodsley had been arrested. Dodsley, footman-turned-bookseller and successful playwright, was Pope's official publisher (Pope had set him up in 1735 with a £100 gift); and Dodsley's premises on Pall

Mall, at the sign of Tully's Head a few doors down from Victor's linen warehouse, was the most important centre of London literary life. Dodsley had a reputation for risking unknown authors: the previous year he had published a satire, 'London', by a young man newly arrived from Lichfield and working for Edward Cave at the *Gentleman's Magazine*. His name was Samuel Johnson. Johnson had been worried enough about the reception of 'London' to lie low for a while after it came out, but the contemporary references in his Juvenalian satire were sufficiently veiled. Not so Dodsley's latest production, a dangerously anti-government poem called 'Manners' by Paul Whitehead which attacked the ministry and praised the Prince of Wales and the politicians around him. Whitehead would have been arrested but he fled – and in any case the government's reaction to his ridicule was probably intended as an indirect warning through Dodsley to Pope, whose own anti-ministerial satires had become more explicit.

Dodsley spent two weeks in jail. During that time Pall Mall was abuzz and little trade in linen went forward at the linen warehouse. Victor, in his element, hurried from club to coffee-house orchestrating support. He claimed that his influence with the Earl of Essex effected Dodsley's release on 20 February after the bookseller had gone down on his knees and begged pardon of the House of Lords. Opposition lords and the 'men of genius, taste and rank' who liked to meet at Tully's Head, browsing the latest books and pamphlets, had their carriages waiting and brought Dodsley back to Pall Mall in triumph.

Dodsley's arrest and the reaction to it marked the beginnings of a sustained and orchestrated opposition to Walpole, led by Lords Chesterfield and Lyttelton with the Prince of Wales as their patron. Victor was well placed to know where to send 'dangerous satire' and these lords had long purses. Responding to demand, he and Mrs Pilkington began concocting verses. Much that they wrote is probably lost, but 'An Excursory View of the Present State of Men and Things. A Satire. In a Dialogue between the Author and his Friend' was published anonymously by Robert Dodsley in August 1739. Mrs Pilkington re-printed it and claimed it as hers in the *Memoirs* although Victor insisted he had written at least 200 lines.

(The poem is just over 300 lines long.) A month later there was another pamphlet, in prose this time, *An Apology for the Minister*. How much each actually wrote cannot be established but clearly both pamphlets owed a good deal to Victor's local knowledge.

'An Excursory View' is an exchange between two voices, 'P' for poet and 'F' for friend, who squabble over the merits of writing risky satire versus safe panegyric and reach a compromise by praising opposition politicians, those

> noble Few, who, in a shameless Age,
> Dare bring heroic Virtue on the Stage.

Victor's tenant Pitt ('What forceful Reason! manly Eloquence!') was named, along with the Earl of Chesterfield, Lord Carteret, Viscount Cobham and the Earl of Stair. The 'pure aethereal Light' cast by these virtuous nobles apparently made Walpole 'sicken' at the sight; and indeed, the poem was prescient in this regard for these men, along with Frederick, Prince of Wales – 'Patron of Learning! Cherisher of Arts!' – brought about Walpole's downfall a few years later.

By the time these pamphlets appeared, eight or nine months after her arrival in London, Mrs Pilkington aka Mrs Meade had established herself as a notable figure in St James's. The country's most prominent politicians, those named in her pamphlets and others, were aware of her existence. She had comfortable first-floor lodgings directly opposite White's Club in St James's Street and could afford to keep a servant. Her writing table with its papers, ink and quill pens was set up in full view of the window from where she could see and be seen by the habitués of White's – scions of the nation's greatest families, top politicians, retired generals, young bloods: any gentleman, in short, of rank and wealth enough to be admitted to membership of one of the most exclusive gambling and drinking clubs in the land. In company, she introduced herself and was introduced as a poet. Callers found her at her desk, writing. In the autumn of 1739, Mrs Pilkington's rooms functioned as a sort of antechamber to White's. There was much toing and froing of notes and poems across the street. Her admirers came and went. She was gathering in a good harvest of guineas.

How had she done it, and what exactly was she doing to earn those guineas? A partial answer lies in Victor's genius for networking; he was key to this transition from the 'great distress' of the months immediately following her arrival in London to relative prosperity. Victor had introduced Mrs Pilkington to Robert Dodsley some time after the latter's release. The experience of prison having temporarily dampened Dodsley's enthusiasm for publishing anti-ministerial satire, he was receptive to a woman poet whose name was guaranteed to arouse a certain kind of interest. Hence, their first approach had been made not on the basis of the satires they were writing together but on Mrs Pilkington's personal appeal and poetic aspirations. (Victor lamented that in the aftermath of Whitehead's 'Manners' 'satire, noble, useful, satire, is no more!') From the store of manuscripts she had brought over from Dublin, they selected a poem written in about 1734: 'The Statues: Or, the Trial of Constancy'. It was revised before submitting it to Dodsley and perhaps the second part of the title, subliminally evoking Mrs Pilkington's recent trial, was added then, along with the direction that it was 'A Tale for the Ladies' – a way of alerting readers, most of whom would be men, that the poem contained exciting sex-war matter presented in a woman's voice and from a female perspective. Dodsley bought 'The Statues: Or, the Trial of Constancy', giving the author at least five guineas for it and possibly ten, which was the sum Johnson got for 'London' and Whitehead for 'Manners'. He published it in April 1739 in a handsome folio edition, putting it out under the imprint of Thomas Cooper of Paternoster Row. Cooper and his wife, Mary, were major distributors, with an extensive network for marketing printed materials. Selling at one shilling, which was the standard price for a medium-length folio poem, 'The Statues' served as a proclamation announcing the arrival of a new poet on the London scene.

When she wrote about 'The Statues' in her memoirs, publishing the full text – a sign of its importance in her career – Mrs Pilkington explained its origins, much as she probably did in company at the time. She said the poem had been inspired by the frustration she had felt at the habitual denigration of women that Swift and her husband indulged in: 'As the Dean, and, after his

Example, Mr Pilkington were eternally satirizing and ridiculing the Female Sex; I had a very great Inclination to be even with them, and expose the Inconstancy of Men.' While this rings true, and illuminates her self-conscious feminism, it was also good marketing. Presenting 'The Statues' in this way was a means of giving it credentials: it advertised her friendship with Swift, suggesting that the poem was written under his aegis and had possibly been read by him and approved of. At the same time, it indicated to readers that the poem was to be located inside the growing volume of literature that protested against Swift's representations of women. By the 1730s it was a standard view that women disliked Swift, an opinion Mrs Pilkington vividly under-lined when she wrote that Swift 'sometimes chose Subjects unworthy of his Muse, and which could serve for no other End except that of turning the Reader's Stomach, as it did my Mother's, who, upon reading *The Lady's Dressing-room*, instantly threw up her Dinner'.

'The Statues' is a vengeful piece adapted from a fable in *Peruvian Tales*, an anthology of 1734 modelled on the *Arabian Nights*. In this fable a princess 'of Origin divine' discovers, while out walking, 'a graceful Youth dissolv'd in Sleep'. She has him carried home to her palace. Her maidens bathe and dress him and bring him before her where, seized with 'Love' and 'Extasie', 'Entranc'd' by her beauty (and she with his) he is invited to speak his wishes. He is in fact a prince and his wish is to be hers:

> Accept my Constancy, my Endless Truth . . .
> Accept a Heart incapable of Change.

The ravishing princess duly offers herself to him. The catch is that his boasted constancy will be tested under extreme pressure. What the prince doesn't know is that forty no less graceful, ardent and self-confident youths have been that way before, married the princess, made love to her and sworn to be faithful. Every one of them, beguiled by a new beauty (the princess/queen is Neptune's daughter and has spells at her command) betrayed her at the first opportunity:

> The Heart of Man the Queen's Experience knew
> Perjur'd and false . . .

Disillusioned but hopeful, the princess agrees to her forty-first marriage and enjoys a night of love. She then announces that she has to go away. The young man, left alone, hopelessly bored, promptly behaves like his forty predecessors and is no less promptly turned into a statue – a fate he had been fairly warned about. But as the princess lectures him:

> Thy changeful Sex in Perfidy delight,
> Despise Perfection, and fair Virtue slight,
> False, fickle, base, tyrannic, and unkind,
> Whose Hearts, nor Vows can chain, nor Honour bind:
> Mad to possess, by Passion blindly led;
> And then as mad to stain the nuptial Bed.

Clearly, it was a poem with a special appeal to ladies who had been ill-treated by men, and perhaps no less to men who ill-treated women. Dodsley appreciated its value, especially given Mrs Pilkington's presence in St James's. Readers who took up the poem with some knowledge of her divorce and the stained 'nuptial Bed' back home would gain additional pleasure, and those who did not would soon be informed by those who did. It was a strong commercial offering. A shrewd businessman attuned to the pulse of public feeling, Dodsley was aware that there was a climate of opinion sympathetic towards ill-used wives. An anonymous pamphlet, *The Hardships of the English Laws in Relation to Wives* written by Sarah Chapone, had been excerpted as the leading essay in the *Gentleman's Magazine* in May and June, 1735, while a number of high-profile cases of husbands abusing their wives had come to court.

Like other poems, 'The Statues' could be bought in the pamphlet-shops 'of London and Westminster' as the title page promised. It was read, read aloud, and talked of in the coffee-houses. Had she been a man, Mrs Pilkington would have taken care to make herself visible at this time, working the important venues. As a woman, she had to rely on friends like Victor to keep up the hum of interest. The word was put about that she was assembling some other poems into a volume-sized collection which she intended to publish by subscription. To this end, she had proposals printed giving the necessary details – a single sheet or half-sheet which Victor and others could distribute. No copy of these proposals survives but she may have used the linen warehouse as her contact address in the way that men customarily used their favourite coffee-house. Perhaps Victor kept a stack on his counter, and perhaps he sold 'The Statues' on her behalf. Promoting her as the coming thing would have appealed to him: he treasured memories of his own early days as a poet when the glamorous 'Clio', Martha Fowke Sansom, introduced him to Aaron Hill. Hill's literary circle included a number of women and perhaps Victor saw himself as the new Hill, a 'most accomplished gentleman' with 'a soul truly disposed to great and generous actions'. Many people commented on Victor's egotism, and spoke contemptuously of him; but if he nursed grandiose fantasies about his role as patron these served Mrs Pilkington well. It was probably Victor's enduring if not always amicable connection with Colley Cibber that opened her path to Cibber, thus bringing into her life a man whose understanding of the publicity machine and the management of image was second to none.

Mrs Pilkington made sure two copies of 'The Statues' went to Edward Walpole at number 71. He wrote to thank her but did not include any payment. She noted in the *Memoirs* that he still owed her two shillings.

Colley Cibber was almost seventy when he took up Mrs Pilkington and began acting for her as something akin to an unpaid agent. The much-mocked laureate ('no Man has ever been more satyrized, or less deserved it,' she wrote) had for almost five decades been at the heart of English theatrical life, as an actor, especially in comic roles, theatre manager, writer and butt of other writers. He loved the limelight and had the capacity to turn the most negative attention to useful ends, as for example, when Pope made fun of him as the character Plotwell in *Three Hours After Marriage* (1717). Cibber went on to play Plotwell. Or, in a different sense, when in 1738 he appeared as a witness at the trial of William Sloper who was being sued by Cibber's son Theophilus for damages for 'assaulting, ravishing, and carnally knowing Susannah Maria Cibber', Theo's wife. It was generally understood – including by

Colley – that Theo was a braggart and a spendthrift who had been living off Sloper, much in the way that Laetitia claimed Matthew had wanted to live off Worsdale, by pimping his wife. Theo's appalling behaviour was such that though the court could not find against him they awarded only £10 in damages. (Theo, unabashed, went back a year later and tried again.) None of the dirt stuck to Colley Cibber, who chose that time to begin writing his memoirs and having his portrait painted. Insouciant, gossipy, full of vitality and fond of finery, he still put on his laced coat and long flowing wig to go to balls and assemblies where he flirted with women half his age; and he spent hours with his cronies at Tom's coffee-house and White's, talking, drinking, gambling. Cibber was the first and thus far only actor admitted to membership of White's. There were those who continued to believe that an actor was, by definition, a low form of life; that he could not be a gentleman and should not expect to come into the company of gentlemen on equal terms. But Cibber had broken through this barrier. The next generation of actors, led by David Garrick who played the gentleman to perfection, were to benefit from his achievement. In Ireland the process was less smooth: the so-called Kelly riots in Dublin during Victor's time as treasurer at Smock Alley partly turned on Thomas Sheridan's insistence on being considered a gentleman.

Out in the world, Cibber played the good-natured fool and the fop. He had no illusions about his abilities as a poet and may not even have been much troubled by Pope's mockery of him in *The Dunciad*; nor was he a passive victim in that long-standing paper war. Complex, high achieving and proud of it, Cibber gave the impression that he lived for pleasure but he had always worked hard; and though officially retired by 1739, he still took parts. He was a serious professional who respected professionalism wherever he found it. Throughout his career he had coached promising actresses (including Mrs Heron), teaching them how to move, how to use their voices. Remarkably, he did not have a reputation as a man who had many affairs though he had a youthful appearance and 'retained the air of a lover long after the age of seventy'. No woman's name has come down to posterity attached to his apart from his wife, Katharine, whom he loved. They were married for forty years. She died in 1734.

Cibber was charmed by Mrs Pilkington and she by him. She wrote that when he first came to visit her he 'ran up Stairs with the vivacity of a Youth of Fifteen'. And the first thing he did was to scold her for not seeking him out earlier:

'And, prithee,' said he, 'why did not you come to my House the Moment you came to London?' 'Upon my Word, Sir, that would have been a modest Proof of Irish Assurance; how could I hope for a Reception?' 'Pshaw,' said he, 'Merit is a sufficient Recommendation to me.'

He asked to see her writings. When he read 'Sorrow' he burst into tears – unashamedly. Cibber, the father of sentimental comedy, liked to laugh; he also as an eighteenth-century man wept freely at tales of distress. Impressed by 'Sorrow', he requested a copy to take away with him and show to others: she readily provided it (this moment must have made up for many laborious hours spent copying out what she had written). And he insisted that he wanted to hear the whole of her 'long, and mournful Story'; he was, she recalled, 'fully determined, to have my History from my own Lips'. He invited her to his house for breakfast the next day.

This was the breakthrough moment. At Colley Cibber's well-appointed house in Charles Street next morning, Laetitia Pilkington gave the performance of her life. She was surprised to find Cibber really was determined, as he had said, to listen. She talked without interruption for three hours, telling him about her early life, her family, marriage, poetry, Matthew, of time spent with Swift and the strange and vivid things he said and did, and of those among the great Dublin families – many of whom Cibber would have known in some degree – who refused to countenance her after the divorce. She stopped when Cibber's servant came in to dress him for dinner with the Duke of Grafton. Cibber, enthralled (he had forgotten about the Duke), told her to come again next day 'and set my Spout a going, for so he merrily called my Mouth', which of course she did and to similar effect: 'The Gentleman neither yawned, scratched his Head, beat Tatoo with his Foot, nor used any such ambiguous Giving-out, to note that he was weary.'

Cibber did not always sit so quietly. Often impatient with new writers (some said envious) he would interrupt readings by making frivolous comments, especially if the writer was present – he called it 'choking singing birds'. He had made an enemy of Henry Fielding in this way. He had no impulse to choke Mrs Pilkington, who kept his attention both by what she had to say and the expressive manner in which she said it. His long experience of auditioning actresses, combined with his practical understanding of stage-writing, including writing parts for himself, give a special significance to Cibber's reactions. He was an acute judge and the best adviser she could have found.

Mrs Pilkington selected her materials carefully. On the second visit, bringing her story up to date, she evidently leaned towards the comic and entertaining rather than the mournful, and it might have sounded, in places, flatteringly like the plots and dialogue of Cibber's own plays. Cibber's *The Lady's Last Stake, or The Wife's Resentment*, a variation on his earlier, successful, *The Careless Husband*, featured a resentful wife, Lady Wronglove, who, as the Prologue explained, was 'No Fool, that will her Life in Sufferings waste', but 'furious, proud, and insolently chaste'. Lady Wronglove's libertine husband behaves badly and she punishes him; in their quarrels, they match each other, insult for insult. Cibber relished witty dialogue and Mrs Pilkington's ability to recall or improvise some of the exchanges that had taken place between herself and Matthew, his wrongdoings and her refusal to tolerate them, delighted him. He became more and more excited, till at last, 'in flowing Spirits' he cried out, 'Zounds! Write it out, just as you relate it, and I'll engage it will sell.'

Cibber's confidence in the saleability of Mrs Pilkington's narrative owed something to his own success. In his memoirs, *An Apology for the Life of Mr Colley Cibber, Comedian,* which recalled his life in theatre and which he was writing at that time, he too made use of a richly personal voice, full of direct address to the reader. High-ranking friends such as Henry Pelham, the future Prime Minister, at whose Esher estate Cibber completed the manuscript during the summer of 1739, approved it. Cibber's experience was extensive. He had been present at or involved in all the important theatrical affairs in the country since the 1690s, had known all the great actors and had interesting and intelligent things to say about them. The book went into a second edition within a month of its publication in April 1740. It made him £1,500.

If Mrs Pilkington's literary ambitions had till then been confined to poetry, Cibber's response encouraged her to think about her material in a new way. The *Memoirs* were conceived at that moment and so too was a heightened sense of her skills as a drawing-room entertainer. Speech could be turned to profit. Her anecdotes about Swift were her prime asset, but her manner of relating them added value, especially when packaged with her own story. There were few precedents for the self-told life story, and none for putting such material on the stage, although actors like Cibber and his son Theo exploited known facts about their own lives in their performances. Throughout her life Mrs Pilkington was more involved in theatrical endeavours than she admitted, but it does not seem that she contemplated becoming an actress. She did not need to. Through Cibber, she had access to an elite circle of men who, in their leisure hours, were as eager as he to sit and be amused by her talk. White's Club, where Cibber was popular and influential was their gathering place. She could not join the club and in that sense could not go to them, but they could come to her.

'As I wanted to make interest with the Great,' Mrs Pilkington wrote, 'I took a Lodging in St James's Street, exactly opposite to White's Chocolate-house.' It was a calculated battle move, like someone laying siege, and Cibber may have suggested it. White's, which had been founded in 1697, was then on west side of St James's Street, at number 69, where the Carlton Club now is. The ground floor was a public chocolate house, above was the exclusive club. Mrs Pilkington's new lodgings were somewhere between numbers 9 and 13 opposite, in a row of smaller houses which have since been destroyed.

Living across from White's, she could watch the parade of members in and out. She could send her servant with a letter to a particular individual, write poems to order, join in the endless, pointless practical jokes that were so heartily enjoyed, receive visits, wave from a window. With Cibber's help she concentrated on building up interest in herself as a personality. 'The Statues' demonstrated her serious intent as a poet and Cibber, ensuring that she provided him with a copy of every new poem she wrote, worked hard on her behalf. Inside White's, the Earl of Chesterfield was one of many powerful aristocrats who read Mrs Pilkington's poems when Cibber handed them to him, and engaged in conversation about her merits. When Chesterfield opined that she must have known Greek and Latin to write English so well, Cibber replied that though he didn't know if Mrs Pilkington had these unusual accomplishments, he could step across and ask her. Through Cibber, Mrs Pilkington was able to send the noble lord her respects and inform him, in an elegant turn of phrase, that though she knew no classical languages, it was the great Dean Swift who had taught her English. Chesterfield concurred that Swift was indeed 'an excellent Tutor'. In these and other ways, Cibber established her as a presence in the club. She became part of the conversation.

Poetry signalled merit (the moral of Cibber's plays was that a woman of merit should not be ill-treated) but poetry apart, Mrs Pilkington's strategies resembled those of the many courtesans and prostitutes who inhabited St James's and with whom men like Chesterfield spent their spare time. The men of White's were at the top of a social hierarchy in which the common prostitute was somewhere near the bottom. To make the kind of 'interest' Mrs Pilkington aspired to, it was vital that she position herself at the upper end of the scale. Reputation was all. As a divorcee she had, of course, lost all claim to reputation in the normal sense of the word, and she was in no position to obtain a husband for herself – the usual means, for a woman, to acquire respectability. Nor, it need hardly be said, could she expect to emulate Cibber's achievement and elicit invitations to the houses, town or country, of the nation's best families. Her location was the *demi-monde* and there she functioned as a courtesan, a woman who made herself available to a group of men for their hours of amusement. Whether, for the men of White's, this meant she was expected to dispense sexual favours remains unclear: if she did, it would have been understood as an inevitable, matter-of-fact by-product of her distress. But it may be that she did not, or not very much. Certainly, the image she later projected was of a woman struggling to survive alone; and her pitch, when endeavouring to persuade people to subscribe to her volume, was that poetry had to keep her from precisely this last resort of a woman in distress. Forced by the oddity of her fate to become a 'Noun Substantive, obliged to stand alone', she made singleness an essential element of the persona she developed.

On the evidence available, Mrs Pilkington achieved something remarkable during her first year in London. She forged a social role for herself as a writer out of two apparently contradictory models, bringing together the ancient tradition of the courtesan-poet with the new sentimental image of virtuous, or at least meritorious, female distress. Like the powerful courtesan, she expected homage from men: she displayed her mettle and flexed her wit and was not to be trifled with. Meanwhile, in her begging letters and petitions, and in personal applications to selected men, she worked the submissive vein. She cultivated the skills necessary to both and performed the parts as required, but the satirist was rarely absent, especially when she was playing courtesan to the leisured gentlemen of White's as lovers.

Even if she did secretly hope to catch a rich keeper, she knew very well that at thirty-plus she needed more than sexual allure, especially given the era's obsession with young flesh. Sir John Ligonier, celebrated general and member of White's, kept four mistresses in his Mayfair house, none older than fifteen. He was not alone in this taste, which also had a sound sanitary principle behind it: given that a virgin was unlikely to transmit a venereal disease (added to which, there was a superstition that sex with a virgin could cure the disease), the age at which girls began to interest men sexually was driven lower and lower. General Ligonier was generous to Mrs Pilkington. He became an important patron, subscribing for twelve copies of her projected poems. He might have warmed to her because of her child-like stature, or because she was Irish – his regiment had been stationed in Ireland for many years and he was one of the few commanding officers to make a point of enlisting Irishmen – or because he was a supporter of the arts. It is conceivable that he valued her for her wit and felt little urge to install her in his harem. The relationship might have been like his 'intimate, bantering' friendship with Lady Mary Coke, he a society gallant and she a society flirt. For Lady Mary Coke, who would dine tête-à-tête with Ligonier and stay weekends at his country house at Cobham, he was 'the best friend I ever had'. She called him 'a gent a hundred years old'; in fact he was ten years younger than Cibber.

Well trained by her years with Swift and her new friendship with Colley Cibber, Mrs Pilkington targeted older men for whom the language of lovers might satisfy without running the risks associated with the deed. Clearly this was not so in the case of General Ligonier whose lechery was still the talk of the town twenty years later when he was in his eighties: a satirical novel, *Chrysal*, depicted his servants procuring little girls for him.

Mrs Pilkington's most important conquest among the company at White's was a less well-known soldier than the great general. Lt Col. John Duncombe of the First Foot Guards (Grenadier Guards) may have been, as she claimed, so old that he had been a page to James II when he was Duke of York, but he was probably in his late fifties. The real point of stressing his age was to emphasise the joke: while so many of the younger members supposedly panted for her attentions, she lavished herself upon the colonel. He was 'droll'; he 'said a thousand witty things in half an Hour', many of them indecent and 'not proper for a female Pen' but wildly amusing. One contemporary observed that Duncombe was 'the most lewd, debauch'd, gaming, swearing, blasphemous Wretch that lived'. He was, in other words, a familiar type. The colonel paid Mrs Pilkington for writing love letters to him which he showed at White's as a proof that he was really a young man. He boasted that she was his mistress and that he supported her, which she said was not true; nor would he pay up his subscription to her poems, though all the men protested at his avarice. Their relationship was a parody, a burlesque of keeper and kept. She wrote a poem about him, 'To the Hon. Colonel Duncombe', which she sent not to the colonel but to Lord Augustus Fitzroy to circulate:

Since so oft to the Great, of my Favours you boast,
When, you know, you enjoy'd but some Kisses at most;
And those, as you say, never ought to be sold,
For Love's too divine, to be barter'd for Gold.
Since this is your Maxim, I beg a Receipt,
To know, how without it, a Lover can eat.
For tho' the fine Heroes, we read in Romances,
Subsisted whole Weeks upon amorous Fancies;
And yet were so strong, if those Writers say true,
That Dragons, and Giants, some thousand they slew;
Those Chiefs were of Origin surely divine!
And descended from Jove, as direct as a Line.
But in our corrupted, degenerate Days,
We find neither Heroes, nor Lovers, like these:
Our Men have scarce Courage to speak to a Lass,
Till they've had a full Meal, and a chirruping Glass.
And so much in myself of the Mortal I find,
That my Body wants Diet, as well as my Mind.
Now, pray, Sir, consider the Case of your Mistress,
Who neither can kiss, nor write Verses, in Distress:
For Bacchus, and Ceres, we frequently prove,
Are Friends to the Muses as well as to Love.

The poem was shown 'to all the Noblemen at White's' and much
fun was had at Colonel Duncombe's expense. The business side of
the matter, from her point of view, was to get more money from
the colonel – who already paid 'handsomely' for the compliments
in her love letters and perhaps more besides – and to bring in
subscribers. Thus she made sure to follow up the success of the
poem with a personal appearance on her balcony. This was an impressively stage-managed moment. She described it in happy detail:

The next Day, as I was sprinkling some Flower-pots, which stood on very
broad Leads, under the Dining-room Window, Colonel Duncombe, the
Duke of Bolton, and the Earl of Winchilsea stood filling out Wine, and
drinking to me: So I took up the Pen and Ink, full in their View; and as I
was not acquainted with any of them, except the Colonel, I sent over to
him these Lines:

> Your rosy Wine
> Looks bright and fine;
> But yet it does not chear me:
> The Cause I guess.
> Is surely this,
> The bottle is not near me.

You shew that Sight
To give delight,
If I may truly judge ye:
But would ye move
My Wit, or Love,
I beg, Sir, I may pledge ye.

Lord Winchilsea bid the Colonel send me all the Wine in the House: 'Ah!'
(said the Colonel) 'that might injure her Health; but I will send her one
Bottle of Burgundy, to chear her Spirits.' Accordingly the Waiter brought
it; the Noblemen all gathered to the Window, so he filled me out a Glass,
which, making them a low Reverence, I drank, and retired.

Duncombe and his friends had all the evidence they needed
that Mrs Pilkington was a poet for she composed for and to the
occasion. Standing in full view she took up the pen and wrote
herself into their company, promising 'wit' and 'love' while at the
same time preserving her autonomy and privacy. We might
suspect she had given the well-turned lines some prior thought
since they capture so well the topographical, social and sexual
distance between her lodgings and White's Club.

Not everybody was convinced, however. Cibber reported that
an Irishman, Joseph Leeson, had spread word at the club that Mrs
Pilkington was merely passing off poems she had stolen from her
husband. Her credit had been damaged. She knew Leeson, a
wealthy brewer's son, and despised him, partly out of snobbery
but also because she believed he had venereally infected his first
wife, his child, the child's nurse and the nurse's husband. She was
furious when Leeson visited and tried to seduce her. His technique
left something to be desired: he appealed to her to be 'charitable'
because his wife was far away and he was desperate; he had chosen
her because she was a gentlewoman and likely to be free of
infection unlike regular prostitutes. She told him she knew too
much about him to risk sharing his first wife's fate. (She was even
more furious a few years later when he boasted to a Dublin nobleman that she had been compliant.) As far as she was concerned he
was tainted, and however 'careless' she had been about her
reputation, she was careful of her 'precious Person'.

Cibber, concerned about the problem Leeson had caused her at
White's, suggested she write some verses on a subject entirely

novel and send them over to the club. Like her first interview with Cibber this was a key moment and, understanding its importance, she gave it a good deal of thought. The idea she came up with was inspired. What could be more novel than to write in praise of the ever-maligned laureate? This would surely be 'the oddest Theme my Muse can find', and one that had never been tried before. The poem she wrote, 'To Mr Cibber', was a lively 'thank you' to her patron that managed to keep herself and her own needs in the foreground while amusingly celebrating him. There were references to Cibber's public quarrels with Pope and others, those 'jealous Bards by Dunces stung', and a few side swipes at the men she now spent her time with:

> Like other Men, you nothing do;
> The World's one Round of Joy to You,

but mostly, in sprightly octosyllabic couplets, she made public how much he had helped her:

> When to the Wealthy and the Great,
> Adorn'd with Honours and Estate,
> My Muse, forlorn! has sent her Pray'r,
> Shunn'd were the Accents of Despair,
> 'Till your excited Pity sped her,
> And with collected Bounties fed her;
> Chear'd her sad Thoughts, like genial Spring,
> And tun'd once more her Voice to sing.

'To Mr Cibber' was a poem which perfectly accomplished its purpose. Like her other occasional verses, it was shown 'to all the Noblemen at White's', and it drew from them a number of subscriptions. Later Cibber incorporated it into his pamphlet, *The Egotist: Or, Colley upon Cibber*, saying nothing about its inception but explaining that it had been written by a female author who had read his *Apology* and wished to praise him. When she printed it in the *Memoirs*, Mrs Pilkington was able to restore to the poem the autobiographical context which lends it bite, for like so many of her poems in the tradition of 'occasional verse' much of the meaning was lost when the lines were no longer embedded in the 'occasion'.

∞

In the summer the rich folk deserted London, abandoning the stinking city for their country estates. Cibber went to Tunbridge. He took with him a supply of Mrs Pilkington's printed proposals to distribute, and promised to collect subscriptions. But in St James's Street the flow of guineas dried up.

From her vantage point across the road Laetitia observed a distant relation, one Captain Meade of the First Foot Guards, going into the public chocolate house part of White's. She sent over a note introducing herself. He came to call, and on the strength of some kind of family connection (and perhaps because she was a favourite of his superior officers) he invited her to spend the summer with him, his wife and four children at Teddington, a mile away from Hampton Court where his regiment was on duty. She quit her lodgings and moved to the country.

The children were 'lovely' and Captain Meade's wife 'pretty' and they seemed a loving couple, if a little over-demonstrative. The captain, a lively man-about-town who supported at least one ex-mistress, was well respected, and their house on the edge of Bushey Park provided a comfortable, economical refuge for the summer months.

Better still, it brought Mrs Pilkington into contact with another willing and well-connected admirer in the person of the local vicar, Dr Stephen Hales. A widower in his sixties, Hales was a celebrated scientist whose experimental work laid the bases of the study of plant and animal physiology. Like many progressive scientists, he conducted experiments for lay audiences. Mrs Pilkington impressed him at once since she was able to show that she had read his books and was familiar with some of the experiments in natural philosophy which he conducted – possibly she had attended demonstration lectures in gravity, electricity or hydrostatics given by her father's friend Samuel Helsham in Dublin. Hales was the first serious intellectual she met in London and the encounter was intoxicating. Invited to his house, she seems to have witnessed some kind of animal dissection designed to show the circulation of the blood. (A typical experiment in Hales's *Vegetable Statics* begins: 'I tied down a live *dog* on his back, near the edge of a table, and then made a small hole through the intercostal muscles into his *thorax*, near the *diaphragm*.') Pope found Hales's dissections of dogs and rats upsetting, but Mrs Pilkington was thrilled, not so much by what she saw – she claimed that nothing she saw then was new to her – as by him and his comments. He was inspired, an enthusiast whose 'comprehensive Mind' was God-like and 'soar'd above this little terrene Spot'; he was second only to Newton, and being in his presence was like being at a 'sacred Banquet'.

Hales's passion for science was combined with an interest in poetry (a combination that perhaps triggered another association with her father) and he at once offered to take some of her proposals. Excited, 'elevated', she could not sleep all night. A poem was forming itself and she gave an account of its genesis which anticipates Coleridge's more famous story about the composition of 'Kubla Khan'. She described going out very early next morning and walking into Bushey Park. She sat down by a waterfall and listened to the falling water so long it seemed to speak. She fell asleep and dreamed that a beautiful water nymph handed her a paper on which was written a poem in praise of Dr Hales. In her dream she read the poem, and then, awakening, remembered it. Happening to have 'a Pencil and Sheet of Paper in my Pocket', she wrote it all down, fifty-eight lines of iambic pentameters.

It was appropriate that Nature herself should write the poem, for Nature was yielding her secrets to Hales:

> Each healing Stream, each Plant of virtuous Use,
> To thee their Medicinal Pow'rs produce.

By animal dissections and other close observation, Hales was removing 'Error, Doubt, and Darkness' from human existence. Nature and God worked together and science was the handmaiden. 'To the Reverend Dr Hales' put into verse what Mrs Pilkington had seen at his house the day before; it betrayed no squeamishness, only a reinforced wonder at God's works:

> When You, with Art, the Animal dissect,
> And, with the microscopic Aid, inspect,
> Where, from the Heart, unnumber'd Rivers glide,
> And faithful back return their purple Tide;
> How fine the Mechanism, by Thee display'd!
> How wonderful is ev'ry Creature made!

Vessels, too small for Sight, the Fluids strain,
Concoct, digest, assimilate, sustain:
In deep Attention, and Surprize, we gaze,
And, to Life's Author, raptur'd, pour out Praise.

She gave the poem to Hales, with the proposals he had asked for, after morning prayers. That evening he visited, bringing with him the minister of Henley upon Thames. Both men subscribed and went on to collect subscriptions from other 'persons of distinction'.

Mrs Pilkington ended the summer in profit, and when she returned to London her first visitor was Colley Cibber who had raised four guineas.

With money in her purse, she was able to move back into her former lodgings in St James's Street which happened to be vacant. One weekend, the landlady's son-in-law, the Rev. Dr George Turnbull who was a chaplain to the Prince of Wales, was due to preach at St James's Chapel. He came to stay, but his mother-in-law now had nowhere to put him except in her own bed. She therefore asked Mrs Pilkington if, as a favour, she could sleep with her for the night. Mrs Pilkington offered instead to let Dr Turnbull have her apartment – 'which was, as may be presumed by the Price, a genteel one' – and squash in with the landlady. Dr Turnbull would not hear of it. Having been in her rooms, however, he had noted that she had books and later he asked if she could lend him something to read. She sent down her own poems in manuscript.

Dr Turnbull made a proper visit after his sermon the following afternoon and they were so entertained by each other that he stayed till midnight and came up again for coffee next morning. From the windows of White's Club, what could be seen was a clergyman walking to and fro in Mrs Pilkington's quarters on Sunday evening and again on Monday morning. The men of White's concluded it could only be the Rev. Pilkington, come to make up. Not wanting to spoil her chances of being taken back into his protection, they stood off (placing bets, probably, on the outcome) until Col. Duncombe, unable to bear the suspense, went to the milliner's shop next door and sent a message up saying that a lady from Ireland wanted to speak to Mrs Pilkington. She, thinking there might be news of her children, hurried down only to find that the colonel was the lady. He was 'full of his usual Gaiety', and heartily amused to learn that his 'dear little one' was conversing with a 'damn'd Parson' of no relation to her.

∞

The first of Mrs Pilkington's anti-ministerial pamphlets, *An Excursory View of the Present State of Men and Things*, had appeared by this time, adding to her reputation as poet and pet of the White's Club coterie that of political satirist. Victor dealt with Dodsley over the printing and proofing, perhaps because she was still in the country, and when *An Excursory View* came out on 24 August, he 'very modestly assured every Person [it] was of his own Composition', which some of it surely was. Given her dependence on the laureate, she might in any case not have wanted to broadcast authorship of a pamphlet that took up the mantle of Paul Whitehead's 'Manners', borrowing its structure and tone, to put into verse a compelling picture of the disastrous 'state of men and things' in 1739. On the other hand, the Earl of Chesterfield, whose accomplished speeches in the Lords made him the hero of the Opposition, was on perfectly cordial terms with Cibber at the club.

The mood of the country had turned against Walpole, whose policy of appeasement towards Spain was widely seen as unpatriotic. The Spaniards had been preying on British ships in the West Indies. Walpole had negotiated a convention with Spain giving limited compensation, which he forced through Parliament, but it included nothing to stop Spain carrying on 'searching' British ships. There was huge public interest in the matter. In March Swift's friend the Duchess of Queensbury and a posse of women, including Mary Pendarves, had forced their way into the House of Lords to hear the debates.

Everybody talked politics that year. In June, negotiations with Spain broke down and in July Admiral Vernon set sail for the West Indies. On 29 September Mrs Pilkington's second pamphlet, *An Apology for the Minister*, was printed anonymously and distributed, one of the snowstorm of such pamphlets that year, as confirmed by a *Letter from a Merchant in London to his Correspondent abroad, in which the Present State of Affairs is Impartially Considered* which described the 'prodigious demand': 'No body asks for the Tatlers and Spectators now. The Belles Lettres lie by the walls ... you'd be astonished at the public spirit that reigns amongst us, anxious for the balance of Europe'.

Mrs Pilkington's twenty-eight-page *Apology for the Minister*, written in the voice of a supporter of the Ministry, professed to be a vindication of its 'wise conduct'. Certain key phrases, however, in its opening paragraphs, made clear how it was to be read while giving nothing for government stooges to fix on. Reference to 'freedom of the press' identified the pamphlet at once as an Opposition production; it was unnecessary to mention Dodsley's name since the events of the spring were still fresh in people's minds. Meanwhile, that 'a certain great man' had become 'obnoxious' was a simple statement of fact. Through the device of ironic inversion, the pamphlet rehearsed familiar critiques: that Walpole rewarded placemen, enriched himself, cared nothing for the people, and allowed the Spaniards to plunder British ships. It sardonically addressed imaginary objections by 'malcontents':

It will, perhaps, be objected by some malcontents, that the barbarities permitted to be exercised with impunity on our sailors, did not so much testify that affection, which I hope I have, by this time, convinced them the M——r has to their persons. To this I answer, that a true patriot has nothing so much at heart, as the good of the publick; to this glorious spirit many have devoted their interest, nay their offspring, and acquired immortal reputation by so doing. With what front can these people presume to censure the M——r? if he chooses rather to let a few slovenly masters of ships, and dirty sailors, fall victim to the rage of their enemies, than expose to hazard all those well-dressed officers, and glittering troops, whom the nation supports for entertainment, for their splendid appearance on every Review Day.

There was more in this vein, smartly expressed but essentially routine. She managed to get in a sarcastic allusion to Edward Walpole's 'generosity' and the last three pages were devoted to plugging her own 'Excursory View', that poem of 'unbounded Freedom' which was the first to brave the censors since Whitehead's 'Manners'.

1 Laetitia Pilkington. Demure yet risqué, the curate's ex-wife depended on her wit after she was thrown out of her Dublin home at 2am. Her *Memoirs* told the story of her life and libidinous times, when men were allowed every sexual licence and women punished for the slightest slip.

2 Jonathan Swift. Dean of St Patrick's, author of *Gulliver's Travels*, Swift was the Pilkingtons' first patron. Later he scratched their names out of his records, calling Mrs Pilkington 'the most profligate whore' in the kingdom.

3 Frontispiece and title page of Rev Matthew Pilkington's 1730 *Poems*. With Swift's help, he was able to publish his poems in this fine edition.

POEMS
ON SEVERAL
OCCASIONS.

CONTAINING

The Progress of Music in *Ireland*.	Translation of *Anacreon*.
The POET's Well.	An ODE on his Majesty's Birth-Day.
An Essay towards a	

To which is added, the

PLAGUE of WEALTH,

OCCASION'D

By the AUTHOR's receiving fifty Pounds from his Excellency the Lord *CARTERET*, for the foremention'd ODE.

With several

POEMS not in the *Dublin* Edition.

By *MATTHEW PILKINGTON*, M. A.

Revised by the Reverend Dr. SWIFT.

LONDON:

Printed for T. WOODWARD, at the *Half Moon* over-against St. *Dunstan*'s Church in *Fleetstreet*; CHARLES DAVIS in *Pater-noster-row*, and W. BOWYER.
MDCCXXXI.

VIVITUR INGENIO

4 *Limerick Hell-Fire Club* by James Worsdale. Rake, actor, painter and perhaps Mrs Pilkington's lover, Worsdale helped found the Dublin and Limerick Hell-Fire Clubs, devoted to drinking and devilry. He included himself in this portrait of hell-raisers. He is the short man attached to the couple at top left. The threesome suggests the relationship Worsdale aspired to have with the Pilkingtons.

5 View of Dublin. According to Mrs Pilkington's *Memoirs,* Dublin was 'a Place of the least Sin, and the most Scandal, of any City in the World.'

Ridendo, dicere verum.

6 Portrait of James Worsdale In vigorous, prosperous, old age. Mrs Pilkington called him 'contemptible' but she needed his help.

7 Hogarth, *A Midnight Modern Conversation*. Hogarth's popular print depicts a club of middle-aged, respectable men, well gone in drink. It was men like these who enjoyed Mrs Pilkington's 'entertaining speech'.

8 Bust of Colley Cibber. The well-connected actor Colley Cibber was Mrs Pilkington's most important helper in London. His gift for getting money out of others was key to her survival.

9 Samuel Richardson. The novelist and printer rescued Mrs Pilkington from dire distress. He also forwarded money from Patrick Delany which Delany didn't want his wife to know about.

10 Joseph Highmore, *Pamela*. Samuel Richardson's *Pamela* was the sensation of 1740. This novel, narrated by a servant girl who virtuously resists the master's advances, helped Mrs Pilkington find a voice for her *Memoirs*.

11 Sketch of Dr Delany. Mrs Delany's sketch of her husband shows a corpulent, comfortable clergyman. Mrs Delany's high-born relations were unhappy that she had married an Irishman.

12 View of Delville, Delany's country estate at Glasnevin. Mrs Pilkington returned to Dublin in 1747 and published her *Memoirs* to general applause, but she was no longer welcomed at Delville. Mrs Delany thought the book 'odious'.

13 Boyle Abbey. Libertine Lord Kingsborough, Mrs Pilkington's generous patron, owned this ruined Cistercian abbey at Boyle, Co Roscommon. Though he lived at King House, he dated his letters to Mrs Pilkington from 'Abbe Boyle' – thereby adding a dash of heretical flamboyance.

In the Crypt
of this Church, near
the Body of her honoured Father
John Van Lewen M.D.
lies the Mortal Part of
Mrs. LÆTITIA PILKINGTON
Whose Spirit hopes for
that Peace, thro' the infinite Merit of
Christ, which a cruel & merciless
World never afforded her.

Died July 29ᵗʰ 1750

14 Mrs Pilkington's memorial tablet in St Ann's church, Dublin, with the words she composed for herself. Though her elder son, William, refused to see her, Mrs Pilkington was comforted in her last illness by her devoted son, Jack, who left a touching account of her death. When asked by a clergyman if she forgave her husband for his treatment of her she replied that she would forgive him if she died but if she lived the quarrel would go on. Peace was never her natural element. The tablet, by the Cork sculptor Ken Thompson, was commissioned and installed in 1997 by the modern editor of the *Memoirs*, A. C. Elias, Jr.

In Brook Street there was a bookshop which lent out books by the quarter and where Mrs Pilkington, as a regular customer, had become known to the owners, a couple called Ryves, 'sensible, well-bred people'. They stocked pamphlets, including hers, and one day a young politician, George Rooke, son of a celebrated naval hero, admiral of the fleet Sir George Rooke, happened to pick up *An Apology for the Minister*. He read it with pleasure, but refused to believe it had been written by a woman. Mrs Ryves assured him she could prove it by producing the author, which she did by sending a note to Mrs Pilkington begging her to make up a table for quadrille with some 'agreeable Friends'. This was a welcome invitation, but when Laetitia was shown into the parlour behind the shop her first impression was that she had made a mistake and exposed herself to 'low' company: she saw an old man whom she recognised as a Grub-Street writer and a young gentleman in plain dress, drinking beer and playing cribbage in a room that smelt of tobacco. George Rooke was slumming. At a loose end having spent some hours in the Mount Street coffee-house, hoping but failing to find company for dinner, he'd invited himself along with 'the old scribbler' to Mrs Ryves's. Once Mrs Pilkington understood Rooke's quality, and he took the measure of her political understanding, they settled down to several happy hours of entertaining conversation, sustained by that 'Chat inspiring Liquor, Green Tea'. He was full of salacious anti-Walpole stories. She adored his easy wit. They flirted, he gave her a guinea for a subscription, and they did not part till well past midnight. He said he would call on her next day. She never saw him again. Shortly afterwards she heard that he had suffered a stroke and on Friday, 23 November, he died. It was a profound shock: 'all Wit, Life, and Gaiety at Night, and dead in the Morning!' She wept for him as if he had been a long-established friend.

War had been declared on 19 October. Known initially as the War of Jenkins' Ear, then the War of Austrian Succession, it was to last eight years (almost the whole of Mrs Pilkington's time in the capital) and take half a million lives. Many of her soldier friends were involved. It was fought in the Low Countries, Italy and Central Europe, and the impact at home was muted though there were fears of invasion. Its most significant contribution to British political life was that it helped end the career of Walpole, whose downfall in 1742 after twenty-one years in power had the unanticipated side effect that there was no longer any money in writing Opposition satire.

CHAPTER EIGHT

Adverse Fate

She was desperate for news of her children, and she was furious that Matthew had sent her no money. She confided in Dr Turnbull who agreed to write to Matthew on her behalf, one clergyman to another. This produced a tirade from Matthew's attorney, James Walsh:

Sir,
In the Absence of my Client, Mr Pilkington, I received your Letter; and he wou'd have you to know, the Woman, you mention, is not his Wife, nor has he any thing to say to the infamous Wretch; she fled from Ireland, where she ought to have been executed, for killing her Father, three of her Bastards, and poisoning her Husband. It does not become a Clergyman to countenance a common Prostitute; if she owes you any Money, you may put her in Jail; for I do assure you, it will never be paid by Mr Pilkington.

Dr Turnbull had returned to his own house in Kensington by the time this missive arrived and Laetitia, opening it even though it was addressed to him, promptly put it away – overcome by a mixture of shame and horror. A few days later, she learned that Josiah Hort, bishop of Kilmore, a worldly, poetry-writing, handsome man, some of whose eleven children had been delivered by her father, was in London. Hort, an Englishman, had first gone over to Ireland in 1709 as chaplain to Philip, Duke of Wharton, when he was viceroy; and Wharton, about whom Rooke had some stories to tell, and who was Edward Young's patron, was once described as the most wicked man in England. Hort himself had pretended to have a degree in divinity to facilitate his rise through clerical ranks. Mrs Pilkington wrote the bishop a letter explaining her circumstances. He sent his servant round with a sympathetic note and some money, apologising that he could do no more as he was leaving for Ireland that day. By chance, Dr Turnbull was back in St James's and paying her a visit, so the messenger found her drinking coffee with a clergyman. This was excellent timing on both counts. The bishop's messenger saw her keeping pious company, while the bishop's compassion and kind recollections of Dr Van Lewen's daughter proved to Turnbull that she was who she claimed to be. It emboldened her to bring out the letter from Walsh and show it to Turnbull, who was duly shocked at so much perfidiousness.

Never one to be discreet, Matthew had an additional reason at about this time to wish his ex-wife dead or rotting in a jail. He had fallen in love. The widow Warren had lost her place to a younger woman. So engrossed was Matthew by Anne, or Nancy, Sandes that he neglected everything but her. Like a lover out of the old romances he carved her name on every tree in his garden and scratched it with a diamond on the windows of his house. The source of our knowledge about Matthew at the time is the unfortunate Jack who was ill-treated by his father and loathed this interloper, regarding her as the negative to all his absent mother's idealised virtues. His mother was 'witty and polite', she was 'hoggish' – dirty, stupid, mean and mercenary. But Matthew's love was real. He wanted to marry Nancy; and though the terms of his separation forbade re-marriage, he was contemplating doing so on the grounds that he could reasonably consider his ex-wife to be dead.

Confirmation of Matthew's behaviour came in another letter from Ireland which Mrs Pilkington stored carefully among her papers. It was from an unknown hand, signed David Lambert, a man whom neither she nor anybody else has been able to trace. Lambert introduced himself as a friend of the father of the young lady Matthew was courting, and explained that he had many times heard Mr Pilkington declare that not only was his wife dead, but so too were his two younger children.

Laetitia probably shared this letter with Dr Turnbull. After carefully making a copy, she sent it to the archbishop of Dublin along with the letter from James Walsh, hoping to stop any planned marriage and to cause Matthew as much trouble as possible with his superiors in the church. Even bishops easy with licentiousness like the bishop of Kilmore did not necessarily want to encourage it among the lesser clergy.

∞

Mrs Pilkington's genteel first-floor apartment in St James's Street cost one guinea a week; expensive, but the location conferred obvious benefits. Colonel Duncombe, for example, had to do little to persuade Charles Spencer, 3rd Duke of Marlborough – 'a lovely Gentleman' – to step across from White's at nine o'clock one evening. The men arrived unannounced to find the poetess seated at her table, writing. It was a momentous occasion. Handsome, young, extravagant, and a Marlborough, Spencer wasted no time in sending the colonel packing: 'Colonel, I shall meet you at White's, either to-night or to-morrow Morning; for I have a mind to have a little Chat with this Lady alone.' The lady was already in 'a little Flutter' when his Grace opened his wallet and pulled out a bank note for £50. 'This,' she wrote, 'was the Ordeal, or fiery Trial; Youth, Beauty, Nobility of Birth, and unsought Generosity, attacking at once the most desolate Person in the World.' She pocketed the cash, trembling but willing to be assured, apparently, that the Duke wanted only to be her sincere and disinterested friend. Rather than impose any 'hard Conditions', he sat while she amused him with her talk, and then he invited her to write some extempore lines making fun of Colonel Duncombe.

Alas, not many of Mrs Pilkington's callers came bearing fifty-pound notes, and as she became known, so she was targeted by the needy Irish who arrived in London in a constant stream and applied to her for help. Typical of these was an ex-footman of Swift's who turned up in 1739. He had a reference from Swift, though it was not immediately obvious that this would help him find a place. Laetitia copied the reference and put it with her collection of materials for future use. Swift had written:

Whereas the Bearer — serv'd me the Space of one Year, during which time he was an Idler and a Drunkard, I then discharged him as such; but how far his having been five Years at Sea, may have mended his Manners, I leave to the Penetration of those who may hereafter chuse to employ him.

She found him well-mannered enough to advise he go to Twickenham and try his luck with Pope who, on being assured that the bearer was indeed the man Mrs Pilkington remembered as footman to Swift, gave him a place which he kept till Pope's death in 1744. Others she fed, some she gave money to. There is no reason to disbelieve her self-description: she was 'naturally liberal' and 'no very great Oeconomist'.

It is hard to form a picture of Mrs Pilkington's finances, just as it is hard to fix the chronology of her movements from one lodging to the next, or know what took place when gentlemen came calling. Quite a lot of money seems to have passed through her hands. She bought furniture – her own bed and coverings, for example; and household goods that displayed her status along with the necessary plates and dishes, tea sets and coffee cups, decanters and wine glasses. Living a semi-public life, she always had to be dressed for company. Her linens and silks needed to be regularly laundered, her jewels out of pawn, and her rooms well-heated and sufficiently lit in winter. (The winters of 1739–40 and 1740–41 were exceptionally cold and the price of coal rocketed: Henry Fielding owed his coal merchant £27 10s. in March 1741.) She had to keep a servant, for appearance's sake as well as need. She was writing seriously, mostly poetry for her planned volume, and some experimental fiction that later became incorporated into the *Memoirs*; and while it was acceptable to be found with pen in hand and papers spread over the table, it would not do to be unwashed, ill-dressed and unready to perform.

The Duke of Marlborough's £50 would be enough to maintain herself for a year in the country. Perhaps it was this gift that made her decide to live 'retired' for a while – relatively speaking – and move from St James's to Green Street.

Green Street, north of Grosvenor Square, was a quiet residential neighbourhood, unlike St James's Street which with its shops, taverns and clubs thronged at all hours. The houses were fresh and new: building had begun in the 1720s when fashionable Grosvenor

Square, the largest in London after Lincoln's Inn Fields, was laid out. Green Street was unfashionable and unfinished, the builder John Green having fallen down a well in Upper Grosvenor Street in 1737. At its west end it looked out over Hyde Park, still virtually open country, and to the east were the large houses of the wealthy. It was respectable; no squalid neighbourhoods pressed up against it.

Dismissing her maid, Laetitia took room and board at 'a very genteel House'. The landlord was valet to the Earl of Stair, a leading politician and member of White's, and his wife was a laundress to families of quality. Here, as Mrs Meade, Laetitia kept company with upper servants and from them she heard much gossip. Among the valets who came to Green Street for dinner on a Sunday was Sir John Ligonier's man, Mr Parkinson, and it was through him that she was introduced to the general who lived round the corner in North Audley Street. Parkinson, having been with the regiment in Dublin at the time of her divorce, recognised her. He joined her after dinner in her ground-floor room which opened on to the garden. There, disdaining alcohol and tobacco, they drank tea and he told her that numbers of people in Dublin lamented her hard fate. True or not, it was a comfort; and combined with Ligonier's twelve guineas which followed shortly afterwards, lifted her spirits.

Mrs Pilkington's initial aim in taking lodgings in St James's Street had been to 'make Interest with the Great' and in this she had succeeded. Marlborough's appearance testified to that; Ligonier's twelve guineas confirmed it. She no longer needed to annex herself to White's. She may have moved to give herself some respite from the pressure of libertine attentions. Or her novelty value may have worn off and if, as seems to have been the case, she was resolved not to go into keeping, the hard whoring men of White's may have felt they'd paid their dues. (The actress Kitty Fisher was maintained 'by the whole club of White's' but Kitty Fisher was an avowed courtesan.) The other possibility is that Mrs Pilkington needed to withdraw and live 'retired' because she was pregnant or infected, but if so there is no mention of a miscarriage, a baby or a salivation treatment.

The laundress and her husband catered to such needs, however.

At Green Street Laetitia made a friend of a pregnant woman who came to lodge there. For two months the woman, who said she was married to a lawyer away travelling the circuit, stayed inside the house and had no visitors. Then a man began coming, but only at night. Suspecting a love affair rather than marriage, and liking the woman and fearing she was being badly treated, Laetitia urged her to confidences, which the woman readily shared. A story of callous marital betrayal was unfolded: the woman's husband had committed bigamy to avoid financial ruin, but loving him still she received him secretly at night in order not to expose him. She was 'in the oddest Situation imaginable', a kept mistress to her own husband. Ominously, however, he had fallen behind in the money he gave for her support.

True or not, the woman's situation, like yet unlike her own, aroused strong feelings of empathy in Laetitia and they became close. When the woman cried, as she did often, she consoled her; and she was ready to do what she could to help in a practical way, taking up the woman's cause so far as to carry a letter to the supposed husband in his office at Ludgate Hill. There she found herself facing 'a polite, handsome Man, of about thirty Years of Age' who received her 'very civilly'. He was less civil when he learnt that she had come to get money out of him for the woman who was about to have his child, and he was disturbed at how much she knew and her readiness to confront him in his office, or, as she hinted, to tell his second wife, but he kept his 'marvellous Assurance'. He informed her he could not possibly give charity to everybody. She had to listen to him rattling off the usual sorts of excuses men made – 'inhumane Speeches, common on those Occasions' – and was even told that the pregnant woman 'ought to work for her Bread, as many of her Betters did'. She was disgusted. She came away with a couple of guineas.

The woman died in childbirth, along with her baby. The contrast between her fate and that of the man Laetitia had met haunted her. He had been able to shuffle off responsibility, blaming the woman and buying his way out of momentary discomfort with a trifle. Now death had done him a favour, freeing him of an unwanted first wife or mistress. It was uncomfortable to reflect that Matthew would be no less pleased were he to get news of *his* first wife's death.

Melancholy at the loss of a friend, Laetitia pondered men's accountability and women's silence. Women bore the consequences of men's pleasures. Why were they so willing to keep secret the way men treated them? Women spoke to other women; but even then the sense of shame was overwhelming. Discarded, duped, ruined women were living 'retired' all around her terrified of being exposed, and yet men – the man on Ludgate Hill, the men of White's, Worsdale, Matthew – went on regardless, civil but selfish. One 'unfortunate lady' sought her out wanting a letter written: she came three times before she summoned up courage and stopped crying enough to tell her story of seduction and betrayal.

Mrs Meade, the Irish gentlewoman off Grosvenor Square, 'with no fortune but my pen', received the wretched and the wronged. She had no family to be troubled by her actions, and, as a woman, no reputation to guard. She listened, observed, advised, wrote letters. The more she heard, the angrier she became. Hardening into an expert in female distress, she registered an important difference between herself and the women whose stories she collected: unlike them, she refused to be shamed into silence.

She read avidly, renting books from Mrs Ryves. Sometimes the two women walked in St James's Park, or they visited an elderly relation of Mrs Ryves who lived across the park in Westminster. He was a doctor who on being told that Mrs Pilkington's father had been a medical man accepted her as one of the faculty and refused payment for his services when she fell ill. Decent and kind, he was like Dr Hales and Dr Turnbull, a man of 'polite' learning with whom she could sit comfortably and talk about books.

Such men were as keen to talk about fiction as other kinds of writing. Mrs Pilkington read the best-known women writers of the day, Swift's friend Delarivier Manley, and Eliza Haywood. It is impossible to know what she thought of them, though clearly she borrowed subject-matter and technique from both. Perhaps she visited Mrs Haywood's shop at the sign of Fame in Covent Garden. Or perhaps she was careful not to, marking out for herself more upmarket literary territory: in the *Memoirs* she damned Mrs Haywood for her sexually titillating fictions – for 'painting up Vice in attractive colours'. The only two women Laetitia acknowledged as having any talent worth noticing were, conventionally, the French scholar Madame Dacier, translator of Homer, and Katherine Philips, 'the Matchless Orinda'. These icons of unassailable virtue functioned as symbols of her own aspiration, although daily life posed questions that were addressed rather more directly in the urban fictions of Manley and Haywood than by Dacier and Orinda.

∞

At intervals, ever since her arrival, Laetitia had written to John Barber. He had ignored her letters. On a personal level she was stung because she thought of herself as having been 'a kind of Favourite' with him; and with regard to her literary aspirations she valued him as an ex-printer who might be able to arrange for her book to be printed cheaply. Furthermore, as an ex-alderman he had many rich friends who might subscribe. Barber was ill throughout 1740, which might be why he did not reply; but, when she pointed out that she had in her possession a vicious satire on him written by Matthew, he invited her to his house and played the charming host.

Barber died shortly afterwards, on 2 January 1741, so she had little scope to extort money from him. Hearing about Barber's death, Matthew moved quickly. He contacted the publisher Edmund Curll, guessing he would be interested in a quick biography, and in the spring sent him a *Life of Alderman Barber*. Curll knew there was another account, Matthew's 'character' written at Swift's behest. This might have been what Laetitia was referring to when she threatened Barber with the 'vicious satire'. Curll seemed to think so, because he visited her one evening, unannounced, pretending to bring news that she had been left a legacy by a long lost relation, and then, 'very gaily', tried to persuade her to have dinner with him in romantic Richmond. When she realised who the 'ugly squinting old Fellow' was it made her laugh, and when she wrote about it she was condescending: 'I comforted myself that Mr Curl had not made a Fool of me, as he has done of many a better Writer, and secured me a Prisoner in his poetical Garret, which the ingenious Mr Fielding charmingly ridicules.' (Fielding made fun of Curll in *The Author's Farce*.) Still, Curll offered a 'handsome Consideration' for materials relating to Barber or Swift and she may have sold him some. At any rate, in July 1741 Curll was able to publish *An Impartial History of the Life, Character, Amours, Travels and Transactions of Mr John Barber, City-Printer, Common-Councilman, Alderman, and Lord Mayor of London*, compiled from a number of sources, the most substantial of which were those that Matthew had written.

A less impartial, more savage character demolition of a biographical subject would be difficult to imagine. Barber is accused of ingratitude ('the blackest ingratitude to his best friend Mrs Manley'), avarice, vanity, envy, pride, insolence and ill-nature. The mayor's chaplain, strangely, emerges from the *Life* of John Barber in a remarkably flattering light.

Single-minded in pursuit of his own good, Matthew had set about restoring his fortunes by cultivating the music and art-loving bishop of Kildare, Charles Cobbe, an Englishman who had been dean of Christ Church and who was to become Archbishop of Dublin. Cobbe, and later his son Thomas, were generous patrons: they gave Matthew the opportunity to develop his expertise as a connoisseur of paintings by employing him to purchase a collection of Old Masters for the family mansion, Newbridge House at Donabate, north of Dublin. That was in the future. To begin with, Cobbe rescued Matthew from his lowly curacy at St Andrew's by giving him the living at Donabate. Installed as vicar in June 1741, Rev. Pilkington's income increased by at least £20 per annum and probably considerably more. In one respect his expenses had diminished: some time near Christmas 1740, ten-year-old Jack, neglected and abused, had run away and managed to get himself to Cork and the temporary safe haven of his mother's Uncle George's house. George Van Lewen took responsibility for the boy, sent him to school and paid for him to have singing lessons.

Laetitia knew nothing of this. Nor had she news of her

daughter Betty who, it is safe to assume, was no less neglected than Jack. When Matthew's duties took him to Donabate, Betty was perhaps put under the care of Matthew's downtrodden mother a few doors away on Lazer's Hill where William, the eldest son, still lived. There was another neighbour who kept some sort of an eye on things: James Worsdale, now listed as one of the company at Smock Alley theatre and self-described Deputy Master of the Revels in Dublin, had taken a house on Lazer's Hill. Worsdale had been touring with a company of singers and actors under John Frederick Lampe, performing (among other things) the enormously popular comic opera *The Dragon of Wantley*, written by Henry Carey and set to music by Lampe. Charles Burney saw them at Chester and laughed so much he went several times.

Whatever scrutiny Worsdale kept over the Pilkington children was occasional and patchy. A shocking accusation reached Laetitia that their grandmother had conspired with Matthew to sell the children into slavery. Irish slavery was big business in the early eighteenth century and Dublin was a popular port for masters of 'kid ships'. Adults could indenture themselves to kid-merchants, putting themselves into bondage for four or five years rather than face starvation in Ireland, and children were sold.

In a panic, barely recovered from a feverish illness that had kept her in a delirium for days, Laetitia wrote at once to every senior church and government official in Dublin who might help, asking them to investigate. No evidence remains, but she claimed she could produce 'a cloud of Witnesses' who would testify to the truth of her account: 'The Letters were delivered Time enough to prevent the Children's being sold to Slavery – the Affair was enquired into, and Mr Pilkington was obliged to refund to the Master of the Kid-Ship the Golden Earnest he had received as the Price of the Innocent.'

Matthew's hypocrisy, and perhaps his happiness, infuriated her. Matthew belonged to a Charitable Musical Society that put on subscription concerts to help the poor, and in 1741 he composed a prologue for a benefit 'To raise the Wretched, to relieve Distress'. She wanted to 'pluck the holy Furr from off his Back' and show the world the 'wicked Priest' within; for 'who that beheld this Man clad in holy Vesture at the Altar, appearing like white-robed Innocence, with Eyes up-turned to Heaven', could believe him capable of such a crime. There is no doubt that those who told her about the kid ship made sure she heard all there was to know about Matthew's love for Nancy Sandes and his success with Bishop Cobbe.

∞

Among the books Laetitia read during the exceptionally cold winter of 1740–41 was Samuel Richardson's *Pamela*, a story of attempted seduction told in letters by a servant girl and subtitled *Virtue Rewarded*. Pursued by her master, Pamela resists, preserves her maidenhead and is rewarded by marriage and a coach-and-six. This fantasy took the town by storm. Not to have read *Pamela* was a sign of 'want of curiosity' according to the *Gentleman's Magazine* in January 1741. Colley Cibber adored it and became friends with the author. Aaron Hill said that like the snow Pamela covered everything with her whiteness, a witty bit of plain speaking from the editor of *The Plain Dealer*, drawing attention to the hilariously unreal moral topography of the novel given that in most households the job of a pretty servant included being sexually available to the master unless otherwise indicated. Actually marrying the master was the stuff of dreams. Still, actresses were managing to marry lords, so why not servant girls? Debate turned on whether Pamela was innocent or calculating: a virgin and good, or sexually experienced and therefore a whore? Henry Fielding had no doubt Pamela was a sham and he burlesqued the story in *An Apology for the Life of Mrs Shamela Andrews*. Fielding's title and fake author, 'Conny Keyber', hit two targets: Colley Cibber, who in his *An Apology for the Life of Colley Cibber, Actor* had attacked Fielding as 'a broken wit', and Conyers Middleton, whose *Life of Cicero* boasted a particularly nauseating dedication to Lord Hervey. Fielding's was not the only parody to appear: Eliza Haywood published her *Anti-Pamela, or, Feign'd Innocence Detected* at about the same time, in spring 1741, describing it as 'a narrative which has really its Foundation in Truth and Nature'. Haywood's ironical imitation of the novel's claims to 'truth' and 'nature' captured the most convincing aspect of *Pamela* for all readers, pro and con the heroine: Richardson's brilliant ventriloquising of her voice.

Pamela provided a new benchmark for what was still a fledgling genre. Over the next two centuries realistic prose fiction would oust poetry and drama as the most significant literary form. In these early days, distinctions between what was 'true' and what was imagined, what had happened and what was made up, as between characters who could be recognised and characters who were fictional constructs, were fluid. In Delarivier Manley's 1709 *The New Atalantis*, for example, fictional characters had been thinly disguised representations of famous people like Charles Spencer's grandfather, the great Duke of Marlborough. In scandal fiction, politics, history, sex and fantasy came together, the text's impact depending on the frisson of recognition for which the publishers provided a handy key. The narrative viewpoint of the *Atalantis* was female, a trend which continued. Defoe's *The Fortunes and Misfortunes of the Famous Moll Flanders* (1721) and his *Roxana, or the Fortunate Mistress* (1724) were 'true' stories of women's lives given in the first person. But it was Richardson who did most to establish the female self and the female voice as the novel's authentic subject-matter and sound. Perhaps even more important was Richardson's commercial skill in promoting the book, what has been described as 'the *Pamela* ad campaign' and 'the *Pamela* media event', to which, of course, the controversy unleashed by Fielding's *Shamela* contributed.

Mrs Pilkington studied *Pamela* closely and learnt from it. She read Fielding and laughed. The energy and immediacy of prose fiction, its capaciousness, its easy incorporation of direct speech and potential for shifting viewpoints, all appealed. A good deal of Pamela and Shamela went to the making of the female persona that eventually emerged as narrator and protagonist of the *Memoirs*. Although she was collecting subscriptions for a volume of poems, it is possible that Laetitia experienced a crisis of confidence in poetry at this time. Her association with Colley Cibber, her 'fellow Grubstreet' as Colonel Duncombe called him, more or less guaranteed critical disdain if ever a book of poems appeared. Added to which the female voice in poetry, though not unwelcome, was more limited in range and expectation. There *were* comic poetesses. There were even scatological ones, such as the 'Miss W —' who answered Swift's 'The Lady's Dressing Room' with 'The Gentleman's Study':

> Four different stinks lay there together,
> Which were sweat, turd, and piss, and leather.

But for a writer already thinking about turning her 'odd adventures' into a book, it was Fielding and Richardson and the complex mix of satire and sentiment which offered the most exciting model.

The *Memoirs* make obvious use of fictional devices and in no way more so than in their depiction of a female adventurer managing against all odds to maintain her virtue. Pamela's essential trait was her innocence. This was not a quality Mrs Pilkington even tried to claim, especially not after a year or two in London, but in describing the decision to move from Green Street to lodgings in a milliner's shop on Fleet Street, she invited her readers to imagine her going there with a Pamela-like innocence. Fleet Street was a station on that busy thoroughfare running from St James's to Ludgate Hill along which prostitutes plied their trade; and if a laundress's house in Green Street catered for discreet childbirth, milliners' shops were notoriously fronts for prostitution.

Perhaps Green Street and the conversation of sober clergymen like Dr Turnbull had become boring. Fleet Street was closer to Grub Street. It was where Curll had his office and garret of driven hacks, and it might have been at this time that Mrs Pilkington wrote for a printer who, she said, 'never examin'd the Merit of the Work, but us'd to measure it' and demand yards more of 'the same Stuff'. The lodgings had been recommended by someone she trusted. The landlady Mrs Smith, a 'likely Dame, of about Forty, very gay', at first sight attracted her. It was only after she had taken rooms that she discovered the house was indeed, in a small way, a brothel. Had she, as she claims, just not noticed anything amiss? Was she, in journalistic fashion, gathering material? Perhaps she had run out of money and was engaging a different clientele. There is a hint of this in the comment that the landlady – by now described as 'a mercenary Town Jilt' – saw in her 'something new to produce to her Customers'. Mrs Pilkington's task, apparently, was to raise the tone of the establishment. The dining room became her office, where she worked at a table covered over with papers, and where she was exhibited by the landlady to poetically minded young lawyers who were interested in paying for some well-bred talk. Thus, as fat Mrs Smith made merry with a sailor, and bowls of punch were downed, sea shanties sung (a 'dissonant and unharmonious Noise') and 'swinish' appetites fed in creaking beds, Mrs Pilkington sat with her 'ingenious' gentlemen. One entertained her by reciting 'several beautiful poetical Compositions of his own' – having politely given her two guineas beforehand for the privilege – and urged her departure from such shocking surroundings.

It was an adventure she relished and which offered freedom of a sort. Amid the bustle of Fleet Street and in the mayhem of the brothel, there was no pressure to be well behaved and nor did she need to strain her shining wit. With an 'amiable Guest' she sipped champagne and discussed history, poetry, 'every Muse-like Theme'. They ranked the glorious dead – 'Milton, Shakespeare, Spencer, and all the British Classics' – and encouraged each other in their dreams. When he left at one in the morning she paced about, her head full of Dryden and Milton, wondering how her life had come to this. And then she made fun of her own posturing and the clichés that sustained it:

In short, I was wrapped in a pleasing Fit of melancholy, and had I been in the Country, midst vernal Airs, and Blooms, should have attuned my rural Minstrelsy to some High Theme; but, alas! Ease and Retirement, those Friends to the Muse, ever were denied to me, being in a populous City pent amidst the busy Hum of Men, obliged to work for daily Bread, and often not obtaining even that poor pittance.

In its debunking comedy, the sketch of the Fleet Street lodgings drew on Fielding more than Richardson, stage farce rather than sentimental fiction. Like Fielding, Mrs Pilkington engaged the reader in a collusion of superiority, sharing a laugh at the contrast between soaring dreams and hapless reality. But low-life scenes were tricky for women. Male authors could picture the poet in his garret, or trawling the many venues where sex was sold, without discomfiting the reader. Artistically Mrs Pilkington was hampered by the conventions of the time. The account is tantalisingly brief; the experiences in the brothel were moralised away. Similarly, when she took a furnished apartment in a tailor's house in Drury Lane, pleased by the low rent of five shillings a week, it was, she claimed, because she had not registered the alarming address. She rapidly moved out. For her, 'of all Persons in the World', Drury Lane was no place to be known to reside: it might be convenient, it might be interesting, the house itself might be respectable, but it was not prudent. Prostitutes of every rank were everywhere in London – the town being so 'overstocked with harlots' was the problem addressed in *Satan's Harvest Home* in 1749 – but it was Drury Lane that hosted the 'corporation of whores', along with coiners, highwaymen, gamesters, pickpockets and thieves of every kind.

If prudence took Mrs Pilkington back to her old lodgings in St James's Street in the spring of 1741, John Monckton, Lord Galway MP, had something to do with it as well. An Englishman, member of White's and one of the Society of Dilettanti, Galway had been given an Irish peerage in 1727 and in 1734 was made a commissioner of the Irish revenue. He had met Dr Van Lewen in Dublin at that time, and admired him. Galway had developed a curiosity about the doctor's daughter, even sending out procuresses to find her. He thought he had succeeded – as she later discovered: Mrs Smith had gone to meet him, pretended to be Mrs Pilkington, and made herself 'so kind, that he could not resist her'. Laetitia learned about this after she returned to St James's, took the not-quite-so-genteel second floor of her former lodgings, and made her presence known by standing at her window. Colonel Duncombe, looking across the street from White's, and happening to be with Lord Galway, asked if he knew the 'little Irish Muse'. Galway, looking and seeing not a large fat lady but a short slight one and realising his mistake, came to visit. She was not surprised to hear his story: 'I told his Lordship, I had the Honour of having many Representatives, which had been of very great Disadvantage to my Character, inasmuch as they were pretty liberal of their Favours.'

Galway was amused by her 'comical Stuff' and for a while he became her most important support. He 'honoured' her with his 'Confidence and Instruction'. 'We bantered half the Nobility,' she wrote, 'either about their Love-Intrigues, or Parliamentary Affairs, all of which were well known to his Lordship.' It was not all banter. John ('Jack') Spencer, younger brother of the Duke of Marlborough, husband of Lord Carteret's daughter Georgiana and 'one of the richest and maddest libertines of the day', felt entitled to a share of Galway's good luck and tried to rape her. He chose a moment just before Galway came to call. Rescued from Spencer whose violence took her by surprise ('in vain for me to remonstrate that he had a fine young Lady of his own'), Laetitia nevertheless failed to convince Galway she was not 'twenty ungrateful Devils, and Jilts'. He dropped her.

Lord Middlesex, amused by Galway's anger and Spencer's vexation, took her up and employed her for practical jokes of his own involving fake letters and love poems. Middlesex was the leading patron of the Italian opera. He was handsome, dissipated and idle about more or less everything except opera, about which he was passionate. Opera was the most costly of the performance arts and though Middlesex was wealthy, his scheme of bringing all things Italian to England, including his mistress, the singer La Muscovita, needed to be underwritten by other wealthy gentlemen. To mount a season of operas, Middlesex raised subscriptions – just as people did for printing books. In spring 1741 he was raising subscribers for the 1741–42 season, asking for twenty-guinea deposits. Edward Walpole was among those who subscribed. Contract negotiations with highly paid singers and musicians exposed Middlesex's limitations and it ended badly. He sued his subscribers. Since it is estimated it cost something like £16,000 to put on a season of operas, and Middlesex finished up paying much of it out of his own fortune, we can guess at the sums of money Mrs Pilkington watched him spend.

As she well understood, all who were dependent on the favours of the great had to comply with their 'Whimsies', of which Middlesex had many. The sort of jokes these men enjoyed playing on each other can be seen in an episode recounted in the anonymous *Memoirs of the Bedford Coffee-House*, where a rake, who thinks he has succeeded in catching the eye of an attractive young lady living opposite, receives a letter, supposedly from her, making an assignation in Birdcage Walk. The letter has in fact been composed by one of his friends to punish him for boasting of his conquests but is written 'in a lady's hand'. The rake gets soaked in Birdcage Walk, receives another letter telling him she will meet him at Windsor and rushes off there; and then another letter says she has gone to Yorkshire. It is just as he is getting ready to set off for Yorkshire that his friend cheerfully confesses what he and the two women in the plot had done to trick him.

This was the sort of writing Middlesex wanted from Mrs Pilkington and with which she obliged him. He paid her but neither he nor other Dilettanti were specially generous. Their prominence gained her some éclat, and as one of their circle she enjoyed exercising such power as she had. When Robert Nugent, an Irish millionaire, made the mistake of applying to her, as if she was a procuress, to choose a whore for him to take into keeping, she got her revenge in a satisfying way. Nugent was hoping to be elected to White's. She disparaged him 'so effectually' that he was blackballed.

The usual visitors came and went. Cibber was present with Colonel Duncombe one day when Loftus Hume, an old Trinity College friend of her brother Meade, came by appointment to meet Duncombe. Hume talked of the old days. Laetitia was pleased that the older men heard him praise her father, especially when Hume recounted how Dr Van Lewen had willingly fed him after he had squandered his entire allowance on a grand party. Cibber, never one to miss the opportunity, pointed out to him that he could show his gratitude by supporting Dr Van Lewen's 'desolate' daughter, at least to the extent of a generous subscription, which was a kindness even strangers had shown her. Hume made his excuses and left.

∞

Summer brought its familiar difficulties – 'oh the dismal Summer (which ever was attended with Want, and all its gloomy Train . . .)'.

Laetitia knew by now that even people who seemed quite well circumstanced suffered when the wealthy folk disappeared to their country estates. Benjamin Victor closed the linen warehouse and took himself off to Tunbridge. Cibber was there in August 1742, 'the gay, blooming Colley', as Victor reported to a friend, 'just arrived from London! As unexpected, as welcome!' They spent a happy evening together, 'and the very next morning, who should kind fortune add to the party, but my worthy, valuable, revered friend Doctor Young!' Victor was ecstatic:

The gaiety of Tunbridge at full season is almost inexpressible! The whole day and night are employed in riding, praying, gaming, dressing, eating, drinking, music, balls and etc and etc and etc. Everyone complies with what is called the fashion. Cibber goes constantly to prayers – and the curate (to return the compliment) as constantly, when prayers are over, to the gaming table!

Such happy sociability required funds. For a woman it also required friends who would provide protection. Had she gone into keeping, Laetitia would no doubt have gone to Tunbridge and been as gay as Cibber and Victor and Edward Young. Solitary in London, she made an ill-fated decision. She moved to nearby Duke Street where her landlady, Mrs Thiffola, 'a most extraordinary painted up, bedizened-out old Woman', heartless and calculating, lived off her lodgers and preyed on the weak. Gradually, Laetitia – never a good judge of character, and still a poor manager – fell into the landlady's clutches, psychologically as well as economically. Somehow, between spring 1741 and autumn 1742, she went from high to low. Mrs Thiffola proved to be her nemesis.

The move to Duke Street may have been prompted, again, by disillusion with life as mascot to White's Club. Neither Cibber nor Duncombe had seen fit to support her in any regular fashion. Cibber could be generous with his time, advice, and other people's money, but he had no intention of providing her with anything more. Unsentimental, often disapproving – he felt she lacked common sense in her dealings with the world – he responded to the drama of her life as a spectacle, but he was a man who was prepared to see his own daughter, the actress Charlotte Charke, starve a few doors away without his help. To him Mrs Pilkington was a 'frolicksome Farce of Fortune'. When the wheel rolled her towards him he did what he could; if she was elsewhere he forgot about her, and besides, his own life in the early 1740s when he was being attacked by Fielding, befriended by Richardson, quarrelling once more with Pope, and serially emerging from retirement to play favourite roles and display his blooming health, absorbed his attention.

Mrs Pilkington might have wanted to live 'retired' again in order to work on a serious literary project. The tomfoolery of titled drunks and dimwits had taken the shine off White's. She had begun writing a blank-verse tragedy, *The Roman Father*, based on an episode in Roman history in which the heroine, Virginia, her honour threatened by the advances of a corrupt tyrant, is killed by her father, Virginius – a theme illustrative, perhaps, of her growing sense that to be female and virtuous and stay alive was a doomed enterprise.

Or she may have decided to distance herself from White's in the hope of presenting a different image of herself to the world and acquiring a different order of patronage. She had heard that one of the country's leading physicians, Dr Richard Mead, had been given £60,000 to distribute in charity. The £60,000 seems to have been mythical, but Mead was a generous benefactor as well as being a noted collector of books, paintings and curiosities. (He could afford it: his fees were reckoned to total £7,000 a year.) She wrote Dr Mead one of her best letters, 'a moving Tale of my Distress'. This had the desired effect and he sent her a note to say that he would call on her next day. She waited but he did not come. Devastated, and also angry, she put her feelings into verse. 'To Doctor Mead' described the ecstasy she had felt when she thought he was coming to visit her, partly because he might give her the money she desperately needed, but also because his response meant that her words had worked. His recognition, the meagre acknowledgement, had revived the poet in her:

> My Hope reviv'd, I wak'd the silent String,
> The Muse, once more, attun'd her Voice to sing,
> Pleas'd, that tho' long deprest by adverse Fate,

193

She yet found Favour with the Good, and Great,
And that her melancholy flowing Strain
To Gen'rous Mead, was not addrest in vain.

All she needed, she told him, was 'one assisting Friend'. She needed a patron whose support would be regular and adequate. She appealed as a poet, someone with whom the 'Good, and Great' had a natural affinity through their shared love of country and desire to enrich its culture. The essence of her problem had been her dependence on the 'whimsies' of those with money, and the endless cycle of application to individuals who, even if they gave a few guineas, never gave enough for permanent relief.

If she hoped Dr Mead would be that 'assisting Friend', she had mistaken her man. On receiving the poem, he invited her to his palatial house off Queen Square. (It stood where Great Ormond Street Children's Hospital is now.) She was thrilled. Letter and poem between them, she thought, had done the job. She was sure he would give her at least ten guineas. But though Mead listened to her story and did not doubt that she was a relation of the Meades in Ireland (of whom there were many), he was unimpressed by her hopes of making money by printing a volume of poetry. Pope might have managed to do so, but she was not Pope. He made her feel a fool, as if she really did think she could emulate Pope. It was a shaming interview and she went away with just two guineas.

Back at her lodgings, disappointed, defiant, Laetitia flung the coins into the air. One of them rolled away and disappeared down a crack in the floorboards. She was never able to retrieve it, and the plan she had formed for paying up and moving on, away from Mrs Thiffola, was abandoned.

Dr Mead had suggested she apply to another formidably wealthy philanthropist and supporter of the arts, his former neighbour Sir Hans Sloane, and gave her a letter of recommendation. An Ulsterman, Sir Hans had recently moved to his manor house at Chelsea, taking with him his valuable collection of books, objects and curiosities that were later to form the nucleus of the British Museum. It was winter when Mrs Pilkington decided to call on him, and Chelsea was a long way from Duke

Street. She walked there in a violent snowstorm, arriving wet to the skin. After waiting in the porter's lodge for two hours, she was escorted through half a dozen magnificent museum-like rooms to 'his Supreme Majesty', a little old man who barely deigned to look at her and wasted no time in courtesies. To him she was just another beggar. He gave her half a crown which she wanted to throw in his face, but she stopped herself. She had no money at all, and little as it was it would buy her a dinner. Cold, hungry, exhausted, she tramped back up to town, promising herself that one day she would get her revenge on the 'conceited, ridiculous, imperious old Fool'.

She pawned what was left of her valuables. Each day posed a challenge, first to find food and second to conceal her distress from her landlady. She would pretend she had been invited out to eat and spent hours walking alone. Westminster Abbey was a favourite place, its gloomy tombs inviting thoughts of death. Comforting herself after these humiliating interviews, she stood and chose the corner where her own memorial should be, between the monuments to Shakespeare and Nicholas Rowe.

She had been living by her wits and now she was at her wits' end. The idea of suicide, though it was a crime, began to haunt her. One soft moonlit night she sat by Rosamond's Pond in St James's Park, a pleasant tree-shaded spot where a number of despairing young women were known to have taken their lives, and resolved to throw herself in. But two well-dressed women, a mother and daughter couple, came and sat on the bench alongside her, their conversation full of the beauties of the scene, the gentle breeze, the fragrant limes in flower, so that it was impossible either to leap into the water or, when they insisted on including her in their remarks, remain taciturn. She soon responded freely. The women were well bred; she was lonely and talking was a comfort. Time passed. None of them noticed that they were locked in. This hardly mattered to the women, for their house backed on to the park which they accessed from their garden. Never suspecting just how 'foodless' she was, they invited her to step inside and have some supper with them.

It was an adventure which turned into an ordeal, only because going into the house she discovered there was a husband, who she guessed to be a wife-beater, who resented her presence and was barely civil. His rudeness reminded her of the way Matthew used to behave towards uninvited guests. A cold supper was laid ready. Liveried servants waited on them. She wanted to leave but she stayed three hours, in a kind of agony on her own and the young wife's behalf.

Another episode in the park suggests she might not always have refused men's custom, although it might also have happened exactly as she told it. Feeling exceptionally melancholy, wondering again why God had singled her out for such crushing affliction, she was startled by a tap on the shoulder. A 'very well dressed Gentleman' accosted her with the words, 'Lord, can this be Mrs Pilkington?' He was an army captain she had met years earlier in Cork. His astonishment at her appearance, his justified suspicion that she was staring at the pond with dreadful intent, upset her. He took her to the Royal Vineyard, a tavern on the south side of the park, where they ate cold chicken and ham, drank champagne, and she told him her 'unhappy' story. Later, he escorted her home and gave her two guineas.

She never saw him again. But Captain Hamilton's concern, his tears as she admitted her suicidal thoughts, and his practical help, were consoling. She felt that God had saved her. She was being tested, but not to the uttermost.

Testing to the uttermost, however, was about to begin. One rainy day in late September 1742, Mrs Thiffola came to her room and smilingly revealed that she knew Mrs Meade had put some valuable things into pawn. She offered to release them for her and keep them until Mrs Meade could pay the 'Trifle' she owed her. This seemed a kindness: Laetitia gave her a note to the pawnbroker and a guinea. Mrs Thiffola went off into the rain, gave three guineas to the pawnbroker and took the goods. Mrs Meade's note proved she owed Mrs Thiffola two guineas, but there was no proof that Mrs Thiffola had stolen her goods, which is what she had done. More seriously, Mrs Thiffola had also taken out a writ to have her arrested for debt.

Everybody lived on credit, yet small debts like these were

treated seriously and could have alarming consequences especially when malice was involved. Surprised at how long Mrs Thiffola stayed out (going through the process of getting the writ), Laetitia suspected nothing and assumed her landlady was sheltering from the rain. Stuck at home, she was lonely and depressed. Upstairs in the garret was an Irish woman even more impoverished than herself with whom she often passed the time and who, as far as she could, she supported. She, however, had gone into league with the landlady, so would not come down. When Mrs Thiffola returned, thirsty from her endeavours, Laetitia, desperate for company of any sort, treated her to a pot of porter. The denouement was not long in coming:

Early next Morning, to my no small Surprize, entered a Couple of ill-favoured Fellows, the Sight of whom struck Terror to my Soul; I demanded their Business, one of them answered, 'Get up, you Irish Papist Bitch, and come along with us.' The other, who had employed himself in looking over my Papers, cried, 'Ay, the Irish Whore, here is something about some Roman Father, that's the Pope, and be damn'd to you, is it?' I was for some Time quite speechless, but, when I recovered Strength enough to speak, I begged of them to leave the Room, till I put on my Cloaths, but my Landlady coming in at that Instant, cried, 'You're damn'd modest; – don't quit the Place'. The Fellows, who had more Decency than she, looked out at the Window while I dressed myself, in which Time my Agony was inconceivable. They called a Coach, and, thrusting me into it, conveyed me to the House of an Officer of Mace at Charing Cross; as I happened to have a Guinea in my pocket I called for a Room and a Pint of Wine, and then considered if I had one Friend I could apply to: My dear Mr Cibber was out of Town, as were likewise most of the Nobility; however, I saw young Mr Cibber go by the Window, and sent to him, but like all the World, when he heard my Condition, he would not come near me: My whole Debt was forty Shillings; Oh, what could I do, but give my Tears vent! which was my only Relief; and next Day, after paying twenty Shillings, I was conveyed to the Marshalsea Prison.

It was 1 October, and she was to stay in the Marshalsea until at least the middle of December.

∞

Life for the destitute inside Southwark's Marshalsea prison was dirty, noisy, drunken, dangerous and expensive. It was the custom for new arrivals to pay 'garnish' at once – a sort of entrance fee – if they didn't want the clothes torn off their backs or worse: this meant a round of drinks from the tap room charged to their account. Other expenses included access to a bed or chamber, which a 'chum' might sell, as well as everyday food and drink. Mrs Meade, obviously a gentlewoman, acquired a 'chum' immediately who rescued her from the mob (a 'Parcel of Wretches') who had at first thought she was claiming to be Dr Mead's wife, and took her to a filthy little room where she threw herself on a bed, remaining there, in a paralysis of misery, for three days.

Throughout the 1720s there had been complaints about unsanitary conditions and overcrowding in the Marshalsea. The latter problem had eased: in the autumn of 1742 there were probably about 130 prisoners (down from 330 in 1729); but it was a stinking, pestilential place, a potential death sentence given the rapidity with which fever spread. Epidemics had ravaged London in the previous two winters, and Laetitia's own bout of fever had been terrifying. She could not afford to collapse. She had to recover from the shock of incarceration, adjust to her surroundings, and apply to the business of release.

Her only resource was to write to everybody she knew. A batch of letters went out, among them one to Dr Mead. Mead, she had discovered, was well known among the inmates of the Marshalsea, less for his philanthropic activities than for his sexual proclivities. It was an ex-mistress of Mead's who had led the clamour against her on account of her name. Dr Mead was a hair fetishist who kept a seraglio of beautiful women who posed naked for him in a variety of 'attitudes', usually combing their hair. They were paid well for this, as was his cast-off mistress, a servant whom Mead had supported and who may have begun blackmailing him when he fell behind in his payments. Certainly she had abused him on the steps of his own house, in front of his servants, thus provoking Mead to arrange for her current lover, a confidence trickster named Dudley Bradstreet who was also her landlord, to put her in the Marshalsea for debt. Bradstreet got £300 and Mead paid the woman two guineas a week. By then she was an alcoholic. Laetitia's first sighting of her had been 'lying dead drunk in a Puddle'. This vision of the hopeless drunk, unjustly imprisoned because she had spoken what men preferred to keep secret, and kept there because men like Mead could buy whatever services they required, seared itself on her imagination. Like the pregnant young woman who had lodged and died at Green Street, the incarcerated ex-mistress symbolised the inequities of a system in which men were directly responsible for female distress. The woman lost everything, beginning with reputation; the man carried on and, in the case of Dr Mead, was revered for his charity.

Did she hint at her knowledge of this in her letter to Dr Mead? She might have done. On 16 October Mead replied to her letter asking for help with a curt note. Its stern severity raises the possibility that he intended her to understand he would not respond to blackmail. He wrote:

To Mrs Meade, in the Marshalsea.

Madam,
I have so many Applications for Charity, that it is impossible for me to relieve all; those from your Country alone are very numerous. The Family of the Meades there, are very rich, and should take Care of their needy Branches; I have, for the last Time, sent you a Guinea.
 I am,
                    Your humble Servant,
                    R.M.

The guinea was welcome. She saved the letter and published it in the *Memoirs* where she gave full vent to her loathing of the charitable Dr Mead, not failing to allude to his range of well-known 'good Works, such as combing the Ladies Heads, &c. &c'.

She wrote, of course, to Colley Cibber who, when he came back to town, sent her a guinea in sixpenny pieces to minimise the possibility of theft and maximise its usefulness. Pragmatic and flippant about her misfortune, he did not visit but he began gathering funds.

Half the time she was starving. In that dismal dank place she pined for want of air and cleanliness. She had nothing, no change of clothing, no books; and even getting hold of paper and ink to write the letters that might persuade her friends to act on her behalf was difficult. Unsurprisingly, she fell ill.

But her days were not all woe. The head turnkey happened to be an ex-servant of John Barber's, who remembered her and was kind. As a favour he let her listen to the trials that were heard inside the prison every Friday, an experience which did nothing to raise her opinion of lawyers and men's laws. Most prisoners were locked up at this time for fear they would escape when the great gates were flung open to let the attorneys' coaches in. Meanwhile, on Sundays, Dr Frend, a clergyman confined in the King's Bench, came and preached. The congregation was rowdy: 'mad and drunk, [they] bade him hold his Tongue', but she was charmed by his oratory and they often sat and talked. She put her own eloquence to good use in drawing up a petition for the release of confined debtors. Every few years, Parliament passed temporary Acts to release debtors, mostly as a response to overcrowding. Her petition was received on 13 January 1743. By then, she herself was free. Another desperate letter to Cibber had roused him to extra exertion. The actor had spoken for her with such passion and pathos he had touched the hearts of 'the Great': sixteen dukes each gave a guinea. Sixteen guineas bought her out. She needed all of it. After paying 'Debts, Extortions, and Dues' she had thirteen shillings left.

Leaving the prison, she was giddy and disorientated. She started walking towards London Bridge but feared she was going to faint. Hunger and confinement made her vulnerable; and perhaps in spite of everything Mrs Thiffola's house felt like home. She rested at a jeweller's shop and asked them to call a coach which she directed to take her to Duke Street. There was a practical reason for going back: her possessions were still there, especially her manuscripts: 'All my Writings, All, the little All! which might make my future Fortune'. And with nowhere else to sleep, no other friends she could apply to, she was grateful to be offered a share in Mrs Thiffola's bed. By morning her pocket had been picked, and when she protested she was turned out of doors.

Dirty, hopeless, she trudged round to Cibber's new house in Berkeley Street. He received her with his usual complacency, fed her and produced some money he had been keeping for her: five guineas from the Duke of Richmond. It was 'a Lottery Prize to one in my unhappy Situation'. She found lodgings in King Street, near Covent Garden, gathered up her possessions, and bought paper and pens and wrote to everybody she could think of. As usual, nothing came of her begging letters to Ireland: 'the best comfort I received, was to be informed, I deserved all that I could suffer here'; but the Duke of Marlborough sent her ten guineas and 'a very genteel Letter, with his best Wishes, and Compliments to me'. She was rich. And then there was more. A little later she received a message that she should call on 'Mr Richardson, a Printer, in Salisbury Court' off Fleet Street. At first she did not connect the name with *Pamela*, and nor, from her knowledge of printers in Ireland, did she expect to find a printer living in a grand house.

Richardson was acting for Dr Delany, whose books he printed. Delany was among those to whom Laetitia had written from prison a full account of her 'calamities', dreading that like her other Irish connections he would rebuff her, but also feeling an angry entitlement to his compassion: Delany more than anyone knew that she was 'a worthy Gentleman's Daughter', who had been 'nurtured in Ease, and Plenty'. On her father's account, if for no other, Delany, with his 'ample fortune', ought to relieve the daughter of his old friend. Perhaps, too, she had heard how in Dublin, at the premier of Handel's *Messiah* in April 1742 (an occasion organised by Matthew's patron Charles Cobbe) Delany had been moved to tears by Susannah Cibber's rendering of 'He was despised', that anguished solo in the second section. Susannah's sufferings as Theophilus Cibber's estranged wife, her frail dignity, the fact that Handel had written the air expressly for her, had all stirred Delany's Christian charity, and as her voice died away he had risen to his feet, opened his arms towards the stage as if to embrace her, and exclaimed, 'Woman, for this all thy sins be forgiven thee!'

Like Delany, Richardson believed in being tender hearted. When Mrs Pilkington presented herself at Salisbury Court, much less well got up than she wished (it had never occurred to her to make herself fine for a printer) she was warmly welcomed. She was given breakfast, introduced to Mrs Richardson and their four daughters, and invited to stay for dinner. After dinner, Richardson took her into his study. There she saw her own letter to Delany. Delany, on his arrival in England in April 1743 bent on marrying Mary Pendarves, had given the letter to Richardson, along with twelve guineas which he asked him to pass on. Richardson did so, and added two guineas of his own. There was one crushing condition: Delany insisted Laetitia was not to write to him again, nor try to contact him directly. He would hear of her only through Richardson.

Still, the turn in her fortunes was thrilling. Now she was able to put into practice a plan that had long been forming: she would use the money to open a little pamphlet-shop. She would turn her stock into trade. By mid-July she was applying to Richardson once more, not for money this time but for a reference. She had found 'a most compleat beautiful shop, in the Strand, exactly opposite to Buckingham-street'. It was available for rent if she could produce 'some person of credit to give me a character'. Flatteringly, she told Richardson that Cibber's name (poet laureate, the most famous actor-manager of the day) had not sufficed; the gentleman who owned the property 'had no opinion of him'.

Perhaps she took the shop in the Strand and built up some expertise and a little capital. Or perhaps, as the *Memoirs* would have it, she went straight to St James's to be 'in the Center of my noble Benefactors'. There were splendid shops up and down St James's Street. The 1749 electoral register lists two apothecaries, two perukiers, three grocers, three tailors, two booksellers and coffee-men, a silversmith and toy-man, three watch and clockmakers, several chandlers, a china-man, a linen-draper, a milliner and a pastry-cook.

A beautiful shop on the Strand, London's main commercial high street, might have been more sensible but St James's exerted its pull. The shop she rented came with a parlour and kitchen behind. It cost £21 per annum, payable quarterly in advance. She was nervous at how much money was needed to fit it out. Shop, parlour and kitchen provided reception areas, public and private, for general socialising, meaning she could economise on lodgings, taking a simple room to sleep in upstairs or nearby. It is unlikely that she slept in the shop, though possible – she kept her clothes there. At five guineas a quarter, it was a cheaper way to be in St James's than the guinea per week lodgings across the street from White's Club, even with the addition of a few shillings for a garret bedroom.

Someone offered her a job lot of prints which she decided she could also sell, 'having some Knowledge in that Way', and she spent a happy weekend arranging the prints to advantage in the window. She composed a poem, a paraphrase of an ode by Horace, in thanks to Cibber for his gift of 'Inestimable Liberty!' and sent it to him which, as she was within striking distance again, brought the 'dear Gentleman' himself. Blithe and cheerful, he gave her three guineas, remarking, 'Faith, Child, you have praised me so, that, I think, it is the least I can do to make you eat for a Fortnight.'

There was another gift pleasing to both: fifty free copies of Cibber's most recent pamphlet, *The Egotist, or, Colley Upon Cibber*. Into this witty dialogue Cibber had incorporated her first poem praising him – the lines written to prove to the men of White's that she, not her husband, wrote her verses.

The shop was her new domain. Remembering its beginnings several years later when she was writing volume two of her *Memoirs* and had become the celebrated writer she dreamed of being, Mrs Pilkington was a little self-conscious. But she put on a bold face, looked her audience straight in the eye and narrated the next instalment of her adventures: 'So, Reader, here was a new Scene, and I, for the first of my Family, took my Place behind a Counter.'

CHAPTER NINE

Poetical Businesswoman

Many women ran small businesses in the eighteenth century. Some ran large ones – Mary Scarth, for example, who had the monopoly on scavenging for the parish of St Giles and employed five men; or the two women in the armaments industry who for some years provided all the gunpowder to the Ordnance. But most women with access to the sort of capital needed for a big business preferred not to be in business at all. Mrs Pilkington joined the ranks of struggling small traders: self-employed milliners, dressmakers, haberdashers, pastrycooks, butchers (there were plenty of women butchers), nurses and laundrywomen with a little capital and equipment who by labouring hard might keep themselves a few notches up from the fruitsellers, milk women, mercury women, hawkers and criers who filled the streets.

She had no training and little of that patience which Daniel Defoe in *The Complete English Tradesman* identified as vital. When the foppish Lord Preston, taking up one of her carefully displayed prints – Shakespeare's monument in Westminster Abbey – offered fourpence for it, she showed her annoyance. The print had cost a shilling and she had priced it clearly at 1s. 6d. Lord Preston, 'dressed a la mode de Paris, with long sloped double Ruffles', left in a huff. Perhaps he had been being deliberately offensive, but this was not the way for her to proceed. Customers expected to haggle. Prices were not fixed but settled by argument, and as Defoe warned, there would always be 'impertinence': the complete tradesman behind his counter 'must have no flesh and blood about him; no passions; no resentments. He must never be angry'.

Then there was the question of credit. One reason for the widespread use of credit was the shortage of coin – as much a problem in England as in Ireland. A fat gold guinea was a genteel coin and there were plenty of them in circulation, but no new silver had been struck and the old coins were wearing thin. Counterfeit and clipped money as well as foreign coins were everywhere and had to be guarded against; meanwhile, the shopkeeper who could not give change either gave credit or turned away custom. The gentlemen Laetitia liked to deal with, her 'noble Benefactors', had never troubled her with requests for small change.

In the *Memoirs* she wrote about the pamphlet-shop as if it were less a business to be run than a new setting for pleasant visits and witty conversation. There were prints in the window and pamphlets on the counter, but she herself was the most important of the goods on display. We learn nothing about day-to-day matters of commerce: who supplied her, what she sold, what hours the shop was open (undoubtedly very long hours, like all shops). It is likely that she had ample time to read: on her first day she was reading a pamphlet of Cibber's – *The Egotist* perhaps, or his earlier *Letter to Mr Pope* which kept up the battle between the two men by asking why Pope seemed so fond of satirising him – when a clergyman came through the door and caught her laughing out loud. She was pleased with her own quick wit when she turned his curiosity about what had made her laugh into a repeatable *bon mot* about herself: the parson (an ex-neighbour of the Van Lewens in Dublin) asking what was new – 'What news?' was the standard question on entering a coffee-house or pamphlet-shop – was told, 'my present Situation'. She recommended the pamphlet with all the familiarity of acquaintance: Mr Cibber was her dear friend, Pope part of her mental furniture, and Dean Swift, to whom Pope dedicated *The Dunciad*, had taught her everything she knew. The clergyman was an ideal customer: he gave a guinea for the combination of pamphlet and conversation, promised to come again, and departed refusing change.

When not reading or entertaining visitors, Mrs Pilkington could write. She worked on her poems, and drafted some recollections of childhood at this time, along with an account of her marriage. She sent a version of what later became volume one of the *Memoirs* to the publisher Jacob Robinson in Ludgate Street who promptly sent it back. There was no market, in his view, for anecdotes about people nobody in London had ever heard of: 'For Madam, said he, what's one Doctor Vanlewen, or one Parson Pilkington to us?' His response suggests that the anecdotes about Swift that were to form so notable a part of the *Memoirs* were not then included.

Stationed at her counter, she was at the mercy of whoever chose to enter. Many Dublin gentry had houses in London and some-times old acquaintances sought her out. Lieutenant Southwell, nephew of Sir Thomas Southwell, 1st Baron Southwell and commissioner of the Irish revenue, was a naval officer related through family connections to the Percivals. He came into the shop one day with a younger friend, Viscount Doneraile. The lieutenant was pleased to see Mrs Pilkington again and was eager to talk, but the viscount's ill manners made that impossible. Doneraile had understood they were going to see someone young – 'a Girl of Sixteen' – to have fun with. He was disappointed and did not hide it: 'My Lord looked on me', Mrs Pilkington recalled, 'with the utmost Contempt, nay, with such an Air, as I had never before met with from any Gentleman.' They left, but as Southwell told her later, Doneraile went on abusing her the rest of that day. As it happened, she knew something of Doneraile from her Dublin days, and still more about his father, a drunk whose refusal to pay his estranged wife (Doneraile's stepmother) a £300 annuity that had been settled on her, had led to a well-publicised chancery case in the House of Lords that had dragged on from 1728 until 1733. The wife's defence for taking a lover was her husband's impotence – possibly a consequence of being, as he said in *his* defence, habitually drunk for days at a time. Doneraile junior had been among the young rakes pestering Laetitia after her separation in 1738. Worsdale, who knew him through the Dublin Hell-Fire club, regarded him as 'a very loose, and a very ungenerous Man'. She claimed she rejected Doneraile's advances then. Now this 'very fine' gentleman, on the hunt for willing young flesh in St James's and finding himself face to face with a worn woman in her mid-thirties, not long out of the Marshalsea, treated her with disdain. She was furious. A vicious anti-panegyric, 'To the Right Honourable the Lord Viscount Doneraile', was the result.

> Satyric Muse! Let me prevail
> On thee to picture Doneraile:
> Fierce, as the surly northern Gale,
> Is proud, contemptuous Doneraile;
> What makes the Artist rot in Jail?
> Trusting the base-born Doneraile;
> The Rose-cheek'd Nymph turns wan, and pale,
> Touch'd by infectious Doneraile;
> Light Gossamer would turn the Scale,
> Weigh'd 'gainst the Wit of Doneraile;
> Nay, were thy Virtues put to Sale,
> A Mite o'er-rates them, Doneraile:
> Honour and Equity shall fail,
> E'er practis'd once by Doneraile;
> For Hell may Charon hoist his Sail
> O'er Styx, to waft curst Doneraile:
> In short, my Subject now grows stale,
> I'm tir'd with Rhymes to Doneraile;
> So were each Fault and Vice combin'd,
> That e'er debas'd the human Mind;
> To sum up all, the black detail,
> I'd name the Scoundrel, Doneraile.

Southwell took the poem and made sure Doneraile read it. It was probably circulated among others too. Doneraile came to remonstrate, held her hand, and assured her he would be a friend if she would cease to write so bitterly against him. Of that there was no chance. The entire episode went into the *Memoirs*, along with a sardonically expressed hope that the young man would, according to his 'true Nobility' (which she had called into question) give her a handsome reward for her 'extraordinary Panegyric!'.

Ordinary panegyric was more profitable. When Henry Pelham became First Minister of the popular post-Walpole coalition government in 1743, Laetitia wrote some flattering lines of congratulation and had them delivered by Pelham's friend Cibber. Pelham sent ten guineas (half a year's rent) and the poem was published in the *Daily Gazetteer*. This newspaper, printed by Samuel Richardson, had on 25 May carried Mrs Pilkington's verses thanking Cibber for effecting her release from prison. Unsigned, and titled 'To Mr. C – BB – R', the poem was offered as a present 'to the Publick' from 'a Soul sincere'. Most of the public would be able to fill in the blanks in Cibber's name and many would have known of his support for 'the little Irish muse'. In forty lines of jaunty octosyllabic couplets, she portrayed her despair – conveying the misery of incarceration and real fear of death,

> Lost in a Prison's joyless Gloom,
> Chearless, and dreary as the Tomb

while at the same time deferring to Cibber's dislike of anything too wretched:

> Oh, let your Gaiety excuse,
> My serious melancholy Muse!
> This World appears a Dream to me,
> Afflictions teach Philosophy;
> And thus, alone, a Christian Heart,
> Its grateful Raptures can impart.

The apology summed up the relationship. Cibber's 'gaiety' was not to be intruded upon.

Sitting in the shop, her bread-and-butter work continued to be ghost-writing of various kinds, especially letters and petitions ('on any subject except the law') for which she charged twelve pence, cash down. All kinds of writing could be bought from Grub Street writers, some of whom were women. We know almost nothing about them, but there must have been others besides Mrs Pilkington writing poems, petitions and pretend billets-doux. Her confidence about what she could offer those less gifted by God, as well as the range of ghost-writing on offer, is displayed in a mock advertisement she drew up which her son believed she intended to publish. Mrs Pilkington projected an authorial persona every bit as superior as Pope's. Beginning with sermons and ending with 'anything in the poetical way', her pen for hire was a worthy instrument in service to those who humbly recognised their own dullness:

If any illiterate Divine, from Cambridge or Oxford, has a Mind to shew his Parts in a London Pulpit, let him repair to me, and he shall have a Sermon, not stolen from Barrow, Tillotson, or other eminent Preachers, as is frequently the Practice with those who have Sense enough to do it, but Fire-new from the Mint. If any Painter has a Mind to commence Bard without Wit, and join the Sister Arts, I also will assist him. If any Author wants a Copy of Commendatory Verses to prefix to his Work, or a flattering Dedication to a worthless Great Man; any poor Person a Memorial or Petition properly calculated to dissolve the Walls of Stone and Flint which environ the Hearts of rich Men, Prelates in particular; any Printseller, Lines to put under his humorous, comic or serious Representations; any Player an occasional prologue or Epilogue; any Beau a handsome Billetdoux from a fair Incognita; any old Maid, a Copy of Verses in her Praise; any Lady of high Dress and low Quality, such as are generally the Ladies of the Town, an amorous melting delicate Epistle; any Projector a Paragraph in Praise of his Scheme; any extravagant Prodigal, a Letter of Recantation to his Honoured Father; any Minister of State an Apology for his Conduct, which those Gentlemen frequently want; any Undertaker a Funeral Elegy; or any Stone-Cutter an Epitaph; or in short any Thing in the Poetical Way; shall be dispatched in the most private, easy, and genteel Manner by applying to me, and that at the most reasonable Rates.

Proud of her independence (gifts like the ten guineas from Pelham secured her freedom from 'Mr Curll's poetical garret') she worked hard, meeting the needs of illiterate prostitutes and ill-educated clergymen.

Still a collector of women's stories, when women came she was partisan. Sometimes she invited the customer into the parlour, sometimes acted on her behalf. A typical case was that of the sister of the valet to Admiral Anson. The admiral, having returned to England in June 1744 after capturing a Spanish treasure-ship, paraded his booty through London in a procession of thirty-two wagons. His valet, however, had not been paid for seven years, nor received any share of the prize money. The valet's sister had nothing at all and was starving. Laetitia wrote the petition and decided to deliver it to the admiral in person at his house in Hanover Square. It so happened that she had access at that time to some valuable jewels that she had agreed to sell for an Irish acquaintance, Henry Fisher, whose father had kept a shop in Castle Street, Dublin. Knowing 'how much Dress commands Respect' she went as a woman of quality: she wore diamond earrings, a diamond necklace, lace and other 'Appurtenance', and instead of walking she took a chair. The admiral came hurrying down to meet her. Unfortunately, the moment he realised she had come with a petition his eagerness disappeared. The navy was notoriously sluggish in paying wages. Admiral Anson was only too used to being petitioned by wives, widows, sisters, daughters, the wounded, the elderly, the infirm. He told her all the money was tied up by the Treasury, there wasn't a shilling he could call his own. Surprisingly, she believed him, or perhaps she was distracted by the pleasure of fine dress and feeling herself the admiral's social equal. She got a guinea for the woman. Whether her own investment of time and chair-money was repaid out of it goes unrecorded.

Begging was costly. An early piece of advice Cibber had given was to think carefully about the timing of petitions to wealthy men: going on a cold foggy morning before breakfast was asking for a grumpy response. Of course, any letter, no matter how well timed and eloquent, was likely to fail given the walls of stone and flint round rich men's hearts, a detail which made its initial cost a matter of some significance. In the *Memoirs* she exposed the true nature of the business, laying out the figures as if in a ledger:

	£.	s.	d.
For Pen, Ink, and Paper	0	0	1½
For a Person to find when his Lordship is at Home	0	1	0
To the Porter	0	10	6
To the Valet	1	1	0
To the Footman who brings the Answer	0	5	0
The amount of which is	1	17	7½

The materials cost almost nothing, but there were no end of palms to be greased along the way. The satire forced uncomfortable truths on the benevolent.

She tried other schemes. One day a well-dressed young Irishman came into the shop, ignorant of London ways but a talented artist, and full of energy and bravado. His name was Nathaniel Bermingham and he later had some success as a pastellist and specialist in cut paper – the art for which Mary Delany is now remembered. Bermingham had much to tell her –

he 'knew every great Family in Ireland, their servants at least' – and they talked for a long while. He produced a sample of his work and it became clear why he had sought her out. He showed her a miniature portrait of Swift, cut from vellum, which was so like the original it needed no caption. She was impressed. Between them they concocted a business plan. He had the skills, she had the contacts; but since they agreed his art would be thought 'more suited to a Woman than a Man', they decided that she should be the one to make the approach to potential customers, passing off the cut-paper portraits, landscapes and coats of arms as her own. In return, she would take a third of the profits. As a project it had potential: high-class, expensive art-works, personally directed at the leading nobility into whose houses Mrs Pilkington had learnt the means of access, even if it sometimes cost her £1 17s. 7½d. Bermingham, unfortunately, gave the game away. The Earl of Stair felt imposed upon by the deceit and Laetitia abandoned the partnership declaring the young artist a fool.

She was 'tolerably content' with her new situation. Her margins were tight but she managed to pay the rent and buy goods to sell. She was able to keep a servant again, a 'little faithful Irishwoman', a Catholic, who could mind the shop when she needed to deliver a petition or wanted to walk in the park or Westminster Abbey. Perhaps it was at this time that she went to be 'electrified'. Entertainments using frictional machines to produce electricity had been popular since the technique was developed in the 1660s. There was a glass globe which, put into motion, made sparks come out of her arm and 'set a Bowl of Sand under it a boiling'. Other excitements included regular trips to the theatre. She saw Garrick play Lear – in Nahum Tate's version with the happy ending which was the only way *Lear* was staged in the eighteenth century. This was a memorable evening. Garrick was the sensation of the early 1740s. He brought a new and naturalistic style of acting, appearing to express feelings of his own rather than performing a ritual set of gestures. When it came to the mad scene Laetitia was so affected she went off in a sort of trance, rising from her seat and 'insensibly' starting to leave the box. A friend – 'the Lady who accompanied me' – had to pull her back by the sleeve. (Garrick's Lear had this effect on people: Joshua Reynolds took three days to recover from seeing his final performance in 1776.)

It may have been at this time, too, that she had her portrait painted by the young Dublin-born miniaturist Nathaniel Hone. It was not the first time an artist had tried to capture her likeness but Hone's was the one she thought most successful. Perhaps she liked the mixed message the picture conveyed: Hone posed her with a silken head covering suggesting a nun-like veil while her gown has slipped off the shoulder on one side. She wears jewels, perhaps those belonging to Henry Fisher.

She made sure she stayed in touch with Samuel Richardson, who encouraged her to write to him. Richardson's interest was not purely philanthropic: like her, he was a collector of women's stories, maintaining a huge correspondence and pasting letters he received into letter books where he reworked them for his fiction. Mrs Pilkington's intimacies with aristocratic rakes and her ear for dialogue and her zestful descriptions of manners and *mores* in circles so removed from his own were useful to Richardson as he began writing *Clarissa* and creating his villain, the libertine Lovelace. He gave practical help by supplying her with paper – something that was easy enough for him to do as a printer.

The Irish arrived in their usual numbers. She had met Michael Clancy in Mallow. A physician who lost his sight in 1737, he was trying to survive much as she was on a mixture of poetry, playwriting and begging. In January 1738, Clancy's comedy *The Sharper* had premiered at Smock Alley just four nights after Mrs Pilkington's appearance in Worsdale's box to hear her 'flaming' prologue to *A Cure for a Scold*. (A few nights after that, at Clancy's benefit, there was a riot.) Swift had valued Clancy and given him money; Laetitia helped him in some way. Clancy turned up in London in spring 1744, hoping to have a play produced. That was unsuccessful, but he did manage to get a benefit night at Drury Lane when he acted Tiresias in Dryden's *Oedipus King of Thebes*. He had attached himself to Thomas Sheridan, Swift's godson, who that summer brought to London a cache of Swift manuscripts that had been among his father's papers and which he sold to Dodsley for £50. The connection served Clancy well: shortly afterwards, through Lord Chesterfield who had become Lord Lieutenant of Ireland, he was awarded an Irish pension of £40. Clancy and Sheridan were to be Laetitia's enemies after she returned to Dublin in 1747 and it is likely that her resentment of their good fortune, starkly contrasting with her own, played a part in hostilities.

Ireland was ever in her thoughts. Visitors bringing news and gossip could not tell her what she most needed to know: what was the fate of her children? A letter to her eldest son, William, elicited no reply but he did pass it on to Betty, then about twelve, who wrote a clumsy but affectionate letter back. Through Worsdale's agency, Betty had been apprenticed to a milliner. It was not to be long before she met the traditional fate of a milliner's girl, but that as yet was in the future. Worsdale had also taken charge of Jack who had been unceremoniously dumped by the Cork relations, finding a place for him with the operatic composer and conductor, Thomas Arne, who was working with Lampe. Worsdale had influence. Based in Dublin, he had been able to help Arne and his wife, the singer Cecilia Young, make a success of their Dublin summer season of concerts in 1742. The connection went back many years, to theatrical circles in London in the early 1730s when Arne had mounted a show with Henry Carey; and it spread wider: Thomas Arne was the brother of Susannah Cibber, Colley Cibber's daughter-in-law. Worsdale fell out with Arne after he abandoned Cecilia, and felt strongly enough about it to register in his will that Arne was 'unworthy of any Man's friendship'.

Laetitia had heard that Worsdale had arranged for Jack to live and study with Arne and she was pleased: her youngest son had prospects. Like his father, Jack was musical. He featured as a boy soprano at Dublin's Aungier Street playhouse in May and June 1743, making his debut at the age of thirteen as a page in *Rosamond*, and in the title role of Arne's burlesque musical, *Tom Thumb*. His formal apprenticeship, seemingly paid for by Worsdale, followed. Unfortunately, Arne's treatment of his apprentices was harsh, and driven by envious suspicion. Charles Burney, who also began his career as an apprentice of Thomas

Arne, left a stinging account of how his master begrudged him any instruction, and hated letting him know anything of the mysteries of the musical craft. Mean and cold, Arne mirrored Matthew Pilkington in his handling of Jack. This may have made it easier for the boy to adjust to life in the Arne household but it cannot have made it comfortable. Later that summer Jack's voice attracted the wealthy music-loving Charles O'Neill of Shane's Castle so much that he scooped him up and took him for his own. O'Neill's interest might have been sexual; at any rate, he rejected the boy when his voice broke. (Another flashpoint might have been Jack's designs on O'Neill's twenty-year-old sister-in-law, Jane Brodrick.) Having travelled the length and breadth of Ireland with O'Neill, the petted singer in a gentleman's retinue, Jack crawled back to the Arnes, an angry, troubled and troublesome teenager.

There was not much harmony among the Arnes that autumn. Thomas Arne was notorious for his infidelities and abuse of his wife and she comforted herself with gin and the tenor Tommy Lowe. Jealous of Tommy and at war with Mrs Arne, Jack stole some music books from a box in the attic, pawned them, and managed to provoke a major domestic tumult. Amid accusations and counter-accusations, Mrs Arne struck Mr Arne, Tommy Lowe called for a horsewhip, and they all beat Jack. Jack ran away again.

This time he stayed in Dublin, getting some sort of assistance from his brother William, though none from his father, who apparently told Thomas Arne to go ahead and prosecute the boy for theft (a hanging crime). Matthew's rejection of Jack encompassed his good fortune as well as his bad: when Jack, brashly confident and beautifully dressed, had passed through Dublin and stepped down from O'Neill's carriage to display himself at Lazer's Hill, Matthew refused to come out. Jack knew he was there; he saw him disappearing up the stairs when William opened the door. For Jack, the contrast between William's life and his own was always painful, even when O'Neill was promising him the earth and he was waited on by servants 'in silver-laced liveries'. William, the only one of the children that Matthew acknowledged, went on to become a prize-winning student at Trinity College, Dublin, and then a respectably obscure clergyman in the Church of Ireland.

Curly-haired Jack, the image of his father, reckless and ill-treated, followed the path of misfortune his mother trod. He called himself 'Jack Luckless' after the character in Fielding's *The Author's Farce* and it is hard not to agree.

In late summer 1744 Thomas Arne was in London. Laetitia called on him expecting to find Jack with him. Instead, she was told about the purloined music books and about Matthew's 'Inhumanity' towards his own son which, apparently, had 'quite shocked' the composer. Jack, of whose musical abilities Arne spoke highly, had made his way to Scotland. Arne had a letter, giving an address in Edinburgh. Thoroughly agitated, Laetitia wrote to Jack at once telling him to come to her in London. She would try through Colley Cibber to get him work at one of the theatres.

Jack had been led to believe his mother was dead. He was thrilled to receive the letter. Seeing her handwriting and reading her 'beloved' name which he had 'kissed a thousand times' was like finding long lost treasure. On 16 September he sat down and wrote a long, lurid, partial account of his sufferings. He complained bitterly about his father's severity towards him, especially when he once broke a window in an ale-house. Matthew had withdrawn him from school, beat him morning and night for six days, took away his clothes, locked him in the dark back kitchen which, Jack reminded his mother, 'was in the Winter overflowed with Water', and ordered the servants not to feed him. (The servants disobeyed.) Then there was all the trouble with the Arnes, none of which had anything to do with him or Mr Arne, 'who is really a good-natured Man', but was all the fault of Mrs Arne's drunkenness and Tommy Lowe's trouble-making – 'a worthless conceited Fellow'. Jack had run away because they were going to put him in prison. They claimed he had stolen candlesticks and jewels. He denied it all. The real problem, he explained, was that he had witnessed Mrs Arne and Tommy Lowe 'toying on the Bed together'.

This letter from Jack, whom she had last seen when he was eight, prostrated Laetitia for several days. It threw her into what she called 'An Hysteric Cholic', a profound digestive upset that foreshadowed the disorder she later died from. She was to learn more, much more, none of it comfortable, of what her youngest child, exposed 'to every Calamity', had experienced in his short life. For the moment she watched and waited, hoping he would shortly turn up. It was not to be. Fourteen-year-old Jack stayed in Scotland. He had arrived there with some money, probably a gift from Jane Brodrick, and a portmanteau full of the gentleman's clothing with which that family had kitted him out. Equipped with the airs and graces of a youth used to fine company (he 'affected the man as much as possible in every serious respect') along with street-urchin cunning, Jack had learned how to gab his way. During his last months in Dublin he had sponged off a Trinity friend of William's, sharing his bed and board, taking the opportunity to catch up on some reading, and haunting tavern and playhouse like any other student. A chancer and a charmer, women young and old warmed to little Jack. If it is true that in Scotland most of his money and clothes went up in smoke in an inn fire from which he barely escaped with his life, perhaps it is also true that the inn-keeper's daughter, having taken a fancy to him, handed over her life's savings in consolation.

Had Jack made his way to London in the autumn of 1744, his mother would have been hard pressed to get him any theatre work. At Drury Lane the manager, Charles Fleetwood, was confined to his house for fear of arrest, as were many of the players, all of whose wages were in arrears. When Fleetwood, hoping to stave off bankruptcy, put up the price of seats there were riots. The interior of the theatre was wrecked. Fleetwood decamped to France, though not before persuading his friend, poet Paul Whitehead, to co-sign a promissory note for £3,000. Whitehead ended up in jail.

Business generally was depressed in the mid-1740s, partly owing to the expensive and unpopular War of Austrian Succession, and partly because of fears of invasion. Ever since James fled England in 1688 and settled in Catholic France, there had been periodic scares. French ships were chased away from the coast of Fife in 1708, in 1715 there was a major Jacobite rising and in 1719 another. Walpole's regime with its network of spies and informers had kept a tight grip throughout the 1720s and 1730s. But early in 1744 the French brought James's son Charles Edward Stuart, the 'Young

Pretender', to France from Italy to front an invasion and return the Stuarts to the throne. Though nothing happened until the following summer when Charles landed in Scotland, it was an edgy time.

∞

For Laetitia, the winter of 1744–5 ushered in a period of remorseless difficulty. Through Stephen Hales, the kindly curate of Teddington, she had gained an introduction to Thomas Herring, archbishop of York, who joined with Hales in recommending her as a candidate for the Royal Bounty. Herring was a youthful-looking fifty, and when Laetitia called on him at his house in Kensington Square and was shown straight in, she did not at first realise that the charming gentleman who received her was in fact the archbishop, 'having join'd the associate Idea of Wrinkles, Avarice, and Pride, to that Title':

his Grace asked me, who I was? I answered, which was Truth, I was a Gentleman's Daughter, of the Kingdom of Ireland; that I had, when I was very young, been married to a Clergyman, that I had three Children living. His Grace, taking it for granted, that I was a Widow, which Mistake it was, by no Means, my Interest to clear up, demanded of me, what I had to support us? I answered, Nothing but Poetry. He said, that was a Pity, because, let it be ever so excellent, Genius was seldom rewarded, or encouraged.

He ordered tea and they chatted 'familiarly' in the handsome drawing room. Thinking him a friendly chaplain she prattled on, omitting the usual ceremonies, and it wasn't until the archbishop's sister entered that she realised her mistake. Herring graciously said he wished it had continued longer; he had enjoyed hearing her 'unawed and uncontrouled'. She probably didn't entertain him with stories about Swift: in 1728 Herring had preached at Lincoln's Inn against *The Beggar's Opera*, famously drawing upon himself Swift's condemnation. Herring's view of Pope's *Dunciad* would have pleased her on Cibber's account: he decried it as a 'peevish effort of wit and inhumanity'. The archbishop took a lively interest in literature, maintaining a correspondence with Richardson's friend, William Duncombe, that was later published.

Applied for annually at around Christmas-time and distributed

at Easter, the Royal Bounty was a fund meant to relieve meritorious distress. No accounts were ever kept of it and it is unlikely
that large sums were involved, but to be a recipient was a mark of
honour. In December 1744, with Hales and Herring as her
sponsors, Laetitia made an application to the Lord High Almoner,
Thomas Sherlock, bishop of Salisbury and Master of the Temple.
Along with her letter, written 'in the most humble and pathetic
terms I was mistress of, or his pride could desire', she presented
him with 'a very curious piece of work' – possibly one of Nathaniel
Bermingham's cut-vellum designs. A scholarly man who in 1756
was to give £600 to renovate the library at his old Cambridge
college, St Catherine's, and who bequeathed all his books and land
to them, Sherlock was a Tory who ran with the Whigs, had been
Sir Robert Walpole's tutor, and had been singled out for satiric
attack by Paul Whitehead in 'Manners'. It was Sherlock who led the
House of Lords in its arrest of Dodsley and attempted arrest of
Whitehead. Identified as she had been with the Opposition
(Laetitia's 1739 pamphlets had not named Sherlock but they had
been contemptuous of Walpole's bishops) it is not surprising that
Sherlock gave her a dusty answer when she tramped round to the
Temple, in the snow, to follow up her application with a personal
appearance. Sherlock, according to her account, left her freezing
on the doorstep, tore her letter to pieces and told her she was a
'foreigner', that there were enough English beggars already and
that he would never do anything for her.

By March 1745 she was at a very low ebb. Anxiety and mal-
nutrition brought on insomnia: Richardson sent some paper and
she did not even open the packet at first, her eyes were so sore
from lack of sleep. In any case, she needed money more than
paper. In May she wrote despondently to tell him that she had to
let her servant go:

The very good woman who bears this to you, I am by the severity of
fortune obliged to part with, as it would be a cruelty in me to detain her,
when I see no prospect either of being able to pay her what is justly due
to her, nor am I even capable of giving her a subsistence. Where *I* shall
find any, I commit to that power who doth the raven feed; yea,
providentially caters for the sparrow.

She had 'resolution' to bear her own misfortunes, but 'I cannot bear another should suffer with me, and for me'. To part with a capable and trustworthy servant, especially one who had been an affectionate companion, cannot have been easy though it happened regularly enough. Richardson was asked to provide a reference for the woman; and presumably took the hint to send something to her starving mistress who dolefully signed herself 'Tristitia'.

Later that month, Cibber returned from a round of visits to titled friends 'in pure health and admirable spirits' and she spent four hours with him plotting, among other things, how to get more out of Richardson – he had become her most reliable support. The quickest way to Richardson's heart (and pocket) was through an interest, real or feigned, in his fictions. In June Laetitia wrote a letter telling him that both she and Cibber were distraught about the proposed ending to *Clarissa* – Clarissa was to be raped and ruined and then die a saintly death. Richardson's 'truly religious and moral' reasons for foisting this fate on his creation had been explained to the tearful old actor by Mrs Pilkington. In an affecting scene, rendered through direct speech, she pictured for Richardson their consternation: Mrs Pilkington wounded by 'the thought of the lady's person being contaminated'; and Cibber raving. She wrote:

'What! (said he) shall I, who have loved and revered the virtuous, the beautiful Clarissa, from the same motives I loved Mr Richardson, bear to stand a patient spectator of her ruin, her final destruction? No! – my heart suffers as strongly for her as if word was brought me that his house was on fire, and himself, his wife, and little ones likely to perish in the flame. I cannot bear it!'

The glaring fact that daily life, for both of them, was customarily passed as much among the contaminated as the pure was acknowledged in a final ringing appeal to the author: 'Spare her virgin purity, dear Sir, spare it! Consider, if this wounds both Mr Cibber and me (who neither of us set up for immaculate chastity) what must it do with those who possess that inestimable treasure?'

It was probably at Cibber's urging that she wrote the poem,

'Verses to a very Singular Gentleman', which figured Richardson as an earthly divinity. Along with effusive flattery there are hints in this poem of self-blame, as when the poet asks the 'singular gentleman':

> Why are th'afflicted still thy constant care?
> E'en tho' they merit all the woes they bear.

Did she think she merited her woes? Or was self-blame part of the persona she adopted for Richardson? There was evidently talk, which she feared had reached his ears. 'I dare say', she wrote to him, 'you would meet with more censure, than applause, for bestowing any favour on one who so little merits it, according to the general opinion.' It is hard to know how far the content and tone of Laetitia's letters to Richardson reflected real woes and how far she performed the needy woman, but it had been a hard winter and she had no reserves. The pressure of poverty had worn her down. She had 'fallen on evil days, and evil tongues'. Angry at God who seemed to have abandoned her, angry at herself, angry at tale-bearers, angry at those who had plenty and refused to give, or gave ungraciously –

> For, O believe me! 'Tis a dreadful task
> To gen'rous minds to be compell'd to ask;
> More dreadful still to have their suit deny'd,
> Or take a wretched alms, giv'n with contemptuous pride –

she was surely also angry at Richardson whose 'heav'n illumined breast' was plump and comfortably clothed, whose table was laden, whose house was warm, whose daughters and wife fussed about him, and whose books were read and praised by everybody.

The first catastrophe was a robbery. She was sitting upstairs with the Countess of Yarmouth's steward's wife one Sunday evening, when the shop was broken into and all her clothes were stolen. It is possible that she had been using her clothes as capital: putting them into pawn whenever she needed ready cash. In any case, the cost of replacing them so that she could appear decently was ruinous. She had no money left over for the rent. The landlord, an obliging and friendly man so long as he was paid on time, seized her stock in lieu, and she left St James's Street for good.

She took lodgings in Westminster somewhere off the Strand near Covent Garden and wrote despondently to Richardson. Then, or on another occasion, the maid whose friendship she valued and whose services she had managed to keep, perhaps with Richardson's help, ran off with all her linen, including sheets, 'everything she could make money of'. Stripped of business and possessions, failing to make any of her projects prosper, socially isolated – 'The greatest unhappiness of desolate poverty to me, is', she told Richardson, 'that I am as it were cut off from human society' – she fell into depression. She couldn't go out because she couldn't maintain the appearance of a gentlewoman, and her lodgings were unsuitable for receiving guests. She had thought she knew about being poor, but this was a further refinement and it took away her confidence in the future. Asking Richardson if he could lend her a copy of Edward Young's gloomy *Night Thoughts*, 'it being a long time since I have been able to purchase a book', she gave a mournful picture of herself: 'a stranger to happiness', 'a poor lost one', convinced that whatever she really wanted she was 'sure to be deprived of'. She felt let down by everybody and thoroughly fed up with herself.

By August she had decided to go back to Ireland. A forlorn and apologetic note to Richardson – 'I think, Sir, I am born to be a troublesome beggar to you' – made what she assured him would be her last request: some gilt paper, some pens and a stick of sealing-wax 'in order to write circular letters to the nobility' to raise enough for the journey.

In Pall Mall, Benjamin Victor was making similar plans and with more success. He had been cultivating Matthew Dubourg, master of state music in Ireland since 1728 who, in London working with Thomas Arne, had been given a position by Frederick, Prince of Wales, to teach him and his brother William the finer points of musicianship. Victor was hoping Dubourg would help him to a place in the prince's household. In the end it was Cibber whose contacts were effective. Once Lord Chesterfield was made Lord Lieutenant, Victor was able to pack up the linen business, settle in Dublin and realise his dream of running a theatre by joining Thomas Sheridan at Smock Alley.

(Victor's other dream, to be made Irish poet laureate, was realised in 1755.) The contrast between what men were able to do for each other and what could be done for a woman like herself fed Laetitia's bitterness.

She remained in London. That summer war fever filled the air. In May 1745 British troops were defeated by the French at the disastrous battle of Fontenoy. (Military historians blame the Duke of Cumberland's inexperience and give General Ligonier credit for the fact that things were not even worse.) In the north, a few Scottish clans joined forces with the Young Pretender and his small band of French and Irish adventurers and began marching southward. In September they defeated government forces at Prestonpans. The news reached London on 28 September and at Drury Lane Thomas Arne's new anthem, 'God Save our Noble King', was sung for the first time. Arne, whose mother was a Catholic, relished the fact that the tune was one he remembered from Mass at the Catholic Embassy chapels that he'd been taken to when he was a boy: the original words had been 'God Save Great James, our King'. Arne liked the irony of this. Nor, as a composer, was he sorry to be able to double his target audience: exile Stuarts always sang it with vigour. Volunteer associations sprang up across the country. Archbishop Herring gave a rousing speech at York and was lauded as the hero of the hour. Prints showed him leading armed clergymen shouting 'King George and the Church of England for ever'. He was, as Laetitia put it, 'a true Son of the Church Militant', having 'nobly taken up Arms in defence of Liberty, Property and the Protestant Religion'. She praised him in a poem which linked him with another of her benefactors, Henry Pelham.

Throughout the autumn, the Young Pretender and his army marched towards London, meeting no resistance but hardly being welcomed either. On 4 December they took Derby, a mere 130 miles from the capital. London was on high alert. Meanwhile, Louis XV had decided to invade across the Channel, but contrary winds and the naval skills of Admiral Vernon caused the French ships to turn back. The Young Pretender's march south had been designed to test the temperature of the nation: was there support for a restoration of the Stuarts? Clearly there was not. Ligonier's regiments were among those recalled from the Continent and sent to the Midlands. The Jacobite army made a brilliant retreat, trudging back north in snow and icy winds to meet their mournful destiny a few months later, in April 1746, when they were slaughtered at Culloden. By then Mrs Pilkington who, like every other Londoner, had at first kept a sharp eye on events, was embroiled in calamities closer to home.

One cold evening in December 1745, she returned to her lodgings off Fleet Street to be told by the landlady that a young woman had called who had 'wept sadly' to learn that she was out. Laetitia recalled asking 'what sort of a Person she was?' and the landlady's reply: that she 'greatly resembled' her. The young woman was her daughter Betty and Betty was eight months pregnant.

In the *Memoirs* Mrs Pilkington passed lightly over Betty's arrival and did not mention the pregnancy nor its catastrophic impact. We know about it from her frantic letters to Richardson, begging his help and making plain that her protective instincts were immediately aroused.

A pregnant unmarried daughter was a source of shame. Respectable families habitually cast such daughters off; little social opprobrium attached to parents who refused further contact. Laetitia, frankly acknowledging that she had 'less authority to blame her than perhaps another mother', took Betty in. The landlady, however, had other ideas. Under the terms of the Poor Law, parishes – meaning rate-payers – were responsible for pauper children born within parish limits. Nobody wanted new paupers. 'My daughter is come to me big with child, naked and desolate', Laetitia told Richardson, 'and because I would not let her lye in the street, my saint-like methodist landlady has padlocked the door, and turned us both there.'

They were evicted. In a grotesque parody of the Christian Christmas story, they tramped the neighbourhood looking for shelter. Without money, or a convincing appearance of money, there was little chance of a decent lodging. By the end of the day they had no option but to take a place in a night-house. Here, for a penny a night, the homeless might have a wooden bed in a stinking dormitory, or no bed and just a crowded room to sit up in, sharing the hours of darkness with drunks and street walkers, the diseased and the insane. It was squalid and frightening.

Betty's condition made it a matter of urgency to find proper accommodation. The prospect of Betty giving birth on foul straw and urine-soaked sacks, in the stink of vomit and faeces, with no linen even to wrap the baby in, was terrifying, not only because of the obvious risk to health but because if the baby died 'the malicious world' might accuse them of infanticide. Mrs Pilkington knew something about the malice of the world by this time. She appealed to Richardson: could he get Betty into one of the charity hospitals? Could he provide her with linens? Richardson sent a boy with money and clothing.

Nine days later they were still in 'the same calamitous night-house' where 'riot and misrule' reigned ('I am surprised that I yet retain my senses'), still sleeping on the floor, still alarmed by every twinge of Betty's belly. Christmas had been and gone, a season of peace and goodwill towards men that had been 'disastrous' for them. And then there was a further threat. The letter thanking Richardson for his 'bounty' told him about an official visit:

I have been terrified with parish-officers demanding security that I shall not be troublesome to them in case of the mortality, either of my daughter, or her child. This, though the girl appears quite hale, is out of my power to answer, and they barbarously threaten to pass her from parish to parish, back to Dublin; if so, she must be lost . . . Here I am at a plunge, and know not what to say to those who are in the insolence of office, and empowered by law to distress the distressed.

It took a month to raise the money that rescued them from the lower depths. Once again the deliverer was Colley Cibber, and as usual the money was not his but coaxed from his friends. Henry Pelham sent five guineas. Henry Furnese, a wealthy merchant, added one. With this she was able to rent a garret in Castle Street, in the house of a turner named Smith – 'a sober reputable house' near the St Martin's parish workhouse on what is now the Charing Cross Road. Redeeming her furniture from the pawnshop, she

only took what was 'absolutely necessary': a bed, no doubt, a chair
and a table perhaps. After what they had been through, to have
their own room, however basic, and some provision for Betty's
lying in, felt like a miracle – as indeed did the fact that Betty had
not yet been brought to bed.

Betty's baby, a boy, was safely born in early February. Swaddled
in the linens that had once wrapped the tenderly raised Richardson
girls, he was not the only new arrival. The garret in Castle Street
was getting crowded. Soon after she became a grandmother, Mrs
Pilkington's 'long-lost' son Jack unexpectedly appeared, ragged,
weather-beaten and absolutely destitute after months at sea on a
privateer. Hers was, indeed, 'an increasing family'. She had prayed
to God to re-unite them and God had in some measure granted her
wishes. How to look after them all, however, was no small puzzle.
She sent Jack, in his rags, round to Richardson in Salisbury Court
with a letter announcing the baby's arrival and reminding her
benefactor that he was, in her view, the nearest thing to divinity
that humanity could boast – unlike her ex-husband, of whose
'inhumanity' to his children she had heard a great deal in recent
weeks from Jack and Betty. In the postscript her joy and pride in
Jack vied with rage at Matthew. 'Tell me what sort of a heart the
father of this lad has, who could use him so cruelly?'

Richardson gave Jack the money to buy a suit of clothes; he also
passed on five guineas from Patrick Delany who on 2 March had
told Richardson he had received a letter from Mrs Pilkington
'complaining of grievous distress'. With Cibber's help, Jack was
able to get a place of some sort at Drury Lane, possibly as a stage-
door keeper; and he was a particularly well-dressed one, having
made sure the tailor gave the most fashionable finish to his suit,
with frogging a la mode and buttonholes just so. The coxcomb in
Jack, as even his mother admitted, was never far below the surface,
a delight in himself that sometimes amounted to arrogance and
generally kept him in high spirits. For Laetitia, his presence was
invigorating. When Richardson learnt that Jack had been parading
about in the latest fashion he felt he'd been duped. But young men
in Jack's position had to cut a dash. When Sam Foote, a comic Jack
was soon to meet, first arrived in London he made sure his

presence was noted. On his first appearance at the Bedford Tavern he went:

dressed out in a frock suit of green and silver lace, bag-wig, sword, bouquet, and point ruffles, and immediately joined the critical circle of the upper end of the room. Nobody knew him. He, however, soon boldly entered into conversation, and by the brilliancy of his wit, the justness of his remarks, and the unembarrassed freedom of his manners, attracted the general notice.

This is what Jack aimed for – including the perfect exit: a carriage pulled up at the door of the tavern, Foote's name was called, and off he went to an elegant assembly.

We hear of no fancy new dresses for Betty. But the father of her child had not entirely abandoned her and he arranged for an aunt of his who lived in London to take charge of the baby and put him out to nurse. With the baby 'disposed of', Betty could go into service. Her mother's connections opened up numerous possibilities. Something had to be done, for by the beginning of April they were starving, all the money spent. They had moved lodgings from Castle Street (the Smiths had let the house) to Great White-lion Street, an even less salubrious area, where Laetitia took a room for £3 a year, paid quarterly in advance. The move had involved some expense and in a new neighbourhood it was difficult to get credit; but eleven guineas – the amount of money we know she had from about the middle of January – was a substantial sum to run through at a time when by her own admission she could, if necessary, manage to get by on a shilling a day. She said she took Jack into company – showing him off and pushing him on – which would have been costly, especially given her impulse to indulge him, although the idea that Jack needed his mother to escort him anywhere seems implausible. It is more likely she handed him money which carried him into places she would never venture.

Richardson was informed that neither she nor Betty had tasted bread for three days – no mention of Jack – but that she was now in a position to resume writing letters and petitions and would publish an advertisement to that effect (meaning: if Richardson would send her paper and some cash). The letter conveyed modest merit struggling against distress. The advertisement appeared: 'At the sign of the Dove, in Great White-lion-street, near the Seven Dials, letters are written on any subject (except the law) by Laetitia Pilkington, price one Shilling. Also, petitions drawn at the same price.' Another idea supported by Richardson, to make and sell decorated paper hats, quickly foundered.

All Mrs Pilkington's letters to Samuel Richardson were designed to press the sympathetic nerve. The originals are lost and the form in which the letters survive, printed in the volumes of Richardson's correspondence edited in 1804 by the blue-stocking Anna Barbauld, make them a problematic source. Mrs Barbauld cut, pasted and possibly embellished to show Richardson in the best light. Richardson was, without doubt, kind-hearted and generous towards a woman whose circumstances in 1745 and 1746 were such as to make her despair: all her schemes had proved 'abortive', her health was causing her concern, and she felt 'as much cut off from society as the dead'. But she was not merely a tiresome Irish beggar and nor was she as friendless as she made herself sound. The episodes of desperation were interspersed with passages of manageable everyday life. Furthermore, Mrs Pilkington was a poet whom others took seriously, who never ceased working on the manuscripts she hoped to publish and for which she gathered subscriptions. One of her concerns when she and Betty were thrown out by the Methodist landlady was for her papers, which the landlady had seized. They were her most important possession. Richardson helped other poets into print but there is no indication that he ever considered giving Mrs Pilkington the most effective kind of help he could give by offering to print a book for her. Perhaps she didn't ask, though that seems unlikely.

Betty went off to her post as a lady's maid. Jack immersed himself in the backstage world of players and prompters, taverns and gamblers, ever on the watch for opportunity. When an old friend turned up, his 'playfellow from his childish days' – a rich young man who was apparently the son of Laetitia's most intimate friend in Ireland but whose identity cannot now be established – Jack attached himself to him and together they planned a Grand Tour. That fell through, though probably not before Jack had used up more of his mother's money than she could spare.

CHAPTER TEN

Looking After Jack

She was crossing Spring Gardens alongside Whitehall early one morning in the summer of 1746 when Laetitia saw a familiar figure. Standing in the open back door of one of the coffee-houses, perhaps Forrest's, or the Green Man which had recently advertised the convenience of its back door as a special feature (for a quick escape into the safety of the gardens – debtors could not be arrested in or about the royal palace and courts of Whitehall), was James Worsdale.

Worsdale had returned to England. The Deputy Master of the Revels had left Dublin for good. Edward Walpole, MP for Great Yarmouth, had at last come up with something and acquired a position for 'Jemmy' as Master Painter to the Board of Ordnance. This brought with it a small but regular stipend and more commissions, including a portrait of King George II himself which when completed Walpole presented to his Yarmouth constituency. Worsdale had rented a house in Mount Street suitable to his status and furnished it, but it had not been long before he ran up debts he was unable to meet. He was lodging in Spring Gardens to avoid his creditors.

The meeting was not a complete surprise to Laetitia and perhaps it didn't really happen by chance. She knew that Worsdale was in London and had written to him but received no answer. Now the man she was later to dismiss as 'contemptible' and 'unluckily interwoven' in her history was all friendliness towards her and she to him. They breakfasted and then had dinner together. There was much to talk about; it was invigorating to be with him. Worsdale's adventuring spirit, his capacity to make up another life, invent another story – or, as George Vertue put it, his 'barefacd mountebank lyes' – and above all his connections with wealthy and well-placed men were a tonic. He told her about the house in Mount Street, furnished and paid for, left in the care of a servant. Brimming with immediate generosity, he invited her to go and live there. She could write for him again. He would pay her one shilling a day. She could begin at once by writing a letter which would help him escape the captivity of Spring Gardens. Worsdale explained that he needed to present himself to the Bavarian ambassador, Von Haszlang. The ambassador had developed a profitable sideline in selling protections against debt. It was a simple stratagem: the ambassador wrote to the Secretary of State to say that the named person was now employed by the embassy and hence had diplomatic immunity. Von Haszlang was notorious for using his position in this way. He maintained himself and a string of mistresses in the highest style for thirty years by combining protections with gambling and smuggling.

The temptation to lean on Worsdale and let him look after her was irresistible. Even as a bankrupt, he was doing better than she was. He was a survivor (he lived into his seventies, and when he died in 1767 he was worth several thousand pounds). It was reasonable to imagine there might be a future in Mount Street, which there certainly wasn't in Seven Dials; being with him was more fun than supplicating Samuel Richardson. Mrs Pilkington penned James Worsdale's letter recommending him as a servant to the Bavarian embassy. Then she gathered up her things and moved to Mount Street.

She went not as a mistress but as a hired writer. Worsdale's theatrical ambitions were as urgent as ever; indeed, his finest hour was yet to come. From her he wanted farces, songs, comic operas, ballads, poems, epilogues. He issued instructions, proposing numerous subjects at once, expecting brilliant compositions to order. The housekeeper was told to let nobody in – an order designed to keep the bailiffs out: by law, bailiffs could not force an entry but they could try to bluff their way in and once admitted, by whatever deception, could arrest the debtor or if necessary re-enter by force thereafter. Laetitia expected the housekeeper to wait on her but the 'old woman' (was she really old?) 'proud, ignorant, and insolent beyond imagination' declined, and instead addressed her as a servant, demanding where she was bred that she could not 'sweep rooms, light fires, and make beds, as well as other servants', and remarking that Worsdale was a fool to hire her, who 'did nothing but write all day long'. Laetitia was left to look after herself, her genteel manners having faded along with her looks.

The independent poet who had been proud of her freedom from Mr Curll's 'poetical garret' in Fleet Street, now found herself writing comedy all day for James Worsdale in a narrow-fronted house in Mayfair. She felt like a prisoner. He came daily, after the hours of darkness when as a debtor he could roam freely, and kept a close eye on what she produced. During this period she worked on several ballad operas for him, including one based on an old ballad, 'A Pennyworth of Wit', which 'exalted the wife over the harlot' and for which, because Worsdale was 'a profest libertine' she wrote a jokey epilogue, to be spoken by a woman, apologising for so much virtue. She made no copies because Worsdale took everything from her as she wrote it. What, if anything, he did with these materials remains a mystery. There is no record of any production. The public appetite for comic operas and ballad operas, so strong in the 1730s in the wake of *The Beggar's Opera*, had been on the wane since Garrick's arrival on the London stage. Worsdale's great success came as Lady Pentweazle in Samuel Foote's 1752 *Taste*, a character he apparently devised as well as acted, and perhaps some of Mrs Pilkington's wit found its way into this triumph of cross-dressed humour.

James Worsdale's application to the Bavarian ambassador was successful (it would be interesting to know how much it cost him – less, evidently, than he owed his creditors). On 6 August 1746 Von Haszlang notified Lord Harrington, secretary of state for the northern department (and a cousin of Lord Chesterfield), that Mr Worsdale was now entitled to '*les Privilèges attachés à ma protection*'. Worsdale could leave Spring Gardens and range as he pleased. He had much work on hand, including a new commission to paint a portrait of Lord Harrington, which he began at once but didn't complete till 1750 and which now hangs in the National Portrait Gallery, London. With other commissions from City merchants and aldermen, it was more convenient to move his studio eastward. He took a floor in a big old house near the Royal Exchange on Cornhill. There amid heavy antique furniture and on a fluctuating income – some days there were beef-steaks, some days not – the two established a domestic life of sorts. Laetitia was given a room that opened off Worsdale's studio. He worked at his canvases until the middle of the afternoon and ensured that she sat in her room and wrote. They had few possessions: she had pawned hers and Worsdale had no interest in making a comfortable home. It was bare, grubby and ramshackle, the antithesis of polite living. Sometimes she felt trapped and sometimes, depending on Worsdale's mood, light-hearted and free. A pastiche married couple, their artistic poverty and perhaps the ludicrousness of ending up, after all, with Worsdale, made her laugh. Their eating arrangements burlesqued gentility:

We had four Play-bills laid for a Table-cloth, Knives, Forks, or Plates, we had none . . . The Butter, when we had any, was deposited in the cool and fragrant Recess of an old Shoe, a Coffee-pot of mine served for as many Uses as ever Scrub had, for sometimes it boil'd Coffee, sometimes Tea, it brought small Beer, and I am more than half afraid it has been applied to less noble Uses.

Scrub was the naïve servant in Farquhar's *The Beaux' Stratagem*, a play about rakes on the make. Pissing in the coffee pot was probably de rigueur for an ex-Satanist who had helped found the Dublin and Limerick Hell-Fire Clubs. With Worsdale everything was theatre. He was a 'facetious Person' the prompter William Chetwood later wrote in an approving description: 'I have been in his Company, when his quick Imagination has struck out several Pieces of Humour that have given great Pleasure in his Manner of Singing . . . he had an inexhaustible Fund of good Humour, good Nature and generosity'. Singing while he worked Worsdale tested out her ballads and songs, interspersing them with successful products from the past such as Henry Carey's lines from *The Dragon of Wantley*:

Zeno, Plato, Aristotle
All were Lovers of the Bottle:
Poets, Painters, and Musicians,
Churchmen, Lawyers, and Physicians,
All admire a pretty Lass,
All require a cheerful Glass
Every Pleasure has its Season,
Love and Drinking are no Treason.

Henry Carey's pleasure in life ended in 1743 when his son Charles died. He hanged himself in his rooms in Coldbath Fields, leaving his pregnant wife and several children destitute.

When Worsdale had finished painting for the day, he was off to the Haymarket, where he understudied, and after that with Sam Foote and Charles Macklin toured the taverns and gaming houses, brothels and bagnios. They were an explosive crew. Macklin, known as the Wild Irishman, had killed an actor in a quarrel over a wig; while Foote's best friend, young and wealthy Francis Delaval, 'that most consummate puppy and unprincipled jackanapes' in Lord Chesterfield's words, was sent down from Oxford for accidentally killing his manservant. Foote himself, brilliant mimic and satirist, had run through three fortunes. One of his creditors was his mother, who had put him in jail. When she herself was arrested and wrote to him, 'Dear Sam, I am in prison for debt: Come and assist your loving mother, E. Foote', he replied only, 'Dear Mother, So am I, which prevents his duty being paid to his loving mother by her affectionate son, Sam Foote.'

Foote's stage career began in Dublin in 1744–5 where, writing his own material and perhaps inspired by Worsdale, he performed satirical monologues in which he imitated well-known personages, including his fellow thespians who loathed him for it. Back in London he devised a show at the unlicensed Little Theatre, Haymarket, which was presented not as a theatrical entertainment but a social gathering: audiences were invited to 'A Dish of Chocolate'. They howled with laughter at Foote's impersonations of preachers, magistrates, quack doctors and the leading actors. A master of self-promotion, this success didn't stop Foote placing anonymous letters in the *Daily Advertiser* threatening Sam Foote with a flogging if he continued his savage mimicry of respectable folk. The show was a sell-out and Foote became a celebrity, cracking jokes in the green room to gentlemen of the first fashion who danced attendance on him (some hoping he would mimic them, some not). Lawless and disruptive, Foote was a bully whose ability to scare people made a great impression on young Jack Pilkington. Garrick, admittedly a victim but also a wise commentator, wrote of Foote that he had 'much wit, no feeling'. The joke always came first and friend and foe alike were sacrificed to it.

How much of Worsdale's social life was shared by Mrs Pilkington cannot be known but that Jack fastened on him and to a lesser extent on Foote is clear. Jack may have shared the house with his mother and Worsdale on Cornhill; we know he lived with Worsdale at some point, either in Dublin or London. He would certainly have done his best to join any parties of pleasure, perhaps taking a boat across the river to Vauxhall Gardens, or hanging on to Worsdale's coat-tails as he skirted the beau monde with Foote, Macklin and the 'mischievous spendthrift' Delaval. In this group, pleasure was one objective but gain was a constant preoccupation. A few years later (after Jack had returned to Dublin with his mother) Worsdale helped orchestrate Delaval's marriage to a rich widow. This involved the kind of pantomime these men relished: Worsdale blacked up as a gipsy fortune-teller to encourage fat and homely Lady Isabella Pawlett into believing handsome Frank loved her for herself alone. The marriage on 8 March 1750, at St George's Hanover Square, brought crowds of apprentices and serving maids out to gawp. So far so good, although when it transpired that Lady Isabella had less ready money than Delaval thought the conspirators pronounced her insane and had her locked up in a madhouse.

Lady Isabella's fate illustrates the dangers women ran when mixing with men like these. By living with Worsdale Laetitia had put herself under his protection. It was never likely to last long. However good-natured he was in company, Worsdale tended to turn on ex-lovers. His will is an interesting document. He provided for some five illegitimate children while at the same time continuing his quarrels with their mothers, his discarded mistresses. Amoral, homosocial and selfish, Worsdale's freedom contrasted with Laetitia's constrained days and made her resentful. Poor health and disappointment along with a fierce competitive striving with men lent added aggression to her wit. They fought. Once when he had gone to Richmond for a few days leaving her in charge of his paintings he was enraged to be told that some potential customers had been impressed by her because she knew poetry, had the hands of a lady not a servant and had declined taking money for showing them Worsdale's pictures. He 'abused me at an unmerciful rate', she recalled, 'and told me, I should not stay in his house, to show my wit and breeding, forsooth, when I had neither; and boast of my family, when it would have been better for me to have been the daughter of a cobbler'. She reminded him that his tendency to claim Sir Godfrey Kneller as his natural father made him the son of a whore.

They railed at each other like husband and wife. It was a stormy relationship and in the big old house near the Royal Exchange it came to an end. Perhaps, catching sight of him in Spring Gardens that summer morning, she had hoped for more. He had, in truth, provided refuge in a time of need, but it had not been long before she felt enslaved in a 'worse than Egyptian bondage'. Any dream of love 'or even common decency' at Worsdale's hands was over.

He had become coarse and brutal. So, perhaps, had she. Or perhaps after being independent for so long she simply couldn't tolerate being treated the way men like Worsdale treated women. When he returned home to find her writing a letter for a prostitute who wanted to convince a client she was pregnant, he accused her of neglecting his business to 'turn secretary for the whores'. His pious indignation amused her. She matched it with a tone of mock innocence: 'I was really surprised, that he of all men, should fall so hard on kind females; and as their money was honestly earn'd by me, and they are generally liberal, I never thought I did anything amiss, in helping them out with a soft Epistle.'

As a doctrine and invariably as a practice, libertinage was profoundly contemptuous of women. Reflecting on it and writing about it, Mrs Pilkington adopted Swift's satirical method of reversal. Neither she nor the prostitutes who filled the streets were deserving of contempt: they were kind and liberal, she was helpful, honest and gentle. So what if the prostitute wanted her to tell a lie? Weren't men deceiving women all the time? From her position on the margins, coolly aloof, she showed society its image: a culture in which a man like Worsdale flourished. She apologised for writing about him at all. He was so contemptible he was 'unworthy even of Satire'.

In any case, she could not give a full account of him and of their life together without compromising the picture she strove to present of herself as a hard-working writer and hard-done-by woman who, 'when turn'd out desolate to the wide World' and abandoned by her 'once dear seeming Friends, and tender Relatives' did not stray from the path of virtue. Had she strayed, she argued, she might at least have hoped for pity, 'and given Necessity as a Plea for Error'. In real life, in Worsdale's bed or out of it, she was but one among many. She was well aware of Worsdale's trail of discarded mistresses.

Jack sought to exonerate Worsdale and he apologised for his mother's critical portrait of him, inviting readers to see in it 'some little Pique' on her part which they should not take seriously but 'only laugh at her Humour'. In an appendix to the third volume of the *Memoirs* which was published posthumously, he depicted Worsdale as a man 'incapable of acting but with Honour, Justice, and Integrity'. One is reminded of Samuel Johnson's abrupt dismissal of Boswell's attempt to defend Lady Diana Spencer, ill-used, adulterous and divorced wife of Lord Bolingbroke who married Johnson's friend Topham Beauclerk: 'The woman's a whore and there's an end on't.' Worsdale was a rake. Richardson gave posterity the template in his fictional character Lovelace. Plunged into the heart of libertine culture at its most extreme, Mrs Pilkington experienced at first-hand what Samuel Richardson could only imagine, but most of what she knew she couldn't write or could only represent in heavily veiled fashion. Jack Pilkington removed the eulogy six months later when he issued the Dublin edition.

Colley Cibber had spent the summer completing a serious scholarly study, inspired by Conyers Middleton's biography of Cicero. Cibber's *The Conduct and Character of Cicero Considered*

had occupied him on and off for years. It was good enough to impress Johnson's friend Thomas Birch who admitted it was 'much beyond what one would expect'. Mrs Pilkington went to visit the old actor. Cibber welcomed her warmly and read some of his manuscript to her. This gave her the opportunity to write a commendatory poem, which she worked on back in Cornhill in full view of Worsdale: he 'had the Confidence' to ask her to give it to him but she 'did not chuse to compliment him with it'. Poem done, she returned and presented it to Cibber. He read it through and congratulated her, and said he would use it in the prefatory materials of the book, but that it needed some corrections. They understood each other perfectly. Cibber took the poem to White's that evening. She called on him next day, full of anticipation:

Well, Madam, said he, there are two Guineas for your Flattery, and one more for the Liberty I took. I blessed my benefactor sincerely, from my Soul; he smiled benevolent: 'Come,' said he, 'I have more good News for you; Mr Stanhope alter'd a Line, for which he desires you will accept of a Guinea: Mr Hervey also pays you the same Compliment, for changing one Monosyllable for another.'

Stanhope and Hervey paid for the privilege of inserting their words into her text. Cibber paid for taking liberties. The words were public property as, implicitly, was her body – as Cibber knew, as she knew. The transaction was a joke, these men paying this woman for words not flesh; and the joke was on those who believed in private integrity, of the person or of the text:

To say the Truth, I only wished every Gentleman at White's had, on the same Terms, taken the same Liberty, till my work, like Admiral Drake's Ship, had been so often mended, that not a Bit of the original Stuff it was compos'd of should remain. I could do no more than (after some joyful Tears) to assure Mr Cibber, that neither his own Favours to me, nor those he had sollicited for me, should ever be forgot, while this poor Machine of mine had any Existence.

Five guineas, to one who had been subsisting on a shilling a day, meant freedom. She quitted Worsdale's house and 'took a little decent Lodging' of her own.

∞

In 1744, at the Battle of Toulon, Vice Admiral Lestock failed to bring his ships forward. Admiral Thomas Matthew, engaging the French and Spanish in some heavy exchanges in the front line, was furious. He suspended his second-in-command and sent him home. A Parliamentary enquiry that opened in March 1745 found that Lestock and other captains of the rear had a case to answer and ordered courts martial which began sitting in September. Public opinion sided strongly with Admiral Matthew who had, after all, fought and won a naval battle; but the court martial acquitted Lestock on a technicality. The man who had done nothing, and who was later described as 'confused, puzzle-headed', unable to cope with complicated battle manoeuvres, was promoted to admiral.

It was Admiral Lestock who, in August 1746, was put in joint command of an expedition to capture the port of the French East India Company at L'Orient, on the coast of Brittany. The ostensible purpose was to seize supplies and damage trading interests. The real purpose, to draw off French troops from Flanders where they were having some success, as at Fontenoy in May that year. An even deeper purpose was to do something – anything – with the massed troops that had been assembled on transport ships at Portsmouth ready for a major campaign, the conquest of Canada, which because of indecision and inefficiency at the very heart of government was delayed; first projected, then abandoned, then resumed and again called off. One of the military commanders was General St Clair, and St Clair's secretary, excited by the 'Romantic Adventure' of driving the French out of Canada, was the philosopher David Hume. At Portsmouth, dependent on the vagaries of winds and Ministers of State, Hume was aghast at the incompetence he witnessed at every level. Instead of invading Canada the fleet was ordered to Brittany, even though the commanders sent word they had no charts, no maps, no information about fortifications, no horses for the artillery, too few troops and no money except some chests of Admiral Anson's Spanish gold. More troops were quickly mobilised in London and on 10 September the 3rd Battalion of Guards sailed from Tower wharf. The Duke of Cumberland was there to see them off and urge them to do their duty against the French. Mrs Pilkington may have been there too, for among the troops on the Man o' War was Captain Meade and along with Meade, helping out with the horses, was Jack Pilkington.

A troopship full of elite Guardsmen famed for the flawless perfection of their uniforms and equipment (results achieved by 'discipline of steel') was an awesome sight. Jack was probably excited at the idea of seeing some action; perhaps he thought of taking the king's shilling. David Hume was hoping to make enough money to finance his future career as a writer. Hume enjoyed the brotherly companionship of the mess and learnt to play whist. In the long run, his friendship with General St Clair was decisive in making him independent. For Jack, the adventure had no such happy outcome.

The fleet consisted of some sixty ships carrying five battalions. Some of them landed just outside L'Orient went ashore and burned a few villages, but they got lost, it rained heavily, and dragging cannon ten miles over poor roads wore out the men, which might not have been so bad had they remembered to take the furnace to heat the shot and enough ammunition to make it worthwhile (the bellows were also left behind on ship). It was a bungled, pointless affair and morale was low. The 3rd Battalion didn't even get that far. It took them twelve days to sail to Plymouth by which time the rest had left. They stayed at Plymouth till the 10th, enduring ferocious storms that on 1 October had dispersed five of the transports off the Brittany coast; their captains, not knowing what else to do, decided to return home. Reinforcements were badly needed, but on 10 October the 3rd Battalion was ordered to sail to the Bay of Biscay and on the 19th they were ordered to sail back. Off Dungeness four days later they were caught in a terrifying storm. Jack had never known anything like it; not even the hardships of the privateer the previous year could compare. Soaked to the skin, clinging for dear life to whatever was screwed down and transfixed by waves that towered mountains high before crashing on the deck, he was convinced they would all drown – as indeed some did. Nor was Captain Meade in a condition to comfort him: panic-stricken,

Meade was begging God to give him one last look at his wife and children and then he would be content to die. The winds abated, the sea grew calm. By 31 October the battalion was able to disembark at Deptford. They marched back to the Tower for a spell of guard duty. Jack, beginning to show symptoms of fever (always as much to be feared as enemy guns) was in a deplorable state. Captain Meade managed to get him to his lodgings at Scotland Yard and put him to bed, and then he went round immediately to report their return to Laetitia. She found Jack delirious. Captain Meade, anxious to travel on to Teddington, paid for a physician and left, giving directions for Jack to follow if and when he recovered. For several days his mother wept and prayed, despairing of her 'poor Wanderer'.

A month or so later, Jack had recovered sufficiently to go down to Teddington. What he found there was a household in utter confusion. He wrote to his mother at once:

Dear Mamma,
I have return'd to what I had just left, *Sickness*. The Captain is in a malignant Fever, beyond any thing I ever saw; he knows nobody, nor has he any Physician; I don't believe he can outlive tomorrow Night: I am really griev'd, as I am sure he lov'd me, and on account of his poor Wife, who is almost distracted; The four little Girls, I fear, will be quite unprovided for. All things are in Confusion: Adieu, my dear Mother. Heaven preserve you to
Your affectionate and dutiful Son,

John Carteret Pilkington

Jack's prediction was correct. The captain died shortly afterwards, his life thrown away on what Horace Walpole sarcastically described as one of 'our glorious expeditions and invasions of France'. On 4 November, writing to Horace Mann, Walpole told him: 'Our Guards are come back too, who never went: in one single day they received four several different orders.'

Disconsolate, Jack stayed at Teddington where the captain's widow began to depend on him for more than ordinary comforts.

Captain Meade's effects were at the Tower and needed to be collected. The captain's widow asked Jack to go and he asked his mother to help him. They were given the keys to the captain's bureau, trunk and portmanteau and they sorted through his possessions. They found two guineas, 'a seasonable relief to the Widow'. It was as they gathered up his regimentals, his sash, his red uniform in which she had so often seen him dressed when alive, that Laetitia burst into tears.

∞

And then came her own bout of fever. Laetitia took to her bed, unable to work for three weeks. She could keep nothing in her stomach and lost a lot of weight. She was so weak that she had to send for Betty to come and take care of her. It was probably at this time that Betty – in one of the few glimpses we get of her in the *Memoirs*, none of them positive – made an unfortunate habit of using her mother's manuscripts to light the fire.

Jack returned from Teddington. As he had some aptitude for painting and drawing, he approached John Millan, the well-known publisher and dealer in books – especially military ones – whose shop was located at the Charing Cross end of Whitehall. Millan gave him engraved prints to hand-colour. These were well enough done for Jack to be given more. Millan paid him decently – better than anything he got at Drury Lane or as a stable boy for Captain Meade. The pleasure of earning money made Jack 'doubly diligent' and, working hard, he took a separate lodging nearby. It had been convenient enough to share his mother's room while she was ill, but once she was up and writing letters again, for herself and her clients, Jack found the coming and going distracting.

Or perhaps Jack's sex life precluded staying with his mother. The captain's widow had come to London and also taken lodgings in the Strand. She was desperate to find a man – she had four children to feed, added to which there was a question mark over her entitlement to the captain's pension. Laetitia had been visited by an officer of the Guards who, in charge of money that the men had collected for the widow, told her that a prior wife had set up a claim. He also mentioned that word had gone around about a boy young enough to be the widow's son. Rumour, which reported that the widow had married the boy, was cooling charity.

There was some foundation to the rumour. Laetitia had seen at least one love letter from Teddington arranging an assignment with Jack at a coffee-house in London, and making an offer of marriage to the sixteen-year-old. She was shocked and blamed the widow entirely: 'Bless me! she amaz'd me!' She also knew that Captain Meade had been paying an annuity of £20 to an ex-mistress. What she didn't know, and what she discovered when she tracked down 'Madam herself . . . deck'd out very gay' to her dingy rooms, was that the captain and his 'wife' had never been married at all. The picture of conjugal bliss had been a fabrication.

This apparently monstrous discovery unleashed Laetitia's scorn. 'Madam', she decided, had over-acted in all departments: as a pious Christian concerned about an inadvertent lie; as a loving wife whose fondness 'seem'd to surpass all things, for she would kiss her Husband's Linen, saying, they smelt of Violets and Roses'; and as a grieving widow who 'yell'd and scream'd to save Appearances', but who privately had received the captain's possessions dry-eyed, though even the soldiers on duty at the Tower had wept at his sad story. Laetitia's own rancour at having been condescended to as a fallen woman fuelled a malicious virtue. Offered a drink – it was nine o'clock in the morning – she refused: she had work to do and needed to keep a clear head. She also refused to do anything to help in regard to the pension. She could not tell a lie. Truth demanded expression, as did some long-stored resentments. The four little girls, all dressed in deep mourning, looked on.

Plainly, she was envious. The captain's widow had found a man and married him (so she claimed) and they set up a punch house together. This gave Jack and his mother something to laugh at, he having lost all respect for a woman whom grief had driven a little crazy, and Mrs Pilkington feeling no need to concern herself about the family's welfare now that Captain Meade was dead. It did not protect either of them from the bitter knowledge that an important support was gone.

By the end of February 1747 Betty's mistress had taken her back, a sign that Betty pleased somebody, and Laetitia was well enough to launch another campaign for funds. Too poor to buy coal, too depressed to make visits, she spent what she had on paper and pens. She had determined that the only option was to return to Ireland with Jack and shame Matthew into doing something for his son. Jack may have urged the plan, having equally unrealistic hopes of Jane Brodrick and other O'Neill connections.

A 'good old woman' did the rounds with a batch of letters. One of the letters went to Colonel Duncombe. On the assumption that because he was so old he was preparing himself for death, and that in settling his accounts with his Maker he might want to tip the final balance towards benevolence, Laetitia sent him a heart-wrenching account of her decay. She told him she was old, cold, sick, hungry and wasted. This was not what he wanted to hear. He brutally set her right: 'You old Devil', his letter began,

When you were something handsome, I told you I loved you, as I told every woman who came in my way; but by God, my dear little creature, I never cared a half-penny for you; and so you now begin to talk to me like a death's head, or a mementi mori. I thought you had more sense than to preach that to me, when I am like yourself, obstinate and old, which I always despised, as you know. You tell me you are in distress: very well: I am not. – And pray, Madam, what's your misfortune to me? Must I break a ten guinea bet at White's, to give you one, because you are unfortunate? That would indeed help to make me so, as I should repent it all my life. – Oh! thou beautiful ruin! thou admirable antique! thou venerable matron! thou poetical sybill! In short, thou dear fine worthy antient gentlewoman! Your most obedient
humble servant,

D –

PS. You want to go eat, I want to go to game; once more your humble servant.

Not a new man like Richardson but an old rake, Duncombe's vicious words told her nothing she didn't already know. He had never pretended to sentiment. He had no interest in compassion and he enjoyed his reputation for avarice, although he had offered the courtesan Teresia Constantia Phillips a £2,000 annuity. Her letter had been badly misjudged, a sign perhaps that she was losing her touch. Playing the coquette was a young woman's game; pleasing men, a basic requirement, had lost its savour. The terms on which Laetitia had tried to live in London were unimaginably hard: fiercely insisting on independence and hoping to maintain it on handouts, with a compromised legal status that made social life awkward, and without an acknowledged protector. (She was never going to do what the captain's widow had done, grab a man, any man.) The beautiful ruin put Colonel Duncombe's letter carefully with her other papers. She would find her form once more when she got back to Dublin.

To Richardson she wrote, 'My head is so bad, it is with infinite pain that I write . . . I am so weak, I am unable to assist myself.' She was 'quite broke', she told him. She had left her previous lodgings in a hurry, before the landlord seized for the rent she had no money to pay. She had to check that Richardson knew where to send to her – at the Blue Peruke, on the Strand. The same information went to Cibber who seems not to have responded. Dr and Mrs Delany were in town, as were the Southwells, Percivals, Donellans and Claytons, among others who had gathered that winter for the wedding of the dowager Lady Kildare's son, James Fitzgerald, 20th Earl of Kildare, to Emily Lennox, fifteen-year-old daughter of the Duke and Duchess of Richmond. (The Richmonds had been unhappy about Emily marrying an Irishman.) The Delanys had taken rooms in Pall Mall, next door to The Cocoa Tree where they paid four guineas a week for three floors – parlour, drawing room with tapestry hangings and crimson damask curtains and chairs, a bedroom looking over the park and two pairs of stair rooms and garrets, 'all very tolerable'. They were not to be approached directly, but Delany was too good a prospect to be left out altogether. His stipulation that he be contacted only through Richardson had to be observed. Explaining that in the hurried move she had managed to keep hold of her bed, her chairs, 'and some few necessaries', but not the good stock of coal laid in, Laetitia gave Richardson his instructions: 'I believe from my knowledge of Dr. Delany's charity, that if he knew I had not even a fire, nor any subsistence, he would take some compassion on me.'

Wit was a casualty along with patience. She was weary, and weary of complaining of her bad luck – 'the world is the world, and I am quite sick of it'. She apologised for her 'tedious epistle' but she did not apologise for expecting former friends, those who had once admired her, who had recognised her merit, to give the little that was needed to keep her alive. Richardson must have remonstrated with her for some earlier complaints. Politely, firmly, angrily, she put him right:

I should be sorry, Sir, to be judged any way ungrateful to Mr Cibber; I owe him many obligations: but my extremity was, and still is, so great, that a trifle, which he could not miss, would have been a relief to me. Violent afflictions made Job himself murmur; so I hope I may stand excused: and thus much I will venture to say, that Mr Cibber never suffered either in fame, or fortune, by his kindness to me.

But neither from you, Sir, nor from him, had I any right or title to expect the favours I have received; but the case is very different with regard to Dr Delany. He indeed (as you might perceive) tied me up from writing my full mind to him, by desiring he might hear from me no other way but by you. Yet considering the long and intimate friendship which was between my father and him, which descended down to me, had he given me from his ample fortune some little annuity, even as much as he pays to his meanest servant, I have richly deserved it from him; and believe me, Sir, I would not presume to say so, had I not a just foundation for it.

She would not sign her name: it was 'lost, barebit and gnawn, by Slander's canker tooth'.

Laetitia felt Delany owed her something and Delany agreed. Through Richardson, he forwarded a generous sum, enough to pay her debts and contribute towards the journey. It was a simple truth that he could easily have afforded an annuity, or to help out in a systematic way as he helped the family of Mary Barber. Such a gesture would not only have been about money: Delany was a key figure in the social and cultural life of Dublin, and when slander's canker tooth chewed Mrs Pilkington's name to shreds *his* name might have countered it. She resented his determination to keep her at arm's length, and Delany knew her well enough to know that if resentment swelled she could do damage. He had reason to be circumspect: his wife's high-born relations were still not convinced that marrying him had not been a complete social disgrace.

Laetitia asked a young woman to carry a letter to Bishop

Clayton. Clayton produced a guinea in memory of Dr Van Lewen, denied all knowledge of the doctor's daughter, but invited the charming young messenger to return in a few days. When she did so he evidently repented his half-formed thoughts of seduction and sent her roughly away. Mrs Pilkington wrote again, in 'not over-courteous' terms – probably threatening him – and his valet called next day bringing ten guineas, out of which the bishop stipulated she was to give him change: for each guinea, she had to give him one shilling back. Presumably this was his idea of a joke.

It was late April and the blossom was out. She and Jack could afford to go, so long as they travelled by the cheapest means, on the Chester wagon, exposed to the elements, and at little more than walking pace. She booked their places. She bought some clothing for them both. She carefully packed her papers: fair copies of poems; the printed version of 'The Statues'; attempts at fiction and autobiography, including at least forty pages of what was to be the first volume of the *Memoirs*; and assorted documents such as the recent letter from Colonel Duncombe and the letter Worsdale wrote from Mallow when she failed to send him a hundred ballads by return of post. Cibber had given her an unbound edition of his *Cicero* and this went in too, though she had not seen Cibber himself for some months and did not tell him she was leaving.

A stinging letter went to Dublin, directed to Matthew's lover Nancy Sandes ('I did the Creature the Honour, Strumpet as she is') to assure her that whatever Matthew might hope, his first wife was very much alive and coming to claim her bond. Matthew was still hoping to marry Nancy Sandes, allowing himself to believe there were reasonable grounds for thinking his ex was dead. No doubt a letter went to Matthew himself, and perhaps one also to his patron Charles Cobbe, archbishop of Dublin. Opening shots in a war of words, they were intended to sow alarm and weaken the enemy's resolve.

On 1 May 1747 the portmanteau was heaved on to the wagon. Mrs Pilkington climbed up after it making herself as comfortable as she could on the straw, and bid a last goodbye to the streets of London.

According to a Mayday custom, ribbons were presented to the wagoners at every inn they stopped at, so that very soon the tired old horses ('our Flea-bitten Nags') were draped in multicoloured stripes and practically blinded. It was a fatiguing journey, hot and dusty. They stayed at humble inns, leaving very early every morning after a breakfast of salt beef and cabbage which the driver and Jack tucked into but she could not. Though there were no luxuries like tea and coffee there were pleasures: nightingales, flower-filled meadows, pretty villages, an inn that served chicken and wine. Once she and Jack sat under an apple tree canopied with woodbine, where a flock of nightingales were singing. When the idyll was interrupted by a snake that curled itself round Jack's leg she took it as a portent. Similarly, the shocking sight of a hanged man in chains on a gibbet whose friends, some twenty or thirty Catholic Irish men and women lying in a dry ditch, frightened her, symbolised 'Albion's' violence towards her homeland.

At Parkgate they found crowds of well-heeled Protestant Irish returning from the wedding and waiting for the wind to bring the boats from Dublin Bay. Lady Kildare was among them, as was her daughter, Lady Margaret Fitzgerald. Keeping them company were the Earls of Granard and Baltimore, and Lord Doneraile, Laetitia's least-favourite peer. Thomas Sheridan was there too. Sheridan had been in London for just a month, shopping for actors for Smock Alley (he got a good bargain on some dancers from Drury Lane) and taking a rest after two brilliant and hectic years. In the 1745–6 season he had persuaded Garrick over to their mutual profit and honour, and more recently in his determination to push through reform he had ridden out the most tumultuous riots in theatrical history. The Kelly riots in January and February 1747 had put Dublin in an uproar. Sheridan emerged triumphant, 'flushed with happy conquest', resolved to continue keeping a firm hold on all aspects of theatre management and to be intimidated neither by mobs of footmen in the gallery nor their noble lords treating the stage and wings as extensions of their own drawing rooms. Actresses were grateful: being groped on stage was not unknown. George Anne Bellamy started her career in Dublin and never forgot 'the horrors of a riot at a Dublin theatre' which she said were impossible to describe.

Laetitia loathed Sheridan. She had known him from a boy and viewed him as a rival. His years at Westminster had given him an arrogance and insolence ill-befitting, in her view, the son of a man who squandered his wife's fortune then, in his will, left her five shillings because she had been 'unkind'. He was a 'beggar's brat' who strutted like a lord. Others used similar terms of abuse, for the theatre manager had many enemies in Dublin whose ranks she swelled once she arrived. Sheridan probably cut her at Parkgate in spite of their many connections through Swift and latterly through Benjamin Victor.

For some people, such as Mary Delany who arrived at Parkgate a week later and also found contrary winds, waiting was no hardship. Mrs Delany enjoyed watching the people passing to and fro. If not sauntering with Dr Delany ('D.D.') in the fields behind the long line of inns and houses that fronted the waterside, she occupied herself with her sketchbook or cut-paper designs. Running out of reading materials was an anxiety; running out of money was not, though they did decide that taking over their own coach and horses had been an expensive mistake.

Laetitia could ill afford to pay for accommodation, and the presence of so many former friends and acquaintances was uncomfortable. She watched for the arrival of the boats with increasing desperation. Sure enough, the last shilling left her purse before the winds changed. Desperate, she sent Jack to beg from Lady Kildare. Did she tell Jack to remind Lady Kildare that Rev. Matthew Pilkington's *Poems on Several Occasions* had been dedicated to her recently deceased and much lamented husband, the 19th earl? Perhaps. Jack came back with a guinea.

On 14 May Lady Kildare and assorted earls and lords boarded the government boat, the *Dublin Yacht*. Lady Kildare's coach was loaded on to the *Racehorse*, a sturdy workaday vessel. Most of the waiting passengers, including the Pilkingtons and Thomas Sheridan, travelled on the *Racehorse*. Jack's spirits were high: he was in his element on board and ran about singing sea shanties. His mother sat on deck, trying to quell sea-sick feelings that incorporated many kinds of queasiness.

The coach came in useful, for that night they were becalmed and Laetitia, Jack and two men – one of whom was a Dublin clergyman named Hudson who recognised Jack because of his resemblance to his father – sat up in it and talked. Laetitia found Hudson a well-read and sensible individual – at least, he showed compassion for her plight although (somewhat to her own surprise) she did not ask him for any money so his compassion was not tested. Her project in returning was to secure Jack's future. Rev. Hudson's agreement that fathers owed such a responsibility to their sons was comfort enough. By daybreak they could see the Irish shore, 'the Mother Land which gave me birth', but it took until the middle of the afternoon to reach Dun Laoghaire, the usual disembarkation point for Dublin. Instead of leaving the boat along with everybody else, and facing the prospect of carriage fare into the city, Laetitia and Jack stayed on board for Ringsend. Again, however, they were becalmed. Again, they took their seats in Lady Kildare's coach and settled down for the night, taking the cloth off the driver's seat for a blanket.

Ships anchoring at Ringsend had to cross the Dublin bar about three miles out, where the channel between the sand bars (the North and South Bulls) could sometimes be as little as six feet deep. In the middle of the night the captain, having gone to sleep, woke them with a volley of curses moments before they hit a sandbank. There was a terrifying crash as they bounced off another boat that was already moored, more or less wrecking it. Luckily, Lady Kildare's coach had been well lashed down. Frightening as this was in the darkness, morning revealed a happy prospect: sun gilding the fields, tide far out, and the little fishing village within easy reach on foot across the strand. And so 'without Expence or Difficulty', carrying the portmanteau between them, 'the little Irish muse' and her son 'Jack Luckless', walked along the beach to Ringsend. She was home. She hoped, as 'the Daughter of a gentleman so universally esteemed as Doctor Van Lewen' that after such a long exile she would find herself among friends.

She tested the proposition at once. She took a room and sent

Jack off into Dublin 'with a Letter to a Nobleman, whom I had formerly seen at my Father's'. This produced a guinea and on the strength of it Jack found cheap lodgings for them in Aungier Street, at Mrs Byrne's near the Ram Inn.

PART THREE

Dublin Again

CHAPTER ELEVEN

Celebrity Memoirs

Dublin was acquiring an outward splendour later visitors would remark upon. The Parliament House had been completed in 1745. There were monumental new piles going up such as the Kildare town house south of the Parliament building to which Lord Kildare brought his new young wife. Some of Kildare's vast wealth was also being poured into a huge Palladian mansion a few miles west of Dublin, at Carton, but in Dublin itself the fashionable direction was eastward. Classical squares and streets of three-bayed, four-storey brick-built houses were laid out by developers with a self-conscious eye to coherence of design. In style it was much like Georgian London but with more available land and cheaper labour the boulevards were wider, the vistas grander. Prosperous, self-confident, Dublin's Protestant elite were putting up a capital city for themselves.

Among the projects for a new and improved Dublin was St Patrick's Hospital, Swift's parting gift. Since at least 1733 Swift had been planning and working for the foundation of a hospital for the mentally ill – the first of its kind in Ireland. He willed his entire estate including the profits from *Gulliver's Travels* to it, though the money came with a characteristic insult. In 'Verses on the Death of Dr Swift' Swift had explained himself:

> He gave the little wealth he had,
> To build a house for fools and mad;
> And shew'd by one satiric touch,
> No nation wanted it so much.

If it was his final satiric touch, there was also a poignant irony.

Swift's mental health deteriorated alarmingly in the last decade of his life, and in May 1742 he was judged of unsound mind. He stayed in the deanery, well looked after but robbed of most of his faculties, until he died in October 1745. At that time, the threat of Jacobite invasion occupied everybody's attention and the great dean's passing made little noise. A year later, St Patrick's Hospital was granted its royal charter and plans began for building on a site in the undeveloped 'rural' western outskirts of the city near Bow Bridge; the architect, George Semple, was to follow Swift's detailed instructions. The committee in charge of the project was headed by Matthew's patron, Archbishop Cobbe.

Within a few months of her arrival Laetitia was able to move to a house in St James's Street by Bow Bridge close to the proposed hospital grounds. For the moment she had no choice but to stay in lodgings in Aungier Street, near William Street where she had grown up, and Molesworth Street where her father died and where Lady Meade still lived, and within shouting distance of Lazer's Hill where Matthew still kept his house. Her arrival made some stir: 'busy Tongues' were soon wagging.

In urgent need of money, she launched a volley of letters to Matthew. The first was what she described as 'a very mannerly Epistle to my beloved Spouse, in which I slightly mentioned his merciless Treatment of me, and his poor Children', and at greater length told him she wanted the £65 she claimed he owed her according to the bond that had been signed and put into the lawyer John Smith's hands for safe keeping. She said that if he gave her the money she would leave Ireland. She probably meant it. There was one condition: he had to promise he would acknowledge Jack and use his position to provide some sort of future for him. In the meantime, while she was manifestly alive and in Dublin he could forget any hope of re-marrying.

Matthew did not reply. She wrote again and still got no reply. His aggressive silence 'a little incensed' her. Her own aggression swelled with self-righteousness: she had taken upon herself the care of both children, had hauled herself all the way home, had starved and begged. She did not intend to be ignored. John Smith was asked to instigate legal proceedings against Matthew. Smith, though willing to help and agreeing that she had right on her side, was unenthusiastic. He knew Matthew. He needed no aggrieved wife come from London to acquaint him with 'Mr Pilkington's Talent, of traducing every Person, who did not act in Compliance to his Inclination'; and nor did he need reminding of the sharpness of Mrs Pilkington's tongue. Smith advised against going to law and offered to write to Matthew himself, reminding him of the exact terms of the settlement. Although we do not know what the financial agreement was nor how much Matthew had undertaken to pay as an annuity – probably £7 or £8 which over nine years would have amounted to about the £65 or £70 she now wanted from him – we do know that in these cases the Church of Ireland required both parties to give an assurance that they would live chastely for the future. Matthew's liaison with Nancy Sandes had been conducted with no more discretion than his earlier affair with the widow Warren. It might be hard for a church court to overlook his conduct. More interestingly, Laetitia's willingness to go to court suggests a confidence that her own behaviour was not such as would undermine her claim. Perhaps she was merely reckless, thinking she had nothing to lose anyway – certainly less than Matthew; or that London was too far away to matter; or perhaps she had nothing to hide.

Through Smith they snarled at each other. Laetitia made little or no effort to patch up relations with other alienated family and ex-friends. She did not seek out her sister, Elizabeth, abandoned by George Frend ten years earlier and mother to a number of small children by somebody else, nor her brother Meade who was, for some of the time at least, in Dublin. Meade was a lieutenant in the 5th Regiment of Foot, the Northumberland Fusiliers, which was on garrison duty in Ireland and often stationed in Dublin. He had married Martha Mercer, the sister of a fellow officer, in Cork in 1741 and they had a daughter, Martha, and possibly also a son, James. The lease of the Molesworth Street house had been transferred to Meade's brother-in-law, Captain Luke Mercer, in 1744. Laetitia would certainly have known these details, as she knew that her eldest son, William, was a student at Trinity. Meade's rejection and William's refusal to have anything to do with her were a source of pain. She told herself that William dared not communicate with her because his father forbade it, but she must have known that he was in touch with Jack. Or she reasoned that having been brought up by his Pilkington grandparents William identified with that side of the family and had become like his father.

Jack at once set about activating old connections. He chose to remember only the happy aspects of his previous stay in Dublin when, after falling out with his patron Charles O'Neill and before taking the boat to Scotland, he had spent some six months in the city, empty of pocket but full of pride and living like a lord at someone else's expense – a Trinity college student friend of William's. At that time Jane Brodrick had come through with cash, but there were others Jack had hopes of. With O'Neill he had kept company with some of the 'first persons of the kingdom'. He went to call on Arthur Hill, brother of the Earl of Hillsborough. Once, travelling from Dublin to Shane's Castle with O'Neill, Jack had spent some days at Hill's country estate where, he later wrote, 'painting, sculpture, architecture, books, music, conversation, with the most hospitable treatment, conspired to show the greatness of the gentleman whose guest we had the honor to be'. An MP and banker, Hill later became Chancellor of the Exchequer and later still was raised to the peerage as Viscount Dungannon. In 1758 Mary Delany described him as '*an old beau,* who has lived much in the world . . . an original'. She found him 'excessively' amusing, an elegant and fine gentleman, but also 'a very honest, hospitable, friendly good man, with a *little pepper* in his composition.' Jack knew Hill would be perfect for his mother. So too was John Bowes, chief justice of the Irish court of exchequer, later Lord Chancellor, also a peer, unmarried and another old beau who adored the company of witty women. Introductions quickly followed.

Although there was a good deal of 'Trouble and Vexation of Spirit' in these first weeks back home, the note that comes through most strongly is not vexation but vitality. Mrs Pilkington was on home-ground and it made her feel animated and confident, brimming with energy and drive, happily belligerent, vivacity restored. There was no more talk of sickness and world-weariness.

She had returned to Dublin as an adventuress with a story to tell and there were many 'persons of taste' who were eager to meet her and be entertained by her. In her usual way, she rose to the occasion. Soon she had a little coterie of admirers, a new circle of ageing men in high office, wealthy, witty and worldly.

If the date of a bragging letter to Colley Cibber is correct, 18 June 1747, it took barely a month for her to declare that her sorrows were at an end. Although since there is at least one exaggeration in this letter – she told Cibber that her memoirs were in the press — we can perhaps treat the further remark that subscriptions were 'pouring in from all quarters' with a pinch of salt. Or perhaps not. Dublin, she told him, was a village; and to prove it, she herself was looked upon as 'a person of consequence'; indeed, so much so that there was no news to tell him for 'I am the chief subject of discourse here, my adventures being impatiently expected'. She entertained her friends 'in the same manner I have had the honour of amusing you, with a particular account of Dr Swift'. She also entertained them with particular accounts of Colley Cibber, letting them borrow her copy of Cibber's *Cicero* into which her commendatory verses had been bound.

From Aungier Street it was a short walk to Crane Lane near Essex Street where the printer Samuel Powell had his shop. Powell made a specialism of subscription publishing. Laetitia paid him a call soon after her arrival, taking what then existed of the manuscript of volume one and a list of names. She convinced him that she could quickly produce a two-volume work that would appeal to readers on both sides of the Irish Sea. It would tell the story of her life in her own distinctive voice. Her recollections of Swift were still her most valuable asset but she could now add to them stories about her encounters with other celebrities. She would incorporate the poems she had once hoped to publish separately; and she would reveal intimate details about the break-down of her marriage and subsequent abandonment. She would name names. Priestly hypocrisy would come under the lash.

Powell seems to have been a Methodist; at about this time he began printing all their materials in Dublin and was on friendly terms with John Wesley. Like many others, not only Methodists, he was disgusted by the ostentation of wealthy clergy and the abuses of place and position in the established church. The view from an ill-used curate's wife willing to dish the dirt on dignitaries like Bishop Clayton as well as her ex-husband, the well-known favourite of the Archbishop of Dublin, was one he was happy to encourage. He agreed to act as agent for the subscription: he would collect money from subscribers, take his share and be her banker for the rest. Proposals were printed and distributed to all the major booksellers, who were also authorised to collect subscriptions. In the *Dublin Journal* of 9–13 June Powell placed an advertisement announcing the memoirs. Well aware that Mrs Pilkington had been collecting subscriptions for almost ten years without producing a book, he promised a refund if no book appeared.

Mrs Pilkington's stories were well worked-up as routines. The challenge, when she set herself seriously to write, was to link them into a connected narrative that retained the 'natural' rhythms of speech. In conversation, her ability to fetch from memory apt poetic quotation or classical reference was admired; on the page it might look over-studied, or – that word dreaded by eighteenth-century authors – 'pedantic'. She had begun to find a textual voice, loosely based on Cibber's in his *Apology*, and a persona that combined his cheerful admission of follies and faults with the rancour of a wronged woman, but there was much still to be done. Jack made himself useful. Acting as his mother's scribe and amanuensis he wrote to her dictation, thus allowing her to compose aloud as if entertaining friends. She then edited his script to produce her own more polished version.

Progress was slow at first. As a prose writer, the skills Mrs Pilkington had cultivated during her exile were those of the petitioner; so now, when she sat down to complete the memoirs that she boasted were already 'in the press' it was letters and invitations to subscribe that flowed from her pen. As always, these were tailored to the individual; it is unfortunate so few survive. Some served to settle scores and as a vent for her own malice. Gloating over the fate of the widow Warren, abandoned by Matthew for Nancy Sandes, it was amusing to write 'in very civil

Terms' inviting Mrs Warren to subscribe to memoirs in which she would feature as one of the villains. There may have been a hint that for a certain sum of money she would not figure in too ridiculous a light. If so, Mrs Warren did not take it. She wrote back in her own hand, an ill-spelt, semi-literate scrawl which Laetitia gleefully saved to transcribe later and publish to all the world as further testimony to Matthew's folly. 'I aboar yow and yowr Filthy Idyous', Mrs Warren apparently wrote. 'As to the Parson yow metown, tis wile nowne what hee iss; he ruinged my Sun by his Ungraitfullness. It is not in your Power to defamatonous my Corrector in your wild Memboirs'. It was a gift. Mrs Pilkington felt herself 'in Duty bound to give my learned Readers a Taste of her excellent Style' by putting it verbatim into her book, although the meaning of 'this elaborate Epistle' escaped her.

Aungier Street was also close to Smock Alley theatre where Benjamin Victor was treasurer and assistant manager to Thomas Sheridan. Laetitia hunted out Victor soon after her arrival, perhaps hoping to get him to do something for Jack. She said they fell at once into the old semi-professional relationship they had established in London when he was at the linen warehouse and she was in St James's: Victor busied himself about her writing plans, they saw each other regularly and were on a 'friendly and familiar footing'. Victor, writing later, claimed he had been careful to distance himself, given 'the badness of her character, and the censoriousness of this place'. At the time, Victor was concerned to keep the peace (and his job) with Sheridan, for whom he had been deputising all spring; however, as someone about whom there was a great deal of talk, Mrs Pilkington was sure of his attention. Dublin had been a good move for Victor. He relished his role in the theatre and it had kept him prosperous enough: he was building a fine new house. Like Sheridan he was flush with victory after their success in putting down the Kelly riots. Victor had been writing pamphlets, using the press, loving the publicity.

Both Victor and Mrs Pilkington were anxious about their friendship with Colley Cibber, a valuable commodity which Victor resented having to share and which Mrs Pilkington may have feared she had lost. Victor was in correspondence with Cibber but Laetitia had left London without even telling him. When she wrote to Cibber on 18 June she knew she had damage to repair. She was also more aware than ever how useful he could be. A letter received from Cibber in return, written in his own hand, would be a valuable object. A personal letter could be passed around the coterie, shared, discussed, repeated, memorised, heard about by others. It would serve as an emblem of friendship and esteem, and it could be incorporated into the memoirs she was writing. 'Original letters' were a key selling-point in books in this period, generally advertised on the title page. (The comedy in printing Mrs Warren's 'scrawl' lay not just in her illiteracy but in the way it burlesqued the fashion for publishing letters by 'polite' writers.) Cibber, understanding these matters, wrote 'By the Return of the Post' an amusing epistle which was immediately communicated to John Bowes and Arthur Hill and others ('Lord Chief Baron Bowes, the Hon. Arthur Hill, Esq., and several Persons of Taste'). Victor could hardly contain his envy, nor Mrs Pilkington her jubilation.

Several transcripts of this letter from Cibber's 'dear Hand' survive. Cibber copied it and seems to have sent it to Samuel Richardson: Mrs Barbauld printed it in her edition of Richardson's correspondence. Laetitia evidently made a number of copies to circulate as well as reserving the original to 'embellish' her memoirs. Lord Orrery came by one, which was later printed in *The Orrery Papers*.

Cibber teased, gave cogent advice, displayed his cynicism and invited her to make as much use of him and his name as she could. As usual, he combined real warmth with profound indifference. 'Thou frolicksome Farce of Fortune,' he wrote, in what was the first of a number of letters that year, each providing her with an occasion to call on her wealthy friends:

What! is there another Act to come of you yet? I thought you had some Time ago, made your final Exit. Well, but without Wit or Compliment, I am glad to hear you are so tolerably alive. I have your agreeable Narrative from Dublin before me, and shall, as you desire, answer every Paragraph in its Turn, without once considering its Importance or Connection. In the first Place, you say I have for many Years been the kind Preserver of your Life. In this, I think I have no great Merit, as you seemed to set so little Value on it yourself, otherwise you would have considered, that Poverty was the most helpless Handmaid, that ever waited on a high spirited Lady. You seem to have a Glimpse of a new World before you; think a little how you are to squeeze through the Crowd, with such a Bundle at your Back, and do not suppose it possible, you can have a Grain of Wit, till you have twenty Pounds clear in your Pocket; with half that Sum, a greater Sinner than you, may look the Devil in the Face.

Few People of Sense will turn their backs on a Woman of Wit, that does not look as if she came to borrow Money of them; but when Want brings her to her Wit's End, every Fool will have Wit enough to avoid her.

On the subject of Matthew, Cibber felt that by arriving in time to prevent his second marriage she had missed an opportunity:

I am not sure your Spouse's having taken another Wife, before you came over, might not have proved the only Means, of his becoming a better Husband to you; for had he pick'd up a Fortune, the Hush, Hush of your Prior Claim to him, might have been worth a better separate Maintenance, than what you are likely to get out of him.

Under other circumstances blackmail might well have been the best option, but there was never anything 'hush-hush' about the Pilkingtons' marital affairs. Cibber's advice was not helpful on that score, but when it came to his own value to her he knew exactly what he was able to offer:

If the Value I have for you, gives you any Credit in your own Country, pray stretch it as far as you think it can be serviceable to you; for under all the Rubbish of your Misfortunes, I could see your Merit sparkle like a lost Jewel. I have no greater Pleasure, than in placing my Esteem on those, who can feel and value it. Had you been born to a large Fortune, your shining Qualities might have put half the rest of your Sex out of Countenance. If any of them are uncharitable enough to call this Flattery, tell them what a poor Devil you are, and let that silence them.

He promised, too, that he would send her 'hints', to help fill out a second volume:

I hope you have but one Volume of your Works in the Press, because if it meets with any Success, I believe I could give you some natural Hints, which, in the easy Dress of your Pen, might a good deal enliven it.

There was, of course, no volume in the press as yet. However, John Smith had squeezed £20 out of Matthew, which may have been what Cibber was referring to. If Cibber sent anecdotes about well-known individuals there is no sign she used them. He signed off with a flourish of compliments about Irish women and their peculiar gift for entertainment:

You pay your Court very ill to me, by depreciating the natural Blessings on your Side the Water: Pray what have we to boast of, that you want, but Wealth and insolent Dominion? Are not the Glory of God's creation there? – Woman, lovely Woman there, in their highest Lustre! I have seen several and frequent Samples of them here; and have heard of many, not only from yourself, but others, who for the agreeable Entertainments of social Life, have not their equal Play-Fellows in Old England.

And pray what would Life be worth without them? Dear soft Souls, for now too they are lavish of Favours, which in my Youth, they would have trembled to trust me with. In a Word, if instead of the Sea, I had only the dry Ground Alps to get over, I should think it but a Trip to Dublin; in the meantime, we must even compound for such Interviews as the Post or Packet can bring or send, to
Your real Friend and Servant,

C. Cibber

⚬∞⚬

By the time these letters were exchanged Laetitia had moved with Jack to the little house by Bow Bridge where there were fewer distractions. The house, though in the unfashionable western end of the city, had a spare room and a charming garden running down to the river. She invited Cibber to stay. Cibber, still keen to play the gallant at Tunbridge – the following year Samuel Richardson described seeing him there, 'as *gay* and lively at seventy-nine as he was at twenty-nine' – was never likely to travel to Ireland. And if he missed Mrs Pilkington's agreeable presence on his side of the water there were plenty of other women available, Elizabeth Chudleigh for one, whose beauty captivated everyone, but who went too far at a masquerade ball at the King's Theatre, Haymarket, when she appeared in 'undress' as Iphigenia ready to be sacrificed, and 'so naked ye high Priest might easily inspect ye Entrails of ye Victim'. Richardson, claiming Cibber was 'over head and ears in love' with Miss Chudleigh, had witnessed his reaction at Tunbridge when

Miss Chudleigh called to him to join her in the tea room: 'his face shone' and all his wrinkles disappeared.

Pleasure-seeking but always pragmatic, Cibber despatched a gift to his old friend: a consignment of copies of his *Cicero*. Just as he had given her copies of his pamphlet to sell in her shop, so he gave his books to distribute as she pleased. It was a generous gift, though one that also served his purposes. She made careful calculations about where best to send them, writing accompanying notes that introduced herself and her circumstances, leaving it for the recipient to judge how much money to send in return. The strategy raised a few more high-ranking friends, a success of which Victor took sullen note, telling Cibber, 'the present you made Mrs P— of your Ciceros has proved a valuable one to her – I must own she disposed of them well, by sending them into the best hands of this kingdom, but from thence arose her advantage, for few returned her less than guineas, and some, moidores [coin worth about 27 *s.*].' When he published his letters Victor, even more sententious than usual, represented himself as having warned the old actor to beware his generous impulses. Thanking Cibber for sending him a *Cicero*, he explained that he had not written earlier because he had been hoping to gather 'some entertaining accounts of that strange being Mrs P— whom you have of late so much served and honoured by your frequent correspondence'. By 'entertaining' Victor meant malicious. The letter continued:

– but, alas! A prostituted body must be the habitation of a depraved and prostituted mind! I wished to have found her an exception to this general rule – but she is taking such abandoned courses here, as renders all acquaintance with her impossible – I will not trouble you with particulars, but think it the duty of a friend to give you this notice, that you may regulate your behaviour to her – I know she is pestering you with ensnaring letters, to extort answers to serve her own mean purposes.

We do not know the 'particulars' of Mrs Pilkington's behaviour in Dublin, nor what precisely (if anything) Victor was referring to by 'abandoned courses', but it is unlikely it amounted to anything we would find shocking; while her 'mean purposes' in this case were merely to print Cibber's letters and make some money –

which Cibber invited her to do. Colley Cibber, of all people, needed no advice on how to 'regulate' his behaviour towards a woman of questionable reputation.

Victor's friendship with Mrs Pilkington had indeed become 'impossible', though not for the reasons implied. Victor had to watch his own back in relation to Sheridan. In early 1748 he found himself forced to take sides in an eruption of theatrical hostilities. The affair, which began with a quarrel over free tickets, quickly escalated into commercial competition after Mrs Pilkington herself turned theatre-manager.

Sheridan had come back from London determined to maintain his strict regime inside the house. Nobody was to be allowed on stage or behind the scenes. The practice of taking 'odd money' – reduced rates for people coming halfway through or just for the afterpiece – was abolished; the late-comers were usually drunk and noisy, so he was happy not to have them at all. Also in need of reform was the abuse of 'silver tickets' and other free passes. In October and November 1747 Sheridan and Victor launched a drive to systematise the issue of free tickets. Silver tickets were tokens issued to members of the court (as Theatre Royal, Smock Alley received an annual payment of £100 from Dublin Castle for command performances and the like) enabling them and their friends and relations to come and go as often as they chose. By 1747 there were ninety-two tokens in use – or lost – and the arrangement was out of control. Sheridan cracked down. He insisted that any lost tokens had to be found or renewed before admission; all tokens had to be deposited in the doorkeeper's hand; no cards or written orders would be accepted in lieu.

As a friend of Victor's, Laetitia felt entitled to a free pass. At Powell's printshop one day Victor had been helping her check the sheets of her book as they came off the press. She asked him for two 'orders' or passes for the play that night. He gave them to her. Two nights later she wanted to go again and Victor, unfortunately, was not on hand. She or Jack wrote themselves an order for four people, for the first gallery, and signed it with Victor's name. That night a full house was expected and Sheridan had said that no orders were to be given so when their obviously forged order

appeared in the accounts that night, the doormen were told to
watch out. A couple of nights later they turned up again with
forged passes and all four – Jack, his mother, and two women –
were stopped from going into the theatre. A constable was called
and they were 'taken into custody' for a moment while Victor was
sent for. When Victor saw who the miscreants were he tried to
smooth everything, but Sheridan wanted to press charges, at least
against Jack. This was no trifling matter: the consequences for Jack
could have been severe.

Victor, to his credit, had Jack discharged and no more came of
it. (There may have been a genuine misunderstanding: George
Anne Bellamy thought Victor had authorised passes for her young
friends in February 1748 because he wanted to fill seats, and was
horrified when she was later billed for £75.) Jack's mother was
enraged at Sheridan. In her view she had done nothing wrong.
Sheridan should have treated her with the respect due to an old
acquaintance of his father, and 'bosom friend' of his godfather,
Swift. Failing that he should have been more careful because she
knew stories about his father and mother that 'were hitherto
unrevealed'. A few days later Jack got into a quarrel with Sheridan's
brother and threatened that his mother would publish scurrilities
about the family. Sure enough, Mrs Pilkington composed and sent
to Victor for forwarding to Sheridan – 'his Mightiness' – an
abusive poem, 'To Mr Sheridan', informing him that his father was
a scoundrel, his mother a whore, and the whole Sheridan clan
sordid and avaricious. Like the anti-panegyric to Lord Doneraile,
'To Mr Sheridan' is thuggish and unpleasant, but both poems
belong to a genre of verse insult which Swift and the elder
Sheridan had enjoyed exchanging. Sheridan senior had occasionally misjudged *his* tone and annoyed Swift; Sheridan junior didn't
see the joke at all. Everybody attacked Thomas Sheridan, including
the young Trinity student Edmund Burke whose play Sheridan
rejected that autumn. Sheridan's strutting gait and high-pitched
voice, his insistence on being regarded as a gentleman though he
was a player (a poor one according to his critics), his moral
crusade for decency and his self-righteous punctiliousness galled
many people. For Mrs Pilkington there was an additional twist.

Poised to get her own back on a self-important, arrogant Protestant elite that had tried to humble her, Sheridan symbolised everything that had made her an outcast. He thought he stood higher than she because of his father's friendship with Swift. Hypocrite, scoundrel, fraud, the gallows was too good for him. As for Victor, she regarded him as a mere underling. She seems never to have had much respect for Victor and any she had disappeared when he allied himself with Sheridan.

All through the winter of 1747–8, subscriptions came in. At first it had been slow because people were nervous about having their names printed as was usual in subscription publishing (and part of the appeal). Realising this, Mrs Pilkington announced she would not print a list of subscribers. It was a good decision. She soon had 'a numerous Contribution, from all the Nobility, Clergy, and Gentry'. Old family friends like the Recorder of Dublin, Eaton Stannard, and senior figures like Henry Boyle, Speaker of the Irish House of Commons, and the Lord Chancellor, Robert Jocelyn, were prepared to support her. Other old friends were not: up at Delville, where a now crippled Mary Barber was once again settled with her family, and where Dr and Mrs Delany sadly witnessed her decline, there was tight-lipped disapproval. Any mention in a book of the sort Mrs Pilkington seemed about to produce was anathema to Mrs Delany whose fear of vulgarity extended even to judgements about her garden: Lady Bell Monck, shown Delville's delights, failed to see that 'it was not a common vulgar garden'. But Dr Delany's kindness in London was still fresh in Mrs Pilkington's mind, and she may even have hoped to become socially acceptable once more in 'Delville's sweet inspiring shade'; she wrote about him in a positive light. Mary Barber explicitly asked not to be named, and was not. Perhaps it was Mrs Barber's friends who threatened to sue: 'When I, in plain English, set down undeniable Facts', Mrs Pilkington wrote indignantly, 'they menace me with Law'. Whoever 'they' were, they had a deterrent effect and some passages were altered after two men paid her a visit.

In the *Dublin Courant* for 19–22 December an advertisement

appeared naming Powell as Mrs Pilkington's agent, giving her address at St James's Street and announcing that she would publish her volumes one at a time. Volume one was 'In the press and will speedily be published'. Volume two was 'ready for the press' and would be published as soon as she was able to 'defray the Expenses of Printing it' – a hint to subscribers to hurry on up with their cash. The *Dublin Journal* carried the same information. Subscribers were asked for a down-payment of five shillings, with the expectation, as Mrs Pilkington later wrote, that any real gentleman would send her at least a guinea and not expect change.

The question of a flattering dedication came next. Having no single patron to be honoured in this way, she opted first to approach one of her Meade relations, Sir John Redmond Freke, stepgrandson of Lady Meade. Sir John's wife was a granddaughter of 1st Viscount Midleton, related by marriage to the Brodricks and O'Neills. Sir John was another person Jack had met through O'Neill. Laetitia wrote Sir John a 'bantering' letter, probably hinting that she knew unflattering stories of him. Sir John, who seems to have had a sense of humour, told Jack that as he had no accomplishments whatsoever people would think he was merely being made fun of if he appeared as the dedicatee to Mrs Pilkington's book. He declined. (She was rude about him in volume three.) He did, however, suggest a likely candidate, the young Sir Robert King, shortly to become Lord Kingsborough, a youth of extreme wealth and flagrantly dissipated habits.

Sir Robert King was twenty-three at the time, with extensive estates in Co. Roscommon, and a seat in the Irish Parliament. Apart from an ability to drink, fornicate and spend money (the baronetcy he was awarded in June 1748 was probably purchased), he was undistinguished. Mrs Delany knew of him as 'a vile young rake'. Writing to her sister at much the same time that Mrs Pilkington was fishing around for a dedicatee, Mrs Delany told the story of King's seduction of a pretty sixteen-year-old, daughter of a tenant. Sir Robert ran off with the girl, but her father, Captain Johnston, chased and caught up with them, 'held a pistol at the knight's head' and swore he would 'shoot him through the head if he did not instantly marry his daughter, which rather than die he consented to do'. Captain Johnston summoned a parson who quickly arrived but before the formalities began Sir Robert's servants rushed in, armed to the teeth, and extracted him. The 'forlorn damsel' was left to trail home with her father. There was an interesting coda to this dramatic tale, however, which Mrs Delany also reported: 'They all appeared at church in Dublin on Sunday morning, and the girl appears at all public places as unconcerned and brazen as if she had acted the most prudent part in the world.' The girl, of course, almost netted herself a lord. The father almost succeeded in forcing the marriage. In chasing the pair, it may be that Captain Johnston was more concerned to secure Sir Robert King's fortune than his daughter's reputation.

Never having met Sir Robert but undoubtedly knowing something of this story, Mrs Pilkington tossed off a general-purpose eulogy expressing pleasure in hearing about a young gentleman 'singularly good' who had 'a Tear for Pity, and a Hand open as Day for melting Charity', and sent it to King's Dublin house in York Street. King accepted the dedication, inviting her to send a servant to call next day. She sent Jack, who came back with two ten-pound notes and a line acknowledging the 'Favour' of the compliment.

Whatever Mrs Delany might think of Sir Robert King, he was a type Mrs Pilkington knew how to handle. Mistress of the burlesque, she could write fawning verses that hymned his 'divinely pure' soul, his 'winning Grace' and open hand, while at the same time including lines like:

> The Peers of Ireland long have been a Jest
> Their own, and ev'ry other Climate's Pest.

King, who was indeed to be her saviour and in monetary terms to deserve every encomium bestowed on him, relieved Mrs Pilkington's distress in handsome fashion. By late spring the following year she had received at least £150 from him along with the invitation to ask his agent, Mark White, for 'any money' she wanted: 'You cannot more effectually oblige me,' Sir Robert explained in proper lordly fashion, than by 'commanding my fortune'. White had been instructed to supply her 'without limit'.

Matthew had dedicated his poems to the Earl of Kildare. Mrs

Barber's *Poems* were dedicated to Lord Orrery, whose 'continu'd Bounty' to her in England and Ireland had made them possible. Now Mrs Pilkington had her own nobleman. Since Sir Robert lived mostly on his country estate at Boyle Abbey she rarely saw him. Her task was to write amusing letters and tell him stories about the young rakes and old soldiers she had known in London's St James's. She managed to keep it up for about a year before she made a horrible and expensive mistake.

Also spending time at his country estate was Charles Cobbe, archbishop of Dublin. In April 1747 Cobbe's ambition to become Primate of All Ireland received a check when George Stone, bishop of Derry, was promoted to the See of Armagh – traditionally the prelude to the Primacy. Cobbe had been planning a palace for himself, commensurate with his anticipated dignity. He had employed James Gibbs to replace his old mansion with a design in the Palladian style for what would have been one of the grandest houses in Ireland. Disappointed, Cobbe gave even more attention to the monument he would leave behind. Newbridge House, a modified version of the original design, was begun in 1747 and is now home to one of the oldest family collections of art in Ireland. Most of the collection was acquired in the 1750s and 1760s by Cobbe and his son Thomas who in 1764 added a gallery on to the house, but buying started in the late 1740s. The agent for both men was Cobbe's secretary and private chaplain, the vicar of Donabate, the Rev. Matthew Pilkington.

As Matthew had once served Swift, so he now served the Cobbes, father and son, except that instead of poring over booksellers' stalls he rushed from painters' studios to picture-dealers' auctions, picking up mostly Flemish and Dutch originals. There is a caricature of him in a one-act farce by Beaumont Brenan, *The Painter's Breakfast*, which represents the Rev. Mr Busy as 'a great wheedler' who has worked his way by foul means to the centre of the art-dealing world. Ruthlessly taking cuts on every sale, he is feared by all. He has a talent for trouble and slander: 'No favours bind him, for he knows no gratitude: and those who treat him kindest, these are they he misuses most.' Brenan's unflattering portrait appeared in 1756, and it indicates that by then Rev. Pilkington was so well known as a collector that Dublin audiences would recognise him in the Rev. Mr Busy. One character, blackmailed out of a couple of paintings that the Rev. Mr Busy wanted for his own walls, comments: 'Why, indeed mr Busy I always thought for a Parson, your morals seem'd queer enough.'

His busy collecting did not diminish Matthew's appetite for reading. The key texts on art history were in Italian, Dutch and German and none had been translated into English. Matthew worked up enough of a facility to read them in the original. He was familiar with Vasari's writings on the Italian Renaissance and Van Mander's on northern Europe; he knew Carlo Ridolfi's *Life of Titian* and Joachim von Sandart's *Teutsche Akademie*, the most important source of information about German painters and artistic life in Rome in the early seventeenth century. The Cobbe family appreciated Matthew's erudition; they may even have paid for him to travel for them on the Continent. Their patronage combined with his endeavours eventually enabled him to produce *The Gentleman's and Connoisseur's Dictionary of Painters*, the first of its kind in English and a landmark work in art history.

The unwelcome return of his ex-wife was a potent distraction. She could never be a serious threat to Matthew's position – as an institution, the Church was solidly behind him – but her ability to bring powerful men over to her side alarmed him. Hearing that she accused him of sending young Hammond to seduce her, Matthew wrote to Hammond, then in England, inviting him to deny the accusation. Hammond replied on 19 March 1748 saying that on the occasion referred to he had merely visited with Dr Walker from Crow Street and that Mrs Pilkington had recited her verses to them. Any other accusation was 'impudently false and groundless'. Matthew circulated the letter, then had it printed as a broadside sheet instructing the printer, Peter Wilson in Dame Street, to capitalise the words 'IMPUDENTLY FALSE' and 'GROUNDLESS'.

By this time volume one of Mrs Pilkington's memoirs had been distributed to subscribers and Mrs Pilkington's story was in everybody's mouth. Matthew threatened to write a narrative of his own, a 'true and impartial' account. No such account appeared but there was a flurry of pamphleteering, some of which he authorised or wrote. In *Seasonable Advice to the Publick, Concerning a Book of Memoirs lately published* it was politely suggested she be whipped through the streets as 'an infamous woman' and 'made a publick Example at the tail of a Cart'. Matthew may have written *The Draper's Letter to Mrs L— P—n concerning her book of memoirs lately Published*, a broadside invoking the memory of Swift. Laetitia thought so, and seems to have answered it in a sheet of her own: *An Answer to a Fool Who Modestly styles himself the Draper*. She also may have responded to Hammond's letter (accusing Matthew of writing it) in *Mrs Pilkington's Answer to the Rev P—son P—ton Who assumes the Name of W. Ham—d, formerly Runner in the Duke of D—set's Kitchen, now an Ensign.* There were probably other exchanges which have not survived, and as none of these were explicitly owned it cannot be said for certain that Laetitia or Matthew wrote them. Supporters on both sides took up cudgels as *The Parson has the Worst on't: or, A Duel between the Cassock and Petticoat* indicates. This pamphlet took for granted Matthew's authorship of *The Draper's Letter* and blamed him for exposing his wife to the dangers of an unprotected life: his duty had been to preserve her from infamy. Beaumont Brenan seized the moment to write a satire, *Congratulatory Letter From One Poet to Another. On the Divorcement of His Wife*, supposedly supporting Matthew and supposedly dating from the time of the Pilkingtons' divorce. Brenan's poem endorsed what he took to be Matthew's point of view, that a wife was a clog to a poet, 'Foe to his Peace, and Bar To his Renown', and congratulated him on having managed to get rid of her:

> It matters not the Means by which 'twas done
> If foul or fair – so she be fairly gone.

Wives were enemies to men's freedom and all men would get shot of them if they could. But one thing puzzled Brenan. Why did Matthew marry Laetitia in the first place?

> What was the Charm then? – Wit – (you reply)
> That Charm was. – Wit! Now help me, or I die,

Ye gracious Gods! – Wit you say? – I'm 'mazed
That ever Man shou'd have a Mind so craz'd.

The duel between the cassock and the petticoat was entertainment of a familiar kind. Most people were prepared to believe Matthew had behaved every bit as badly as Mrs Pilkington's *Memoirs* claimed. His continued refusal to countenance Jack was a mark against him in some people's eyes, especially given the physical likeness between father and son. There was admiration and sympathy for Mrs Pilkington, as a wit and as a wife – a response that the tone of volume one, especially in its representation of Matthew, was carefully designed to elicit.

Victor reported to Cibber that the book had been well received. All over Dublin, Mrs Pilkington's recollections and adventures amused and intrigued readers. Her fate had been harsh but the tone in which she described it was not. Matthew was a villain but he was also a fool. There was warmth in the descriptions of their early life together. As a young poet favoured by Swift, the perverse – in Matthew's values, Matthew's follies – was to be expected. When Mrs Pilkington wrote, for example, 'I could reckon up numberless Instances of Mr Pilkington's Aversion to me' the subtext was Swiftian perversity, a man who might just have preferred a horse to a pretty young woman. She made the same point when opening up intimate domestic scenes for the readers' delectation. One episode at the family dining table, 'no body but my Husband and Children present', told how when a pin in her gown had pricked her and to find it she uncovered her breast, the sight made Matthew feel so sick he had to leave the table. The scene was skilfully done, at once an invitation to voyeurism and an appeal to a more gallant male readership. Lovers of poetry would also recognise an allusion to a poem by another Matthew, Matthew Prior, in which the poet, properly ravished by the sight of his lover's breast, ceases to be angry at her. Like the 'solemn' declaration that Robert Adair was in her bedroom because of a shared love of books rather than bodies, the wit made literal truth seem merely dull. It also subtly redirected the question: not, was the wife unfaithful but was the husband an authentic man and poet?

People who remembered the events of October 1737 were

amused at Mrs Pilkington's rendering. Even if it were true, as Victor told Cibber, that 'almost every person in Dublin' knew she had glossed the details it still made them laugh. Victor wrote: she was 'so determined to be supposed a woman of virtue, that she has falsified the fact in which her husband publickly discovered her, with at least a dozen persons attending him, most of whom are now living here'. The twelve still-living nightwatchmen must certainly have been a problem. But in what was to become a much-quoted passage of the *Memoirs*, Mrs Pilkington drew on popular comedy to give her version of the events of that cataclysmic night. David Garrick's comedy, *Miss in her Teens*, which had a successful run in Dublin in the spring and summer of 1747, featured a foolish character, Fribble. Wanting to shift the focus from her behaviour to that of her husband, she likened Matthew to Fribble, an actor in a farce entering on cue and in costume. It was a brilliant touch, which reinforced her accusation that he had stage managed the whole event:

At length the fatal Hour arriv'd, when Mr Pilkington's Machinations wrought the Effect he so long desired, namely, my Destruction; and, as he never did Things by Halves, that of his own Children also; to whom his Barbarity has exceeded anything I ever either heard, or read of; but that in due Place.

I own myself very indiscreet in permitting any Man to be at an unseasonable Hour in my Bed-Chamber; but Lovers of Learning will, I am sure, pardon me, as I solemnly declare, it was the attractive Charms of a new Book, which the Gentleman would not lend me, but consented to stay till I read it through, that was the sole Motive of my detaining him. But the Servants being bribed by their Master, let in twelve Watchmen at the Kitchen Window, who, though they might have open'd the Chamber-Door, chose rather to break it to Pieces, and took the Gentleman and myself Prisoners.

For my own Part, I thought they had been House-breakers, and would willingly have compounded for Life, when enter'd Mr Pilkington, with a Cambric Handkerchief tied about his Neck, after the Fashion of Mr Fribble, and with the Temper of a Stoic, bid the authoriz'd Ruffians not hurt me: but his Christian Care came too late; for one of them had given me a violent Blow on the Temple, and another had dragg'd two of my Fingers out of Joint. The Gentleman at the Sight of Mr Pilkington, threw down his Sword, which he observing, made two of the Watchmen hold him, while he most courageously broke his Head.

After this heroic Action, he told me, who stood quite stupefy'd between Surprize and Pain, that I must turn out of Doors; but observing that I was fainting, he brought up a Bottle of Wine, and kindly drank both our Healths.

She was a married woman and she was found with a man not her husband in her bedroom late at night. In control of the narrative, as she manifestly had not been in control of the events of that night, she managed to make herself seem dignified and put upon yet lady-like; her husband, technically in the right, a cowardly figure of fun responsible for a cruel charade.

Mrs Pilkington might not be welcome in certain drawing rooms but her book found its way. Whatever people thought about her as a woman, they loved her as a writer, even if what some of them loved was how indignant she made them feel.

Gratified by the generally positive response, Laetitia decided to move back into the centre of the city. Her complacency did not survive the move, which took place in February or early March 1748. Having found suitable rooms for herself and Jack in Abbey Street, she sent her furniture and possessions on ahead. Arriving at the house that night expecting to find the beds put up and other things arranged she discovered instead that a fellow lodger, a clergyman named John Vesey, had objected to sharing a house with her and ordered the landlord to throw her things out. Her belongings were piled in the passage. The Vesey family feature prominently in the list of subscribers to Matthew's *Poems*, so John Vesey may have been acting on Matthew's behalf. He did not stop at preventing Mrs Pilkington's move to Abbey Street. When Jack, next day, found lodgings in Big Butter Lane (now Bishop Street) and Laetitia ordered her furniture to be sent there, Vesey followed and reviled her to the owners. They refused her entrance. With Jack she was forced to trail back to Bow Bridge where a friendly neighbour took them in, forty shillings poorer and livid with rage. At the third attempt, a house in Golden Lane, it was Dr Van Lewen's name which did the trick: the landlady was a grateful former patient. Also living in Golden Lane was an obstetrician, Fielding Ould, who honoured the memory of Dr Van Lewen. A feverish cold and some weeks of sickness followed these upsetting events. Dr Ould took care of her.

Readers in England did not have to wait long for Mrs Pilkington's entertaining book. In April *The Gentleman's Magazine,* the most widely distributed periodical of the day, carried a long extract serving as a trailer and publicity-boost for London publication of the *Memoirs* in June. The selection had been carefully made and sent, apparently, by one 'G. F.' – initials which could stand for George Faulkner. Whether Faulkner was actually involved or not, as Swift's printer his initials gave an imprimatur to what was listed in the contents as 'Private Anecdotes of Dr Swift from Mrs Pilkington's memoirs'. Most of the stories about Swift were there, including his roughness as a tutor. If Faulkner judged it 'an authentic picture of that eminent person' as the headnote declared, others might surely not cavil.

The 1747–8 season at Smock Alley was a lively one. Along with the usual complaints about Sheridan's 'puppet-like strut' and risibly unconvincing dying on stage, there was disapproval (or pretended disapproval) of the tumblers, dancers, singers and acrobats that were introduced as between-the-acts entertainments. Pantomimes were a special feature that winter because handsome Henry Woodward, comedian and harlequin, had come over from Covent Garden. Playing alongside George Anne Bellamy in her third season at Smock Alley, Woodward was good box office. Sweet-tempered, physically beautiful, tall and strong, he was a favourite on and off the stage. Hence, when short, fat, acerbic Sam Foote arrived early in March and took the Capel Street theatre to launch a Dublin version of the satirical sketches that had been so successful in London, Woodward was one of his targets. As before, Foote advertised his show as an invitation to take tea or chocolate with him. Imitations of David Garrick, Peg Woffington, Sheridan – now out of town – were all part of his repertoire. Eager to pick up whatever was topical and give a local flavour to his imitations, Foote welcomed contributions from his old friends the Pilkingtons, mother and son.

Jack was excited at Foote's arrival and may have been the driving force behind what became some sort of collaboration. He had probably had hopes of work at Smock Alley and been disappointed. Foote's belligerence was a tonic and Jack studied him closely. The Capel Street shows drew good audiences and when Woodward retaliated by putting together an afterpiece of his own, a 'Tit for Tat' threatening Foote, his 'brother Atall', with 'a Dish of his own Chocolate' audiences became even better. There were considerable profits to be made by all parties. We know Woodward made sixty guineas from his 'Chocolate' shows, bringing his total earnings that season to about £600. When Foote returned to London after three busy weeks, Mrs Pilkington and Jack decided to keep up the action at Capel Street. A notice went into the *Dublin Journal* for 22–26 March announcing 'Foote the Second'. Two sketches featuring Jack and written by his mother were to be performed: 'A Club for an Epilogue' and 'Harlequin Turned Newsboy, or Bays in Distress'. They were not enough to carry an evening's entertainment (and nor perhaps was Jack's comic talent) so there was a delay while the tyro managers, having leased the theatre, put together a company and a main play. The next issue of the *Dublin Journal* carried an apology: 'Mr Pilkington hopes his generous and noble benefactors will not be offended that he is obliged to defer his benefit until Tuesday 5 April, as he has had a violent fever, and cannot hope to be able to perform until then.' On the 5th the benefit was announced for the 20th when 'at the particular desire of several persons of distinction' Dryden's comedy *The Spanish Fryar* was to be presented, with Jack playing the lecherous Lorenzo and Mr Barrett from the Theatre Royal, London, playing the 'fryar'. Tickets were available from Mr Pilkington at his house in Golden Lane. The evening was to conclude with *A Dish of Imperial Tea*, 'written by Mrs Pilkington'. Confusingly, on 12 April another apology appeared: a benefit scheduled for the 12th had been put off twice because of Mr Pilkington's illness. Addressing the 'many persons of distinction' who had been 'disappointed' Jack gave notice:

that at the particular Desire of the Quality in general, he will on Tuesday 26th April perform a new comedy, written by Mrs Pilkington, and called

The Turkish Court. With a new Prologue. And by particular desire, Mr Pilkington will give The Club for an Epilogue, which met with such universal applause. The whole house to be fitted up with Scenes, Machines and etc and all the characters intirely new dressed; and on the night of performance, the whole house will be illuminated with wax.

An afterthought was added at the bottom of the paragraph, following the usual information about prices: 'There are people from London who perform the parts. '

Jack, or 'Foote the Second', had in fact appeared on 12 April which is when the afterpiece 'Harlequin Turned Newsboy, or a Club for an Epilogue' met with enough favour to be puffed in this advertisement. The piece, though never printed, was clearly an attack on Henry Woodward, a generally peaceable man but one who if struck could be relied upon to return the blow. For commercial reasons, the Pilkingtons hoped to provoke him. Woodward obliged at his benefit on 25 April at Smock Alley. Playing Harry Wildair in Farquhar's *The Constant Couple*, he followed it with a new afterpiece: 'A Dish of Atall's Chocolate, a Dish of Imperial Tea, and a Dish of Fresh-roasted Strong Coffee To settle the head of Madam Pill-Kill-Tongue.'

Madam Pill-Kill-Tongue liked the soubriquet so well she used it in the advertisement for her new comedy: 'Mrs Pill-Kill-Tongue begs leave to inform Mr Mar-word that she is of opinion his own head was a little out of order when he attacked hers.' She advised him to take some strong coffee.

All did not go as smoothly as hoped in preparing *The Turkish Court; or, The London 'Prentice* for its opening night. Bills had been printed for Tuesday 'without Mr Pilkington's knowing' by 'the unhappy young gentleman in the Marshalsea' (probably William Chetwood) but the opening was put off to the following day. Never printed and now lost, *The Turkish Court* was a rushed job: the production was hastily put together, the sets were scrappy and the actors under-rehearsed and poorly costumed, but the writing, according to Chetwood who may be biased, was admired. For the afterpiece Jack again did his mimicry of Woodward and others.

Feuding was kept up through May and June as the season

wound down. Mrs Pilkington boasted of an exposé about Woodward's sex life; it was 'in the press'. This seems not to have appeared but a broadside on Woodward 'the Coffee Tosser' survives, signed 'Hibernicus' and presented as a letter to Mrs Pilkington with her answer appended. This broadside, *The Bloody Murder of Sir Harry Wildair*, attacked Woodward's poor acting (his 'bloody murder') in the part, but the question at stake was why Mrs Pilkington, whose wit was so excoriating, didn't lash Woodward harder. Her answer: he was nothing but a tumbler with an 'agile heel' whose strong body and weak mind – 'very proper recommendations to some of the fair' – made him too 'low' a target for her. More likely she was anxious about balancing profit and loss, the good effects of abuse with the bad. Woodward's impersonations of Mrs Pilkington hissing, 'Subscribe, or else I'll paint you like the Devil', made audiences laugh. She sent him a crown for a box ticket claiming to be 'well diverted' by being distinguished in this way. It was excellent publicity, but it could easily backfire; and when Woodward added some scurrilous verses to the script in honour of her presence she may have decided she couldn't compete. He was a popular man, he commanded the most important stage, he had Sheridan and Victor behind him, his audiences were surely bigger than Jack's and he was a better performer. Her last throw was probably a pamphlet, *Faddle Found Out: Or, The Draining of Hal W—dw—d's Coffee-Pot*, which suggested that Woodward should have asked for her services if he wanted witty abuse, for she was 'a very Wag' and 'would as soon write against, as for herself'. It was reckoned that Woodward had won. The anonymous *Letter to Mr W—dw—rd, Comedian* congratulates him on overcoming his competitors in Capel Street and making money at the same time. Whether the Pilkingtons made or lost money from these ventures is unknown.

CHAPTER TWELVE

Lord Kingsborough

Mrs Pilkington's public profile throughout 1748 was high and the traffic of people and paper in and out of her lodgings reflected it. She was a figure of note. Proposals for the second volume of her memoirs were in circulation along with a printed list of subscribers. Stories went the rounds. Churchmen, lawyers, Trinity College fellows and students, peers of the realm and country squires discussed her doings and sayings. Work came in. She was asked to write poems, give her opinion about legal matters, lend her name to a new play, comment on fistfuls of verses. Pamphleteers quoted her, or made up lines and attributed them to her. She was teased by 'impertinent Visitors, who make any Sort of an Excuse to see so great a Curiosity as my little Ladyship'; and gratified by receiving 'as many Pacquets of a Day, as a minister of State, some praising, and some abusing'. This change in her status was thrilling.

There was so much demand for her book that on 2 May a second edition was printed in Dublin – in small format, handy-size. She sold it from her house at Golden Lane 'over against the Golden Heart', and it was available in the usual way at Powell's in Crane Lane. On 22 June the London edition was published by Ralph Griffiths, who also published John Cleland's *Memoirs of a Woman of Pleasure*. Griffiths regularised some of the phrasing, taking out Hibernicisms such as ' 'Tis', so that the overall effect was more formal. No money came to the author.

Mrs Pilkington had signed off her first volume with a flourish and a lie. People had said she had nothing to publish: 'I hope this will convince the World,' she concluded grandly, having told the story of her birth, parentage, marriage and divorce, and leaving readers with an image of a sorrowing woman sadly crossing the Irish Sea to an unknown fate in England, 'that Mrs Pilkington was never yet reduc'd to the Meanness of Falshood or Tricking'. That her second volume, dealing with her adventures in London, might be 'infinitely more entertaining' was always possible; that it was 'now ready for the Press' was not true. It was still not true when she advertised it as 'now in the press' in May. In June she informed a surprised public that she was unable to proceed because she had 'so very few subscriptions paid in'. She blamed Powell, with whom she seems to have fallen out. An advertisement in *Esdall's Newsletter* on 29 June gave her name only, not his, though he had been acting as her agent, and complained that she couldn't promise the second volume yet because she had been 'so often wrong'd by those she empower'd to receive subscriptions for her'. Victor thought she had damaged the subscription by her 'falsehoods' (which might have been wishful thinking on his part), while Lord Orrery told Thomas Birch in London that she had 'squandered away the money she gained by her first volume', and that was why she couldn't print the second.

Victor couldn't imagine what she would put into a second volume anyway. In his view, 'the remarkable part of her life' – scandalous divorce and friendship with Swift – had all been written about in volume one. He feared that like other writers she would fill it out with her private correspondence. She had letters from Colley Cibber and Samuel Richardson, and then there were his own: 'I must have wrote her many heedless letters within the compass of ten years, which must be unfit for the public eye.' Mrs Pilkington agreed. None of Victor's letters was fit to be included but she did have in her trunk copies of verses she had ghost-written for him to present at Court. There was an ode on the Princess of Wales's birthday, and 'a Lilliputian Ode' on the birthday of young Prince George which was sweet and inane:

> The Flow'ry Prime,
> Delights a Time,
> The hopeful Bloom,
> Sheds rich Perfume,
> Then Fruits appear,

To crown the Year;
So, lovely Boy,
Thy Spring employ,
That thy sweet Youth
Be crown'd with Fruits of Wisdom, Virtue, Truth.

These were part of the story she intended to tell about being a Grub-Street hack. Nobody knew how much men like Victor depended on women and men like herself. Victor had paid her five shillings for the verses. Since her return to Ireland he had twice informed her she was a fool. More fool him then 'to apply to a Fool for Wit'.

Matthew had written to her – 'a most stupid epistle' – accusing her of trying to ruin his career, a conclusion no reader of the *Memoirs* could quarrel with. There was an incident in Dublin, however, which suggests some ambivalence. Laetitia was invited, along with Jack, to dine at a widower's house and they were waiting in the parlour for their host to arrive. A fellow guest was also waiting, and he was reading her book. As it happened the guest, a Mr Edwards, had a suit against Matthew going slowly through the courts which he had not tried to hurry because he felt sorry for him. Now, reading her version and convinced Matthew was a villain, he was resolved to show him no more mercy. He would press for what was owed even if it meant throwing the parson into prison. At this, Jack jumped up and swore he would shoot any one who did any such thing and Mrs Pilkington burst into tears. Mr Edwards, touched by their generosity towards a man who had treated them both so harshly, retracted.

Another reader moved by her tale of distress was a country schoolmaster named Bernard Clarke. Clarke taught at Navan in Co. Meath, in one of the English Protestant Working Schools that were given the Royal Charter in 1733. His pupils, 'bred up in dirt, insolence and ignorance', were poor and so was he. A progressive on the subject of women's education, Clarke read the *Memoirs* and pictured a woman possessed of what in his view were male attributes: knowledge, judgement and wit. These could have made her the perfect wife, he thought, had Matthew been a better husband. (Early eighteenth-century feminism tended to imagine its ideal women as having the qualities of virtuous men.) Pitying Mrs

Pilkington's fate, Clarke composed near eighty lines of iambic pentameters hailing her 'spotless, but much injur'd Name' and singing the praises of her 'sprightly Parts'. The schoolmaster had his own ambitions: he was trying to gather enough subscribers for a volume of verse. The bishop of Meath supported him; and sundry merchants and attorneys, a brewer, a seal cutter, a staymaker, a wine cooper and a cutler were among those urging him on.

During the autumn of 1748, while she worked hard at volume two, Mrs Pilkington kept up a correspondence with Bernard Clarke which he was later able to publish. They exchanged letters in the character of poets. She told him his 'poetical Favour' had pleased her; to have an admirer in the country was a comfort. It made her feel young again and she played up to it:

Pray, Sir, come to Town, lest, like a Female Quixote, I should visit your rural Retreat in Quest of some agreeable Adventure; or, as all we poetical Folks border on the romantick, and sometimes on the enthusiastick Strain, I should fancy myself some fair silver-shafted Nymph, clap on my Tragedy buskins, and pay you a Visit, who generously feel so much Tenderness for me.

You see, Sir, a little encouragement is likely to engage you a troublesome correspondent.

In response, the schoolmaster gave a downbeat description of himself: approaching thirty, of average height and 'tolerably corpulent', afraid of being dull, good-natured, free of conceit, and with no money. Glad to find misfortune had not depressed her, convinced that women had 'naturally an easier flow of words than men', he was nevertheless surprised and intimidated by her 'pretty Sallies'. He hoped his lack of fortune would not turn her off. Not at all, she assured him. Being a poet was to be generous and 'above little sordid views'. She did not want him to send her money; gold from the rich, poetry from poets. Proudly resembling Swift's Vanessa, she urged him to come to Dublin and visit her, for

> Men of Sense have free Approach
> Altho they come not in a Coach.

Then she matched his self description with one of her own, beginning with a fib about her age:

I am, alas-a-day! in my thirty-seventh Year, and one of the most diminutive Mortals you ever saw, who was not a Dwarf or disproportioned. As all the Beauty I ever had consisted in Complexion, 'tis pretty much faded, and my auburn Locks are here and there besprinkled with Gray. The Hand of Time has silvered what was Gold. O! he is a bad Alchymist.

Her spirit, however, was undiminished: 'I have too much vivacity to think of sackcloth and ashes'; and if she was going to repent it would be 'in Falstaff's Manner; In new Silk and old Sack, like a merry Body as I am'.

Writing to Clarke was an opportunity to show off. At one moment, 'a mere old Coquette' who spread her snares for men of sense and who would be 'in the vapours' if he did not at once reply, next she was the harassed hack, multi-talented and multi-tasking. She let him know she was in constant demand, endlessly interrupted:

A country Squire, taking me for a Lawyer, wanted me to write out his case. A stripling from the College wanted Prize Verses; and a Player a Prologue. Well, to mend the Matter, here's the Printer wants more Copy: This must give us a Pause; so he's gone, and now I return very willingly to you.

She was 'hurried', languishing for 'sacred Leisure', had 'scarce a Moment to devote to you and Friendship', wished he was nearby so that he could help her, told him of a 'stupid' letter she had received which declared that none but whores and rakes would countenance her – 'a handsome Compliment to the Nobility, Clergy and Gentry of this Kingdom' – and promised she would insert his poem in the prelims of volume two. She explained to him the rules of coquetry: it was about giving and withholding, winning and losing. There was no fun in getting victory over a fool, all the delight was in 'tyrannizing over a Man of Wit'.

Clarke did his best to match her tone. Mostly anxious to be understood as a '*Platonick* admirer', on being told that she intended to print his poem he rose to a risqué joke: 'I think it reasonable we should be intimate,' he ventured, 'while we are together in the sheets.' She welcomed his compliments and laughed at his seriousness: 'I am in great hopes you are in love with me, and as it is a pleasing Pain, a Sweet Madness, I wou'd not have you cur'd, which you will certainly be the Instant you behold me.' When 'a gentleman from the college' gave her some Latin verses, a recipe for kisses, she asked the schoolmaster to provide her with a response: 'It will give me an opportunity of bantering my friend, and making him think I have a knowledge of Latin by intuition.' But he was too young to be Platonic she told him; and so, indeed, was she. She warned him:

It may not be yet safe for either of us to indulge even an ideal Love too far. I have known such Amours end with less seraphick Purity than they commenced. The Mind, where it is strongly engaged, is very apt to draw the Body after it: So I believe we must only converse thus till you are threescore, and yet, to own the Truth, I am not half satisfied with it; for I want to see you, which seems a little carnal; and you may observe by Cadenus and Vanessa

What dangerous things are Men of Wit

And the good Doctor leaves it very doubtful how their Platonick Amour ended. But however, I am a Woman of Courage, and if I have a mortal Heel, or a fallible part, it is only to be assailed by magick Numbers [i.e. poetry]

Such strains as warbl'd to thy string
Drew iron tears down Philo's cheek,
And made hell grant what love did seek.

And truly I am at least as susceptible of the softest Passions as his grim Majesty. You see I have such Confidence in you, that I dare send you any Whim, Gaiety or Gallantry which occurs to my Mind, expecting your favourable Allowance for all my Sallies as you very justly style them.

Did she want to see him? Were her wishes carnal? Perhaps. But she was an old trouper playing a part. The lines from Milton's *Il Penseroso* have an odd misquotation: it was not Philo, a Stoic philosopher, but Pluto, god of the underworld, whose cheek was stained with tears. Pluto's sexual demands symbolised Persephone's death, Demeter's grief, and wintry dearth.

Clarke seems to have had a girlfriend, a Miss L. O'More, and he stayed in Navan. He shared the letters with his friends who joined with him in drinking the lady's health. Then he stored them carefully with the fair copies of his own poems.

∞

Although she only admitted to thirty-seven Laetitia was forty, old enough to be Lord Kingsborough's mother. At first Kingsborough enjoyed playing the poet-patron. He visited her in her lodgings. She showed him some of the manuscript of the second volume and entertained him with stories about Colonel Duncombe and others. Her gallantries and gaiety were exactly what he wanted. They laughed and talked about her memories. In a book for polite readers, decency did not permit her to display Duncombe's real character, his speech full of oaths and expletives, but in the privacy of her rooms she could reproduce it for her noble visitor. Kingsborough may have sought other freedoms, she may have allowed them, they may have been carrying on an intrigue, but it seems implausible. At Boyle Abbey he pictured himself stealing away from 'company who can be happy with a bottle' to write a letter and 'enjoy the more rational felicity of conversing with Mrs Pilkington'. He thanked fortune that he was rich because it gave him the chance to serve her. It was a mystery to him how the world could have been so long blind to her exalted merit. She in return recognised in him a 'humane lovely gentleman, formed in the prodigality of Nature' – whatever that meant.

Kingsborough's boredom threshold was low. He did not want to be nagged and he was flatly uninterested in hearing about misery and woe. When he received from her what she called a 'true' letter, explaining that repeated grief had overcome her spirit and that she was 'incapable of enjoying anything on this side of the grave', he was aghast. 'Madam', he replied,

Your letter found me alone, I expected a fund of humour and entertainment on the receipt of it; but, good God! How much was I affected at your alteration of stile. Surely, Madam, you are troubled with vapours, and this must be the effect of them. When I last had the honour to see you, you were in full health and spirits; neither did I ever see more vivacity in any person living. For heaven's sake, Mrs Pilkington, be yourself, and think no more of quitting the world, wherein the longer you live the more you will be admired.

She had told him she was worried about her son, her 'only joy', nursed at her bosom and 'cruelly abandoned' by his father. She had described her feelings, a mixture of guilt and fear; shared with him the duty she felt to work her contacts – of whom he, of course, was chief ('prayers to heaven . . . interest upon earth') to put something in place for Jack's future. Fatigued by so much information, Kingsborough reverted to his favourite subject: the old rakes at White's Club. He was happy to throw money at the Jack problem, though not to the extent of a formal 'provision', which is what she wanted, and she was told he would do something when he came to town. But he was in the country. He needed amusement. He reminded her of the letter from Colonel Duncombe that had been so blisteringly callous and had made him laugh. 'I shall take it extremely kind, Madam, if you will, at a leisure hour, send it to me'; and in case he had not made himself absolutely clear he added a PS: 'I beg, dear Madam, you'll send something to raise my spirits, which your last has much depressed'.

She replied:

My Lord
As you desire me to be merry, whether I will or not, my duty obliges me to comply with your injunction, and rattle out everything I think entertaining, without once considering who I am prating to. I assure you, my Lord, if I was not old enough to be your mother, the world would say we carried on an intrigue; nay, those who have not seen how roughly master time has handled me give shrewd innuendoes, that it is not for nothing some people are so great. Your Lordship's hand and seal is already known in the post-office; and, but for the causes aforesaid, there might possibly be an action of damages against you, or a formal citation to appear in Facie Ecclesiae, and good reason. Why, forsooth, if a reverend gentleman of the gown chose to distress his wife, why should any flirting young nobleman take upon him to protect and defend her?

Why indeed. Kingsborough was infatuated with an idea of himself as a glamorous rake, living in the moment, warm-hearted, witty and benevolent. Her ability to turn out platitudes such as 'generous Minds delight in generous Actions', kept him amenable (the aside, 'and you know our Irish Nobility seldom touch our Souls that Way', went to her schoolmaster pen-pal, Bernard Clarke). Kingsborough enclosed £20 in a note delivered in person by his younger brother, Edward. He thanked her for 'the infinite delight your last has afforded to myself and friends, who unanimously join with me, in confessing you are, as I have ever esteemed you, Madam, unrivalled in wit, ease and vivacity', and promised a whole afternoon of his company when he next visited Dublin.

Edward King, a cooler character who had to watch the family wealth being squandered on others besides Mrs Pilkington, was unresponsive to her charms. With no desire to ape the Colonel Duncombes of this world, he delivered the note and prepared to go. She told his brother:

I intreated he would condescend, as his noble brother had frequently done, to bless my humble abode with his presence; and would you believe me, my Lord, I put your dear letter into my breast, and suspended even a woman's curiosity to know its contents, in hopes to engage him in a little chat . . . But he pulled out his watch, and told me he was absolutely obliged to go in ten minutes. I told him I hated a watch, and could not see how that machine was useful to any, except those who were tied to hours . . . Well, Madam, said he, but I am one of that number, and therefore must depart.

Late in September an anti-Sheridan pamphlet appeared. It was presented as a letter 'to the Admirers of Mr S—n' and contained the usual abuse. On the reverse side were advertisements for some recent publications:

This day is publish'd by Augustus Long, Printer and Bookseller, under Welsh's Coffee-house in Essex-Street (Price Three pence) A LETTER from Mrs L-t-t-a P-lk-ngt-n to the celebrated Mrs Teresa Constantia Phillips. Containing many <u>Remarks</u> and <u>Observations</u> on that Lady's *Apology for her Conduct.* Together with some curious ANECDOTES of her LIFE.

She knows the Heat of a Luxurious Bed;
Her Blush is Guiltiness, not Modesty.

Shakespeare.

The letter 'from Mrs L-t-t-a P-lk-ngt-n', if it existed at all, was probably not by Mrs Pilkington. The announcement was a plug for a little book called *The Parallel; Or, Pilkington and Phillips Compared, Being Remarks upon the Memoirs of those two celebrated Writers. By an Oxford Scholar* which had appeared in London and which Long rushed out for Dublin readers.

The Parallel drew a parallel between Mrs Pilkington's *Memoirs* and the memoirs of the courtesan Teresia Constantia Phillips, whose *Apology for her Conduct*, issued in instalments from her house in Covent Garden, featured a villainous husband, long-drawn-out litigation over large sums of money, corrupt lawyers and high-ranking lovers including one, 'Thomas Grimes', thought to be Lord Chesterfield but actually Thomas, Earl of Scarborough. Like Mrs Pilkington, Mrs Phillips was intelligent, articulate and aggrieved. (And had been admired by Colonel Duncombe.) There were clear, if unfortunate, parallels between the two women and at least one important difference: though famously witty, Mrs Phillips was not literary and had no ambitions to be a writer. Her beauty and personality were the selling points. Her book had been written by a ghost writer: Laetitia's old acquaintance, Paul Whitehead.

Long's actual advertisement for *The Parallel* was in rhyme, easy to learn and delicately lewd:

> Two Ladies learn'd, in diff'rent Islands born,
> Themes in their Turns of Rapture and of Scorn.
> Letty and Conny, pious, precious pair!
> Now wise and witty, as once young and fair;
> To the whole Town, their naked Thoughts expose,
> And tempt Applause, at once in Verse and Prose.
> With how much Justice, with what failings too.
> How great their Merits, and their Faults how few.
> How like their Paintings, and how like their Tales?
> Where Nature dictates, and where Art prevails.

To be linked with 'Conny' in this way was probably not something Laetitia welcomed and in the long run it did her a disservice. At the time, however, she recognised its value in promoting sales of her own work. Whoever wrote *The Parallel* (Laetitia suspected James Worsdale's hand in the background) produced a well-executed piece of literary criticism based on close reading of both books and making sensible comments about the literary culture which produced them. Moreover, the pamphlet was well distributed: Bernard Clarke came by a copy in Co. Meath. He thought the author had a cheek putting Mrs Pilkington in such company. She saw the matter differently. In London as well as Dublin, people were talking about her.

By driving her pen hard all summer, Laetitia had substantially finished her second volume. She had a public and it was waiting. Reading *The Parallel* gave her pause for thought. Like Woodward's 'Tit for Tat', it was likely to be good for business. If it was meant to be a satire, she could find no sting: the writer complimented her on her 'well drawn' characters and 'easy, natural and picturesque' style. She was criticised for remarking that Pope was envious of other writers and for showing Swift as a brute, also for including her own poems which interrupted the flow of her narrative, but the overall judgement was that she had written about an ordinary life in an interesting way – or as she summed it up, 'I have even made a dull Story entertaining by the Force of a sparkling Wit, and retentive memory.' She might not be a match for Mrs Phillips 'either in Beauty or in Art', but in terms of selling her own product, the rattling, combative, witty 'Mrs Pilkington', she had done comparably well. She had not, however, made as much money as Mrs Phillips made from her *Apology*. Mrs Phillips's first volume, sold in six separate parts at a shilling a part, had grossed £2,400.

Laetitia took stock. She had written more than enough to fill a second volume, mostly about her London adventures. But she still had material she wanted to publish in some form: poems that had not found a place in the first volume, the completed first act of her tragedy, *The Roman Father*, more stories about Swift. A third volume, which would enable her to keep up the momentum of her relationship with her readers, was the obvious solution. Around a central core of stories she could put a miscellany of poems sent to her by others; and letters, such as those she was writing and receiving from Clarke and Kingsborough. Decision made, she took out some of what had been intended for volume two and put it aside for volume three, filling up the space with a mixture of dusted off old writings like *The Roman Father* and some Richardsonian 'to the moment' new commentary. Through October and November she wrote. She told Bernard Clarke she was having to manage without Jack: 'I have no Amanuensis, no Assistant; but must, like the Silk-worms, spin all out of my own Bowels; or rather Brains, if I have any.'

She strove to produce the impression of spontaneous conversation on the page, and it was hard, unremitting work. Making
herself stay at home to write, she was distracted by the antics of
the household, telling Clarke,

I wish to Heaven you were to pass one Day with me, and then I am
certain you wou'd be convinced I am really unhappy. My landlord is a
Quaker, his Wife a Papist, his Son a Fool, and his Daughter a Whore. Had
I my dear Benefactor Cibber's comic Genius, I might make an Audience
(low as they are) laugh at them.

Feeling dull, she lost confidence in herself. Clarke's praises were
vital; she looked for his letters: 'I tell you sincerely I long for Post-
day, and if I have not a Letter from you, I give you in my Mind a
bad Wish, find fault with every Thing about me'. She could be 'as
ill-tempered' as if she were 'a Lady of the first Quality'.

Some of this strain made its way into the newly written parts of
the second volume which, while full of sprightly asides and
digressions, is less guarded in its venom. She took the opportunity
to answer criticisms of her first volume. To those who had said she
used too many quotations, that there was too much Milton, Swift
or Shakespeare, she modestly gave thanks for the compliment:
evidently they wanted more from her 'superior Pen'. Those who
had tried to go one better in wit, as Bishop Clayton had apparently
done by joking about her claim that he had seduced her maid, she
lambasted. People said she had written bitterly against the clergy
in general: they were wrong, her spite was reserved for individuals
who forgot their high calling. Over several pages she railed at
Clayton, angry because he had refused to acknowledge her in
London (though he had sent her £16 which she never thanked him
for); and because he had criticised Jack for the extravagance of his
dress. 'Were not you a little censorious, think you?' she sweetly
asked, given that the bishop himself, though hardly young, still
had 'a strong Dash of the Coxcomb, and might excuse it in a Boy'.
In Clayton it revealed itself not in fashionable buttonholes but in
fornicating with 'Juggy Macshane, the Chairman's Wife' and
making her son a parson. Clayton's joke, that he had seduced not
only the maid but the mistress too, on the carpet, was turned
against him. Mrs Pilkington wrote in the voice of the discarded

lover, telling the bishop he didn't have to 'be a Blab', that if he had made her husband a cuckold he ought now to make him a dean, ('you know it was in that sweet Hope I yielded up my Heart') and that if he had to tell the world their secret he ought to get his facts right:

I am much offended that you should say, when I was last at Shrift with your Holiness, that we had no better Accommodation for our Feast of Love, but a Carpet, whereas I insist on it that the Penance you enjoined me was as easy as a Down-bed could make it.

Who was to be believed? The Mrs Pilkington whose adultery was witnessed by twelve nightwatchmen but who swore she was only reading a book – and kept a straight face as she said so? Or Bishop Clayton? Carpet or bed, book or body, satire or sincerity? It was for the reader to judge.

The insults were crude, but the delivery was full of panache. What did it matter what anybody said about her sexual reputation now? She had acquired reputation of a different sort. She was a writer:

Now says my Reader, if he be a Giber, how this prating old Woman, who certainly never had any Temptation, boasts of Chastity: Ay, 'tis no Matter, I have had so many amorous Epistles, Odes, Songs, Anacreonticks, Saphics, Lyricks, and Pindaricks, in Praise of my Mind and Person too, since I came to Ireland; that I believe some Gentlemen, tho I cannot, have found me out to be a marvellous proper Woman.

Some of her 'learned Correspondents' accused her of being a plagiarist – she agreed: all writers were plagiarists. They said there was nothing new in what she wrote, that her vanity was intolerable, and in any case she didn't write her own memoirs: men, she retorted, couldn't tolerate so much talent in a woman. In a quickfire monologue, she mimicked men discussing the relative virtues of beauty and mind. Was 'external Loveliness' the 'nobler Part'? Was mind in a woman 'of little Consequence?' Well, 'Dr Young seems of a different Mind; but great Authors sometimes vary'. In any case, she was in such demand there was hardly time to waste on these stale debates and hackney themes. The present pressed into the text:

Hey-day, the Devil rides on a Fiddle-stick! fresh News arriv'd! all my Letters to Worsdale to be published, oh terrible! well, I hope he will publish every Poem that was enclosed in them, that I may come by my own again; let him return to me three Operas, twenty-five Odes, the Letters I wrote for him, the Poem which begins, 'To distant Climes, while fond Cleora flies'. And then he has my full Leave to publish every Letter of mine that he thinks will serve his Purpose.

Like *The Parallel*, anything Worsdale published would promote her *Memoirs*.

There is a vehemence in these passages in the second volume, with rapid changes of tone and voice, which make it hard to follow the narrative at times – not least because wrong-footing the reader was part of the point, like tyrannising over men of wit. Literary success was a 'mighty' conquest. Mrs Pilkington had 'signal Victories' to celebrate and she made sure people knew. She took the pen-name 'Euphrosine' as a mark of her status. She was so confident she even wrote a prologue to be spoken before the play at Smock Alley on the king's birthday at the end of October. Sheridan refused to use it, saying her lines were blasphemous. Given that her panegyrical impulse went so far as to place the monarch above God –

> Not the Great Ruler of the genial Year,
> Whose radiant Beams the whole Creation chear,
> Inspires such Joy, such Rapture, such Delight,
> As swells each Bosom at their Monarch's Sight!

– it's hard to disagree although it still might have been a trumped up reason. No prologue was spoken at all that night, to the monarch's apparent displeasure. Sheridan put a notice in the *Dublin Journal* blaming the 'Neglect of the Person who wrote the Prologue, in not sending it in Time'. This incident raises the suggestive possibility that Mrs Pilkington's prominence was such that Sheridan felt he had to countenance her, and that some mixture of his reluctance and her tardiness lay behind it.

Sheridan paid Michael Clancy for a prologue, and gave him a benefit at Smock Alley. Ominously, Clancy was also having some success in persuading Lord Kingsborough to be his patron.

Mrs Pilkington's search for a dedicatee to the second volume proved profitable. Lord Kingsborough did not want it dedicated to him but he continued generous. Having already given her forty guineas in the summer he came to breakfast one morning and informed her she had made a poet of him. He handed her an envelope in which he said were written four lines of poetry, but she was not to look at them until he had left; it would wound 'his Maiden modesty'. In fact, the paper contained a bank note. At least so she told her distant admirer Bernard Clarke, Lord Kingsborough's 'rival', who was advised to tremble at the competition. (Another of the 'sallies' that might have been lost on the schoolmaster.) She wrote some flattering lines to John Bowes, chief baron of the Irish court of exchequer. Bowes gave her a sum of money not to print the lines or name him. Others of her gentlemen friends did likewise. Nobody wanted the honour of the dedication. Undeterred, she embellished the verses written in praise of Samuel Richardson some years earlier and recycled them as a panegyrical poem to Lord Kingsborough, explaining in a note that he had prohibited a dedication and begging pardon for her presumption. She followed this with a preface which included a short letter from Bernard Clarke which usefully directed readers to the correct response: 'Madam,' Clarke had written, 'When I read the First Volume of your Works, I was touch'd with a feeling Sense of your uncommon Misfortunes, and am convinced, the Villainy of a Priest, and Envy of some of your own Sex, gave Birth to all your Afflictions.' Then came Clarke's own poem, as promised, blaming Matthew, dubbing her 'strictly innocent', and praising Kingsborough.

In England, the respectable bluestocking Elizabeth Montagu was waiting impatiently for the second volume. She was not alone. Mrs Pilkington's promise of even more entertainment in the continuation meant there were many like Mrs Montagu who on reading volume one 'could not help laughing' at the 'saucy' author's severities on the clergy and others, and looked forward to more of the same. Mrs Montagu judged Mrs Pilkington to have 'a pretty genius for poetry', and 'a turn of wit and satire', along with the degree of vanity required to display them. She wasn't convinced of her innocence but she didn't particularly mind that: 'one sees through her character,' she wrote to Ann Donellan, who of course knew Mrs Pilkington's character well, 'but at the same time one imagines nature meant her well in the gifts it gave her, and that a bad education, bad company, and a bad husband, perverted her.' The depiction of James Worsdale she found specially amusing: 'By the by, what a ridiculous light she makes Mr Worsdale appear in! A beau dressed from Monmouth-street would not make so absurd a figure as a man setting up for a wit with purchased poetry.' (Monmouth Street was a market for the most tattered and threadbare lace shirts and fancy coats.)

Laetitia would have enjoyed reading that remark. She might also have had interesting things to say about Mrs Montagu's thoughtful observations on the difficulties of being a female wit. Mrs Montagu sensed that an era was coming to an end:

It is often said that wit is a dangerous quality; it is there meant that it is an offensive weapon that may attack friend as well as enemy, and is a perilous thing in society; but wit in women is apt to have other bad consequences; like a sword without a scabbard it wounds the wearer, and provokes assailants. I am sorry to say the generality of women who have excelled in wit have failed in chastity; perhaps it inspires too much confidence in the possessor, and raises an inclination in the men towards them, without inspiring an esteem; so that they are more attacked and less guarded than other women.

Immensely wealthy, married, and in the inner circle of English aristocracy – that class for whom maintaining the stability of society was simple self-interest – Mrs Montagu spoke from a position of extreme protectedness. The freewheeling Irish woman's aggression alarmed her; but in fact, having 'failed' in chastity, wit was Mrs Pilkington's most important source of esteem and therefore defence.

In Dublin there was a high level of anticipation. After eighteen months back home Mrs Pilkington was a fixture. Her account of her life in volume one had given Dublin back an image of itself. Who would be mentioned in volume two? What shocking things would be said? Friends as well as enemies knew success had made her bolder and that she sought revenge. Matthew, after the pamphlet exchanges of spring and summer, was keeping quiet probably on the advice of Archbishop Cobbe.

Some time in that autumn, while volume two was going through the press, Laetitia and Jack moved house again. They went to Fownes's Street, centrally located off Dame Street and 'opposite to the Golden Cup', where they stayed for about a year. While at Fownes's Street she was able to afford to keep at least two servants. Jack bought many new suits.

The second volume of Mrs Pilkington's *Memoirs* was ready in December. Copies were distributed and there was more or less simultaneous publication in London on 15 December. *The Gentleman's Magazine* quickly extracted the poem in praise of Dr Hales for its December issue, 'from the second volume . . . just published'.

In Dublin Laetitia expected an army of critics to rise up and so it did. A Mrs Ir—d—ll published several papers, now lost, and one anonymous pamphlet printed by K. Wentworth recorded the fact that drawing rooms across the city echoed with the sound of Mrs Pilkington's name. This pamphlet, *Remarks on the Second Volume of the Memoirs of Mrs Pilkington, with some particulars of that lady's life which she has omitted*, by 'an impartial hand', appeared early in 1749 and it complained that Mrs Pilkington's book was spoiling good conversation in Dublin: nobody wanted to talk about anything else. The author was unhappy about a number of things, chiefly how well Mrs Pilkington had been getting on. She was working her way back into favour. The barriers were beginning to go down. The pamphlet revealed its true agenda in its attack on Mrs Pilkington's 'vanity', 'impertinencies' 'impudence' and 'insolencies': the real beef was how 'undeserving' she was of 'the favour she has met with, not only as to her behaviour as a woman, but her merit as a writer'. Colley Cibber was called a blockhead and pickpocket (picking the pockets of noblemen to get money for a 'Female Scandal-monger') and Mrs Pilkington's claim to have maintained herself by her pen was snappishly dismissed: ' 'Tis a likely Story, that People would give their Money to a young, single Woman without asking a Favour'.

Far away at Caledon, his country house in the north, the Earl of

Orrery read both Mrs Phillips and Mrs Pilkington – 'Con and Pilky' – not because he wanted to but 'to adapt myself to the conversation of my neighbours, who have talked upon no other topic, notwithstanding the more glorious subjects of peace, and Lord Anson's Voyage'.

Perhaps some of his neighbours (or their servants) also got hold of *The Ladies Advocate: or Wit and Beauty A Match for Treachery and Inconstancy* which retold both stories as romantic sagas for a popular readership. In this book Mrs Pilkington became 'the fair Pilkmena' while Matthew was 'Pilkmenon'.

Mrs Pilkington's 'merit as a writer' outweighed her failure as a wife, although it was generally agreed that the tone of volume two was coarser than that of volume one, the invective harsher. Bernard Clarke was among those who thought she would have more friends if she dealt less in scandal. A more worldly reader, John Cleland, having been lent both volumes by his publisher Ralph Griffiths, was more sympathetic to the criticisms of male behaviour. Cleland found 'a great deal of nature' in the story, and a convincing picture of a legal and social environment that allowed men to mistreat women with impunity. He observed to Griffiths:

This woman would have, in all probability, made an irreproachable wife, had she not been married to such a villain, as her whole history shows her husband to have been: and indeed to do that sex Justice, most of their errors are originally owing to our treatment of them.

No such thoughtful reflections about the difficulties of being a woman in a man's world oppressed Benjamin Victor. He complained that the representation of him showed 'malice' and that he felt a 'small degree of resentment', but he assured Colley Cibber his resentment contained 'not the least taint of revenge'. This was not true, though Victor's thirst for revenge might have expressed itself earlier had she not been meeting quite such favour. Kingsborough's protection, and his wealth, inhibited him.

Mrs Pilkington had been too busy to keep up her own correspondence with Cibber. She also seems to have made the mistake of lending out some of his letters to 'a Man of Distinction' (possibly Kingsborough) without first having them copied. They never came back. In the spring she wrote to Samuel Richardson, asking him if he could tell her anything about the reception of her books in London. Like any author, she was interested, but her motive for writing was likely to have been to prod Richardson into sending replies which she could use in the third volume. Jack had copied out Kingsborough's letters and they had talked about the pros and cons of including them. While Kingsborough remained generous it was unwise to risk offending him.

Subscriptions for volume three began coming in as soon as volume two hit the streets: many people quickly subscribed as a way of buying their names out of the next volume. At the end of April Mrs Pilkington called in at Samuel Powell's printshop to gather up some of the money he was holding. She had complained about Powell, but he was probably doing honestly by her and they were then on friendly enough terms for him to invite her to stay for dinner. There was another client in the shop, a stiff-looking man dressed in black, without a wig, whom she assumed was a parson. He too was invited. Powell told her he was 'the great Dr Wesley' the Methodist preacher and that she would enjoy his conversation. John Wesley knew exactly whom he was meeting when Powell introduced him: the little woman was 'the famous Mrs Pilkington'.

Wesley and Mrs Pilkington each reported on this unlikely encounter. Their stories do not tally. A recent historian of Methodism flatly states, 'Wesley's account is almost entirely a fiction', while noting that Mrs Pilkington was more 'credible' though she also embellished because her purpose was to entertain Lord Kingsborough. Wesley situated the meeting in Mrs Pilkington's lodgings where he figured her as a repentant prostitute and potential convert. He claimed he 'talked with her seriously' for about an hour and they sang a hymn together – Charles Wesley's 'Happy Magdalene'. Wesley commented that she 'appeared to be exceedingly struck', by his words, but 'How long the impression may last, God knows'.

In her *Memoirs*, Mrs Pilkington took several swipes at Methodists. It was a Methodist landlady in London who had thrown her out on to the street when Betty arrived. Wesley himself does not feature and she chose not to make any reference to this meeting. She wrote about it in a long letter to Kingsborough, a patron unsympathetic to Methodism. (She kept a copy which Jack later published.) It had been a dull dinner with the Powells, she told Kingsborough, lank-haired Wesley largely silent, and she having to keep some sort of 'general conversation' going. All Wesley would say was that he wanted her to go and hear him preach. She declined, telling him:

For my part, Sir, when I go to church, it is to that established by law; to which, notwithstanding that some of her clergy are little better than they should be, I am so heartily reconciled, that it will be a hard matter now to make a Methodist of me.

However, the man she had been assured was 'a gentleman and a scholar' did want to visit her at her house where they could talk privately. She invited him to breakfast next morning. Wesley said he would come if God was willing and if there was a hope of seeing her 'a sister in Christ'. She thought him a 'sanctified levite'.

He came at eight, a transformed creature. Where all had been flat and blank the day before was now charged with energy. Wesley, she wrote, made her a courtly bow, the muscles in his face were 'braced up to their proper functions, and he appeared a sprightly young fellow'. And then he explained that his behaviour the day before had been a performance:

I never suffered more pain, Madam, said he, than I did yesterday, lest Mrs Pilkington should believe me the stupid animal I affected: but I may be sincere enough to tell you, Madam, this seeming sadness and solemnity is of the utmost use in my vocation; and you know, Madam, as Falstaff says, 'May not a man labour in his vocation?' Powel and his wife were Anabaptists, but are now followers of me; and 'tis natural to suppose I'll obtain as many as I can, as well as Mrs Pilkington endeavours to fill her subscription list; upon which, Madam, I beg to be in cog; and so saying, he presented me with a couple of guineas. – Now, Doctor, said I, do you consider what you have been about? How do you know, that the moment you depart, I may not take the pen and publish all this? Madam, said he, I know by your writings, that it is not in your nature to do a premeditated injury to one who has reposed a confidence in your honour and understanding; and besides, not one of my followers would believe a syllable of it, I have so effectually gained an ascendancy over their faith.

After these agreeable preliminaries, they settled down to talk about books, plays, music, painting, statuary, 'and in short, every subject that could convince me he was a man of taste and true breeding'. She had never, she told Lord Kingsborough, 'received more satisfaction from the discourse of any divine in my life, nor ever knew one who was half so honest and ingenuous'. Wesley, she concluded, was an honest hypocrite following a trade not dissimilar to her own. If he was a prophet, she could see no difference between him and other men except that he wore his own hair not a wig, and instead of taking tea with milk for breakfast he asked for warm milk and water.

Had she known about Mrs Grace Murray, Wesley's companion on the Irish tour, a widow with whom he had fallen in love and to whom he was secretly engaged, she would surely have shared the morsel. Methodists in the north of England, where Mrs Murray managed the Newcastle Orphan House and was a noted preacher, had some concerns. Wesley's animation in Mrs Murray's presence had led to talk; they had been seen holding hands. Mrs Pilkington may not have known the details but she was a trained observer of men in a state of sexual excitation and she caught the mood. Wesley, meanwhile, was stimulated by an encounter that confirmed his belief in the power of female ministry, a cause he championed. Mary Magdalene, after all, was the first person to see the risen Christ and in Charles Wesley's hymn 'Happy Magdalene' she is the favoured one whose task was to spread the gospel and 'Teach the Teachers of Mankind'. Mrs Pilkington's *Memoirs* had barbed words for Methodists but they were as nothing to her righteous attack on the established church. Unlikely as it might seem, John Wesley and Mrs Pilkington probably were as pleased with each other as she reported.

Keeping Lord Kingsborough amused was a full-time job. When she referred slightingly to her old enemy Joseph Leeson, the brewer's son whose first wife 'died of his love', Kingsborough told her off: Leeson was a friend. Another friend of Kingsborough, John Browne of the Neale, a moving spirit behind the Kelly riots, was in jail awaiting trial for murder after killing a man in a duel. On Kingsborough's behalf she visited him and reported back that he was in good form and had 'absolutely made love' to her and written a sonnet in her praise. Browne, apparently, ordered her not to mention a syllable of it to Lord Kingsborough, so she was 'ready to die with impatience to let your Lordship into the secret', and copied out Browne's verses so Kingsborough could decide whether the style was Platonic or carnal. Browne's poem opens with an image of 'Euphrosine' leaning forward and displaying her breasts:

> Fortune's malice I defy
> While my beautious fair one's nigh
> Let Euphrosine encline,
> Are not both the Indies mine?

Commenting that it was strange someone under threat of death should be so 'volatile', Mrs Pilkington added: 'I fancy it was written more to shew our friend's wit and politeness, than to make a conquest of an old woman'. Browne was released later.

An artist, possibly Robert Hunter who later did a series of portraits of the Kingsboroughs, asked her to sit for him. She thought he produced a good likeness, which nobody had ever managed to do before except Nathaniel Hone. She offered to send the painting to Kingsborough and he politely replied he would be delighted to place it 'where I would the original, might I have the happiness of her company, in my best apartment.'

Mostly what she was required to serve up was fictional flirtation, semi-soft porn, for a young man who continued to send money and ask for stories. When he recalled some verses she had written on 'an unfortunate lady' and asked her to copy them for him, she tried to get out of it. The poem was 'irregular and indigested'. No matter. Kingsborough wanted it. It featured 'the most beautiful and accomplished young lady' Mrs Pilkington had ever beheld, in attitudes of melting distress and sexual arousal. The poem told the story of the young lady's fall: an angelic youth had stimulated passion in her. Weeping, sighing, loving, longing, she was contrite and ashamed, but sexually awakened and hence in fantasy attainable, murmuring,

> Can I forget the still, the solemn night,
> Scene of my joy, my ruin, my delight?

These pleasing images heated Kingsborough so much that he

learnt the lines by heart. It was part of the fiction that he should wish to 'rescue' the woman, or perhaps buy her services: he sent two fifty-pound notes for Mrs Pilkington to pass on, having praised the poem in conventional terms: 'You know, Madam, I am neither connoisseur or critic, yet I can certainly feel what enraptures my sense, and melts my soul to a feminine weakness'. Labouring to fill the page with the language of criticism, Kingsborough had one thing on his mind. He added a PS: 'If you should not readily hear of the lady, do me the favour, Madam, to dispose of the bills as you think proper.'

Was he asking her to procure such a 'beautiful and accomplished young lady' for him? It may be so, which might account for Mrs Pilkington's unusual reluctance to take the money. She was offended at being told she could apply to his agent, Mark White, for whatever she wanted. This proof of her patron's 'unlimited kindness' made her uncomfortable she told him, though the discomfort probably had more to do with the services required. 'I can't help thinking, my Lord, it would manifest great want of modesty in me to make the least use of so noble an indulgence,' she wrote, adding that she couldn't work out what use so much money could be 'but to serve those who are in distress'. His recent bounty of £50 was not yet exhausted. She hadn't spent it, she told him, because she didn't have expensive tastes; she spent nothing on amusements or dress, she herself wore what was decent and convenient, and if she was 'superfluous in any point' it was only extravagance 'in dressing out my son'. For this she knew she was censured. She was unapologetic. Jack loved clothes; it gave her an opportunity to annoy Matthew and 'his partizans'; and it was a way to display her good fortune in having Lord Kingsborough as her patron.

Performing the satisfied client, Mrs Pilkington may have been hoping to direct Lord Kingsborough's attentions to Jack. She herself had been placed above need. Money, in fact, was raining down on her. 'I have had so much money of late, ' she rather unwisely told Kingsborough, 'that I have been at a loss what to do with it. B—ps, P—ts, and D—ns [Bishops, Prelates, Deans?] liberally supply me, without my being at the pains to sollicit their benevolence. I receive sums of money from unknown hands; nay, even the ladies now begin to honour me with their correspondence and contributions.'

Glad that the world was penitent for 'the injuries it has offered to the greatest and best of her sex', Lord Kingsborough proposed a subject for her poetic talents. He invited her to take 'the world' as her subject for a panegyric. Telling her she was sent on earth 'as a pattern of vivacity, for dull authors to imitate and improve by', he promised that he personally would be able to rustle up 500 subscribers. At this point it was hard for Laetitia to disguise her impatience. She (mis)quoted Hamlet at him

> Fie on't, oh fie
> 'Tis an unweeded garden that grows to weeds.
> Things rank and gross in nature possess it merely

and sent him a poem, 'from the bottom of my soul', which showed no vivacity or enthusiasm for the world whatsoever.

Either success or despair made her reckless. In her real ambition, to get a secure provision for Jack, she had made no progress. Out and about in his fine new clothes, voluble and brash, Jack was a target for envy. His own account of himself suggests a talent for self-destruction. Blind Michael Clancy may or may not have heard Jack and his mother speaking disrespectfully of Lord Kingsborough but that they did so is wholly plausible. That Jack boasted he would print the noble lord's letters one by one in halfpenny sheets and have them cried by hawkers in the streets is also plausible. Clancy, leagued with Sheridan and angling for Kingsborough's patronage, made sure the word reached Boyle Abbey. He then paid Mrs Pilkington the compliment of stealing her idea. Clancy had begun writing his memoirs. In late May he ran advertisements soliciting subscriptions and promising a fund of anecdotes about 'Persons of the first Distinction'. The book would be printed by Powell.

Kingsborough probably wanted to disassociate himself from Mrs Pilkington by now, especially after she had named him in the dedication to volume two when he had expressly declined. Returning to Dublin he went to her at Fownes's Street and without preamble, 'in a sort of commanding Tone', gave her ten guineas and demanded she give him back his letters. She was stunned. She managed to retain enough composure to respond politely and hand over to him just a handful from a drawer. He took them 'abruptly' and left, telling her to find the rest and have them ready in the morning when he would send a messenger for them. She tearfully registered that she had been sacked. Luckily, 'some agreeable Company' arrived and dissipated melancholy thoughts. These friends may have spent the evening helping her transcribe any uncopied letters she still had.

Early next morning there was a chairman at the door, storming and swearing, and with instructions not to leave without the cache of letters. His noise woke her up. She was furious. She sent an angry note to Kingsborough, complaining of this treatment. It was a 'fatal Epistle'. The moment it was out of the house she knew she had made a mistake. Another messenger was despatched to catch the first but it was too late. The letter reached Lord Kingsborough and his lordship took offence.

Mrs Pilkington's letter seems to have contained threats which Kingsborough at first scorned to acknowledge – his reply was a terse, ''Tis very well'. She passed a sleepless night, cursing Clancy and her own impulsive folly. She tried to recover by composing a grovelling poem and begging forgiveness but Kingsborough coldly put her in her place. 'Madam,' he wrote, 'I am extremely honoured, by that Esteem and Friendship which you profess for me in your really fine Copy of Verses; yet, when I reflect on a late Letter of yours, which I still have by me, I cannot help thinking myself as unworthy of your Praises, as I was of your Threats.'

She blamed herself. She had handled it badly. Bored and irritated by the requirements of the relationship, she had made a serious professional error. There was no way back into Kingsborough's good graces and no more access to his open-handed benevolence. All hope that he would provide for Jack after her death was at an end.

CHAPTER THIRTEEN

Last Days

The break with Lord Kingsborough in the summer of 1749 precipitated a depression. Illness played a part. Racked and sleepless, Laetitia was surprised at how agitated she felt. 'I did not believe', she wrote, 'that after all the Anguish of Mind I had sustained through my Life, any thing could move my Philosophy (which had made me determine never to be overjoyed or surprised at any Advancement in Life, or dejected or cast down at any Adversity on this Side Futurity), so much as this.'

Kingsborough's rejection may have re-activated feelings and fears from twelve years earlier when she was caught with Robert Adair and turned out of her home. Matthew rejected her then, and Robert Adair abandoned her shortly after. And perhaps she had been more overjoyed at her recent 'Advancement' than she cared to recognise, drew more comfort from it than she could easily give up – not just financial comfort but social acceptance. After so many years on the margins as a disowned daughter of family and class, to find herself feted in her home city, to be able to boast that 'even the ladies' were writing and subscribing and perhaps inviting her to dinner, was a triumph. It is little wonder that she felt remorse as she contemplated the potential damage that had been done and her own contribution to it.

She had failed, in the end, to manage an awkward client–patron relationship. It had needed effort, and her impatience had been showing for some time. To Kingsborough's silly proposal that she 'write on the world', for example, Mrs Pilkington had responded sourly with a poem that began by saying no:

Call me not to a world I hate,
Call me not to perverse mankind,
Move me from folly and deceit,
Content and virtue let me find.

This 'retirement' poem, forwarded to Kingsborough as requested (carefully copied and stored first), urged the superiority of solitude over society, and direct communion with God over anything 'perverse mankind' might offer. It contained no softening flatteries, unlike the placatory verses 'To the Right Hon. the Lord Kingsborough' that were sent in the desperate attempt to win him back. In 'To the Right Hon. the Lord Kingsborough', Kingsborough was assured that one smile from him made

rich Amends,
For shatter'd Fortune, and the loss of Friends.

There was no such promise in 'Call me not to a world I hate'; indeed, it could be considered wilfully ungrateful:

Know all you splendid rich and gay,
Know all ye wretches, worldly wise
Like mine your span is but a day,
And flatt'ring hopes are mere surmise.

I know you all, you know not me,
Beneath your ken, by fortune plac't
My sorrows with disdain you see,
And my distresses with distaste

Curs'd be the head that first devis'd
A bar from each sublimer tie;
Bid wealthy knaves, and fools be priz'd,
And merit in oblivion lie.

Is it a boast to say thy hand,
Almighty guardian of the just,
Made me the strokes of fate withstand,
While e'er in thee I plac'd my trust?

No – let me to an age deprav'd
An age of infidels declare,
Thy servant never was deceived,
When fondly she confided there.

I seek the cot, I seek the cell,
I seek the mountain, stream or grove;

Lead me contentment where you dwell,
With concord, piety and love.

Lead me to some inspiring vill,
Near a romantic structure rear'd;
Where virtue and religion still
Bloom by corruption unimpaired.

Where health and jollity robust
Spreads a rich glow o'er evr'y face;
Where not the meanest sold his trust
For title, grandeur, wealth or place.

If there be such a spot on earth,
Oh! God of an all-searching eye;
Tho' not from such I drew my birth,
In such contented let me die.

Kingsborough was one of the 'wealthy knaves and fools', the 'splendid rich and gay', from whom she had hoped great things and upon whom, she now told him, she wanted to turn her back in disgust. The hermit's cell, the mountain stream, her own merit and God's providential care, were to compose a new dream of contentment. Kingsborough, though he made no comment on these lines, might have justifiably remarked that the dream was only made possible by his money.

'Call me not to a world I hate' condensed a lifetime's disappointments. It was one of the last poems Laetitia wrote, and like so much of her work it was written to and for a specific individual. Detached from context the deceptively simple, polished lines enunciate conventional themes; read in the knowledge of this particular client–patron relationship they gain complexity. Traditionally, the poet's role was to raise the tone, pointing the patron's mind towards eternity during his lifetime and celebrating him in deathless verse for future generations. The reward was protection and mutually reflected glory. There was always tension between the claims of merit and the vantage of birth, but the poet–patron relationship was not usually that between a middle-aged woman and a young rake. Laetitia performed clientage as an old coquette but her laurels had been earned by merit. With cash in her purse, a celebrated poet and writer, she had begun to wonder what kind of lustre Kingsborough – true product of 'an age deprav'd' – was likely to spread over her name.

Like her earlier poems 'Sorrow' and 'Expostulation', which gave dignified voice to unbearable loss as she contemplated the ruins of her reputation in the aftermath of divorce and faced the prospect of leaving Ireland and her children, 'Call me not to a world I hate' angrily bid farewell. Perhaps Kingsborough had read and understood.

Along with the turmoil Kingsborough's abrupt dismissal provoked, there were other threats to Laetitia's peace of mind in the summer of 1749. Her health, never robust, had begun to give serious cause for concern. Over the years she had endured recurring stomach trouble, complaining of what she described as 'an extreme bad Stomach, and Digestion'. Poor nutrition, anxiety, insomnia all contributed. She may have suffered from stomach ulcers. She may have had cancer or some other disease.

Then there was the absent brother-in-law, George Frend, and his abandoned wife, Laetitia's sister Elizabeth. After thirteen years on garrison duty in the Mediterranean the sunburnt soldier, now a captain, returned with his regiment to Dublin. This was in July. Captain Frend had long regretted his youthful indiscretion but it is likely that Elizabeth, hearing of his return, made financial demands. Frend had no intention of supporting her. The fact that she had several children gave him grounds for claiming that she was living 'a scandalous, dissolute and adulterous Life'. His son born in 1735, Jack's fourteen-year-old cousin, he was prepared to acknowledge, but no-one could accuse him of fathering any of the other children; and he wanted to follow the example set by Matthew Pilkington and obtain a formal separation through the Consistory Court. Elizabeth may have become a prostitute, as Frend's charges implied, and as perforce many women did; she may simply have settled down with another partner which would have been enough to warrant the adjectives 'scandalous', 'dissolute' and 'adulterous'. Whatever her actual behaviour, any upsurge of talk about her was irksome to her estranged sister.

∞

In the autumn of 1749 Laetitia was well enough or sufficiently in need of funds to return to the manuscript of her memoirs and think seriously about the third volume. She placed an advertisement in *Esdall's Newsletter* for 23 November thanking her supporters and advising them that the third and last volume was in the press and would be 'speedily' published. She promised letters from Colley Cibber and more anecdotes about Swift. A good deal had been written the previous year so even if the bleak combination of ill health and low spirits disinclined her to work much she might have thought she had enough for Powell to begin printing. Cibber himself was wondering what had happened to her. He wrote to ask Victor, 'When does the next Volume of our poor Devil's Memoirs come out?' and 'what is become of her?'

She was still living at Fownes's Street when she advertised. Some time towards the end of 1749 or early in 1750 she and Jack moved across the river to Phraper Lane (now Beresford Street) where they took two floors of a house which belonged to a former parish clerk of Matthew's at Donabate, Patrick Sheile. This may have been a simple coincidence. Sheile had left Donabate some years earlier and pursued a living as a farrier and then as an untrained, unlicensed doctor. Meanwhile, most of his income came from letting out rooms to lodgers. Laetitia and Jack paid half a guinea a week for their two apartments. 'Doctor' Shiel's house cannot have been very grand: it was rated at £5. The lowest charge on the rate was £1 or £2; Lord Kingsborough, living nearby in Henrietta Street, paid £60 but that is certainly an unfair comparison.

In this house, through the winter and spring of 1749–50, Mrs Pilkington's health steadily worsened. She began to lose weight. Increasingly weak, she stayed inside the apartment and as spring turned to summer she kept to her bed. At some point a nurse was hired to tend to her. Of these months of terminal illness we know nothing, but Jack left an account of her last few days in which he indicated that she had been declining for some time and that when he went upstairs to sit with her they would talk freely about her approaching death. 'She never seemed in the least uneasy at the Knowledge of her approaching End,' he wrote, 'often declaring, that if she could take me with her to Felicity, she would leave this World without Reluctance.'

It was a hot summer. Some time about the middle of July, Jack had a bout of fever. It began as a heavy cold and quickly went to his lungs. Breathing was painful, he was running a high temperature and coughing and retching so badly he feared for his life. He sent for Dr Fergus who agreed he should have called him earlier and applied the usual remedy: bleeding, four times that day. Then Dr Fergus went up to see Mrs Pilkington. Jack recalled his mother asking the doctor's advice on both their cases. The doctor did not prevaricate:

He told her a little too frankly, that Nature might do something for my recovery, but that her Death was inevitable; she smiling, said to him, That the worms would have but a poor Feast of her, she being quite worn away.

Jack had a steady girlfriend, a 'Miss C—m'. The doctor's visit had pepped Jack up, and when Miss C—m came next day she was delighted to see him much recovered, though still in bed. She stayed. The nurse brought Laetitia down to Jack's apartment, lifting her 'like a Child, in her Arms', and placed her in an elbow chair by Jack's bed. Jack described a devout scene in which Miss C—m knelt by the chair and declared her love for Jack, asking for his mother's blessing and saying that she hoped they would have a wedding from the house not a burial.

Jack could see that his mother was doing her best to be cheerful for their sakes, though he also made a point of saying that she kept her spirits and good humour to the last. She gave her blessing to their proposed marriage. There was chicken for dinner, of which she took a little, but could not keep it down. She was soon carried back upstairs to her own bed.

Jack's misery is very apparent in what followed. He, too, tried to be cheerful. Next morning going into his mother's room he found that she had a cast over one of her eyes. She told him that she was seeing double. Shocked, he pretended there was nothing there and that in fact she seemed to him better than she had in a long while. He was feeling better himself and he proposed that the three of them take a trip. They could go to Chapelizod, a pleasant country jaunt just beyond Phoenix Park. The doctor might have 'given her over' but together, Jack declared, if they followed his prescription, they might be able to make 'a Fibber' of the doctor. Pleased with the idea, Laetitia ordered a landau. 'In the morning,' Jack wrote,

> she was up and dressed before me, and was as sprightly as I had ever seen her, tho' quite weak, insomuch that she was obliged to be carried into the Coach and out again.

> We set out before Breakfast, and went thro' the Phoenix Park, it was a fine Day, and we had the Landau opened, the fresh Air vastly revived her, and she repeated a good many Lines of the Poem on Windsor-Forest; she even complained of being hungry. When we came to the Tavern, I ordered some Tea; and to my infinite Surprize, my Mother called for a Plate of Ham, and some Oil and Vinegar, ate very heartily, and drank two Glasses of White wine.

They walked, though she had difficulty, into the flower garden. She was weak and in pain. Her eyes hurt. Back at the tavern, Jack ordered duckling and green peas for dinner. Laetitia went to lie down and slept a little. When dinner was ready she ate 'very hearty'. There were two gentlemen in the tavern whom they knew; they came over and joined them. Probably shocked at the sight of Mrs Pilkington, they nevertheless laughed at her stories and nodded in agreement when she told them the doctor had said there was no hope but she intended to outlive them all. She entertained them with 'twenty agreeable Stories' and Jack felt joy and pride.

They stayed till ten. When they left it was cooler. Before they had gone a hundred yards, Laetitia began coughing uncontrollably. She coughed all night.

Jack thought the air had been 'fatal' to her but she had probably caught his cold. Jack also blamed their landlord, Sheile, 'this Blood-hound', this 'inhuman Cannibal' for frightening his mother with threats to throw her on the street for the three weeks' rent that was owing. There was a scene that had left her trembling and pale. She had been forced to give Sheile the keys to her drawers and let him take her valuables for security. Perhaps he took some items of clothing. Jack had already removed the real valuables, his mother's manuscripts, and stored them elsewhere for safe keeping.

Jack found one more poem, 'the last she ever wrote', after he had persuaded her to drink some mulled wine and try to sleep. It was on the table and it was a prayer. She had written:

> My Lord, my Saviour, and my God
> I bow to thy correcting Rod;
> Nor will I murmur or complain,
> Tho' ev'ry Limb be fill'd with Pain;
> Tho' my weak Tongue its Aid denies,
> And Day-light wounds my wretched Eyes.

The cough kept her awake and she became feverish. When she mixed up present and past, and told Jack that her father had taken in subscriptions for her, it gave him 'the most piercing Anguish'; and when, after dozing, she related a 'mighty agreeable Dream', they both understood its import. In the dream, her father had come to her,

in a Mourning Coach and six; and told her he was very angry she had been so long ill, and yet never sent for him whom she knew was always ready to assist her; I am come, continued he, to bring you out of all your Troubles; and with that, took her in his Arms, like a Child, and carried her away in the Coach.

Next day Laetitia sent Jack for the local curate. She had always said she would never let any of the Church of Ireland clergy near her during her last hours 'except dear Doctor Delany' (who was out of town). Now she feared people would add 'Impiety' to all the other things they had said of her, and she wanted comfort. The local curate was a young man, twenty-five-year-old George Antrobus. He spoke a prayer then stayed for a glass of wine and 'a good deal of Discourse'. Antrobus was curious to know if Mrs Pilkington forgave her husband, Matthew. In answer, she told him a joke about a dying Irish Catholic seeking absolution who would forgive everyone except a man who stole his cow. When the priest explained he had to forgive him too, the man replied that if he died he would forgive him, but if he lived he never would. The priest agreed it would have to do. 'So, Sir,' Laetitia told Antrobus, 'if I die I do forgive him; and I wish the God whom he has offended may do the same; but if I live, mark you that, Master Parson, I never will.' Like the priest in the joke, Antrobus agreed that would have to do.

There was no forgiveness, even after death. She made Jack swear that when she died he would make sure she was buried with her father in St Ann's church. Matthew might try to bury her in his own family burial place and if Jack allowed that he would have his mother's curse; 'Nay,' she assured him, 'if it's possible, I will come from the Grave to resent it,' and added that if he ever grew rich he was to put up a marble stone and have the following inscription carved on it:

Here lyeth, near the Body of her honoured Father, John Vanlewen, M.D. the Mortal Part of Mrs Laetitia Pilkington, Whose Spirit hopes for that Peace, thro' the infinite Merit of Christ, which a cruel and merciless World never afforded her.

In acute pain, ceaselessly coughing, by evening she began to be incoherent. Jack sat up with her. In the early hours of the morning her breathing became more laboured. Her eyesight failed. Jack, taking her hand, which seemed to him to have no life in it, asked her if she knew him and she said, yes, he was William, her eldest son, come from the college to ask her blessing. Uttering William's name made her agitated. 'It seemed as if her not being permitted to see him disturbed her last Moments,' Jack wrote. Kneeling by the bedside, he held her hand till it grew cold and heavy.

It was Sunday, 29 July 1750. Jack had lost his mother for the second time.

∞

The funeral took place at St Ann's church. Matthew provided a decent oak coffin and shroud and paid the costs of interment. Less than a month later, on 27 August, he married Anne Sandes. Her father, Pigott Sandes, gave £700 as her marriage portion.

Twenty-year-old Jack looked into the future and saw nothing but 'the Malice of Fortune'. For over five years he had depended on his mother. He had worked with her, learnt from her and, for an all too brief period, enjoyed the comforts of success with her. It was natural that he should try to do alone what they had done as a pair, and that she should continue to be his 'Prop and Succour'.

Jack possessed the completed manuscript of volume three, numerous poems, and many bundles of letters from senior figures in church and state. His first resort was to his father. The landlord, Sheile, advised Jack to send all his mother's papers to Matthew as a peace offering and promised he would mediate between them. Sheile was confident he could persuade Matthew to pay Jack £20 a year. Credulous, but not that credulous – 'as to Twenty Pounds a Year, my Father would as soon give Twenty of his Teeth' – Jack did invite Sheile to negotiate a deal for him: if his father would give him a flat payment of £50 he would hand over everything that remained, leave Ireland and never trouble him again. Matthew laughed at the offer. 'He said I had not my Mother's Genius, and must quickly fall into Contempt,' Jack recalled, 'therefore he very fairly set me at defiance; and should I dare to print any Thing against him, he had Interest enough to send me over the Water.'

Spurned by Matthew, Jack wrote a round of letters. If his father didn't want to buy his stock there were other concerned individuals who might take it off him piece by piece. One of those who responded was Nathaniel Clements, MP, a wealthy banker and property-developer and one of the most powerful figures in the administration. Clements had known and respected Dr John Van Lewen and he had supported the doctor's daughter, which is why Jack had a number of letters written by him. Clements invited Jack to call at Phoenix Lodge, his palatial residence in Phoenix Park. There, Jack was given a comprehensive dusting-down, delivered with 'the utmost good manners' and ending with an undisguised threat that echoed his father's words. Clements spoke not only on his own behalf but for all those other 'Persons of the most eminent Stations in this Kingdom' who had complained, beginning with the Primate, Archbishop Stone. These men had been annoyed by Jack's letters. His writing 'very much in the Stile' of his mother was a 'Liberty' that would not be tolerated. Clements spelled it out. They had imagined, after Mrs Pilkington's death, that they would hear no more of her, but Jack 'seem'd to keep her Spirit alive'. The brash boy was reminded of his place. It was to be a humiliating exchange:

Now, young Man, said [Clements], consider you are not a Woman, from whom ev'n a Blow cannot hurt Honour. We tolerated those Things in her, which, in you, would be culpable in the highest degree; in short, if you have any Talents, as I am told you have, apply them to make Friends, instead of troubling your Head about the Follies of Mankind; find out their Virtues, and make that your Theme. Indeed, Sir, that, said I, will be a difficult Matter. In short, Sir, continued he, if you do not apply your Genius, according to the Will of your Superiors, Care will be taken to send you out of the Kingdom before you are aware of it.

The lesson Jack had to learn was that his mother occupied a special category and he did not. She had been tolerated but if he tried blackmail and satire he would be run out of town.

Many people vented their resentments on Jack; and the anxiety he described himself feeling as he was 'traduc'd' and 'plung'd into a World of Calamities' had real causes. To these rebuffs and rejections we owe the survival of the third volume of Mrs Pilkington's *Memoirs*.

Over the next few years we catch only glimpses of Jack, keeping body and soul together as a grubbing writer and gentlemanly player. He dreamed not of fame but of an annuity of £40. He took what work he could. On 16 October 1750 he was a featured singer in an outdoor benefit concert for the composer and violinist Giovanni Angelo Battisto Putti, originally announced for the 9th but postponed because of rain. He may have taken other singing engagements. He was on friendly terms with his brother William who by this time was finding it 'an Herculean labour' to put up with Matthew's 'caprice and peevishness'. We know nothing about Betty.

Jack was probably aware of events in his aunt Elizabeth's life: her ecclesiastical divorce on 12 July 1751; the deliberations of the Irish House of Lords committee on 25 November 1751 which considered George Frend's petition for a full divorce and took evidence from Meade Van Lewen on George's behalf; and on 21 April 1752 their approval of a bill based on Frend's petition. Free to re-marry, Elizabeth married a Dublin apothecary named John Turkington.

Jack also married. He broke with Miss C—m, and on 7 July 1753 he married Ann Smith at St Peter's, Dublin. He fathered one and perhaps two children. Later there was another wife, Dorinda, and perhaps more children.

Jack had decided to follow the advice he had been given and become a 'profess'd Sycophant'. On the strength of his mother's genius he was able to raise funds during these years. His cache of manuscripts gave him social access to 'Persons of Fortune and Humanity' who were willing to help him, some of whom had already subscribed and were committed to the appearance of a third volume of Mrs Pilkington's *Memoirs*. Judging by his success it was a role that suited him. (Later, he raised an even more impressive list of subscribers for his own memoir, *The Real Story of John Carteret Pilkington*.) Ranged against Jack were his father's supporters. It may have been their opposition which made him decide to go to London in the autumn of 1753 to see what support could be garnered there; or it may have been his own writerly ambitions. Before leaving he had talks with Powell about printing volume three. He tidied up the manuscript, possibly adding to it here and there where fulsome praise might bring him some reward, and discussed whether they should provide a key to the blanked out names in earlier volumes. Bearing in mind what Clements had said, this seemed unwise. A death-bed scene would play better. Jack wrote a heart-rending account of his mother's last days, stressing her Christian resignation and his own filial devotion.

Powell insisted on keeping hold of the manuscript. Jack owed him money.

In London, Jack had proposals printed, wrote letters and did a round of visits to previous subscribers, especially those mentioned in volumes one and two. He presented himself to Sam Foote, then having success with his *Englishman at Paris*, searched out James Worsdale, and seems to have managed, quite quickly, to antagonise both of them; his own envy was probably a factor. He was furious that Foote, who breezily promised a hundred subscribers, did nothing when it came to it. More pleasing was his reception by Sir John Ligonier, who agreed to accept the dedication and paid handsomely for it. The Duke of Marlborough gave him a generous sum.

By January 1754 Jack was able to write a preface (mostly attacking Sam Foote) and arrange for publication with Ralph Griffiths who had issued the London versions of volumes one and two. Having subscribers to satisfy on both sides of the Irish Sea, he probably crossed over more than once. He paid Powell what he owed him and liberated the manuscript for initial publication in

London in June. In Dublin it was advertised as 'In the press' that same month but did not actually appear until September. In London, *The Gentleman's Magazine* judged Mrs Pilkington's *Memoirs* the most attention-grabbing book to appear that summer and made use of it for their front page leading article in July with a follow-on in August. Over several pages in these two issues, *The Gentleman's Magazine* ran condensed accounts of Mrs Pilkington's story as told in volumes two and three. There was no editorial commentary except in a concluding paragraph which moralised that the companion of Swift had become 'the tool' of Worsdale.

For Mary Delany, one word sufficed: the third volume was 'odious'. Dr Delany (who was well praised) seems not to have minded; he continued to take an interest in Jack and to send him money. Mary Barber, not only named but mocked for the dullness of her poems, was probably past caring; after long illness, she died the following year.

We can perhaps get some idea what Matthew thought of the renewed publicity by the fact that he drew up his will that year for the express purpose, it would seem, of cutting off the children from his first marriage. He left £5 to William, acknowledging him as his son – 'my son William Pilkington' – but denying that he had behaved in a son-like way: 'who never felt a filial affection'. The younger children were not acknowledged. They were 'those two abandoned wretches John Carteret Pilkington and Elizabeth Pilkington', and each was left one shilling. Matthew only named them to protect himself: 'I should abhorr to mention them in any Deed of mine, if it were not to prevent all possibility of Dispute or litigation'. The will is a chilling document, though it does testify to Matthew's continuing love for Nancy. She gave birth to a child sometime after the marriage, which may also have prompted the will. At least one other child was born to the couple. None survived beyond infancy.

Jack seems to have lived mostly in London after 1754. Without the formal education William had received, he could not enter the professions and was more or less forced into dependence on that 'dangerous' implement, the pen. As he put it, 'from a poetical father and mother, what inheritance could a second brother hope, but a pen?' But for all its difficulties, Jack enjoyed the business of putting out his mother's third volume. He liked addressing 'the polite World', in person and in print. Projecting an image of himself as a 'poor lost one' in need of protection, he worked hard at cultivating all those who had shown the slightest willingness to be involved in the Pilkington family drama and traded on the reputations of both his parents. 'The writings of my mother,' he later wrote, 'added to the candour and indulgence of her readers, has procured her a place in the temple of fame; and my father's poetical productions, tho not received with so much applause, are yet allowed to be pretty enough'. His credit raised by the appearance of the book, Jack's benefactors (and perhaps his creditors) encouraged him to emulate his mother further by writing up his own adventures. Readers of *Tom Jones* and *Roderick Random* thought Jack's life had all the ingredients of a picaresque novel: his running away to Cork at the age of ten, falling in with a variety of characters, seeing high life with the O'Neills, experiencing several miraculous escapes and sudden transformations of fortune. Jack knew what he would call it: *The Adventures of Jack Luckless*. It would contain no satire, no personal abuse, only 'rational and inoffensive' anecdotes.

In the meantime, money came and went. There was much recourse to the pawnshop. At the end of 1754 Jack found himself following his mother's path into the Marshalsea for a 99 shilling debt. He was there for four weeks beginning 9 November. The following winter he was incarcerated again, from 4 December until 7 February. That time he owed £9 11s., which may be why it took longer to get out. His health suffered.

Over in Ireland, Lord Kingsborough died in 1755. Kingsborough's will, witnessed by a servant, a drunken porter and a prostitute named Mrs Jones, was disputed by his younger brothers, Edward and Henry. The vast Boyle estates were not to be settled for many years, a matter of no concern to Jack Pilkington who could, however, now consider publishing the correspondence between Lord Kingsborough and his mother which he had copied and kept.

Jack's uncle Meade was in England with his regiment in 1756. Captain Meade had had his own brush with the courts after killing a fellow officer in a duel. Tried for murder, he was acquitted on 30 August 1753. It seems unlikely that Meade would have taken any interest in his nephew's affairs. Later his regiment was posted abroad. He died in 1765, during the British occupation of Spanish West Florida, at Mobile, in what is now Alabama.

There is no record of Jack making contact with Colley Cibber, although he had some acquaintance with Cibber's son Theo. Cibber died in 1757. Theophilus Cibber did not long survive his father: he drowned en route to an engagement with Victor and Sheridan at Smock Alley the following year. The *Dublin Trader*, overloaded and with an inadequate crew, went down in a storm taking with it Theo, several acrobats and a crowd of wealthy linen and wool merchants returning from the Chester Fair. Smock Alley foundered shortly afterwards. Victor returned to London where he later became treasurer at Drury Lane.

Lord Carteret, now Earl Granville and the most prominent elder statesman in the land, was immensely rich. Jack had been named for him. Jack's parents had hoped the noble lord would sponsor the child. Granville kept aloof, as was his way, and it was irksome to Jack that he could not make more of what he considered his right. However, Carteret's daughter Georgina, whose 'goodness' Mary Barber had celebrated, proved susceptible. Georgina's first husband, dissolute Jack Spencer who had tried to rape Mrs Pilkington, had died in 1746 and in 1750 she married the second Earl Cowper. Georgina, Countess of Cowper, took up the mantle and did what her father disdained to do: she became Jack's patron.

By autumn 1757 Jack was living in Margaret Street and feeling pleased about the responses he had been getting to his plans for *Jack Luckless*. He wrote to Baron Dawson and the Earl of Clanricarde asking them to subscribe to a book which may or may not by then have been written. Still, Jack was entitled to be pleased. He had an extraordinary list of subscribers, testimony, as he boasted, to the 'publick good opinion and private esteem' in which he could consider himself held. The list was so starry that when he drew up the formal proposal the following spring, dated in humorous fashion 1 April 1758, Jack printed many of the names in a long list. Two copies of Jack's proposal for *The Adventures of Jack Luckless* survive in the British Library, on one of which *The Adventures of Jack Luckless* is heavily inked out, leaving *The Real Story of John Carteret Pilkington* as the final title. The change is significant. 'Jack Luckless' was nobody (or everyman) but John Carteret Pilkington was the son of Mrs Pilkington whose fame had grown through the 1750s. In 1755 many of Mrs Pilkington's poems had been extracted from the *Memoirs* and given wide circulation in an anthology of whose title she would undoubtedly have approved: *Poems by Eminent Ladies*. Meanwhile, through his patron as well as his name, Jack had a connection to the illustrious Carteret family which it was useful to advertise. Both copies of the leaflet are covered with handwritten names, added in the margins as people paid in their subscriptions. Subscribers were promised at least 500 pages of adventures interspersed with 'poetical essays on different subjects'. There would be entertaining characters 'drawn from real life', a new comedy, and 'remarks on and explanations of Mrs Pilkington's *Memoirs*'. The book would be printed on 'superfine' paper, neatly bound in Turkey leather with gilt lettering, and carry a frontispiece portrait 'scraped by Houston from an original picture'. Subscribers were assured the volume was 'in the press' which it wasn't.

Jack never did grow rich. He died in 1763, 'abroad', having probably fled to the Continent to escape his creditors. But he did produce his book. *The Real Story of John Carteret Pilkington* appeared, elegantly printed though not quite as full as promised, in 1760. It did not include remarks on the *Memoirs* as such, and indeed the story of Jack's adventures stopped before Jack was re-united with his mother in London; but in a substantial Appendix he printed the all-important correspondence with Lord Kingsborough which he had saved, and the unpublished poem, 'Call me not to a world I hate'. For the frontispiece Jack used not the picture of himself (now lost, if it ever existed) but a portrait of his mother.

∞

In 1760, old general Ligonier received the twenty copies of *The Real Story of John Carteret Pilkington* for which he had subscribed. Later, he went to the Haymarket to see Sam Foote and caught a feverish cold. Among the doctors treating him was Robert Adair, one of 'the most distinguished medical men' of the day.

Ligonier rallied and lived on until 1770. When he died, a huge monument was erected to his memory in Westminster Abbey.

During her years in London, Laetitia Pilkington often walked in Westminster Abbey. Once, she claimed, she was accidentally locked in overnight and, terrified of rats, pulled the carpet off the communion table to wrap herself in. She spent the night in the pulpit and dreamed dreams of violence, power, poetry and money. This may have happened, although being locked inside Westminster Abbey and having meaningful dreams was a fictional motif used in a well-known piece in the *Gentleman's Magazine*. The Abbey appealed when she wanted 'to indulge a pleasing Fit of melancholy' and had time to wander 'through the Cloysters, reading the Inscriptions'. The contrast between the lavish memorials and the dust beneath had its cheering aspects. She knew it was a joke when she identified the spot where she wanted to be interred – between the monuments of Shakespeare and Nicholas Rowe – although in the 1740s it was not so far-fetched to imagine such a thing. Actresses like Mrs Bracegirdle were buried in the Abbey; Aphra Behn's tablet can still be seen there. Laetitia had chosen her epitaph: an adaptation of Pope's lines in his 'Elegy to the Memory of an Unfortunate Lady' which mourned the lonely death of another outcast – possibly a suicide – whose fate was 'unpitied' and whose passing, in a 'foreign' land, was unmarked. She changed the pronoun from 'thee' to 'me':

> How lov'd, how honor'd once, avails me not,
> To whom related, or by whom begot;
> An Heap of Dust alone remains of me,
> 'Tis all I am, 'tis all the Proud shall be.

Death, the great leveller, would do her work of revenge for her.

There was, of course, to be no memorial in Westminster Abbey. But the inscription Mrs Pilkington hoped Jack might put on a marble stone over her grave, naming her as the daughter of Dr Van

Lewen and delivering a few parting words of reproach to a 'cruel and merciless World', can now be seen on a tablet in St Ann's church, Dublin. It was provided in 1998 by A. C. Elias, the modern editor of Mrs Pilkington's *Memoirs*, her lasting memorial.

A Note on Laetitia Pilkington's Early Literary Reception

An enthusiasm for anthologies of poetry developed in the mid-eighteenth century which served Mrs Pilkington well. Her poems were excerpted from the *Memoirs* and given wide circulation in collections such as George Colman and Bonnell Thornton's 1755 *Poems by Eminent Ladies*, which went through several editions. Lady Mary Wortley Montagu read Mrs Pilkington's *Memoirs* and scribbled in her copy that the poetry was as good as Pope's. There was no scandal attached to being a woman poet. Memoir-writing was another matter. Mrs Pilkington's literary reputation suffered from her association with Constantia Phillips and Lady Vane. Samuel Richardson, for all his personal kindness, condemned her as one of the 'Set of Wretches' who wrote memoirs 'wishing to perpetuate their Infamy'. Richardson called on 'proper' women like Mrs Chapone and her bluestocking friends to provide an 'Antidote to these Womens Poison!' Similarly a clergyman, Richard Graves, was inspired to write a poem, 'The Heroines: or, Modern Memoirs', in which Laetitia featured as one of the 'modern whores . . . Renown'd Constantia, Pilkington, and Vane':

> Without a blush, behold each nymph advance,
> The luscious heroine of her own romance;
> Each harlot triumphs in her loss of fame,
> And boldly prints – and *publishes* her shame.

Richardson's friend John Duncombe reiterated the theme in *The Feminiad* (1754): writing and publishing memoirs was the shocking thing.

By the end of the century, memoir-writing as a genre had

become even more firmly associated with courtesans and actresses. Scandal was big business for an expanded press. Negotiations over financial settlements between ex-lovers were closely followed, and an ex-mistress with a way with words who possessed a cache of letters – such as Mary Robinson, who as 'Perdita' captivated the young Prince of Wales – had bargaining power. There were sensational pay-outs; and some obstinate refusals of blackmail as when the Duke of Wellington told Harriette Wilson to 'Publish and be damned'. Retrospectively, Mrs Pilkington suffered again by association, though her threats had never been directed at ex-lovers and when people hurriedly subscribed to keep their names out of her book it was because they feared her wit rather than exposure of their sex lives.

Most readers probably knew Mrs Pilkington from extracts in periodicals and books. In 1759 many of her anecdotes were recycled in a commercial production, *Mrs Pilkington's Jests: Or the Cabinet of Wit and Humour* which was successful enough to be put out again five years later as *The Celebrated Mrs Pilkington's Jests*. The *Memoirs* themselves continued to be valued for their vivid portrayal of Swift in his later years. Not everybody acknowledged their use of Mrs Pilkington. Patrick Delany borrowed anecdotes when he wrote his *Observations on Swift* in 1754, and in 1784 Thomas Sheridan took from Delany for his *Life of Swift* what Delany had taken from Mrs Pilkington. Thackeray depended entirely on her for his account of Swift in *The English Humorists*, 1853.

A three-volume set of the *Memoirs* was reprinted in Dublin in 1776, two years after the death of Matthew Pilkington. There was no nineteenth-century edition. The first modern edition was in 1928, the year of female suffrage, edited and introduced by Iris Barry.

A Note on References

The main source throughout is the 1997 edition of Laetitia Pilkington's *Memoirs* edited by A. C. Elias Jr. This is in two volumes: volume one prints all three volumes of Mrs Pilkington's *Memoirs* first published in March and December, 1748 (vols one and two) and 1754 (vol. three). Elias's volume two provides substantial notes to Mrs Pilkington. My page references indicate the volume in Elias's edition not in the original three-volume publication of the *Memoirs*.

Jack Pilkington's *The Real Story of John Carteret Pilkington*, London, 1760, tells the story of his life as a series of picaresque adventures. It includes, as an appendix, his mother's correspondence with Lord Kingsborough.

These are abbreviated as *Memoirs* and *Real Story* respectively.

FURTHER ABBREVIATED REFERENCES IN THE NOTES

Richardson, *Letters* *The Correspondence of Samuel Richardson, Author of Pamela, Clarissa, and Sir Charles Grandison, Selected from the Original Manuscripts, Bequeathed by Him to His Family*, Anna Laetitia Barbauld (ed.), 6 vols, London, 1804. Mrs Pilkington's letters to Richardson are in vol. 2, pp. 113–57.

Clarke, *Poems* Bernard Clarke, *A Collection of Poems upon Various Occasions. Never Before printed. To which is added, An Epistolary Correspondence with a Lady of Singular Wit and Humour*, Dublin, 1751.

Ehrenpreis, *Swift* Irvin Ehrenpreis, *Swift: the Man, his Works, and the Age*, 3 vols, London, 1983.

Swift, *Letters* *The Correspondence of Jonathan Swift*, Sir Harold Williams, (ed.), 5 vols, Oxford, 1963–72.

Delany, *Letters* *The Autobiography and Correspondence of Mary Granville, Mrs Delany*, Lady Llanover (ed.), 6 vols, London, 1861–2.

Victor, *History* Benjamin Victor, *The History of the Theatres of London and Dublin. From the Year 1730 to the present time*, 2 vols, London, 1761.

Victor, *Original Letters* Benjamin Victor, *Original Letters, Dramatic Pieces, and Poems*, 3 vols, London, 1776.

Barber, *Poems* Mary Barber, *Poems on Several Occasions*, London, 1734 [actually 1735].

Pilkington, *Poems* Matthew Pilkington, *Poems on Several Occasions*, Dublin and London, 1730.

ODNB *The Oxford Dictionary of National Biography.*

Notes

PROLOGUE

xv 'Knobs and Flames of Fire' *Memoirs*, vol. 1, pp. 146–7.

xvi in flagrante   The discovery scene is ibid., pp. 88–9.

— 'our seducers'   Ibid., p. 67.

— 'little Irish muse'   This is the nickname she was given by the coterie at White's Club in London.

xvii Swift repudiated them   this came in a letter to John Barber. Swift, *Letters*, vol. 5, p. 95.

— 'a Lady of Adventure'   *Memoirs*, vol. 1, p. 213.

— Moll Flanders   Virginia Woolf invites us to imagine Mrs Pilkington as 'a very extraordinary cross between Moll Flanders and Lady Ritchie . . . between a rolling and rollicking woman of the town and a lady of breeding and refinement'. See 'Laetitia Pilkington', in Virginia Woolf's 'The Lives of the Obscure' in *The Common Reader*.

— 'scandalous memoirists': this is the conventional classification. Mrs Pilkington is linked with the courtesan Constantia Phillips and the scandalous Lady Vane, all of whose stories were avidly read in the mid-eighteenth century. See Thompson, *The 'Scandalous Memoirists'* and Goulding's thoughtful article, 'Claiming the "Sacred Mantle", The *Memoirs* of Laetitia Pilkington'.

xviii 'immaculate chastity'   When writing to Samuel Richardson about Clarissa, and begging him not to kill his character off, Mrs Pilkington assured him she and Colley Cibber, 'who neither of us set up for immaculate chastity', agreed in hoping Clarissa would be allowed to live. Richardson, *Letters*, vol. 2, p. 130. And see below, chapter 9.

— praised by critics   For recent evidence of Mrs Pilkington's standing as a poet see Backscheider, *Eighteenth-Century Women Poets*, pp. 238 and 262–3, and Staves, *A Literary History of Women's Writing*, pp. 278–83.

— 'a minor classic'   A. C. Elias makes this judgement in his introduction to the *Memoirs*, vol. 1, p. xvi.

xviii 'lemon and sugar'   Ibid., vol. 1, p. 263.
xix 'poor Laetitia'   Ibid., vol. 1, p. 319.
— 'If ever a woman'   Woolf, 'Laetitia Pilkington'.
xix 'bastard Sons'   *Memoirs*, vol. 1, p. 267.
— 'a faithful history'   *Gulliver's Travels*, part 4, chapter 12, 'The Author's Veracity'. On the question of Mrs Pilkington's veracity, see the discussion in A. C. Elias's introduction to the *Memoirs*, vol. 1, esp. pp. xxxiv–viii.

CHAPTER ONE

3 'his faithful Mistress'   *Memoirs*, vol. 1, p. 12.
— 'descended of an antient'   Ibid., p. 10.
— actual parents   All details about Meade and Van Lewen family history are taken from the notes to Mrs Pilkington's *Memoirs*, vol. 2, p. 363 and passim.
4 'that natural Contempt'   Ibid., vol. 1, p. 10.
— 'a handsome Fortune'   Ibid., p. 12.
5 'Coop up your hens'   *Real Story*, p. 32.
— 'no man for the future'   *Memoirs*, vol. 2, pp. 369–70.
6 the local cess list   Eighteenth-century cess (short for 'assessment') lists show taxes levied on householders according to the valuation of their property.
— 'strictly followed'   *Et seq.*, ibid., vol. 1, p. 13
8 'sensible and cheerful'   Delany, *Letters*, vol. 1, p. 327.
9 'I never forgot'   Ibid., vol. 1, p. 13.
— 'two young Ladies'   *Et seq.*, ibid., pp. 14–15.
10 'poor illiterate country people'   *Et seq.*, ibid., p. 17. For more on Constantia see A. C. Elias Jr, 'A Manuscript Book of Constantia Grierson's'. Elias (p. 50) writes, 'Of Mrs Grierson herself, the outlines of her life, we know very little. In her transcript poems, out of the darkness of near-anonymity, we can still hear a genuine voice.'
11 'seldom asunder'   *Memoirs*, vol. 1, p. 18
12 'continual Application'   Barber, *Poems*, Preface, pp. xlv–viii.
13 'of obscure Birth'   *Et seq.*, *Memoirs*, vol. 1, pp. 14–15.
14 one estimate   The cost of a clergy training: Barnard offers this estimate for the cost of training in *A New Anatomy of Ireland*, p. 82.
16 'amorous Correspondence'   *Memoirs*, vol. 1, p. 20.
17 'a Scratch'   Ibid., p. 20.
— 'A Pastoral Elegy' by Matthew Pilkington can be found in Foxon, *English Verse 1701–1750*, p. 281, and Matthew Pilkington, *Poems*, pp. 89–95.
— 'which, with a Cat'   *Et seq.*, *Memoirs*, vol. 1, p. 21.

CHAPTER TWO

19 'a good wainscoted' *Memoirs*, vol. 2, p. 380.
— 'One Ev'ning' 'A Pastoral Elegy', Matthew Pilkington, *Poems* pp. 89–95.
20 'The Petition of the Birds' *Memoirs*, vol. 1, pp. 21–2.
— 'said it so often' Ibid., p. 22.
21 'how severely' Ibid., p. 24.
— 'there is not in the King's Dominions' Ibid., vol. 2, p. 382.
22 Matthew's interests The *ODNB* gives a good account of Matthew Pilkington.
— 'The Candle' Matthew Pilkington, *Poems*, pp. 56–9.
23 'To Lycidas in the country' Ibid., pp. 83–6.
— 'always a-breeding' *Memoirs*, vol. 1, p. 310.
24 'To Miss Laetitia Van Lewen' Ibid., pp. 18–20.
25 'the best tuition' *Real Story*, p. 3.
— 'The Irish represented' Ehrenpreis, *Swift*, vol. 3, p. 152.
26 'the griping landlords' Ibid., p. 157.
27 'a scene too little' Delany, *Observations on Lord Orrery's Remarks on Swift*, p. 218. Quoted in Ehrenpreis, *Swift*, vol. 3, p. 5.
— 'epidemical frenzy' Ehrenpreis, *Swift*, vol. 3, p. 248.
28 'the people rescued' Ibid., p. 270.
— 'the poor young Couple' *Memoirs*, vol. 1, p. 24.
— 'a Favour' Ibid.
29 Mary Barber See Fagan, *A Georgian Celebration*; Budd, ' "Merit in Distress": the Troubled Success of Mary Barber' and Christopher Fanning, 'The Voices of the Dependent Poet: the Case of Mary Barber'.
— 'Senatus Consultum': a sample poem by Patrick Delany, summoning the group, is quoted in *Memoirs*, vol. 1, p. 283.
— 'The Lost Muse' Matthew Pilkington, *Poems*, pp. 36–40.
30 'Delville' *Memoirs*, vol. 1, p. 25.
— 'Unhappy Child' A. C. Elias Jr, 'A Manuscript Book of Constantia Grierson's', p. 45.
— 'Occasion'd by seeing some Verses' Barber, *Poems*, pp. 38–40.
31 'Written for My Son' Ibid, pp. 13–16. See also Lonsdale (ed.), *Eighteenth-Century Women Poets*, pp. 118–29 for this and several other poems.
— 'I pity poor Barber' 'Conclusion of a Letter to the Rev. Mr C—.' The whole poem is in Lonsdale (ed.), *Eighteenth-Century Women Poets*, pp. 122–4
32 'Ode on His Majesty's Birthday' Matthew Pilkington, *Poems*, pp. 155–62.
— '*The Plague of Wealth*' Ibid., London edition. pp. 163–84.
33 diminutive size it is also worth noting that the kingdom's most famous poet, Pope, was of stunted growth and tiny.

33 'The Invitation' Matthew Pilkington, *Poems*, pp. 41–6.
35 'we both invoked' *Memoirs*, vol. 1, p. 38.
— 'every thing disagreeable' Ibid., p. 299.
— 'Can you boast' Swift, *Letters*, vol. 3, p.369.
— 'so hopefull' Ibid., vol. 4, p. 57.
36 'As I spoke' *Memoirs*, vol. 1, p. 26.
— 'Give me my Due' Ibid.

CHAPTER THREE

38 'several prettinesses' Mrs Delany, July 1744, quoted in Hayden, *Mrs Delany: her life and her flowers*, p. 85. Hayden reproduces a number of Mrs Delany's sketches of the garden.
— 'a magnificent Portico' *Memoirs*, vol. 1, p. 27.
39 'a man of the easiest' Sherburn (ed.), *The Correspondence of Alexander Pope*, vol. 3, p. 109. Quoted in Ehrenpreis, *Swift*, p. 646.
40 'What,' says he *Memoirs*, vol. 1, p. 27.
— Of that Sunday visit a full description of this first Sunday at St Patrick's deanery is ibid., vol. 1, pp. 27–31.
44 'Lilliputian Palace' Ibid., p. 38.
— 'a very odd companion' Delany, *Letters*, vol. 1, p. 396.
45 'by Agreement' *Memoirs*, vol. 1, p. 309 and passim.
46 'After receiving' Ibid., p. 311.
47 *Letter to a Young Lady* Ehrenpreis has an interesting discussion of Swift's letter in his biography of him, vol. 3, pp. 396–404.
— 'which by the bye' *Memoirs*, vol. 1, p. 30.
— 'sans consequence' Ibid., p. 24.
— 'It was owing' Ibid., p. 33.
— 'of middle understanding' Swift, *Letters*, vol. 3, p. 285.
— 'the Pains he took' *Memoirs*, vol. 1, p. 45.
48 'submit to any punishment' Swift, *Letters*, vol. 4, pp. 179–80.
— 'all that could not be saved' See the footnote to Mrs Delany's letter, ibid., p. 179.
— 'special good Cover' *Memoirs*, vol. 1, pp. 33–4.
50 'a freeman among slaves' Swift, *Letters*, vol. 4, p. 73.
— 'despotic' power Ibid., vol. 3, p. 172.
— 'friends, side by side' Sherburn (ed.), *The Correspondence of Alexander Pope*, vol. 2, p. 426.
— 'The Dean' *Memoirs*, vol. 1, pp. 36–7.
52 'to speak my Sentiments' Ibid., p. 45.
— 'or rather trolled' Ibid., p. 35.
53 'poetical people' *Real Story*, pp. 5–6.
— 'a Lady in the Country' Barber, *Poems*, p. 132; see also pp. 99–102. Mary Barber's was only the second volume of poems by a woman to appear by subscription. She eventually gathered 918 subscribers – a huge

number, especially considering how illustrious were some of the names and how low her social status.

54 'Fly the fair, delusive Nine' 'Sent as from a Schoolfellow to my son, Anno 1727', ibid., p. 103.

55 'a melancholy, drooping young woman' Delany, *Letters*, vol. 2, p. 316.

— 'I was Gaming' Swift, *Letters*, vol. 4, p. 206.

— 'Britons void of care' Barber, *Poems*, p. 189.

56 'To Tell the Reader' Mary Davys, *The Merry Wanderer*, in *The Works of Mrs Davys*, 1725, vol. 1, p. 161. Mary Davys was a widow whose husband had been a curate in the Church of Ireland. Swift gave her some financial support. *The Merry Wanderer* was a revised version of her earlier work, *The Fugitive* (1705), which had been dedicated to Esther Johnson, Swift's 'Stella'.

— 'Written on the Rocks' Barber, *Poems*, pp. 147–8.

— 'To Mr —' Matthew Pilkington, *Poems*, pp. 49–51.

57 George Vertue For Vertue on Worsdale see Vertue's *Note Books*, III, pp. 59, 61. William Whitley, in *Artists and their Friends*, vol. 1, p. 105, says Worsdale was the only man of whom Vertue spoke contemptuously except the sculptor Scheemaker.

— white prison bars The story about Worsdale painting lines on his portraits is in Anthony Pasquin, *An Authentic History*, pp. 21–2.

— 'Say, Worsdale' 'On the Duchess of Newcastle's Picture', Barber, *Poems*, p. 77.

59 'young poetical parson' Swift, *Letters*, vol. 3, p. 328.

60 'But guessing' *Grub-Street Journal*, 31 December 1730.

CHAPTER FOUR

63 'foolish Scribble' *Et seq.*, Swift, *Letters*, vol. 3, pp. 491–2.

65 'Mrs Barber acted weakly' Ibid., p. 457.

— to forge Swift's signature Mary Barber's letter, known as the 'counterfeit' letter to Queen Caroline, is printed in Appendix XXIII Swift, *Letters*, vol. 5, pp. 259–60.

— 'I have the honour' Four letters from Matthew Pilkington to William Bowyer are printed as Appendix XXII in Swift, *Letters*, vol. 5, pp. 252–6. All quotations from Matthew to Bowyer are from this source.

66 'An Infallible Scheme' Swift–Pope, *Miscellanies*, vol. 3, pp. 112–24.

68 'drank a little caudle' A caudle was a warm, spiced gruel for invalids. *Memoirs*, vol. 1, pp. 315–16.

— 'How thoroughly' Ehrenpreis, *Swift*, p. 732.

69 'begun an acquaintance' Delany, *Letters*, vol. 1, p. 301.

— 'We were not very merry' Ibid., pp. 335–6.

— Constantia Grierson See Barber, *Poems*; and A. C. Elias 'A Manuscript Book of Constantia Grierson's'.

69 'self-willed', 'plagu'd' *Memoirs*, vol. 1, pp. 47 and 48.

70 'I believe there never was' *Memoirs*, vol. 1, p. 282.
— 'a young gentleman' Ehrenpreis, *Swift*, p. 732.
72 Swift had become increasingly unhappy The complicated manoeuvres regarding the Pope–Swift *Miscellanies* are exhaustively explored in Ehrenpreis, *Swift* pp. 727–51.
— servilely complaisant *Et seq.*, *Memoirs*, vol. 1, pp. 50–1.
74 'These Lines' *Et seq.*, ibid., pp. 52–3.
76 'extraordinary regard' *Et seq.*, ibid., vol. 1, pp. 53–4.
78 'a very agreeable ingenious man' Swift, *Letters*, vol. 4, p. 101.
— the lawyer John Smith For Matthew's envy, see *Memoirs*, vol. 1, pp. 48–50.
79 She wrote poems 'Verses Wrote in a Library', and 'Solitude' are included in a clutch of poems apparently written during Matthew's absence. *Memoirs*, vol. 1, pp. 57–62.
80 A coolly pragmatic Barber, *Poems*, p. 233.
— 'a fine Eagle Quill' *Memoirs*, vol. 1, p. 46.
81 'Squander vast' 'To the Hon. Mrs Percival, on her desisting from the Bermudan Project', in Barber, *Poems* pp. 141–2.
82 a swipe at Mrs Barber In the third volume of her *Memoirs*, published posthumously, Laetitia Pilkington wrote: 'Mrs Barber, whose Name, at her earnest Request, I omitted in my first Volume, and who was the Lady I mentioned to have been with me, at my first Interview with the Dean at Dr. Delany's Seat, was at this time writing a Volume of Poems, some of which I fancy might, at this Day, be seen in the Cheesemongers, Chandlers, Pastry-cooks, and Second-hand Booksellers Shops. However, dull as they were, they certainly would have been much worse, but that Doctor Delany frequently held what he called a Senatus Consultum, to correct these undigested Materials; at which were present sometimes the Dean (in the Chair), but always Mrs Grierson, Mr Pilkington, the Doctor, and myself.' *Memoirs*, vol. 1, p. 283.
— 'trimmed with plumes' Nokes, *John Gay, a Profession of Friendship*, p. 534.
— 'Mr Pilkington gains' Swift, *Letters*, vol. 4, p. 110.
— 'I like the Young man' Ibid., p. 128.
— a major campaign for Barber's part in the Excise affair see Rivington, *'Tyrant': The Story of John Barber*, p. 162–74.
83 'I will not deny' Swift, *Letters*, vol. 4, p. 149.
84 'I did so' *Memoirs*, vol. 1, pp. 54–5.
85 'had he lived in the city' Swift, *Letters*, vol. 4, p. 208.
— 'impartial' description Matthew's account is in *An Impartial History of . . . Mr John Barber*.
86 'a set of ungrateful monsters' Swift, *Letters*, vol. 4, p. 109.
87 Swift was tireless For Swift's letters in support of Mary Barber, see, e.g., Swift, *Letters*, vol. 3, p. 464, vol. 4, pp. 56, 176, 188, vol. 5, p. 479.

88 'London has very attractive Charms' *Memoirs*, vol. 1, p. 63.

CHAPTER FIVE

90 'very obligingly' *Memoirs*, vol. 1, pp. 63–7 covers the London trip.
92 'until the nineteenth century' Stone, *Road to Divorce*, p. 13. Explaining why it was rarely wives pressing for separation upon the breakdown of marriage, Stone writes (p. 4) 'a separated wife faced exceptionally severe penalties . . . she was in practice virtually an outlaw'.
94 'swallow-like risings', Victor, *History*, vol. 2, pp. 183–4.
95 'a Place of the least' *Memoirs*, vol. 1, p. 109.
96 Lord Abergavenny see Stone, *Road to Divorce*, pp. 272–3.
98 'To Strephon' *Memoirs*, vol. 1, p. 61.
— 'A Song' Ibid.
99 'Why Mr Pilkington' Swift, *Letters*, vol. 4, p. 209.
— 'I should have scorned' *Memoirs*, vol. 1, p. 68.
100 'a primate will toast' *Correspondence of Horace Walpole*, vol. 37, pp. 35–6.
— 'the first to attack' *Memoirs*, vol. 1, p. 68.
— 'the Government's star' Fischer, 'The Government's Response', p. 53.
101 'better acquainted' Sheridan, *Life of Swift*, p. 277.
— 'The Notion of' Et seq., *Memoirs*, vol. 1, pp. 68–9.
102 'bade me let' Ibid., p. 69.
103 'pray Mr Dean' Swift, *Letters*, vol. 4, p. 232.
— 'intervening, officious' Swift, *Letters*, vol. 4, p. 253.
104 'poor' Mrs Barber Delany, *Letters*, vol. 1, p. 473.
105 'my humble Service' Swift, *Letters*, vol. 4, p. 532.
107 'a bon companion' *Real Story* p. 40.
108 'fifty pounds at Mallow' Ibid., p. 51.
— 'The Mirror', *Memoirs*, vol. 1, pp. 71–2.
109 'Verses Wrote in a Library' Ibid., pp. 57–9.
111 'telling us to our Faces' Ibid., p. 200.
— 'Fear and Terror' Ibid., p. 199.
— George Frend For Elizabeth's marriage to him, see *Memoirs*, vol. 2, p. 459. Dean Madden was a benevolent, pious and perhaps somewhat unworldly clergyman, ibid., p. 462.
— 'great sociableness' Delany, *Letters*, vol. 1, pp. 291–2.

CHAPTER SIX

114 'at all Hazards' Et seq., *Memoirs*, vol. 1, pp. 72–3.
116 'I rose from' Ibid. The account of Dr Van Lewen's accident and lingering death is taken from *Memoirs*, vol. 1, pp. 73–9 and vol. 2, pp. 456–66 unless otherwise stated.
118 'put out his tongue' *Real Story*, pp. 40–1.
122 'and as nothing but my Death' *Memoirs*, vol. 1, p. 79.

123 Dublin Hell-Fire Club   Jones in *The Clubs of the Georgian Rakes*, p. 8, observes that in the 1730s, 'the rakes were very active in all three kingdoms' and specially wild in Dublin. Ashe in *The Hell Fire Clubs*, p. 59, writes: 'a wave of blasphemy swept over the small, close knit world of the Anglo-Irish', inspired by Wharton but more violent. He suggests that Samuel Richardson drew on his memories of Wharton for the character Lovelace in *Clarissa*.

— 'rackets, brawls'   *Real Story*, p. 143.

— 'vile, atheistical'   Vertue, *Note Books*, III, 106, 109. Lens was accused of Devil worship.

124 'a club, for which'   quoted in Brewer, *Pleasures of the Imagination*, p. 257.

— 'a very troublesome coxcomb'   *Memoirs*, vol. 1, pp. 79–81.

— Hammond later denied   See *A letter from William Hammond . . .*

125 'quite in an Uproar'   Et seq., *Memoirs*, vol. 1, pp. 82–4.

127 'no enemies but his passions'   Anon., *Memoirs of the Life of Robert Adair*, p. 4.

— 'singular, sudden and violent'   Ibid., p. 13.

128 'sat like Statues'   *Memoirs*, vol. 1, p. 89.

— 'administering Christian'   Ibid., p. 110, and see vol. 2, pp. 498–9.

— she 'was found'   Ibid., vol. 2, p. 476.

129 'I started up'   Ibid., vol. 1, p. 90.

— 'When those worthy'   Ibid., p. 92.

— 'To Counsellor Callaghan'   Ibid., pp. 96–7. Callaghan seems to have been George Frend's uncle.

130 double or quits   Ibid., vol. 2, p. 487.

— 'matron-like'   Ibid., vol. 1, p. 93.

131 'no Protector'   Ibid., p. 90.

— ' "Sorrow" '   Ibid., pp. 90–2.

132 'forced me'   Swift, *Letters*, vol. 5, p. 95.

— 'from striking on the'   Anon., *Memoirs of the Life of Robert Adair*, p. 9.

133 'strange ambition'   *Memoirs*, vol. 1, p. 95.

134 *A Cure for a Scold*   Ibid., vol. 2, p. 501.

— 'a flaming prologue'   Ibid., vol. 1, p. 222.

135 Worsdale acted as a go-between   Ibid., vol. 1, p. 102.

136 'the Temptations'   Ibid., p. 103.

— 'in concealed'   Ibid., vol. 2, p. 493.

— *No Death but Marriage*   Ibid., vol. 2, pp. 500–1.

— Worsdale went to Mallow   Ibid., vol. 1, pp. 104–15; vol. 2, pp. 493–6.

137 'Subalterns'   Ibid., vol. 1, p. 95.

138 'I lived the Life'   Ibid., vol. 1, p. 115.

— 'To a Lady'   Ibid., pp. 111–2.

139 'This Lady sent'   Ibid., p. 110.

— 'plunder'd his Wife'   Ibid., p. 109.

140 'Expostulation'   Ibid., pp. 115–6.

141 'To the Honourable' Ibid., pp. 113–4, and vol. 2, pp. 499–500.

CHAPTER SEVEN

145 'The sense' *Real Story*, p. 6.

— 'all the Treasure' *Memoirs*, vol. 1, p. 116.

146 'Chastity enough' Ibid., p. 117.

147 'who was really' and the journey from Chester to London, ibid., pp. 129–31.

150 'a sort of right' Victor, *Original Letters*, vol. 1, p. 148. See also *Memoirs*, vol. 2, pp. 527–30.

152 'An Excursory View' *Memoirs*, vol. 1, pp. 151–5.

154 'The Statues' Ibid, pp. 39–44.

— 'As the Dean' Ibid., p. 39.

155 'sometimes chose' Ibid., p. 314. In 'The Lady's Dressing Room' Swift catalogues the excremental and other messes in 'Celia's' room where 'Celia shits'. *The Poems of Jonathan Swift*, Williams (ed.), vol. 2, pp. 524–30.

157 'a most accomplished' On Hill and Victor see Gerrard, *Aaron Hill*, pp. 75–6 and 148–50.

— 'no Man' *Memoirs*, vol. 1, p. 158.

— 'assaulting, ravishing' Mary Nash, *The Provoked Wife*, p. 138.

158 'retained the air' Victor, *History*, vol. 1, p. 150.

159 'And prithee' *Memoirs*, vol. 1, pp. 158–60.

161 'As I wanted' Ibid., p. 132. In the background of Plate 6 of *The Rake's Progress*, Hogarth pictures White's – changing the name to 'Black's'. The gamblers are all too busy gambling to see that the club is on fire. Swift, in his *Essay on Modern Education*, wrote: 'the late Earl of Oxford never passed by White's Chocolate-house (the common rendezvous of infamous sharpers and noble cullies) without bestowing a curse upon that famous Academy, as the bane of half the English nobility.' *The Prose Works of Jonathan Swift*, vol xi, p. 53.

163 'a Noun Substantive' *Memoirs*, vol. 1, p. 226.

164 'intimate, bantering' Whitworth, *Field Marshal Lord Ligonier*, p. 179.

— 'droll' *Memoirs*, vol. 1, p. 136.

— 'the most lewd' This description of Duncombe is in an anonymous 1749 pamphlet, *Remarks on the Second Volume of the Memoirs of Mrs Pilkington*.

— 'To the Hon.' Ibid., p. 137.

165 'The next Day' Ibid., p. 138.

166 Joseph Leeson Ibid., pp. 302–3; and *Memoirs*, vol. 2, pp. 691–2.

167 'To Mr Cibber', *Memoirs*, vol. 1, pp. 134–6.

169 'To the Reverend Dr Hales', ibid., pp. 133–4.

171 'full of his usual Gaiety' Ibid., p. 142.

— 'very modestly' Ibid., p. 151.

173 'all Wit' Ibid., p. 173.

CHAPTER EIGHT

175 'In the Absence' *Memoirs*, vol. 1, pp. 160–1.
176 'witty and polite' *Real Story*, p. 9.
177 'Colonel, I shall meet you' *Memoirs*, vol. 1, p. 139.
— 'Whereas the Bearer' Ibid., p. 287.
178 Henry Fielding owed Battestin, *Henry Fielding, A Life*, pp. 288–9.
179 'a very genteel House' *Memoirs*, vol. 1., p. 162.
180 'in the oddest' Ibid., p. 167. The woman's story is told pp. 164–8.
182 'painting up Vice' Ibid., p. 227.
— 'very gaily' Ibid., pp. 192–3.
183 'the blackest ingratitude' [Barber], *An Impartial History*, p. 24.
184 Deputy Master of the Revels No official record naming Worsdale has
been found, in spite of extensive searches through almanacs of the
period. Traditionally the post seems to have gone to the manager of
Smock Alley. See Hitchcock, *An Historical View of the Dublin Stage*,
vol. 1.
— Charles Burney Burney was a boy at school in Chester at the time. He
describes seeing Worsdale in *A General History of Music*, vol. 4, p. 662.
— 'a cloud of' *Memoirs*, vol. 1, p. 176.
185 like the snow Aaron Hill, *The Works*, vol. 2, p. 294.
187 'The Gentleman's Study' Lonsdale, *Eighteenth-century Women Poets*,
pp. 130–4.
— 'never examin'd' *Memoirs*, vol. 1, Preface, p. 7.
— 'likely Dame' And Fleet Street brothel scenes, ibid., pp. 177–82.
189 'of all Persons' Ibid., p. 183.
— 'overstocked with harlots' Anon., *Satan's Harvest Home*, p. 4. This
1749 pamphlet blames masters, footmen, journeymen, lodgers and
apprentices for debauching women servants and then sending them on
to the streets. It quotes a West Country rhyme: as the girl sets out for
London, the coachman says,
> Now Hussy a month's wages or a month's warning
> And to bed to your master every morning.
It also reminds us how very young many of these 'harlots' are: 'What a
deplorable Sight is it, to behold Numbers of little creatures pil'd up in
Heaps upon one another, sleeping in the publick Streets, in the most
rigorous Seasons, and some of them whose Heads will hardly reach
above the Waistband of a Man's Breeches, found to be quick with Child',
p. 2.
189 'so kind' Et seq., *Memoirs*, vol. 1, pp. 186–8.
190 Lord Middlesex As patron of the opera, see Taylor, 'From Losses to
Lawsuit'.
191 *Memoirs of the Bedford Coffee-House* Anonymous pamphlet,
pp. 64–70.

191 'so effectually' *Memoirs*, vol. 1, p. 189.

— 'desolate' Ibid., pp. 191–2. Loftus Hume made up for it later: when Mrs Pilkington returned to Dublin, he became a generous supporter. She thanked him in her third volume, *Memoirs*, vol. 1, p. 286.

192 'the gay' Victor, *Original Letters*, vol. 1, p. 71.

— 'a most extraordinary' *Memoirs*, vol. 1, p. 194. In the *Memoirs* the landlady's name is spelt 'Trifoli' but in the Palace Court records it is clearly given as Thiffola.

193 'frolicksome Farce' *Memoirs*, vol. 1, pp. 326–7.

— 'a moving Tale' Ibid., p. 194.

195 'his Supreme Majesty' Ibid., p. 196.

196 A 'very well dressed' Ibid., p. 201.

197 'Early next Morning' Ibid., pp. 201–2.

199 'To Mrs Meade' Ibid., pp. 203–4. In *The Life and Opinions of Tristram Shandy* (1760) Laurence Sterne made fun of Mead's hair fetishism, giving him the name Dr Kunastrokius. Criticised for this, Sterne protested that he was only writing about 'a droll foible' in Mead's character and that it was hardly secret, 'but known before by every chamber-maid and footman within the bills of mortality'. See Curtis, *Letters of Laurence Sterne*, p. 89. Dudley Bradstreet later wrote his memoirs, *The Life and Uncommon Adventures of Capt. Dudley Bradstreet*. It was printed by Mrs Pilkington's Dublin printer, Samuel Powell, and supported by the man who had been her generous patron, Lord Kingsborough.

200 'mad and drunk' *Memoirs*, vol. 1, p. 206.

— 'All my Writings' Ibid., p. 207

— 'a Lottery Prize' Ibid.

201 Handel's *Messiah* For Delany's presence there see Nash, *The Provoked Wife*, pp. 175–6.

202 'a most compleat' Richardson, *Letters*, vol. 2, pp. 116–17.

203 'having some Knowledge' *Memoirs*, vol. 1, p. 210.

— 'So, Reader' Ibid.

CHAPTER NINE

204 Many women ran small businesses For these and other details about women in business in London see Earle, *A City Full of People*, chapter 4, 'Women's Work' and especially the subsection, 'Women in Business', pp. 146–50. For Mary Scarth see pp. 206–7.

— 'dressed a la mode' *Memoirs*, vol. 1, p. 210.

— 'impertinence' Defoe, *The Complete English Tradesman*, p.114.

205 'my present Situation' *Memoirs*, vol. 1, p. 210.

206 'For Madam' *Real Story*, p. 216.

— 'a Girl of Sixteen' *Et seq.*, *Memoirs*, vol. 1, pp. 219–22, and vol. 2, p. 248.

207 'extraordinary Panegyric' 'To the Right. Hon. Henry Pelham', *Daily*

Gazetteer, 24 December 1748.

208 'If any illiterate Divine'   *Memoirs*, vol. 1, pp. 346–7.

209 'how much Dress'   Ibid., pp. 220–1.

210 'for Pen, Ink, and Paper'   Ibid., p. 286.

211 'knew every great Family'   Ibid., p. 223.

— 'little faithful Irishwoman'   Richardson, *Letters*, p. 121.

— to be 'electrified'   *Memoirs*, vol. 1, p. 290.

212 'insensibly'   Ibid., p. 329.

213 'unworthy of any Man's friendship'. Worsdale's will is in the National Archives. He left instructions for his funeral at St Paul's, Covent Garden, requesting that his body be carried by six journeymen painters, who were to be dark clothed and wearing felt hats with a band, and gloves, and be paid five shillings each for their trouble. He bequeathed £50 to Edward Walpole and £200 apiece to his five children by five different mothers. He seems to have maintained connection with at least two of his four sons, three of whom were named James. Mrs Pilkington does not mention them.

— Arne's treatment of his apprentices   Burney, *The Memoirs of Dr Burney*, vol. 1, pp. 12–13.

214 'in silver-laced liveries'   *Real Story*, p. 86.

215 'Inhumanity'   *Memoirs*, vol. 1, p. 212.

— a long, lurid, partial account   Jack's letter is printed ibid., vol. 1, pp. 214–16.

216 'affected the man'   *Real Story*, p. 96.

217 'having joined'   *Memoirs*, vol. 1, p. 144.

— Herring had preached   For Herring on Gay and Swift, see Ehrenpreis, *Swift*, vol. 3, p. 559.

— 'peevish effort'   Thomas Herring, *Letters to William Duncombe, from the Year 1728 to 1757* (1777) pp. 145–6. Earlier, Herring had admired Pope, though he felt he lacked 'good nature', p. 29.

218 'in the most humble'   *Memoirs*, vol. 2, pp. 538–9.

— 'The very good'   Richardson, *Letters*, vol. 2, p. 121.

219 'truly religious and moral'   Ibid., p. 127–31.

— 'Verses to a very Singular Gentleman'   Ibid., pp. 125–7.

220 'I dare say'   Ibid., p. 124.

221 'everything she could'   Ibid., p. 132.

— 'The greatest unhappiness'   Ibid., p. 135.

— 'it being a long time'   Ibid., p. 134.

— 'I think, Sir'   Ibid., pp. 135–6.

222 'a true Son'   *Memoirs*, vol. 1, p. 143.

223 'wept sadly'   *Et seq.*, ibid., vol. 1, p. 274.

226 'dressed out in'   Fitzgerald, *Samuel Foote, A Biography*, p. 29.

227 'playfellow from his'   Richardson, *Letters*, vol. 2, p. 147.

CHAPTER TEN

229 'contemptible' *Memoirs*, vol. 1, p. 288.

230 'barefacd mountebank lyes' Vertue, *Note Books*, vol. 3, 61.

— the Bavarian ambassador For the dashing Von Haszlang, see *Memoirs*, vol. 2, p. 664, and *Town and Country Magazine*, II (1770), pp. 513-20.

231 'proud, ignorant' *Et seq.*, *Memoirs*, vol. 1, pp. 275-6.

232 'We had four Play-bills' *Memoirs*, vol. 1, p. 276.

— 'facetious person' Chetwood, *A General History of the Stage*, pp. 252-4. Chetwood lists Worsdale's publications on p. 185.

— Henry Carey See Dane, 'The Life and Works of Henry Carey', which praises Carey above all for his 'superb achievement in the genre of the mock heroic'. Dane is also one of the best sources for Worsdale.

232 'Zeno, Plato' The poem is in Carey's *Dramatic Works*, p. 98.

— 'that most consummate' Askham, *The Gay Delavals*, p. 15.

— 'Dear Sam' Trefman, *Samuel Foote*, pp. 3-4.

234 'much wit' Spencer and Dobson, *Letters of David Garrick and Georgiana Countess Spencer*, p. 39. Dr Johnson said of Foote, 'he never lets truth stand in the way of a jest', quoted in Stone and Kahrl, *Garrick, A Critical Biography*, p. 588.

— 'Lady Isabella Pawlett' See Trefman, *Samuel Foote*, pp. 52-5.

235 'abused me' *Et seq.*, *Memoirs*, vol. 1, p. 277-8.

236 'when turn'd out' Ibid., p. 290.

— 'incapable of acting' Ibid., pp. 347-8.

— 'The woman's a whore' Boswell, *Life of Johnson*, p. 537.

237 'much beyond' *Orrery Papers*, vol. 1, p. 309.

— 'had the Confidence' *Et seq.*, *Memoirs*, vol. 1, pp. 288-92.

238 The philosopher David Hume For his 'Adventures on the Coast of France', see Mossner, *The Life of David Hume*, pp. 187-204. For Jack's adventures, *Memoirs*, vol. 1, p. 292. Other details from Richmond, *The Navy in the War of 1739-48*, pp. 28-35.

240 'poor Wanderer' *Et seq.*, *Memoirs*, vol. 1, p. 292.

— 'our glorious expeditions' Walpole, *Correspondence*, vol. 19, p. 327.

241 'a seasonable relief' *Memoirs*, vol. 1, p. 295.

— manuscripts to light the fire On Betty's burning manuscripts: 'It is a very great Loss to me, that by the Ignorance of my Daughter, half of my Writings were burned, for she never scrupled if even the Fire was bad, to take a whole bundle of them to enliven it.' *Memoirs*, vol. 1., p. 225.

— Jack's sex life For Jack and the captain's widow, see *Memoirs*, vol. 1, pp. 292-7.

243 'You old Devil' *Real Story*, p. 233.

244 'My head is so bad' *Et seq.*, Richardson, *Letters*, pp. 154-5.

246 'not over-courteous' *Memoirs*, vol. 1, p. 321.

— She and Jack could afford to go The description of the return journey is in *Memoirs*, vol. 1, pp. 321–5.

247 Thomas Sheridan   For Sheridan and the Kelly riots, see Sheldon, *Thomas Sheridan of Smock-Alley*, chapter 4, 'Dublin in an Uproar'.

248 'the horrors of a riot'   Ibid., p. 88.

— 'beggar's brat'   *Memoirs*, vol. 1, p. 329.

— Mary Delany   For the Delanys at Parkgate, see Delany, *Letters*, vol. 2, pp. 457–8.

CHAPTER ELEVEN

253 'Verses on the Death of Dr Swift'   Swift, *Works*, vol. 2, pp. 551–72.

254 'busy Tongues'   *Memoirs*, vol. 1, p. 251.

— 'a very mannerly'   Ibid., p. 325.

255 her eldest son   For William see ibid., p. 212.

256 'painting, sculpture'   *Real Story*, pp. 123 and 125–6.

— 'an old beau'   Delany, *Letters*, vol. 3, p. 514, and *Memoirs*, vol. 2, p. 724.

— 'Trouble and Vexation'   *Memoirs*, vol. 1, p. 326.

257 'I am the chief'   Richardson, *Letters*, pp. 158–61, and *Memoirs*, vol. 2, pp. 722–3.

258 'in very civil Terms'   *Memoirs*, vol. 1, p. 110.

259 'friendly and familiar'   *Memoirs*, vol. 1, p. 328.

260 'By the Return'   *Memoirs*, vol. 1, p. 327.

— Several transcripts   For Cibber's letter see *Memoirs*, vol. 1, pp. 326–7. Richardson, *Letters*, 161–7. *Orrery Papers*, vol. 1, pp. 314–17.

262 'as gay and lively'   Eaves and Kimpel, *Samuel Richardson, A Biography*, p. 181. Richardson's correspondent Lady Bradshaigh considered Cibber a 'Shameless Old Man', ibid., p. 182.

— 'so naked'   Gervat, *Elizabeth, the Scandalous Life of an Eighteenth-Century Duchess*, p. 44. The person quoted is the witty bluestocking Elizabeth Montagu.

263 'his face shone'   Eaves and Kimpel, *Samuel Richardson, A Biography*, p. 181.

— 'the present you made'   Victor, *Original Letters*, vol. 1, pp. 137–9.

264 free passes   The affair of the theatre passes is in Victor, *Original Letters*, vol. 1, pp. 145–50; and *Memoirs*, vol. 1, pp. 327–8.

265 George Anne Bellamy   The dispute is mentioned in Sheldon, *Thomas Sheridan of Smock-Alley*, pp. 127–8.

— 'To Mr Sheridan'   *Memoirs*, vol. 1, pp. 328–9.

266 'a numerous Contribution'   *Memoirs*, vol. 1, p. 330.

— 'it was not a common vulgar garden'   Hayden, *Mrs Delany: her life and her flowers*, p. 87.

— 'When I, in plain English'   *Memoirs*, vol. 1, p. 232

267 a 'bantering' letter   Ibid., vol. 1, pp. 330–1.

— 'a vile young rake'   *Et seq.*, Delany, vol. 1, 482. *Memoirs*, vol. 2, pp. 359–61.

268 'divinely pure'   *Memoirs*, vol. 1, pp. 123–4.

269 'a great wheedler' *Et seq.*, Beaumont Brenan, *The Painter's Breakfast*, p. 6. For Matthew Pilkington's contribution to the Cobbe collection, see Laing (ed.), *Clerics and Connoisseurs*, pp. 50–2. See also Bryant, 'Matthew Pilkington and the Gentleman's and Connoisseur's Dictionary of Painters of 1770: A Landmark in Art History', ibid., pp. 52–62, and Mark Broch's thesis, 'Matthew Pilkington, auteur van The Gentleman's & Connoisseur's Dictionary of Painters'.

271 a flurry of pamphleteering Elias summarises these in *Memoirs*, vol. 2, pp. 626–7. The British Library has them bound in a large volume of tracts and pamphlets, BL 1890.e.5.

272 'I could reckon up' *Memoirs*, vol. 1, p. 85.

— 'no body but' Ibid. For those who did not remember their Prior, she quoted the relevant lines from 'A Lover's Anger' which end:
So saying, her Bosom she careless display'd:
That Seat of Delight I with Wonder survey'd,
And forgot ev'ry Word I design'd to have said.
Matthew Prior, *Poems on Several Occasions*, 1718, p. 85.

273 'almost every person' Victor, *Original Letters*, vol. 1, p. 141.

— 'At length' *Memoirs*, vol. 1, p. 88.

275 'an authentic picture' *Gentleman's Magazine*, April 1748, pp. 153–9.

— the Pilkingtons, mother and son For their theatrical ventures see *Memoirs*, vol. 2, p. 565; Sheldon, *Thomas Sheridan of Smock-Alley*, pp. 125–7, and Burke, *Riotous Performances*, chapter 6, 'The Capel Street Opposition of 1748–50', pp. 183–208.

CHAPTER TWELVE

279 'impertinent Visitors' Clarke, *Poems*, p. 70.

279 'as many Pacquets' *Memoirs*, vol. 1, p. 125.

— 'I hope this will' Ibid., p. 117.

280 'now ready for the Press' For delays in publishing volume two, see *Memoirs*, vol. 2, pp. 642, 644–5, 723.

— 'I must have wrote her' Victor, *Original Letters*, I, p. 137.

— verses she had ghost-written These verses are printed with disparaging comments in *Memoirs*, vol. 1, pp. 148–51.

282 'spotless, but much injured' Clarke's letter and poem form the preliminaries to Mrs Pilkington's second volume. *Memoirs*, vol. 1, pp. 125–8.

— 'Pray, Sir' Clarke, *Poems*, p. 53. A fragile copy of Clarke's *Collection of Poems upon Various Occasions*, issued in four instalments and bound into one slim volume printed by Samuel Powell for the author in 1751, is in the British Library. Mrs Pilkington is not named but she was unquestionably the 'Lady of Singular Wit and Humour' whose correspondence with him Clarke advertised on the title page. There are a dozen undated letters in all, which were probably exchanged between spring 1748 and December that year. The two had never met, and when they did – presumably in or soon after December 1748 – it had the effect of ending the correspondence. Clarke wrote, 'after that Time, I never heard from her more'.

282 'tolerably corpulent' Ibid., pp. 57–8.
— 'above little sordid' *Et seq.* See Mrs Pilkington's second letter to Clarke, ibid., pp. 61–3.

283 'I have too much vivacity' Ibid., p. 88.
— 'A country Squire' Ibid., p. 62.
— 'a handsome Compliment' Ibid., p. 70.
— 'tyrannizing over' Ibid., p. 88.
— 'Platonick' Ibid. p. 65.
— 'I am in great hopes' Ibid., p. 70.

284 'It may not be yet safe' Ibid. pp. 79–80.

285 'company who can be' *Real Story*, p. 225.
— 'humane lovely' Clarke, *Poems*, p. 89.
— 'Your letter' *Real Story*, pp. 230–1.

286 'My Lord' Ibid., pp. 231–4.
— 'and you know our Irish' Clarke, *Poems*, p. 81.
— 'the infinite delight' *Real Story*, p. 237.

287 'I intreated he' Ibid., p. 239.
— 'This day is publish'd' Full-page advertisement on the reverse of 'A Letter to the Admirers of Mr S[herida]–n', BL. 1890.e.5 (151).
— *The Parallel* for Constantia Phillips see Thompson, *The 'Scandalous Memoirists'. Constantia Phillips, Laetitia Pilkington and the shame of 'publick fame'*.

288 'Two Ladies learn'd' This poem is printed as part of Long's advertisement on the reverse of 'A Letter to the Admirers of Mr S[herida]–n', BL.1890.e.5 (151).

289 'well drawn' *Memoirs*, vol 1, p. 248.
— 'I have no Amanuensis ..' Clarke, *Poems*, p. 72.

290 'I wish to Heaven' *Et seq.*, ibid., p. 99.
— Bishop Clayton *Memoirs*, vol 1, p. 228–31.

291 'Now says my Reader …' *Et seq.*, ibid., p. 303–4.

292 'Hey-day, the Devil' Ibid., p. 250.
— 'Neglect of the Person' Ibid., vol 2, p. 633.

293 'his Maiden modesty' Clarke, *Poems*, p. 82.
— 'Madam,' Clarke had written, 'When I read' *Memoirs*, vol 1, pp. 125–8.
— 'a pretty genius' *The Letters of Mrs Elizabeth Montagu*, vol. 3, pp. 96–9.

295 'from the second volume' *Gentleman's Magazine*, December, 1748, pp. 565–6.

296 'to adapt myself' *Orrery Papers*. Quoted in *Memoirs*, Introduction, vol. 1, p. xvii.
— 'a great deal of nature' William H. Epstein, *John Cleland, Images of a*

Life, pp. 97–8. Epstein comments that Mrs Pilkington's *Memoirs* 'give an especially horrifying account of some of the problems facing an eighteenth-century woman'.

— 'malice and . . . resentment' Victor, *Original Letters*, pp. 146 and 149.

297 'Wesley's account' John C. English, 'John Wesley Meets Laetitia Pilkington', *Methodist History*, vol 42:2 January 2004, p. 88. Wesley published his account in 1756 as an 'Extract' from his Journal.

298 'For my part, Sir' *Real Story*, p. 262.

— 'I never suffered' Ibid., pp. 263–4.

299 Mrs Grace Murray See John C. English, 'John Wesley Meets Laetitia Pilkington', pp. 94–5.

300 'absolutely made love' *Et seq.*, These and the following exchanges are in *Real Story*, pp. 243–69.

302 stealing her idea For Clancy's competition, see *Memoirs*, vol. 2, pp. 733–4.

— 'in a sort of commanding Tone' The final break with Kingsborough, *Memoirs*, vol. 1, pp. 332–4.

CHAPTER THIRTEEN

304 'I did not believe' *Memoirs*, vol. 1, p. 332.

305 'Call me not' *Real Story*, pp. 270–72.

— 'rich Amends' *Memoirs*, vol. 1, p. 333.

307 'an extreme bad Stomach' Ibid., p. 335. See also p. 216 for the 'Histeric Cholic' she suffered in 1744.

— 'a scandalous, dissolute' These are the words in Frend's submission to the Consistory Court, quoted in his petition to the Irish House of Lords in 1751 when he applied to them for a full dissolution by Act of Parliament. *Journals of the House of Lords*, III, p. 792, 25 November 1751.

308 'When does the next' Victor, *History*, pp. 207–10.

— Phraper Lane *Memoirs*, vol. 2, p. 737.

— 'She never seemed' *Et seq.*, ibid., vol. 1, p. 335. Subsequent details of Mrs Pilkington's death are from Jack's account in the appendix, pp. 335–40.

312 £700 Ibid., vol. 2, p. 685.

— 'the Malice of' *Et seq.* Jack described his attempts to wring money from his mother's name in the appendix, *Memoirs*, vol. 1, pp. 340–48.

314 'an Herculean labour' *Real Story*, p. 123.

— Free to re-marry *Memoirs*, vol. 2, pp. 487–8.

— Jack also married Ibid., vol. 2, p. 736.

316 'the tool' of Worsdale *Gentleman's Magazine*, July and August, 1754.

— 'odious' Delany, *Letters*, vol. 3, p. 312, 17 December 1754.

— Matthew . . . drew up his will This was transcribed and published by Ball in *Notes & Queries*. The original burned in the Four Courts fire in 1922.

316 'from a poetical' *Real Story*, p. 2.
317 'the writings' Ibid., pp. 2–3.
— 'rational and inoffensive' Proposals for Printing by Subscription, In London and Dublin, The Adventures of Jack Luckless. Being the *Real Story* of John Carteret Pilkington, Son to the Reverend Mr Matthew, and the ingenious Mrs Laetitia Pilkington. Written by Himself . . . London, 1 April, 1758. (British Library, Newcastle papers, Add. MS 32891 ff. 96–99 and 157–61.) Filed with these proposals are the covering letters written by Jack's wife, Dorinda.
318 'publick good opinion' Ibid.
320 Westminster Abbey *Memoirs*, vol. 1, p. 216–18. *Gentleman's Magazine.*
— Pope's lines *Twickenham Edition of the Poems of Alexander Pope*, vol. 2, pp. 71–4.

A NOTE ON LAETITIA PILKINGTON'S EARLY LITERARY RECEPTION

323 'Set of Wretches' Eaves and Kimpel, *Samuel Richardson*, p. 179. Quoting this, they add: 'A person inclined to carp might point out that Richardson's help to Mrs Pilkington was never enough to end her distresses.'
— 'Without a blush' *General Advertiser*, 16 March 1751. See also *Memoirs*, vol. 1, Introduction, pp. xliv–xlix.

Bibliography

Anon., *Memoirs of the Bedford Coffee-House*, By a Genius (London, 1751)

Anon., *Memoirs of the Life of Robert Adair* (London, 1790)

Anon., *Remarks on the Second Volume of the Memoirs of Mrs Pilkington. With some particulars of that lady's life which she has omitted* (Dublin, 1749)

Anon., *Satan's Harvest Home* (London, 1749)

Anon., *The Ladies Advocate: or Wit and Beauty A Match for Treachery and Inconstancy* (London, 1749)

d'Arblay, Frances (nee Burney) *The Memoirs of Dr Burney, arranged from his own Manuscripts, from Family Papers, and from Personal Recollection, by his daughter* (London, 1832)

Ashe, Geoffrey, *The Hell Fire Clubs: a history of anti-morality* (Stroud, Sutton, 2000)

Askham, Francis, *The Gay Delavals* (London, Jonathan Cape, 1955)

Backscheider, Paula, *Eighteenth-Century Women Poets and Their Poetry, Inventing Agency, Inventing Genre* (Baltimore, Johns Hopkins University Press, 2005)

[Barber, John] *An Impartial History of the Life, Character, Amours, Travels and Transactions of Mr John Barber . . . Written by Several Hands* (London, for E. Curll, 1741)

Barber, Mary, *Poems on Several Occasions* (London, 1734) [actually 1735]

Barker, Richard H., *Mr Cibber of Drury Lane* (New New Haven, Columbia University Studies in English no. 143, 1939)

Barnard, Toby, *A New Anatomy of Ireland: The Irish Protestants, 1649–1770* (New Haven and London, Yale University Press, 2003)

— *Making the Grand Figure: Lives and Possessions in Ireland, 1641–1770* (New Haven and London, Yale University Press, 2004)

Barnett, Louise, *Jonathan Swift in the Company of Women* (Oxford, OUP, 2007)

Battestin, Martin C., with Ruthie R. Battestin, *Henry Fielding, A Life* (London, Routledge, 1989)

345

Belden, Mary, *Dramatic Works of Samuel Foote* (New Haven, Yale Studies in English no. 80, 1929)

Bellamy, George Anne, *An Apology for the Life of George Anne Bellamy, Late of Covent-Garden Theatre. Written by Herself*, 5 vols (London, 1785)

Boswell, James, *Life of Johnson* (Oxford, OUP, World's Classics, 1980)

Bradstreet, Dudley, *The Life and Uncommon Adventures of Capt. Dudley Bradstreet. Being the most Genuine and Extraordinary, perhaps ever published* . . . (Dublin, 1755)

Breashears, Caroline, 'Scandalous Categories: Classifying the *Memoirs* of Unconventional Women', *Philological Quarterly*, vol. 82, 2003, pp. 187–212.

Brenan, Beaumont *A Congratulatory Letter from One Poet to Another on the Divorcement of his Wife, Written some years since and now made public. Plus a humorous new ballad called 'The Female Combatants'. By B. B.* (Dublin, 1747)

— *The Painter's Breakfast. A Dramatick Satyr* (Dublin, 1756)

Brewer, John, *The Pleasures of the Imagination, English Culture in the Eighteenth Century* (London, Harper Collins, 1997)

Broch, Mark, 'Matthew Pilkington, auteur van The Gentleman's & Connoisseur's Dictionary of Painters' (unpublished PhD thesis, Amsterdam Free University, 2004)

Bryant, Barbara, 'Matthew Pilkington and the Gentleman's and Connoisseur's Dictionary of Painters of 1770: A Landmark in Art History', in Laing (ed.), *Clerics and Connoisseurs*, pp. 52–62

Budd, Adam, ' "Merit in Distress": the Troubled Success of Mary Barber' in *The Review of English Studies*, NS, vol. 53, no. 210 (Oxford, OUP, 2002)

Burke, Helen M., *Riotous Performances: the Struggle for Hegemony in the Irish Theater, 1712–1784* (Notre Dame, Indiana, University of Notre Dame Press, 2003)

Burney, Charles, *A General History of Music, from the Earliest Ages to the Present Period*, 4 vols (London, 1789)

Carey, Henry, *Dramatic Works* (London, 1743)

Carpenter, Andrew, (ed.) *Verse in English from Eighteenth-Century Ireland* (Cork, Cork University Press, 1998)

Charke, Charlotte, *A Narrative of the Life of Mrs Charlotte Charke*, Robert Rehder (ed.), (London, Pickering & Chatto, 1999)

Chetwood, William Rufus, *A General History of the Stage: From its Origin in Greece down to the Present Time* (London, 1749)

Cibber, Colley, *An Apology for the Life of Colley Cibber, with an Historical View of the Stage during his Time*, B. R. S. Fone (ed.), (Ann Arbor, University of Michigan Press, 1968)

Clark, Peter, and Raymond Gillespie, *Two Capitals: London and Dublin, 1500–1840* (Oxford, British Academy, OUP, 2001)

Clarke, Bernard, *A Collection of Poems Upon Various Occasions. Never*

Before printed. To which is added, An Epistolary Correspondence with a Lady of Singular Wit and Humour (Dublin, 1751)

Clarke, Norma, *Dr Johnson's Women* (London, Hambledon, 2000)

— *The Rise and Fall of the Woman of Letters* (London, Pimlico, 2004)

Curtis, Lewis P., (ed.), *Letters of Laurence Sterne* (Oxford, 1935)

Dane, Henry James, 'The Life and Works of Henry Carey' (unpublished PhD thesis, University of Pennsylvania, 1967)

Davys, Mary, *The Fugitive* (London, 1705)

— *The Works of Mrs Davys* (1725)

Defoe, Daniel, *The Complete English Tradesman, in Familiar Letters; Directing Him in all the several Parts and Progressions of Trade* (London, 1725)

Delany, Mary, *The Autobiography and Correspondence of Mary Granville, Mrs Delany*, Lady Llanover (ed.), 6 vols (London, R. Bentley, 1861–2)

Doody, Margaret Anne, 'I am an Irregular Verb', *London Review of Books*, 22 January 1998, pp. 22–3

Earle, Peter, *A City Full of People: Men and Women of London, 1650–1750* (London, Methuen, 1994)

Eaves, T. C. Duncan, and Ben D. Kimpel, *Samuel Richardson, A Biography* (Oxford, Clarendon Press, 1971)

Egmont Diaries Manuscripts of the Earl of Egmont, 1730–38, 2 vols (Historical Manuscripts Commission, 1920)

Ehrenpreis, Irvin, *Swift: the Man, his Works, and the Age*, 3 vols (London, Methuen, 1983)

Elias, A. C. Jr, 'Laetitia Pilkington on Swift: How Reliable Is She?' in *Walking Naboth's Vineyard: New Studies of Swift*, Christopher Fox and Brenda Tooley (eds), pp. 127–42 (Notre Dame, Indiana, University of Notre Dame Press, 1995)

— 'A Manuscript Book of Constantia Grierson's', *Swift Studies*, 2 (1987) pp. 33–56

— 'Men's Hormones and Women's Wit: The Sex Appeal of Mary Goddard and Laetitia Pilkington,' *Swift Studies*, 9 (1994) pp. 5–16

English, John C. 'John Wesley meets Laetitia Pilkington', *Methodist History*, vol. 42: 2 (January, 2004) pp. 88–97

Epstein, William H., *John Cleland, Images of a Life* (New Haven, Columbia University Press, 1974)

Fagan, Patrick, *A Georgian Celebration: Irish Poets of the Eighteenth Century* (Dublin, Branar Press, 1982)

Fanning, Christopher, 'The Voices of the Dependent Poet: the Case of Mary Barber', *Women's Writing*, vol. 8, no. 1, 2001

Field, Ophelia, *The Favourite, Sarah, Duchess of Marlborough* (London, Hodder & Stoughton, 2002)

Fielding, Henry, *Joseph Andrews and Shamela* (Oxford, World's Classics, 1999)

Fielding, Henry, *The Modern Husband, a comedy* (London, 1732)

Fischer, J. I., 'The Government's Response to Swift's Epistle to a Lady', *Philological Quarterly*, 65 (1986), pp. 39–59

Fitzgerald, Percy, *Samuel Foote, A Biography* (London, Chatto & Windus, 1910)

Foxon, D. F., *English Verse 1701–1750: A catalogue of Separately Printed Poems*, 2 vols (Cambridge, CUP, 1975)

Gerrard, Christine, *Aaron Hill, The Muses' Projector 1685–1750* (Oxford, OUP, 2003)

Gervat, Claire, *Elizabeth, the Scandalous Life of an Eighteenth-Century Duchess* (London, Arrow Books, 2004)

Glendinning, Victoria, *Jonathan Swift* (London, Hutchinson, 1998)

Goldsmith, Netta, *The Worst of Crimes: Homosexuality and the Law in Eighteenth-Century London* (Aldershot, Ashgate, 1998)

Goulding, Susan, 'Claiming the "Sacred Mantle": The *Memoirs* of Laetitia Pilkington', in *Lewd & Notorious: Female Transgression in the Eighteenth Century*, Katharine Kittredge (ed.), (Ann Arbor, University of Michigan Press, 2003)

Griffin, Dustin, *Literary Patronage in England, 1650–1800* (Cambridge, CUP, 1996)

Hammond, William, *A letter from William Hammond, Esq, in Justification of Himself, from the False and Scandalous Aspersions of Mrs Pilkington in her Memoirs* (Dublin, 1748)

Harvey, Karen, *Reading Sex in the Eighteenth Century: Bodies and Gender in English Erotic Culture* (Cambridge, CUP, 2004)

Hattersley, Roy, *John Wesley: A Brand from the Burning* (London, Little, Brown, 2002)

Hayden, Ruth, *Mrs Delany: her life and her flowers* (London, British Museum Press, 1980)

Herring, Thomas, *Letters to William Duncombe, from the Year 1728 to 1757* (1777)

Hill, Aaron, *The Works of the Late Aaron Hill, Esq.*, 4 vols (London, 1753)

Hitchcock, Robert, *An Historical View of the Dublin Stage*, 2 vols (Dublin, 1788)

Hogwood, Christopher, *Handel* (London, Thames & Hudson, 1984)

Hume, Robert, *The Rakish Stage: The London Theatre from the Beggar's Opera to the Licensing Act* (Carbondale, Southern Illinois University Press, 1983)

Johnston, Charles, *Chrysal* (London, 1761)

Jones, Louis, *The Clubs of the Georgian Rakes* (New York, Columbia University Studies in English, no. 157, 1942)

Keymer, Thomas, and Peter Sabor, *Pamela in the Marketplace: Literary Controversy and Print Culture in Eighteenth-Century Britain and Ireland* (Cambridge, CUP, 2005)

Koon, Helene, *Colley Cibber, A Biography* (Kentucky, University Press of Kentucky, 1986)

Laing, Alastair, (ed.), *Clerics and Connoisseurs: The Rev Matthew Pilkington, the Cobbe Family and the Fortunes of an Irish Art Collection through Three Centuries* (London, English Heritage and Azimuth Editions, 2001)

Langford, Paul, *The Excise Crisis: Society and Politics in the Age of Walpole* (Oxford, OUP, 1973)

— *A Polite and Commercial People: England 1727–1783* (Oxford, OUP, 1989)

Lewis, Jeremy, *Tobias Smollett* (London, Jonathan Cape, 2003)

Lewis, Peter, *Fielding's Burlesque Drama, Its Place in the Tradition* (Edinburgh, Edinburgh University Press, 1987)

Lonsdale, Roger, (ed.), *Eighteenth-Century Women Poets* (Oxford, OUP, 1989)

Mack, Maynard, *Alexander Pope, A Life* (New Haven, Yale University Press, 1985)

Mahony, Robert, *Jonathan Swift, the Irish Identity* (New Haven and London, Yale University Press, 1995)

Malcomson, A. P. W. *Nathaniel Clements: Government and the Governing Elite in Ireland, 1725–75* (Dublin, Four Courts Press, 2005)

Montagu, Matthew, (ed.), *The Letters of Mrs Elizabeth Montagu* (London, 1813)

Mossner, E. C., *The Life of David Hume* (Oxford, OUP, 1980)

Nash, Mary, *The Provoked Wife, The Life and Times of Susannah Cibber* (London, Hutchinson, 1977)

Nokes, David, *Jonathan Swift, A Hypocrite Reversed* (Oxford, OUP, 1987)

— *John Gay, A Profession of Friendship* (Oxford, OUP, 1995)

Orrery, Earl of, *The Orrery Papers, ed. the Countess of Cork and Orrery* (London, Duckworth and Company, 1903)

The Oxford Dictionary of National Biography, eds H. C. G. Matthew and Brian Harrison (Oxford, OUP, 2004)

The Parallel: Or, Pilkington and Phillips Compared, Being Remarks upon the Memoirs of those two celebrated Writers. By an Oxford Scholar (London, 1748)

Pasquin, Anthony, *An Authentic History of the Professors of Painting, Sculpture & Architecture, Who have Practised in Ireland* (London, 1796)

Phillips, Hugh, *Mid-Georgian London: A Topographical and Social Survey of Central and Western London About 1750* (London, Collins, 1964)

Pilkington, Jack, *The Real Story of John Carteret Pilkington* (London, 1760)

Pilkington, Laetitia, *Memoirs of Laetitia Pilkington*, A. C. Elias (ed.), (Athens, University of Georgia Press, 1997)

Pilkington, Laetitia, *An Apology for the Minister*, pamphlet, British Library Tracts, T.1110. (7.)

Pilkington, Matthew, *Poems on Several Occasions* (Dublin and London, 1730)

Place, Geoffrey W., *The Rise and Fall of Parkgate, Passenger Port for Ireland 1686–1815* (Chetham Society, Manchester, 1994)

Pope, Alexander, *The Twickenham Edition of the Poems of Alexander Pope* (London and New Haven, Methuen and Yale University Press, 1961–9)

Relke, Diana M. A. 'In Search of Mrs Pilkington' in *Gender at Work: Four Women Writers of the Eighteenth Century*, Ann Messenger (ed.), pp. 114–49 (Detroit, Wayne State University Press, 1990)

Richardson, Samuel, *Pamela: or, Virtue Rewarded* (London, 1740)

—*The Correspondence of Samuel Richardson, Author of Pamela, Clarissa, and Sir Charles Grandison, Selected from the Original Manuscripts, Bequeathed by Him to His Family*, Anna Laetitia Barbauld (ed.), 6 vols (London, 1804)

Richmond, H. W., *The Navy in the War of 1739–48* (Cambridge, CUP, 1920)

Rivington, Charles A. *'Tyrant': The Story of John Barber 1675–1741* (York, William Sessions, 1989).

Rubenhold, Hallie, *The Covent Garden Ladies: Pimp General Jack and the Extraordinary Story of Harris's List* (Stroud, Tempus, 2005)

Samuels, A. P. I., *The Early Life, Correspondence and Writing of the Rt. Hon. Edmund Burke LL.D* (Cambridge, CUP, 1923)

Scouten, Arthur H. *The London Stage, 1660–1800* (Carbondale, Southern Illinois Press, 1961)

Sheldon, Esther K., *Thomas Sheridan of Smock-Alley* (Princeton, Princeton University Press, 1967)

Sherburn, George, (ed.), *The Correspondence of Alexander Pope*, 5 vols (Oxford, OUP, 1956)

Sheridan, Thomas, *Life of Swift* (London 1784)

Smollett, Tobias, *Roderick Random* (London, 1748)

Solomon, Harry M., *The Rise of Robert Dodsley: Creating the New Age of Print* (Carbondale and Edwardsville, Southern Illinois University Press, 1996)

Spacks, Patricia Meyer, *Privacy: Concealing the Eighteenth-Century Self* (Chicago, University of Chicago Press, 2003)

Spencer, Earl Edward John, and Christopher Dobson, *The Letters of David Garrick and Georgiana, Countess Spencer* (Cambridge, CUP, 1960).

Staves, Susan, *A Literary History of Women's Writing in Britain, 1660–1789* (Cambridge, CUP, 2006)

Stone, George Winchester Jr, and George M. Kahrl, *David Garrick, A Critical Biography* (Carbondale and Edwardsville, Southern Illinois Press, 1979)

Stone, Lawrence, *The Family, Sex, and Marriage in England, 1500–1800* (London, Weidenfeld and Nicolson, 1977)

— *Road to Divorce, England 1530–1987* (Oxford, OUP, 1992)

Swift, Jonathan, et al *Miscellanies*, vol. 3 ['Last volume'] (London, Motte and Bathurst, 1736)

Swift, Jonathan, *Prose Works of Jonathan Swift*, Temple Scott (ed.),
(London, George Bell & Sons, 1907)
— *The Poems of Jonathan Swift*, Harold Williams (ed.), 3 vols (Oxford,
1937)
— *The Prose Works of Jonathan Swift*, Herbert Davis et al. (eds), 14 vols
(Oxford, OUP, 1939–69)
Taylor, Carole, 'From Losses to Lawsuit: Patronage of the Italian Opera in
London by Lord Middlesex, 1739–45', *Music and Letters*, 68, 1987, pp. 1–25
Thompson, Lynda M. *The 'Scandalous Memoirists': Constantia Phillips,
Laetitia Pilkington and the shame of 'publick fame'* (Manchester,
Manchester University Press, 2000)
Tillyard, Stella, *Aristocrats: Caroline, Emily, Louisa and Sarah Lennox
1740–1832* (London, Chatto & Windus, 1994)
— *A Royal Affair: George III and his Troublesome Siblings* (London,
Chatto & Windus, 2006)
Timbs, John, *Clubs and Club Life in London* (London, 1872)
Todd, Janet, *Rebel Daughters, Ireland in Conflict 1798* (London, Penguin,
2003)
Trefman, Simon, *Samuel Foote* (New York, New York University Press, 1971)
Tucker, Bernard, (ed.), *The Poetry of Mary Barber* (Lewiston, NY and
Lampeter, Edwin Mellen Press, 1992)
— ' "Our Chief poetess": Mary Barber and Swift's Circle', *Eighteenth-
Century Ireland*, vol. 7 (1992–3)
Uglow, Jenny, *Hogarth, A Life and a World* (London, Faber and Faber, 1997)
Vertue, George, *Note Books*, 6 vols (Oxford, The Walpole Society, 1930–55)
Victor, Benjamin, *The History of the Theatres of London and Dublin. From
the Year 1730 to the present time*, 2 vols, (London, 1761)
— *Original Letters, Dramatic Pieces, and Poems*, 3 vols (London, 1776)
Walpole, Horace, *The Yale edition of the Correspondence of Horace
Walpole* W. S. Lewis et al. (eds), 48 vols (New Haven, Yale University
Press, 1937–1983)
Whitworth, Rex, *Field Marshal Lord Ligonier: a story of the British Army
1702–1770* (Oxford, Clarendon Press, 1958)
Williams, Basil, *Carteret & Newcastle: a Contrast in Contemporaries*
(Cambridge, CUP, 1943)
Williams, Sir Harold, (ed.), *The Correspondence of Jonathan Swift* (Oxford,
OUP, 1963–72)
Woolf, Virginia, *The Common Reader*, 1st series (London, Hogarth Press,
1925)

Index

LP refers to Laetitia Pilkington, MP to Matthew Pilkington

Jonathan, 67–8; entertains Mary
Pendarves, 69; distressed at idea of MP
spending a year in London, 71, 72–4;
encourages Swift to smooth things over
between Pope and MP, 76–7; uses MP's
absence to write, socialise and maybe
more, 78–9; MP's physical distaste for
her body, 79, 272; poem on Swift's birthday published, 80; reaction to Grierson's
death, 81–2; leaves for London without
telling anyone in Ireland, 88–9; MP
encourages Worsdale's attentions to,
90–1, 92–3, 95–7; goes to see Heron act,
94–5; recognises failure of marriage, 98;
returns home alone to face disapproval,
99–100; faces the Dublin music for MP's
supposed betrayal of Swift, 101–2, 104–6;
repudiated by Swift, 105–6; goes to stay
in Cork and Mallow with uncle, 106–9;
systematic reading programme, 109–10;
deteriorating home life, 110–11; parents
fall out with, 114–15; father's accident
and death, 115–21; MP desires to rid self
of, 122–3, 124–6; caught in flagrante with
Adair and evicted, xvi, 126–8; becomes
prey of rapists and madams, 128–32;
Adair abandons, 132–3; Worsdale pays to
write for him, 133–4, 137–8; divorce,
135–6; gives birth to daughter, father unknown, 135–6; possibly writes play, 136;
plans to go to London, 138–41; journey
to London, 145–8; Edward Walpole
won't help, 148–9; taken up by Victor,
149–51; writes anti-government
pamphlets, 152–3, 171–2; success with
poetry, 153–7; Cibber takes up, 157,
159–62; origin of Memoirs, 161; summer
at Teddington, 168–70; MP refuses her
money and tries to declare her dead,
175–7; and women writers, 181–2;
possibly sells Swift and Barber materials
to Curll, 182–3; hears rumours MP has
tried to sell their children into slavery,
184–5; Pamela's influence on Memoirs,
185–7; taken up by Galway and
Middlesex, 189–91; moves to Duke
Street, 192–3; imprisoned in Marshalsea
for debt, 197–200; Richardson gives her

money from Delany, 201–2; opens
pamphlet and print shop, 202–7; ghost-
writing, 208–9; scheme to pass self off
as artist fails, 210–11; urges Jack to come
to London, 215; applies unsuccessfully
for Royal Bounty, xv, xvi, 217–18; at low
ebb, attempts to get money from
Richardson, 218–21; robbery forces her
to give up shop, 220; decides to return
to Ireland, 221–2; Betty arrives in
London pregnant, 223; LP's landlady
evicts them both, 223–4; Cibber raises
money to rehouse them, 224–5; lives
with Worsdale as hired writer, 229–33,
234–7; writes commendatory poem for
Cibber's Cicero, 237; collects Captain
Meade's effects from the Tower, 240–1;
Betty uses her MSS to light fire, 241;
raises money for journey to Ireland,
242–6; the journey, 246–50; wrangles
with MP for money, 254–5; makes little
effort to contact family, 255–6; coterie of
admirers in Dublin, 256–7; prepares
Memoirs for press, 257–9; takes up again
with Victor, 259; uses acquaintance with
Cibber to raise her reputation, 259–64;
row over theatre passes with Victor and
Sheridan, 262–4; more work on
Memoirs, 266–9; appearance of first
volume, 270–2; Memoirs' rendering of
end of her marriage, 272–4; long extract
from Memoirs published in England,
275; sparring with Woodward at Capel
Street theatre, 276–8; success of first
Memoirs volume gives her high public
profile, 279–80; correspondence with
Clarke, 281–4, 286, 289, 290, 293;
relations with Kingsborough, 285–7,
299–302; book published comparing
Memoirs to those of Phillips, 287–8;
tone of second volume, 289–93; public
anticipation and reception, 293–7; meets
Wesley, 297–9; Kingsborough breaks
with, 302–3; depression caused by break,
304–7; serious health problems, 307;
decline and death, 308–12; last poem,
311; funeral, 312; Jack fails to sell her
papers, 312–14; Jack publishes third

292; helps Clancy engineer
Kingsborough's break with LP, 302;
biography of Swift, 101, 324

Sherlock, Thomas, Bishop of Salisbury,
xv, 218

Sican, Elizabeth, 29, 35, 58, 69

Sloane, Sir Hans, 194–5

Sloper, William, 157–8

Smith, Ann *see* Pilkington, Ann

Smith, Counsellor John, 78, 120, 121,
254–5, 262

Smith, Mrs (madam and LP's landlady),
187–8, 189

Smock Alley theatre, 158, 221, 247–8,
264–6, 275, 292, 318

Society of Dilettanti, 124

'A Song' (LP), 98

'Sorrow' (LP), 131–2, 140, 141, 159

Southerne, Thomas, 81

Southwell, Lt, 206, 207

Spain: relations with Britain, 171, 173–4

The Spanish Fryar (Dryden), 276

The Spectator, 12

Spencer, Charles *see* Marlborough, Duke of

Spencer, Lady Diana, 236

Spencer, Jack, 190, 318

Stair, Earl of, 153, 179, 211

Stanhope, Charles, 141, 237

Stannard, Eaton, 110, 266

'The Statues' (LP), 145, 154–7, 162

Steele, Richard, 12, 149

Sterne, Laurence, 337

Stone, George, Bishop of Armagh, 269, 313

Stuart, Charles Edward, 216–17, 222–3

Swift, Jonathan
GENERAL: appearance and demeanour,
39; attitude to women, 36–7, 47, 52–3,
154–5; conversational style, 41–2; health,
47; love of wordplay and practical jokes,
41–2, 43–4, 45–7, 52–3; relationship with
Pope, 49–50, 72, 75
LIFE: background as popular hero, 26–8;
support for Mary Barber, 29, 31, 35, 54,
60; letter to Pope about Dublin Triumfeminate, 35; relationship with LP, xvii,
9, 36–53, 68, 69–70, 83–4; early
relationship with MP, xvii, 28, 32, 35–6,
38–47, 50–1, 58–9, 62–3, 65–6, 67, 69–70;

presents from famous friends, 40; letters
from famous correspondents, 48–50;
disagreements with Pope over the
Miscellanies, 50, 72, 75; support for
Davys, 331; support for Grierson, 60;
smoothes over row between Tickell and
MP, 63–4; apologises to Pope on Mary
Barber's account, 64–5; Mary Barber
forges testimonial in his name to queen,
65; helps MP become chaplain to Lord
Mayor of London, 70–1; plans for MP to
act as his agent in London, 72; smoothes
over problems between Pope and MP so
MP can remain of use to him, 76–7; 1732
birthday celebrations, 80; reaction to
Gay's death, 82; becomes symbolic
political figure in London, 82–3; MP
places poems of his in London press,
83–4; MP passes off own works as his,
84; causes problems between MP and
John Barber, 85–6; continues to strongly
support Mary Barber, 86–7; Mary
Barber brings some poems of his to
London which put all associated with
them in prison, 100–6; repudiates
Pilkingtons, 105–6; on bargain selling,
108; LP systematically reads his works,
109; LP praises in verse, 110; reaction to
breakdown of Pilkington marriage, 132,
135; on Worsdale, 133; LP's use of his
name to advance herself, 155, 161, 162,
205; ex-footman of his applies to LP for
help, 177–8; Bermingham's miniature,
211; gives Clancy money, 212; Sheridan
sells MSS, 212–13; condemnation of
Herring, 217; wills entire estate to build
hospital for the insane, 253–4; decline
and death, 253–4; LP's depiction in
Memoirs, 275, 289; other biographers'
borrowings from LP, 324

Taafe, Theobold, 130

Taste (Foote), 231

Tenison, Margaret *see* Delany, Margaret

Thackeray, William Makepeace, 324

Thiffola, Mrs (LP's landlady), 192, 196–7

Thornton, Bonnell, 323

Three Hours After Marriage (Pope), 157